UNDERSTANDING AND COUNSELING ETHNIC MINORITIES

UNDERSTANDING AND COUNSELING ETHNIC MINORITIES

Edited by

GEORGE HENDERSON, Ph.D.

S.N. Goldman Professor of Human Relations
Professor of Education
University of Oklahoma
Norman, Oklahoma

CHARLES C THOMAS • PUBLISHER

Springfield • Illinois • U.S.A.

Published and Distributed Throughout the World by
CHARLES C THOMAS ● PUBLISHER
Bannerstone House
301-327 East Lawrence Avenue, Springfield, Illinois, U.S.A.

© *1979, by* CHARLES C THOMAS ● PUBLISHER
ISBN 0-398-03916-X
Library of Congress Catalog Card Number: 79-11118

With THOMAS BOOKS *careful attention is given to all details of
manufacturing and design. It is the Publisher's desire to present books that
are satisfactory as to their physical qualities and artistic possibilities and
appropriate for their particular use.* THOMAS BOOKS *will be true to those
laws of quality that assure a good name and good will.*

Printed in the United States of America
V-OO-2

Library of Congress Cataloging in Publication Data
Main entry under title:

Understanding and counseling ethnic minorities.

Includes index.
1. Minorities--Education--United States.
2. Minorities--United States--Social conditions.
I. Henderson, George, 1932-
LC3731.U5   371.9'7'0973   79-11118
ISBN 0-398-03916-X

PREFACE

IN order to improve the quality of education for all students, school personnel must understand the cultural backgrounds which shape the behavior of students long before and after they enter school. Unfortunately, except for a few courses usually focusing on "ethnic studies" or "special problems," most teacher/counselor programs provide future educators with very little basic understanding of ethnic minority histories and life-styles. Fewer still provide an overview of counseling issues and techniques centering on ethnic minorities.

Groups whose members share a common social and cultural heritage passed to each successive generation are known as *ethnic groups*. Ethnic groups are generally identified by distinctive patterns of family life, language, and customs which set them apart from other groups. Above all else, members of ethnic groups feel a sense of identity and common fate. While ethnicity is frequently used to mean race, it extends beyond race.

It is foolish to talk about educating the whole child if we do not understand the social and physical environmental forces affecting each child. Various pieces of these human puzzles are found in the social sciences and education courses. However, without a careful design, these pieces remain disparate.

Rather than assume that members of the various helping professions will somehow become familiar with minority history, familial patterns, school achievement, and counseling needs, these four crucial areas have become the foundation upon which this book of readings is built. Unlike some texts that focus almost exclusively on blacks and Chicanos as the minorities to be counseled, this volume includes Puerto Ricans, American Indians, Chinese Americans, and Japanese Americans. Together these groups represent more than 20 percent of our total population and more than 80 percent of our ethnic minority population.

Specifically, this book is written for counselors, school psychologists, teachers, administrators, social workers, psychiatric consultants, and anyone else concerned with understanding and improving the lives of ethnic minority individuals.

G.H.

ACKNOWLEDGMENTS

I AM grateful to the following authors and publishers for permission to reprint their material.

Aguilar, Ignacio. Initial Contacts with Mexican-American Families. *Social Work*, 1972, 17:66-70. Copyright 1972 by the National Association for Social Workers, Inc. Reprinted by permission.

Christensen, Edward W. Counseling Puerto Ricans: Some Cultural Considerations. *Personnel and Guidance Journal*, 1975, 53:349-356. Copyright 1975 by the American Personnel and Guidance Association. Reprinted by permission.

Clark, Margaret. Mexican-American Family Structure. *Health in the Mexican-American Culture*. Los Angeles, Cal.: University of California Press, 1970. Copyright 1959, 1970 by the Regents of the University of California; reprinted by permission of the University of California Press.

Connor, John W. Acculturation and Family Continuities in Three Generations of Japanese Americans. *Marriage and Family*, 1974, 36:159-165. Copyright 1974 by the National Council on Family Relations. Reprinted by permission.

Delgado, Melvin. Puerto Rican Spiritualism and the Social Work Profession. *Social Casework*, 1977, 58:451-458. Copyright 1977 by the Family Service Association of America. Reprinted by permission.

Maldonado-Dennis, Manual. Puerto Rico, Puerto Probe: The First Three Centuries of Spanish Domination. *Puerto Rico: A Socio-Historic Interpretation*. Trans. by Elena Vialo. New York: Vintage Books, 1972. Copyright 1972 by Random House, Inc. Reprinted by permission.

Forbes, Jack D. The Mexican Heritage of the United States: An Historical Summary. *Mexican Americans: A Handbook for Educators.* Berkeley: Far West Laboratory, 1967.

Ghali, Sonia Badillo. Culture Sensitivity and the Puerto Rican Client. *Social Casework,* 1977, 58:459-468. Copyright 1977 by the Family Service Association of America. Reprinted by permission.

Goode, Kenneth G. *From Africa to the United States and Then.* Glencoe, Ill. Scott, Foresman, 1969. Copyright © 1969 by Scott, Foresman and Company. Reprinted by permission.

Higgins, Earl E., and Warner, Jr., Richard W. Counseling Blacks. *Personnel and Guidance Journal,* 1975, 53:382-386. Copyright 1975 by the American Personnel and Guidance Association. Reprinted by permission.

Hirata, Lucie Cheng. Youth, Parents and Teachers in Chinatown: A Triadic Framework of Minority Socialization. *Urban Education,* 1975, 10:279-296. Copyright 1975 by Sage Publications, Inc. Reprinted by permission.

Horse, John G. Red; Lewis, Ronald L.; Feit, Marvin; and Decker, James. Family Behavior of Urban American Indians. *Social Casework,* 1978, 59:67-72. Copyright 1978 by the Family Service Association of America. Reprinted by permission.

Huang, Ken, and Pilisuk, Marc. At the Threshold of the Golden Gate: Special Problems of a Neglected Minority. *American Journal of Orthopsychiatry,* 1977, 74:701-713. Copyright © 1977 by the American Orthopsychiatric Association, Inc. Reprinted by permission.

Hsu, Francis L. K. Parents and Children. *Americans and Chinese.* New York: Doubleday, 1953. Copyright © 1953 by Doubleday & Co., Inc. Reprinted by permission.

Jackson, Gerald G. The Emergence of a Black Perspective in Counseling. *Journal of Negro Education,* 1977, 46:230-253.

Kaneshige, Edward. Cultural Factors in Group Counseling and Interaction. *Personnel and Guidance Journal,* 1973, 51:407-412. Copyright 1973 by the American Personnel and Guidance Association. Reprinted by permission.

King, James R. African Survivals in the Black American Family: Key Factors in Stability. *Journal of Afro-American Issues*, 1976, 4, 153-167.

Lewis, Oscar. The Ríos Family. *La Vida*. New York: Vintage Books, 1965. Copyright 1965 by Random House, Inc., and Martin Secker & Warburg, Ltd. Reprinted by permission.

López, David E. The Social Consequences of Chicano Home/ School Bilingualism. *Social Problems*, 1976, 24:234-246. Copyright 1976 by the Society for the Study of Social Problems. Reprinted by permission.

Maes, Wayne R., and Rinaldi, John R. Counseling the Chicano Child. *Elementary School Guidance and Counseling*, 1974, 8:278-284. Copyright 1974 by the American Personnel and Guidance Association. Reprinted by permission.

Mahan, James M., and Criger, Mary K. Culturally Oriented Instruction for Native American Students. *Integrated Education*, 1977, 15:9-13. Copyright 1977 by the Center for Equal Education. Reprinted by permission.

Maldonado, Bonnie M., and Cross, William. Today's Chicano Refutes the Stereotype. *College Student Journal*, 1977, 11:146-152.

Onoda, Lawrence. Personality Characteristics and Attitudes Toward Achievement Among Mainland High Achieving and Underachieving Japanese-American Sanseis. *Journal of Educational Psychology*, 1973, 51:407-412. Copyright 1973 by the American Psychological Association. Reprinted by permission.

Rodriguez, Clara. The Structure of Failure II: A Case in Point. Reprinted from *The Urban Review*, Volume 7, Number 3, July 1974, published by APS Publications, Inc., New York.

Ruiz, Aurelino Sandoval. Chicano Group Catalysts. *Personnel and Guidance Journal*, 1975, 53:462-466. Copyright 1975 by the American Personnel and Guidance Association. Reprinted by permission.

Saslow, Harry L., and Harrover, Mary J. Research on Psychosocial Adjustment of Indian Youth. *American Journal of Psychiatry,* 1968, 125:224-231. Copyright 1968, the American Psychiatric Association. Reprinted by permission.

Schwartz, Audrey J. The Culturally Advantaged: A Study of Japanese-American Pupils. *Sociology and Social Research,* 1971, 55:341-351.

Shade, Barbara J. Social Psychological Characteristics of Achieving Black Children. *Negro Educational Review,* 1978, 29:80-86.

Sue, Derald Wing, and Sue, Stanley: Counseling Chinese Americans. *Personnel and Guidance Journal,* 1972, 50:637-645. Copyright 1972 by the American Personnel and Guidance Association. Reprinted by permission.

Wright, Kathleen. *The Other Americans: Minorities in History.* Los Angeles: Lawrence Publishing Company, 1969.

Youngman, Geraldine, and Margaret Sadongei. Counseling the American Indian Child. *Elementary School Guidance and Counseling,* 1974, 8:272-277. Copyright 1974 by the American Personnel and Guidance Association. Reprinted by permission.

Finally, I am indebted to Michele Alicia Henderson for reviewing and commenting on the articles cited above, and Cass Bittle for secretarial assistance.

G.H.

CONTENTS

UNDERSTANDING
AND COUNSELING
ETHNIC MINORITIES

Chapter 1

OVERVIEW

GEORGE HENDERSON

EACH minority-group student comes to school as a distinct individual with his or her own attitudes, beliefs, values, and goals. Because classroom and counseling interactions reflect each student's personality, whatever adjustment is made in these interactions represents an alteration in personality. It is imperative that school personnel never forget that when minority-group students leave school, they carry these changes with them.

While the major focus of this book is on ethnic minority-group students, many of the observations and recommendations are applicable to majority-group students too — especially in desegregated schools where white students are the numerical minority group.

TOWARD CONFORMITY

If we assume that a minority-group student's personality is holistic, somewhat more and somewhat different from the various elements that comprise it, we immediately are made aware of the enormous task of trying to understand and effectively counsel ethnic minority students. To be successful, counselors must identify the elements of a student's personality that can be measured so that counseling activities can be evaluated and, if needed, changed. A few words of caution are appropriate: throughout this book we will be talking about unique human beings who defy precise categorizations. That is, minority-group students are not likely in all instances to behave according to our generalizations.

The term *ethnic minority personality* refers to the relatively constant behavior patterns adopted by minority-group

3

members through the process of living as second-class citizens. This type of personality distinguishes minority-group from majority-group persons. Thus the ethnic minority personality is the outcome of a minority group's basic drives for success in societal activities and a majority group's inhibiting forces.

Minority-group children quickly learn that they have low status and little esteem from the perspective of the majority group. Through verbal and nonverbal communication minority-group children learn and internalize socially prescribed and extremely limiting roles. Only an extremely sensitive person is able to discern the personal style of behavior that distinguishes each minority-group individual.[1] Small group interaction within the school can be quite painful for the non-middle-class minority child. These children are viewed as outsiders by their teachers and majority-group peers.

The arrival of an outsider changes a school's group dynamics, setting in motion the process of mutual adjustment. A large number of minority students referred to counselors have school adjustment problems. Often maladjustment is the result of dysfunctional interaction between factors associated with a classroom group and a minority student newcomer. Nowhere is this more evident than in newly desegregated schools enrolling their first few minority-group students.

Formal and informal group norms set parameters for patterns of adjustment. A general principle of expansion is: "Given a clear group organization and the addition of a new member, a set of forces operates which tends to preserve, with the minimum alteration, the essentials of the state of the organization before the addition."[2] Rejection of minority-group students maintains the majority-group hierarchy, while minority-group acceptance breaks down the status quo. Interpersonal and intergroup problems usually center on the inability of nonwhite students to crack white cliques and vice versa. Peer acceptance is a paramount need of all students.

The larger the proportion of new members introduced at a single time, the greater will be the disruption of the ongoing group process.[3] The pledge procedure of a typical fraternity or sorority exemplifies the process of majority group members maintaining their homeostatis while admitting minority-group members. For instance, if a group of fifty white members initiate ten black pledges, there is a possible threat to the "white" values characterizing the organization. To counter this threat, the white members are likely to insure that the black members either have or acquire values and behaviors similar to theirs. Consequently, black students who survive the initiation rites talk, dress, and otherwise behave like their white brothers and sisters. Minority-group students undergoing this type of change tend to lose their ethnic identity and frequently are in need of counseling to help them sort out and resolve questions of their own identity and guilt.

If most members of a class have been together for a long time, they will have developed a style of operation that accomodates their needs. Students with high status positions (usually majority-group students in desegregated schools) will accept newcomers only if they perceive them not to be a threat to their own position. Furthermore, ethnic minority group students have to demonstrate compliance and acceptance of group norms and, if status-conscious, will be encouraged to seek a position not held by a majority-group student.[4] The stacking of minorities in a few competitive positions creates additional ethnic minority tensions.

Group relationships are based on history, and it is not surprising that nonwhite ethnic minority students in predominantly white schools feel like the outsiders they are. They do not possess the experiences and stories or folklore that bind the white students together. Minorities in this situation learn to exercise considerable care in the early stages of membership. Furthermore, they learn to somehow present themselves as being moderate, nonradical persons. To their chagrin, majority group acceptance tends to make them ordinary, conforming members with little ability to alter the character of the group. Or as a dejected black student said, "I lost my black neurosis and gained a white psychosis." (The growing number of middle-class blacks who commit suicide provides documentation of the substance of this comment.)

Regardless of ethnic background, most students are ordinary

persons who are not behavior problems. This fact surprises ethnic minority students who have been taught to believe in their inferiority, and it upsets white students who have been taught that they are superior to ethnic minority people.

In the school setting each student acts on the basis of his interpretation of the situation. He categorizes the social transaction in which he is involved, locates himself within it, and therefrom derives responsibilities and obligations. The consistency with which members of an ethnic group define their social status comes from sharing the same or similar environmental experiences. Once a particular point of view is adopted, it becomes a working conception of the world, and this frame of reference is brought to bear upon each new situation, including counseling.

The manner in which minority-group students participate in a counseling session also will depend on their personal evaluation of themselves. This value assessment is a crucial dimension of the counseling process. If a student regards herself as a capable person, she acts with confidence. If she regards herself as inadequate, she avoids situations in which her inadequacies may be revealed. Therefore the manner in which ethnic minority students relate to their teachers and counselors reflects this self-evaluation.

Implicit in the preceding examples is the complexity of each individual's phenomenal world — the sum total of his or her perceptions, experiences, and dreams. A helping relationship is achieved by counselors only when they can synthesize relevant portions of a minority student's world. Language, tone of voice, and manner of dress are but a few of the things that facilitate or impede the helping process.

Nor should we overlook the importance of rhetoric or purposive communication (verbal or nonverbal) carried on by one person to alter the beliefs or behavior of another. Communication within the counseling setting is rhetorical on two levels. First, the counselor has personal needs and goals congruent with his or her own values. Therefore consciously or subconsciously the counselor will model behavior that says to the student, "My way is the correct way. Follow me and you'll achieve a degree of self-actualization." In order to meet a counselor's rhetorical requirements students must submit to a modicum of organization, curb their tendencies to digress or fight, and engage in a face-to-face interaction. Of course, the second rhetorical level involves the student's personal needs, some of which may include not to self-disclose or become friendly with the counselor.

The figure-ground dimensions of counseling shift during various stages of interaction.[5] The dyadic relationship in one-to-one counseling is much more functional for confrontation tactics. The figure-ground concept holds that an individual can pay attention to or hold in clear figure (focus) only one object, event, or person at a time. Thus in individual counseling there are a greater number of personal response possibilities than in group counseling. It is easier for a person to hide in a group. However, because the roles of communicator and listener are rapidly interchanged in individual counseling, the chance of interpersonal failure is maximized. Most minority-group students feel more comfortable in a group setting where they can support each other. This is especially true of students who are nonverbal students in formal settings. (They usually are quite verbal among their peers in informal settings.)

In order to be optimally successful, counseling must include both individual and group counseling. Some minority subcultures consider it a sign of weakness for an individual not to be able to solve his or her own problems. Furthermore, in order to survive, most minorities have learned not to reveal themselves psychologically to strangers.

As noted earlier, individual counseling is a one-to-one interaction between a counselor and a client. Usually it is oriented toward abating specific problems. Some of the problems minority-group students bring to the sessions involve personal identity (who am I?), goal setting (what do I want to be when I grow up?), clarifying feelings (why do I hate and also feel attracted to white people?), and testing hypotheses (perhaps I am failing because I can't read and not because I'm not white).[6]

Group counseling is more effective in assisting students through involvement to resolve interpersonal and intergroup conflicts. When using role play or other carefully selected and monitored interventions, group counseling helps students to explore various strategies for change. The key words are "involvement" and "strategies for change."

Initially the language of the student in counseling is conditioned by previous similar experiences and is stylized by the kind of victories won in verbal and nonverbal combat. Unless we are careful, a counseling situation will become a competitive situation where each victory for the speaker is a loss for the listener. For example, inner city black youths tend to use jive talk to make their points, and reservation Indians resort to silence. Part of the counselor's challenge is to enable minority-group students to maximize their psychic victories but not at the expense of their environmental coping skills. Demands for immediate self-disclosure frighten minority students. The initial fear of self-disclosure has much to do with personal and familial privacy and nothing to do with racial or ethnic inability to disclose.

The new wave of affective techniques in counseling initially may not be suited for minority-group students whose cultures teach them not to publicly discuss family or personal problems. For example, Asian American students from traditional families are taught to hide their feelings and not to discuss potentially disruptive emotions. Thus for these students an action-oriented approach, as opposed to an affectively oriented counseling approach, is more palliative.

A structured, action-counseling approach is more in line with most minority students' highly structured patriarchial family interactions.[7] Counseling procedures that are vague by design will inevitably conflict with most minority American cultures.[8] There must be some clearly perceived pay-off in terms of individual success (but not at the expense of family relationships) *before* minority counselees will become actively involved in the counseling process.

If words hold societies together, it is not less true that words are crucial to the success of a counseling relationship.[9] One of the most important abilities of the counselor is his or her use of words. Jargon and polysyllabic words intimidate minority students. Simple words, such as "I believe" or "that must hurt," are more effective than jargon.[10] Some counselors go so far as to establish the norm that analytical or intellectually oriented statements are to be avoided during counseling sessions. Joseph Conrad gave the following advice to counselors concerned with using effective language: "He who wants to persuade should put his trust not in the right argument but in the right word. The power of sound has always been greater than the power of sense."[11] But the right word does not mean that the counselor must adopt the students' speech mannerisms or dialects. Minority students generally view this kind of role reversal as demeaning.

ROLES, STATUS AND ACHIEVEMENT

At the turn of the century Charles Horton Cooley, a pioneer in the study of group membership, wrote about the existence of multiple group memberships. He described the individual in modern society as "a point through which numerous arcs, representing different memberships, pass."[12] Minority group students know full well the meaning of being *of* but not *in* the mainstream of community life. Grudgingly, they learn to adjust to being nonpersons within majority-group institutions. The classroom is a microcosm of this sometimes not-too-subtle process of group rejection.

In 1973 the U. S. Commission on Civil Rights examined the verbal behavior of Anglo and Mexican American teachers with Anglo and Chicano students in 429 classes and 52 schools in California, New Mexico, and Texas. The Commission's study showed that while teachers addressed a great deal more non-criticizing talk to Anglo students than to Chicano students, they gave significantly less praise and encouragement to Chicano students. In addition, the ideas of Chicano students were accepted and used less often by teachers than were the ideas of Anglo students, and teachers spent significantly less time asking Chicano students questions. Perhaps most important, the study found that Chicano students expressed themselves less often in the classroom than did Anglo students, both in terms of responses to teacher questions and their own initiations.[13]

Similar conclusions regarding negative attitudes on the part of teachers toward black students were drawn by W. J. Barnes who observed social studies classes in several desegregated high schools. He found that teachers had more direct contact with white students than with black students; teachers indicated that they believed the quality of the interactions of black students in the classroom was not as high as the quality of white student interactions; teachers asked more prodding questions and sustaining follow-up questions of white students than they did of black students; teachers gave more process feedback to white students than they did to black students; whites were named as the best students by both blacks and whites; and blacks were described as the students who did not have the opportunity to express themselves to any appreciable degree in the classroom.[14]

In both the Commission on Civil Rights and Barnes studies it is apparent that the schools had merely redistributed majority and minority-group bodies without significantly changing the basic attitudes of either teachers or students in a positive or humane way. While information is lacking as to whether the schools were plagued with racial disturbances (a major indicator of minority-group alienation), the teachers whose behaviors were examined showed a substantially less caring attitude toward Chicano and black children than they did toward Anglo children. It is highly likely that most Chicano and black students in these schools learned each day to care just a little less for their teachers, administrators, Anglo classmates and, above all, themselves.

George M. Gazda succinctly described the importance of teachers caring for all students regardless of their race, ethnic or socioeconomic background: "If a student is to learn from a teacher he must be valued by that teacher, he must be understood by that teacher, and the teacher must be able to communicate with him and present a good model for him to imitate."[15]

William James once declared that a human being has as many social selves as there are distinct groups of persons about whose opinion he or she cares.[16] It is extremely painful for minority-group students to care about the opinions of school personnel only to be rejected by these significant others. Continued rejection or low status will cause the student to stop seeking majority group recognition. Minority group militants are created out of a series of majority group rejections and put downs. These precepts suggest a form of centrality in which minority-group students who receive recognition conform most clearly to the norms or standards of their school. They also are the minority-group persons who have the highest status within the school. Nonwhite students achieve a disproportionate amount of high status by conforming to athletic and music norms, while white students achieve a disproportionate amount of success in scholastic activities.

Differentiation of status usually results in differentiation of conformity. As we have seen, conformity may lead to status mobility. Middle-class minority students have little difficulty adjusting and conforming to white middle-class norms. The relation between status and conformity is direct under some circumstances and curvilinear under others. It tends to be direct for white students and curvilinear for nonwhite students. However, conformity is not without its price. Or as Robert N. Linder concluded, "Man is a rebel. He is committed by his biology not to conform."[17] Consequently, ethnic minority student gains won by conforming to majority group norms may be illusory. In winning, minority students risk losing their minority-group status and identity. However, few minority-group students have to worry about this happening to them within their classrooms. Why? Because they will not be accepted by their teachers and majority-group peers as equals.

Too often in the traditional classroom a seating arrangement is used which does not best serve the minority group student. Observation has shown that certain locations in a seating arrangement result in greater amounts of interaction, both in receiving and imparting information. These locations are the central and front positions: students located at the back and on the sides (where a disproportionate number of minority-group students are seated) are virtually left out of the mainstream of the learning that takes place from group interaction. Compounding this inequity, it has been found that most teachers seldom visit student locations; and when they do, the locations visited are the central, front-line positions.

Bernard W. Mackler undertook a project to determine what students have to do to succeed under the above conditions. In observing the progress of 1,000 black ghetto students in New York City for five years, he concluded: "Observations and test scores indicated that students have to behave in a socially-acceptable or school-acceptable way to succeed. The school staff wants pupils to be passive, polite, to listen and to adhere to the rules."[18] How hopelessly circumscribing this appears when compared with the goals of humanistic education which focus on promoting self-identity, involving the whole student, building upon student needs and interests, promoting a sense of personal effectiveness, and educating for change!

Data from other research indicate that in the traditional classroom most minority-group children do not ask questions, while their teachers ask incredibly large numbers of questions. The questions teachers ask usually are factual ones requiring "right" or "wrong" answers that simply are a matter of memory and regurgitation of appropriate portions of textbooks. Most minority-group students are free to initiate, conduct, and evaluate their own projects only about 5 percent of the time, while 95 percent of school projects are teacher-evaluated.

Rather than meeting individual needs, most teachers teach to an aggregate; instead of distributing their attention equally, teachers pay far more attention to high achievers or low achievers, neglecting the average achievers. Instead of inculcating a sense of responsibility for their own learning, teachers usually require that students be docile, polite, listen, and adhere to school rules. Instead of helping students to improve their group skills, teachers dominate and direct class discussions which focus primarily on low-level cognitive activities. Instead of being concerned with learning, most teachers and administrators are concerned with classroom control or management.

The following disturbing inference that can be drawn from analyzing research pertaining to the failure of education to meet the needs of ethnic minority students: Those inadequacies that are vividly apparent in educating ethnic minority students are applicable to majority-group students who also are not achieving their full potential.

Four areas of need constitute a framework for understanding low status minority-group students. Some students have a *dependency need* which is characterized by dependence on persons in position of authority for succorance. Others have a *status need* as exemplified by seeking to gain recognition from significant others. The *dominance need* manifests itself in expressions of intellectual superiority or physical control. Still other students display the *need for personal unburdening*, that is, making continual references to their strengths and weaknesses. Most minority students display a combination of these needs.

Competition is built into almost every school situation, and except for Asian Americans, the minority-group students discussed in this book are not given the cultural tradition needed to succeed in classroom competition. For example, prior to their contact with whites, destructive competition was alien to most of the more than 400 Native American tribes. Yet only a naive counselor would assume that today's Indian students do not need to develop skills in competitive activities. Basic survival dictates that at least a balance must be maintained between competition and cooperation. This is difficult for the culturally-oriented noncompetitive student.

> To succeed . . . the child must learn to maintain both competition and cooperation in a delicate balance of forces, and he must develop this balance through the learning situation itself. More exactly, he must learn kind of covert competition, more strenuous to keep up than open competition or abandonment of competition altogether: he must compete but he must not be competitive.[19]

POWER

Bertrand Russell wrote: "Power is sweet, it is a drug the desire for which increases with the habit."[20] The importance of power as it pertains to ethnic minority-group students cannot be overemphasized. Power is the ability to cause or prevent change. Since counselor preparation is mainly concerned with effecting positive change, it is imperative that counselors understand the kinds of power operative in their schools. It also is necessary to explore the effects of powerlessness as well as the role of counselors in alleviating its effects.

George Bernard Shaw said, "Power does not corrupt men; fools, however, if they get into a position of power, corrupt power."[21] It is in the context of power as a positive force that we can best understand its opposite — powerlessness. Both forces are present in the educative process. The student-teacher relationship has long been structured to make minority students submissive rather than active partners in the learning process. The danger of this situation can be understood if the relationship that exists between impotence and violence is clearly drawn. Violence does not generally arise out of an excess of power but in fact when a sense of powerlessness to act becomes the central emotion.

In today's schools, with their computerization, machine sectioning and unilateral audiovisual communication, a growing number of students are developing a sense of isolation, depersonalization, and powerlessness. The mass of multiethnic bodies thrown together in an academic arena often do not become an in-group of any kind but instead becomes encapsulated, discrete specks of humanity who feel they have no recourse against the decision-making apparatus controlled by some nebulous force that wears the label "educators."

In order to relate power to counseling it is helpful to explore the different facets of power of two of its most commonly interchanged synonyms: *influence* and *force*. One of the chief reasons the term power has been denigrated has been its association with force. Force, in turn, has been made an integral part of aggressive acts such as rape, war, homicide, and slavery. Some writers use the term power to mean the "restructuring of action without altering preferences; you are made to do something irrespective of whether it is your preferred course of action."[22] In terms of humanistic counseling, influence is preferable to force.

One of the best descriptions of the kinds of power with which counselors must cope, both in individual and group counseling, is offered by Rollo May.[23] He differentiates five basic kinds of power: exploitative, manipulative, competitive, nutrient, and integrative. May describes *exploitative power* as the most destructive kind of force — it subjects others to whatever use we have of them, regardless of their well-being. Exploitative power is synonymous with raw force, and it always presupposes violence or the threat of violence. Usually there is no choice or spontaneity on the part of its victims. This is the kind of power minority groups see in city slums and rural depressed areas.

May describes *manipulative power* as being power *over* another person. One of the best examples of this kind of power is set forth by B. F. Skinner who states that because much of human life is manipulative, manipulation should be applied on a mass scale for socially justifiable ends. Specifically, Skinner asserts that counselors are justified in manipulative intervention to alter student responses:

> We change the way a person looks at something, as well as what he sees when he looks, by changing something called perception. We change the relative strengths of responses by differential reinforcement of alternative courses of action; we do not change something called a preference. We change the probability of an act by changing a condition of deprivation or aversive stimulation, we do not change need. We reinforce behavior in particular ways, we do not give a person a purpose or an intention. We change behavior toward something, not an attitude toward it. We sample and change verbal behavior, not opinions.[24]

May is very critical of Skinner's operant conditioning proposals in which educators would use manipulative power in order to construct a patterned society and bring all of its members into predetermined conformity. On a smaller, less systematic scale most students are being conditioned by passing or failing grades.

Competitive power or power *against* another person is the third kind of power. Instead of creating a climate of cooperation, competitive power pits the energies of group members against each other. In its most negative sense, majority-group students achieve at the expense of minority-group students. However, May recognizes the positive aspects of competitive power that can give zest and vitality to human relations. "It is worthwhile to remind ourselves," May reflects, "that the great dramas of Aeschylus, such as *Oresteia,* or Sophocles' *Oedipus* trilogy and many of the works of Euripides were produced in competitions. The implication is that it is not the competition itself that is destructive but only the *kind* of competitive power."[25]

The fourth kind of power is *nutrient power* or the power *for* the other person. Nutrient power derives out of concern for the welfare of the individual or group for which one feels responsible. Examples of nutrient power include a counselor or teacher's nurture and care for her students or a superintendent exerting power out of concern for the well-being of her staff. Most counselors are trained to use nutrient power so that student objectives are achieved without forcible intervention. Martin Luther King, Jr. used nutrient power in his nonviolent civil rights campaigns. He stated that this method "has a way of disarming the opponent. It exposes his moral defenses, it weakens his morale, and at the same time it works on his conscience. He just doesn't know how to handle it."[26] Power has many faces, and the type that nurtures minority students without forcibly violating their basic right of self-determination is both humane and effective.

The fifth kind of power, *integrative power* or power *with* another person, is operative when an individual aids or abets his or her neighbor's power — when there is a cooperative relationship between people who have reached a state of trust. This kind of reciprocal power leads to emotional understanding and growth. It expands itself to include not only the acceptance of others but also an effort to assist them in realizing their full potential. Love and power, which are usually cited as opposites, become one. Integrative power necessarily involves the inclusion of other people — especially minorities. In this process social interaction is viewed not as a threat but as a promise, the fruition of which will accrue to the mutual benefit of all parties. The intimacy that counseling provides is an ideal environment for the exercise of integrative power.

Compassion, a primary emotion, derives from integrative power. It has been described as the feeling of community or emotional acceptance. In the words of May, "Compassion gives us a basis for arriving at the humanistic position which includes both power and love . . . It gives us the basis for judging someone without condemning him. Although loving one's enemies requires grace, compassion for one's enemies is a human possibility."[27] It can be utilized in verbal and nonverbal interaction. Jacob Bronowski stated, "We are all lonely . . . We've learnt that nothing remains to be discovered except compassion . . . At the end of years of despair, there is nothing to grow in you as tall as a blade of grass except your own humanity."[28] From the foregoing comments it is apparent that the power found in counseling should reside in individuals who have special training in the art of caring.

One of the most challenging aspects of counseling for constructive change pertains to self-concept and its relationship to a sense of personal power. Researchers in this area offer numerous, though sometimes disparate, opinions. Some researchers report significant personal gains through counseling for minority-group students, particularly in terms of improvement in self-concept. Other researchers caution that such gains are transitory. Still other researchers cite data supporting the possibility of negative changes in students' self-concepts.

Self-concept refers to the composite of attitudes, beliefs and values a person holds pertaining to himself/herself and the interrelating environmental forces. The self-concept determines an individual's reaction to other people and is shaped by their reaction to him or her. Minority students who feel abused, neglected, or rejected tend to abuse, neglect, and reject other people, including their counselors.

Power seems to be a strong antecedent or predicator of the direction of self-concept changes. Minority students high in power tend to change toward a more positive self-concept. Students exhibiting dominance in school activities maintain positive self-concepts because they usually are given the opportunity by school personnel to talk at length uninterrupt-edly, and they have numerous opportunities to validate their individual self worth. A sense of self-power also appears to provide minority-group students with an attitude of usefulness or competence in understanding other students and making suggestions which might prove helpful to them.

The relationship between attention received or prominence during counseling and positive change in minority student self-concept may be attributed to two factors: (1) the attention paid to minority-group students contains helpful or supportive in-formation and (2) attention *per se* tends to cause minority stu-dents to infer that they are people whom their counselors value. Thus attention can provide a positive change in a minority student's self-concept because it has intrinsic gratification for the counselee. In any case, it appears that power in the class-room and counseling sessions is a very decisive variable in shaping the self-concepts of minority-group students.

Minority students with a high need for achievement tend to privately set goals of intermediate difficulty so that they will succeed. For example, instead of setting a goal of "B" or "A" on a test, minority-group students more so than majority-group students are likely to set their sights on a "C," thereby reducing the odds for failure. The major emphaisis is not placed on success but avoiding failure. This has much to do with histor-ical conditions of minority-group students with a high need for achievement and power. It is important for these students to publicly beat the system and prove that they are as good as white high achievers. The desire for public verification of their abilities causes them to take greater risks then their peers who only manifest the achievement need. Counselors should ascer-tain whether a scholastically oriented minority student's pro-clivity is for achievement or power or both.

In an article entitled "Counseling for Power," Stanley Char-nofsky discusses individual differences within groups and what counselors can do to alleviate negative results such differences tend to produce.[29] In many instances, being "different" in America results in a catastrophic sense of despair and power-lessness among ethnic minorities. Certainly being a member of a low-status ethnic minority group has negative ramifications. Counselors desiring to help minority students who feel powerless must be able to accept them as individuals of equal worth. Above all else, counselors need to function in a way that degraded and powerless minority students can feel safe and free enough to find and express a personal and positive sense of their own worth and power.

Most discussions of the mental health of minority students, especially blacks, focus on social and psychological pathologies. Few counselors seem to realize that out of minority communities characterized by inordinate environmental and psychological stress have come a majority of children with healthy coping mechanisms. Admittedly, rage, anger, and depression are not uncommon. In fact there may be something quite wrong with minority-group children who do not exhibit at least a small amount of these defense reactions.

> Many children growing up in the black community learn a certain kind of mental toughness. They learn survival skills. They know how to jive the school principal and they show a lot of psychological cleverness and originality in the particular style they merge with. They know how to deal with hypes and pimps. But most professional institutions have not yet learned how to appreciate and capitalize upon this particular kind of style.[30]

Rather than accept low-achieving minority-group students as creative persons with the potential and ability to achieve success in school, too many educators blame the students for their problems rather than the structural inequalities institutionalized in their environment. This is commonly known as *blaming the victim.*

CROSS-CULTURAL COUNSELING

There are two broad responsibilities for anyone who counsels ethnic minority students. First, the counselors should try to promote optimal personal and intellectual growth of the students. Second, they should assume responsibility for the psychological welfare of their counselees. Being empathic is not enough. As students engage in self-disclosure and goal setting they are vulnerable to additional failures. Consequently, counselors should create a psychologically and physically safe environment for growth.

Minority-group students who seek help outside their peer group and family do so because they cannot help themselves and neither can their friends or family help them. Ideally, the counselor will offer help that is consonant with students' abilities. This type of reality-based counseling is clothed in empathy. If the counseling garment woven in the counselor-counselee interaction is a good fit, the students come to better understand themselves and their problems. Furthermore, they develop meaningful alternatives of action.

> The process of change will be more humane if the stimulators for change realize that feelings and emotions are of primary importance. These prime movers must realize that the individuals they are asking to change are first of all humans; they have deep underlying feelings, wishes, and defenses, and fears that must be considered. Those involved in change must be allowed to be authentic persons, living, breathing, human beings. They must be allowed to think for themselves, to initiate, to imagine, to work without constant "over-the-shoulder supervision"; they must learn to be empathetic; they must be willing to show concern and compassion. And they must be supported and trusted as they risk themselves in openness.[31]

Counselors who are most different from minority-group students in terms of culture generally have more difficulty communicating empathy, congruence, respect and acceptance than counselors who share or understand the students' cultural perspective. To be more specific, white counselors who understand the psychological and sociological backgrounds of nonwhite students are better able to counsel such students than their colleagues who lack this knowledge. A meaningful relationship with a white counselor representing the dominant society can do much to reduce hostile minority student feelings. Indeed, the counseling process is a rare opportunity for understanding ethnic group differences and similarities.

Contrary to popular notion, little empirical evidence supports the assumption that race *per se* is related to the level of understanding between counselors and minority students. Generalizations about race and effective cross-cultural counseling should be made with great caution. At best, the literature on this subject is inconclusive. Several studies suggest that cultural barriers make the development of successful cross-cultural counseling highly improbable.[32] Yet other studies conclude that well-trained, empathic white counselors can establish effective relationships with nonwhite clients.[33] Even the issue of trust, which precedes self-disclosure, is not conclusively settled by research. For several years it was assumed that blacks involved in counseling disclosed less than whites.[34] However, a recent study conducted by Bertha M. Williams concludes that age, race, and sex were not the critically important variables that they have been considered in the development of trust and disclosure in the counselor-client relationship.[35]

Bilingualism and biculturalism presents another kind of block or bridge (depending on one's perspective) to cross-cultural counseling. Mexican Americans and Puerto Ricans have the largest number of bilingual-bicultural students in schools.

> ... language, culture and ethnicity play the most important role in the formation of the self-concept, and in the development of cognitive and coping skills. The three concepts are analytically different, yet they are interrelated.[36]

Most bilingual-bicultural subcultures have not assimilated into the American melting pot because they prefer not to assimilate. Only black Americans (who are not bilingual-bicultural in the true sense of the terms) have mounted national civil rights campaigns to gain integration and assimilation with white Americans.

Ethnic minority students living in traditional families have to function at two demanding levels of consciousness: according to the norms of their kinship and also according to the dominant society's norms. This conflict was vividly captured by D'Arcy McNickle when he summarized the dilemmas of traditional Indian students:

> The problem of being Indian, and being obliged to function
> at two levels of consciousness, for many individuals reduces
> itself to this: They are aware that their communities, their
> people, their kinsmen are Indians and are held in low esteem
> by the general society. The young people especially recognize
> themselves as Indians, but they do not want the low-status
> equivalent. They look for some way in which they can share
> in the status acribed to middle-class Americans without
> ceasing to be Indian.[37]

The net result of ethnic minorities living outside their ancestral lands and maintaining their cultural heritage is a less than
pure culture. The African American culture is not African culture; the Chicano culture is not Mexican culture; the mainland
Puerto Rican culture is not Puerto Rican culture; the Chinese
American culture is not Chinese culture; and the Japanese
American culture is not Japanese culture. These cultures have
become a synthesis of their own native and adopted American
cultures. (Even the Indian cultures have been altered.) Older
immigrants tend to be less Americanized than the new im-
igrants. Of all the non-Indian groups, Mexican Americans,
because of the close proximity of Mexico, have retained more of
their cultural heritage.

Ethnic group language shapes one's philosophy of life. Consider the following example: In English the clock runs; in
Spanish *el reloj anda* (the clock) walks; and for Indians it just
ticks. Thus the concept of time and structuring relationships
around clock-measured appointments vary according to culture. Bilingual counselors tend to be more appreciative of this
fact.[38]

Counselors who do not know the various social class dimensions of ethnic minorities also are unlikely to know that despite
common language, color, and historical backgrounds, all
members of a particular minority group are not alike. It is
presumptuous or counterproductive to talk about *the* black or
the Indian or *the* Chinese as if members of these and other
groups have only one set of behavior characteristics. While this
text will focus on ethnic group characteristics, the reader is
reminded that social class differences often are more determinant of a minority student's behavior than ethnic back-

ground.

Minority-group children from middle-class oriented families are burdened with the need to succeed in school — not just for themselves but for all members of their ethnic group. This cultural press for academic success is vividly seen in Japanese American and Chinese American students. Scholastic failure brings shame and disgrace to Asian American families, especially traditionally oriented families with a high success orientation. As a group, Asian American students work harder and devote more time to school subjects than other ethnic students. Counselors aware of individual and cultural needs to succeed seek ways to get low-achieving minority students to make better grades or to accept their current grades if they represent the highest level of ability. But then all students need this type of guidance.

Although focusing on Native Americans, Charles W. Ryan offers the following practical guide for counselors who want to understand a minority group:[39]

1. Study carefully the local history of the minority group. This may involve a review of appropriate social science literature.
2. Spend time as a participant observer in process observation of local minority customs.
3. Analyze data regarding school achievement and work histories of minority youth representing the ethnic group.
4. Analyze carefully your feelings regarding the minority group.
5. Study the attitudes of local Caucasians as well as other minority groups. How do they feel about the minority group you are researching?

Finally, some thought should be given to ethnic minority counselors who ostensibly have everything working for them — cultural experiences, language and color needed for ethnic minority empathy. However there are several factors which frequently mitigate against them being effective counselors. Most ethnic minority counselors are white, Anglo-Saxons in terms of their training and professional associations. They are, in short, very much like their white colleagues. Of course, some minority counselors are able to maintain their ethnic identities with minimum loss in credibility. Many minority counselors, however, appear condescending to minority-group students in terms of their verbal and nonverbal language.

In other instances, minority-group counselors feel quite marginal — estranged from whites and no longer comfortable with members of their own ethnic group. These counselors appear cold and detached to both white and nonwhite students. Besides, there is always the possibility that minority students will displace to minority counselors their hostility toward whites.

A related issue seldom explored in depth is the lack of empathy and sensitivity ethnic minority counselors have for minority groups other than their own. Indians, for example, display considerable hostility toward blacks, and Mexican Americans frequently reject close associations with Japanese Americans. No doubt you can think of other instances of minority groups displaying a lack of acceptance. It is worth stating at this juncture that all Americans are products of institutionalized racism and to be aware of this condition will allow the counselor to deal with his or her own racism.

Caucasian counselors — the overwhelming majority of members in professional counseling organizations — are beginning to come to grips with their own racism and that of their colleagues. Hopefully such introspection will not lead to a repression or denial of hostile feelings. Nor should a counselor who is trying to understand his or her white racism be immobilized by guilt. *Proactive* rather than reactive or inactive counselors are needed if the vicious circle of racism is to be broken.[40]

None of the observations made in this book should be interpreted as obviating the need for higher education institutions to recruit and train considerably more ethnic minority counselors. Too few Caucasian counselors seem to have the interest or skills needed to effectively counsel ethnic minorities. For this reason a growing number of minority counselees are expressing preference for counselors from their own ethnic background. While not discussed in this book, the sex of the counselor is another important variable.[41]

In the end, however, ethnic and sex similarities are not adequate substitutes for counselors who are (1) linguistically compatible with ethnic counselees, (2) empathic, and (3) well-trained. This means that the initial edge a minority counselor may have with a minority counselee will be lost if the counselor cannot get beyond ethnic history and identity. Problem solving must result from the ensuing information and interaction.

REFERENCES

1. Gerald M. Phillips and Eugene C. Erickson, *Interpersonal Dynamics in the Small Group*, New York: Random House, 1970, 168.
2. Theodore M. Mills, ed., *Readings on the Sociology of Small Groups*, Englewood Cliffs, N.J.: Prentice-Hall, 1970, 162.
3. Dorwin Cartwright and Alvin Zander, *Group Dynamics: Research and Theory*, Evanston, Ill.: Row, Peterson, 1953, 53.
4. Phillips and Erickson, *op. cit.*, 58.
5. Arthus W. Combs and Donald Snygg, *Individual Behavior*, New York: Harper & Bros. 1949.
6. Raymond A. Ehrle, An Alternative to "Words" in the Behavior Modification of Disadvantaged Youth, *Vocational Guidance Quarterly*, 1968, 17:41-46.
7. Derald W. Sue, Ethnic Identify: The Impact of Two Cultures on the Psychological Development of Asians in America, in Stanley Sue and N. N. Wagner, eds., *Asian Americans: Psychological Perspectives*, Palo Alto, Cal.: Science and Behavior Books, 1973, 141.
8. See Raymond T. Garza, Affective and Associative Qualities in the Learning Styles of Chicanos and Anglos, *Psychology in the Schools*, 1978, 15:111-115; and Joseph F. Rychlak, C. William Hewitt, and Jean Hewitt, Affective Evaluation Word Quality, and Verbal Learning Styles of Black Versus White Junior College Females, *Journal of Personality and Social Psychology*, 1973, 27:248-255.
9. Stuart Chase, quoted in George Seldes, ed., *The Great Quotations*, New York: Pocket Books, 1972, 984.
10. Michael Jay Diamond, From Skinner to Satori? Toward a Social Learning Analysis of Encounter Group Behavior Change, *Journal of Applied Behavioral Science*, 1974, 10:145.
11. Joseph Conrad, quoted in Seldes, *op. cit.*, 984.
12. Cartwright and Zander, *op. cit.*, 249.
13. United States Commission on Civil Rights, *Teachers and Students: Report V: Mexican-American Education Study: Differences in Teacher Interaction with Mexican-American and Anglo Students*, Washington,

D. C.: United States Commission on Civil Rights, March, 1973.

14. W. J. Barnes, Student-Teacher Dyadic Interactions in Desegregated High School Classrooms, Unpublished Doctoral dissertation, Austin: The University of Texas at Austin, 1973.

15. George M. Gazda, Systematic Human Relations Training in Teacher Preparation and Inservice Education, *Journal of Research and Development in Education*, 1971, 4:50.

16. Cartwright and Zander, *op. cit.*, 249.

17. Robert M. Linder, quoted in Seldes, *op. cit.*, 209.

18. Bernard W. Mackler, WIN, *Psychology Today*, 1971, 4:61.

19. John R. Seeley, R. Alexander Sim, and Elizabeth W. Loosley, *Crestwood Heights*, New York: Basic Books, 1956, 229.

20. Bertrand Russell, quoted in Seldes, *op. cit.*, 755.

21. *Ibid.*

22. Peter Nettl, Power and Intellectuals, in Conner C. O'Brien and William D. Vanech, eds., *Power and Consciousness*, New York: New York University Press, 1969, 17.

23. Rollo May, *Power and Innocence*, New York: W. W. Norton, 1972, 105-106.

24. B. F. Skinner, *Beyond Freedom and Dignity*, New York: Random House, 1971, 90.

25. Rollo May, *op. cit.*, 108.

26. Martin Luther King, Jr., quoted by Kenneth B. Clark, *Dark Ghetto: Dilemmas of Social Power*, New York: Harper & Row, 1965, 183.

27. Rollo May, *op. cit.*, 253.

28. Jacob Bronowski, *The Face of Violence: An Essay with a Play*, Cleveland: World, 1967, 161-62.

29. Stanley Charnofsky, Counseling for Power, *Personnel and Guidance Journal*, 1971, 49:354.

30. Joseph White, Guidelines for Black Psychologists, *The Black Scholar*, 1970, 1:53.

31. Robert L. Heichberger, Toward a Strategy for Humanizing the Change Process in Schools, *Journal of Research and Development in Education*, 1973, 7:78.

32. See George Banks, The Effects of Race on the One-to-One Helping Interviews, *Social Service Review*, 1971, 45:137-146; Ralph W. Heine, The Negro Patient in Psychotherapy, *Journal of Clinical Psychology*, 1950, 6;373-376; Marylou Kincaid, Identity and Therapy in the Black Community, *Personnel and Guidance Journal*, 1969, 47:884-890; and Clemmont E. Vontress, Racial Differences: Impediment to Rapport, *Journal of Counseling Psychology*, 1971, 18:7-13.

33. See Donald S. Arbuckle, The Counselor: Who? What? *Personnel and Guidance Journal*, 1972, 50:785-790; David N. Aspy, Empathy-Congruence-Caring Are Not Singular, *Personnel and Guidance Journal*, 1970, 48:637-640; Jerry Atkin, Counseling in an Age of Crisis.

Personnel and Guidance Journal, 1972, 50:719-724 and M. H. Jones and M. C. Jones, The Neglected Client, in Reginald L. Jones, ed., *Black Psychology*, New York: Harper & Row, 1972.

34. See Sidney M. Jourard and Paul Lasakow, Some Factors in Self-Disclosure, *Journal of Abnormal Social Psychology*, 1958, 56:91-98; Richard E. Dimond and David T. Hellkamp, Race, Sex, Ordinal Position of Birth, and Self-Disclosure in High School Students, *Psychological Reports*, 1969, 25:235-238.

35. Bertha M. Williams, Trust and Self-Disclosure Among Black College Students, *Journal of Counseling Psychology*, 1974, 21:522-525.

36. Marta Sotomayor, Language, Culture, and Ethnicity in Developing Self-Concepts, *Social Casework*, 1977, 58:195.

37. D'Arcy McNickle, The Sociocultural Setting of Indian Life, *American Journal of Psychiatry*, 1968, 125:119.

38. See Guadalupe Gipson, An Approach to Identification and Prevention of Developmental Difficulties Among Mexican American Children, *American Journal of Orthopsychiatry*, 1978, 48:96-113.

39. Charles W. Ryan, Counseling the Culturally Encapsulated American Indian, *Vocational Guidance Quarterly*, 1969, 18:125.

40. See Judy H. Katz, *White Awareness: A Handbook for Anti-Racism Training*, Norman, Okla.: University of Oklahoma Press, 1978.

41. See Mary Lee Smith, Influence of Client Sex and Ethnic Group on Counselor Judgment, *Journal of Counseling Psychology*, 1974, 21:516-521.

Part I. African Americans

INTRODUCTION

Normality is socially defined. What is normal and functional behavior in one subculture may be abnormal and dysfunctional in another. When culturally encapsulated counselors assume that they can effectively counsel black clients without modifying their style of counseling, the result usually is something less than helpful. In short, counselors who do not realize that black societies structure the behaviors and attitudes of their members overlook valuable clues to individual stress.

AFRICAN AMERICAN CULTURAL CONDITIONING

African Americans are the most difficult ethnic group to categorize. The difficulty stems mainly from slavery, where African heritages were almost entirely lost through Caucasian acculturation. Even so, there are some general behaviors that typify black cultural conditioning.

EXTENDED FAMILY. The black family is sometimes extended bilaterally but often it is maternally oriented. The black extended family is a closely knit group, frequently consisting of grandparents, cousins, aunts, uncles, nieces, and nephews. Within the black family roles are interchanged more frequently than in most non-black families. This sharing of decisions and jobs in the home stabilizes the family during crisis situations.

KINSHIP BONDS. Children born in and out of wedlock are loved. Legitimacy refers to parents; it has little to do with black children being accepted. Children are proof of an individual's manhood or womanhood and caring for them are proof of his or her humanity. When children marry or otherwise reach adulthood, they leave home but often settle close to their parents or other relatives. Family unity, loyalty, and cooperation are part of the black life-style. (This is true for the other ethnic groups discussed in this book).

AUTHORITY AND DISCIPLINE. Childhood in the black community revolves around assertive behavior and challenging authority. There is a constant crossing of wills. Through this process the black child learns the acceptable outer limits of his or her behavior. Discipline tends to be strict and preoccupied with teaching children respect for their elders, respect for authority, responsibility for oneself, and an understanding of what it means to be black in America.

ACHIEVEMENT AND WORK ORIENTATIONS. Contrary to popular notion, most black parents pass on to their children high achievement aspirations. However, many black homes are deficient in middle-class role models. The desire to survive has forced most black families to internalize a strong work orientation which makes palliative the unskilled and semiskilled jobs characterizing the discriminatory job market within which most blacks must work.

READINGS

Kenneth G. Goode provides a comprehensive historical review of American black explorers and the evolution of slavery. The scope of the history extends from precolonial times through the 1860s with considerable attention given to the conditions of slaves. Of special merit is the succinct description of the cultural attributes of African Americans, including a brief section on the structure of the slave family.

The thesis that black Americans have been able to survive because of their adaptability is exposued by James R. King. Specifically, he focuses on African life-styles which are evident in contemporary black families. However, there are differences between American black families and West African families.

Barbara J. Shade concludes that although family income makes some difference in black school achievement, the most significant differences between black achievers and nonachievers are found in the behavior of parents or guardians. The family, she maintains, sets the stage and provides the nurturing environment for children to develop personality traits needed for school achievement. Ms. Shade compares black students with their minority counterparts and concludes that student achievers are generally stereotyped by their teachers.

Gerald G. Jackson provides an extensive review of literature which suggests a new perspective, a black perspective, for counseling black students. The new roles, techniques, and behavior advocated are juxtaposed with traditional counseling approaches.

Earl B. Higgins and Richard W. Warner examine position papers and research generated by guidance workers concerned with counseling black students. They underscore the importance of understanding black culture. Finally, they point out several practical considerations which counselors should be aware of and techniques to utilize when counseling black students.

By answering the following questions after reading about each ethnic minority group, the various pieces to the ethnic minority puzzle will fit into a clearer whole.

1. Which statements are based on subjective biases and not objective analyses?
2. How accurate and relevant are the chapters?
3. What specific cultural characteristics do ethnic minority groups have in common?
4. Which readings contradict data and/or recommendations found in other chapters or materials that you have read? How do you reconcile these contradictions?
5. Cite examples of effective teaching methods and counseling techniques that appear to be applicable to all ethnic groups. Which methods and techniques appear to have unique or limited value?
6. What unanswered questions do you have after reading each chapter? Where can you go to get the answers to your questions?

Chapter 2

FROM AFRICA TO THE
UNITED STATES*

KENNETH G. GOODE

BLACKS IN AMERICA DURING PRECOLONIAL TIMES

THE purchase of twenty blacks in 1619 by the colonial government at Jamestown, Virginia, was not the first contact of blacks with the Western Hemisphere. According to some authorities, long before Europeans established a claim to lands in the Western Hemisphere, black Africans had visited its shores and penetrated far into the interior.

More important is the fact that blacks had a place among the exploits of the European pioneers who many years later explored North and South America. Pedro Alonso Nino, a pilot in Columbus' fleet, has been referred to as a black. In the discovery of the Pacific Ocean, Balboa's party included thirty blacks. In the conquest of Mexico, Cortez was aided by many blacks, one of whom planted some grains of wheat and thus made himself a pioneer in wheat raising in the New World. Blacks assisted in the exploration of Guatemala and the conquests of Chile, Peru, and Venezuela. Blacks were with Lucas Vasquez de Ayllon in his expedition from Florida northward and figured prominently in the establishment of the settlement of San Miguel at the mouth of the Pee Dee River in South Carolina. They accompanied Narvaez and his successor, Cabeza de Vaca, through what is now the southwestern part of the United States. They were with Alarcon and Coronado in the conquest of what is now New Mexico, and they were ordered imported by De Soto, the explorer of the lower Mississippi

*From *From Africa to the United States and Then ... A Concise Afro-American History* by Kenneth G. Goode. Copyright © 1969 by Scott, Foresman and Company. Reprinted by permission.

Valley.

Blacks were also with the early French explorers. Although there is not concrete evidence that they were with Cartier and Champlain, it is certain that they did accompany the Jesuits in Canada and the Mississippi Valley during the seventeenth century. They also constituted a considerable element in the exploration and settlement of Louisiana.

The majority of blacks who accompanied the Spanish, Portuguese, and French explorers were slaves who served as laborers and domestic servants. But there were also a few free blacks, some of whom were skilled artisans. The most celebrated black man during precolonial times was Estevanico, or "Little Stephen." Estevanico was a member of the Narvaez expedition. He preceded the main force and sent back messages as to the direction the expedition should take as well as to observations he had made. He was the first non-American to cross what is now New Mexico, Arizona, and northern Mexico.

EVOLUTION OF THE INSTITUTION OF SLAVERY

In August 1619, the colonial government at Jamestown, Virginia, purchased twenty blacks from a Dutch frigate and thus commenced the importation of black people into North America for the purpose of servile labor that was to last for some 250 years. During the first forty years some Afro-Americans were accorded the status of indentured servants — a status given to whites who had bound themselves for a number of years to work for those who had paid for their passage to the New World. Some of these Afro-Americans served out their terms of indenture, became free men, acquired property, and became the owners of indentured servants and slaves. From 1640, however, there is evidence that some Afro-Americans in Maryland and Virginia were being held as slaves.

As the demands for labor increased and as the colonists found that the use of white indentured servants and Indians for servile labor was unsatisfactory, they began to look to the blacks, the supply of whom seemed inexhaustible, whose temperament was said to be suited to chattel slavery, and whose physical characteristics prevented them from becoming indistinguishable in the community. Consequently, each of the colonies began to give recognition to the institution of slavery. By custom, court decision, or legislation, the Afro-American's status was reduced to that of a slave. In some, and perhaps all, of the English colonies the idea that blacks would be enslaved was reinforced by the example set by the Spanish and Portuguese — from whom the English borrowed the term "Negro," which meant "black."

From its inception slavery was an economic success in the southern colonies. With its mild climate and fertile soil, the South reaped many benefits by using slaves to cultivate the crops that were then in demand. Hence, the vast majority of slaves were used on plantations in the cultivation of the great staples — rice, indigo, and tobacco. Other slaves worked as domestics or as unskilled laborers in nonagricultural pursuits. Because of the acute shortage of white artisans and mechanics, many slaves were also trained in the skilled trades.

As an economic institution slavery in the middle colonies and New England never became deeply entrenched. The predominantly commercial and mixed-farming economy in this area did not encourage the large-scale employment of slave labor. In certain areas such as Rhode Island and the counties around New York, however, there were appreciable numbers of blacks. For the most part they worked as farm hands, domestics or unskilled or skilled laborers in the urban centers. Because of the thin soil, the harsh climate, and the relatively commercial nature of the area slavery never developed into an important economic institution in the northern colonies. But even though slaves were not used in large numbers, it should be remembered that many northern shippers and merchants gained the benefit of the slave trade and its allied industries during the first half of the eighteenth century. In Rhode Island, especially, enslavement of Africans throughout the British colonies helped support a major domestic industry, the distilling of rum.

SLAVE RESISTANCE IN COLONIAL TIMES

Historians who have pictured slavery as a beneficent or necessary institution have had little or no place in their works for accounts of the efforts by slaves to avoid or challenge the system. Because the institution was inherently brutal, the basic attitude of slaves was very often one of recalcitrance and sometimes of active defiance. The record is replete with evidence indicating that from the earliest times blacks fought courageously against being enslaved. In the slave wars of Africa, they fiercely resisted. On the slave ships they mutinied whenever the opportunity presented itself. And they carried their struggle for freedom to the colonies in North America — into a society that did everything it could to suppress them.

The resistance of slaves took many forms. Many ran away, idled at their tasks, feigned illness, and damaged or stole property. Some burned crops, barns, and houses; others killed whites, usually their owners or overseers; and some even maimed or killed themselves in desperation.

The form of resistance that whites dreaded most was the revolt. Generally, revolts were small and ill organized, but there were several that were fairly extensive and well planned. Regardless of size, however, most were discovered prior to fruition and quelled with tyrannical ferocity. More slaves than white men died in these struggles for liberty.

COLONIAL SLAVE CODES

With the legalization of slavery and the increase of the slave population, the colonies began to adopt slave codes. The codes, sometimes an outgrowth of the laws governing indentured servants and sometimes patterned after the West Indian slave codes, were negative in character and were aimed at repressing slave insurrections as well as controlling slave conduct. In the southern colonies they were very elaborate and generally deprived the slaves of virtually all civil, judicial, economic, social, political, familial, and intellectual rights.

Some features common to the more complete codes were:

a. Slaves were declared to be chattel property, which could be bought and sold at the will of the owner.

b. The avenues of manumission were greatly restricted.

c. All business dealing of slaves had to be done through their white masters.
d. Slaves could not bear firearms.
e. Slaves could not buy or consume alcoholic beverages.
f. Slaves could not vote.
g. The right of assembly was restricted.
h. The right of free speech was nonexistent.
i. The right to travel was restricted.
j. The right to a fair and impartial trial was nonexistent.
k. The right to obtain an education was nonexistent.

The types of punishment meted out to a slave for violation of the codes depended on the nature of the crime, the colony in which the crime took place, and the time when the act was committed. Except for capital crimes, during peaceful times there was a tendency to work slaves hard and to pay little attention to the law. But during and after an actual or rumored insurrection the codes were usually rigorously enforced.

The slave codes of the southern colonies, especially of South Carolina and Georgia, were enforced with brutal discipline. Capital crimes were numerous, and burning, branding, maiming, cropping, and whipping were the usual means of punishment. In comparison to the codes of the southern colonies, the codes of the northern colonies were not extensive, especially in Pennsylvania where the Quaker influence was predominant. There were fewer capital crimes and the customary means of punishment was the whip.

Some colonies had laws that restricted the conduct of the masters with reference to the treatment of their slaves. But if a master were brought to trial for mistreating a slave, very rarely would he be convicted, because no slaves could testify against white men; even if he were convicted, the punishment was usually a small fine.

THE UNWANTED FREEDMAN

At the turn of the nineteenth century there were approximately sixty thousand free Afro-Americans, constituting 7.9

percent of the total Afro-American population. The majority of the free Afro-Americans lived in the urban centers of the north and in Maryland and Delaware.

This segment of the Afro-American population came about as a result of Afro-American indentured servants completing their terms of indenture; some slaves being freed after serving in the armed forces; slaves being freed as a result of the passage of legislation providing for emancipation; and slaves who were freed by private acts of manumission, by deed of gift, by self-purchase, by will, or by flight.

In the South the free Afro-American was totally unwanted. He was thought to have criminal inclinations, to be improvident, and likely to become a public charge. The chief objection to his presence was that it endangered the institution of slavery. The free Afro-American was said to be guilty of an entire catalogue of sins, including receiving stolen goods from slaves, selling slaves liquor, harboring runaway slaves, and inciting slave revolts.

Increasingly, by law and court decision, attempts were made to control the conduct of the free Afro-American. From state to state, county to county, and city to city, the extensiveness of the controls and their application varied, depending primarily on the number of free Afro-Americans and the temper of the times, but some controls common throughout the South were as follows:

1. A free Afro-American had the burden of proving that he was not a slave. This he did by carrying a certificate of freedom. An uncertified Afro-American was treated as a runaway slave, subject to being jailed, hired out, or sold at public auction. In some states a free Afro-American had to have a white guardian to whom he reported periodically.
2. A free Afro-American could be reduced to servitude if he failed to pay his debts, taxes, fines, or court fees.
3. A free Afro-American could not hold public office, and in most states he could not vote.
4. Generally, a free Afro-American could not testify against a white person nor was he permitted to possess or purchase

firearms without special permission.

5. A free Afro-American could not purchase liquor without a recommendation from a "reputable" white person.
6. A free Afro-American had to observe curfew laws and was generally denied the right of assembly.
7. A free Afro-American was often segregated in places of public accommodation and educational institutions.

Even in the face of the many restrictions, however, there were opportunities for free Afro-Americans in the South to make a living. Because of the acute shortage of white skilled laborers, the free Afro-American had the opportunity to work in the trades. A few were able to accumulate substantial amounts of property, and some even became the owners of slaves.

In the North, because the doctrine of white supremacy was held as tenaciously in the North as in the South, the status of the free Afro-American in the North was not unlike that of his southern counterpart. Nevertheless, he encountered fewer restrictions, he could sometimes protest against them, and he had somewhat greater opportunities for self-expression. As in the South, laws and court decisions governed his conduct. In many states a free Afro-American could not vote, he could not testify against whites, he was barred from jury service, places of public accommodation were closed to him, and he had to attend segregated schools or none at all.

In making a living the free Afro-American faced more difficulties in the North than in the South. His fields of employment were generally confined to common labor and domestic service, and after 1830, even these menial jobs were increasingly unavailable, since they were being taken by the almost five million white immigrants who arrived between 1830 and 1860. Furthermore, trade unions were closed to him. Despite the many laws, court decisions, and the established custom, a few free Afro-Americans became "well-to-do." Most northern cities had their Afro-American food caterers, barbers, tailors, and small businessmen. There were also a few Afro-American fur traders and farmers.

As the number of free Afro-Americans increased it was felt by many that they must be sent out of the country. In the South, slave owners believed that complete discipline of the slaves was impossible as long as the free Afro-Americans remained. In the North it was felt that the two races could never live together in peace and harmony. Consequently, the possibility of colonizing the Afro-American arose. Serious proposals were first frequently advanced after the Revolutionary War, especially in Virginia. The great majority of Afro-Americans and northern abolitionists were adamantly opposed to colonization and especially to the American Colonization Society, which was founded in 1816. With the aid of the federal and state governments, the Society established the colony of Liberia in 1821 for Afro-Americans who wished to leave the United States. The efforts of the Society to deport Afro-Americans were unrewarding, for it is estimated that less than fifteen thousand Afro-Americans were relocated outside the United States.

BLACK SELF-IMPROVEMENT

In the early 1800s, the atmosphere in which Afro-Americans lived, whether North or South, was oppressive. In the South, the institution of slavery was becoming more entrenched, and the status of many free Afro-Americans was not much better than that of the slave. In the North, where laws were fast putting an end to the institution of slavery, Afro-Americans still could not express much optimism or any great faith in the future. In this atmosphere ladened with subservience and subordination, Afro-Americans had to seek ways of bettering their lot, independent of the white man.

Some of the first Afro-Americans to achieve some measure of intellectual freedom and economic self-sufficiency were Jupiter Hammon (writer), Gustavus Vassa (writer), Phyllis Wheatley (poet), Benjamin Banneker (mathematician, astronomer, and surveyor), and Paul Cuffee (shipowner). These and others were pointed to as examples in refuting the growing charges that Afro-Americans were inherently inferior to whites.

In the effort to improve their status in the post-Revolutionary War period, Afro-Americans found it necessary to establish separate institutions. Independent churches sprang up, and in a number of northern cities, organizations of a benevolent and fraternal nature were established. Afro-Americans took advantage of and benefited from the general trend to establish and improve schools, though frequently they were excluded. Afro-Americans founded literary societies, libraries, and reading rooms in their struggle for self-improvement.

After 1830 Afro-Americans throughout the nation began to meet and collectively protest against their status. This movement, called the Negro Convention Movement, gave free Afro-Americans the opportunity to petition collectively the state and federal governments and otherwise apprise the nation of the Afro-American's stand on public issues. But after the national conventions had adjourned, the delegates dispersed, doing very little in their communities to carry out plans they had adopted. Furthermore, some Afro-Americans refused to participate in the Movement because they felt that an organization made up exclusively of Afro-Americans tacitly accepted segregation.

THE SLAVE FAMILY

The slave family was very unstable because the forces inherent in the American system of slavery worked against its stability. With few exceptions, slave marriages were not legally required, slave fatherhood was not legally recognized, legal prohibitions against dividing slave families were uncommon and where they did exist they were conveniently ignored, customary "courtship" and "engagement" seldom existed, and many slave owners were very reluctant to allow "marriages" between slaves who lived on different plantations.

Whatever recognition the slave family received was voluntary on the part of the master. A few owners insisted on religious ceremonies to unite slave couples, and other owners informally sanctioned the relationship of slave couples. In addition, where there were children involved, the slave family sometimes tended to be more stable, and a few states had laws forbidding the selling of mothers away from their children who were under a certain age. However, this did not apply to fathers. It should be recognized that in all cases where the maintenance of a stable family was detrimental to the economic interest of the master, the slave family was inevitably divided. Wives would be sold away from their husbands and children, husbands from their wives and children, and children from their parents, brothers, and sisters.

Because of the difficulty in establishing and maintaining a "normal" stable slave family, cohabitation, sometimes forced, was widespread. In such cases a close family relationship had little chance to develop, for very seldom did the parties want or have time to learn to care for each other. Children of such relationships also suffered the pangs of nonaffection, since their parents, especially the mother, had little time for child-rearing and in many instances she was largely relieved of this responsibility. However, whenever possible the slave mother did everything she could to maintain a stable family, and she grieved very deeply when the family was divided.

Despite laws against it, miscegenation was extensive, especially between white men and slave women (slave women had no rights and few means to protect themselves against the sexual desires of white men). Concubinage and polygamy were so widespread in some cities in the South that they almost gained social acceptance. The rape of a slave woman was not a crime but merely a trespass on the property of her master. Children of such relationships were slaves and were generally treated accordingly. In a few instances, however, white fathers emancipated them and provided for them. The extent of such miscegenous relationships is evidenced by the mulatto slave population, which in 1860 was estimated to be 410,000 out of a total slave population of approximately 4,000,000. The proportion of mulattoes among the "free" Afro-American population was considerably higher.

Slave breeding also contributed to the instability of the slave family. The prohibition of the African slave trade after 1808, the decline of the value of certain cash crops, the deterioration of the soil in the upper South, and the expansion of the Cotton Kingdom all made slave breeding inevitable. To a small extent, it had existed since the beginning of the institution of slavery in North America, but after the turn of the nineteenth century, when the demand for slaves reached its peak, slave breeding became a common means of gaining profit, especially in the states of the upper South.

Slaves, male and female, were purchased especially for breeding purposes. Sometimes no regard was paid to the preferences of slaves in matters of mating, but generally slave owners preferred to let slaves pick their own mates since this made the slaves more "contented" and more likely to produce offspring. Breeding slaves were pampered, well fed and clothed, and treated less brutally. They were generally not overworked; in fact some were given bounties at the birth of each child, and occasionally women were emancipated if they gave birth to a specified number of children.

In view of the instability of the slave family and the almost total absence of slave marriages, the slave women tended to become the head of the family, for it was she who provided what little degree of stability that existed in the "home." One fact of slavery that has not yet been adequately treated in the literature is the heroic efforts on the part of slave fathers and mothers to maintain stable family relationships despite impossible odds. That many of them succeeded is a most remarkable aspect of the black experience in America. And the fact that the overwhelming majority of black families have achieved stability in a short span of one hundred years suggests that the abolition of slavery, more than any other social act, contributed to this stability. It also suggests that the best way to further enhance the stability of black families would be to abolish all the remaining vestiges of bondage black people now experience in this country.

Chapter 3

AFRICAN SURVIVALS IN THE BLACK AMERICAN FAMILY: KEY FACTORS IN STABILITY*

James R. King

WHEN Europeans and Africans migrated to America, voluntarily or not, they brought many of their family traditions from the Old World. Immigrants tended to look at the new environment with expectations conditioned by the environment from which they came. Since the family is the basic unit in most societies, it should not be surprising that Old World family customs tended to persist in the New World. It was from families that one received the kind of security needed to enable one to survive in a strange environment. The structure of the typical American family, consisting of a biological mother, father, and child(ren) in one household, has developed into a more and more isolated nuclear family unit. West Africans, on the other hand, view the family unit as a cooperative community encompassing not only living relatives but also those not yet born and those already dead. Many practices exist in black American communities which can be traced back to West Africa. This paper shall concern itself with a general view of African survivals, African survivals in the black American family and the impact of African survivals on contemporary black American families.

A GENERAL VIEW OF AFRICAN SURVIVALS

African cultural traits can be found in many areas of American

*From "African Survivals in the Black American Family: Key Factors in Stability" by James R. King, *Journal of Afro-American Issues*, 4:153-167, 1976. Reprinted by permission.

life. Certainly one can see the influence of African survivals in many American dances. For many American Negro forms of dancing are basically African. Motion pictures taken of the rites for the ancestors of a chief of an Ashanti village showed a perfect example of the Charleston. And films taken of Africans dancing in Dahomey and among the Yorubas demonstrated the resemblance to many styles of Negro dancing in America.[1] Another area which contains African survivals is that of Negro music.

African survivals exist in both secular blues and spiritual music in the Negro world. It is, however, in the spiritual world that one can find the greater influence of Africanism. It was the singing of the blues and spirituals which gave comfort and meaning for life to many black Americans whose only solution was to sing away their troubles. And since most Negro songs, like their African counterparts, serve functional purposes, it is not surprising that songs are an integral part of American Negro life. Black Americans as well as Africans use songs to influence courtship, to make life's tasks easier, to communicate with God, etc. Songs, then, to Africans and black Americans, are functional music. There are other African survivals which are expresses in black oral culture.

African folklore and proverbs are ever present in black American life, for oral cultures express themselves through the use of folklore and proverbs. One of the best known African folktales in (black) America is that of the Tar Baby story from the Anansi folk stories of the Ashanti. There are also many African survivals in black poems and essays.[2] African survivals are to be found also in many black Americans' concept of time.

Many white Americans say that black people have no regard for punctuality because black people tend to be late for appointments. But a closer look at black people's concept of time will demonstrate that black people are punctual but in a different way. This can be briefly explained by dividing time up into actual time, potential time, and no time.

In black America, as in traditional Africa, time has to be experienced in order for it to be real. A black person gets up and goes to work or school. The idea of getting up and going to school is the actual time, for the person made time by doing something. Black people and traditional Africans control time by making it happen. Time is, thus, meaningful at the point of events and not at the mathematical moment. To tell a traditional African or some black Americans to get up at 6:00 AM and get to work by 8:00 AM makes no sense in their concept of time. For time for them begins when they make it happen; that is, when they perform the events. So in the lives of traditional Africans and black Americans, any period of time is reckoned according to its significant events.[5] Traditional African concepts of potential time and no time have had much effect on black Americans.

For example, black Americans view potential time or the future as events that are likely to occur soon. Those events which are not likely to occur fall into the category of no time. One can see, then, that for many black Americans, time has two dimensions: the present and the past, with actual time being the present and the past. The future does not exist in this sense because it has not been experienced.

This concept of time, then, is crucial to helping one understand many black Americans.

Many other African survivals can be found in black American cookery, in the black church where call and response occurs between the black preacher and his congregation, in black mannerisms, etc. But for this study the main focus shall be on African survivals in the black family.

AFRICAN SURVIVALS IN THE
AFRO-AMERICAN FAMILY

In the social reality of both traditional African societies and black America, families can be described as a particular philosophical orientation which can be perceived as the survival of the family (tribe) and the *Oneness of Being*. This oneness of being can be defined as relating to the whole black community (tribe). In such relationships one finds that the traditional black family (tribe) system is structurally "stretched horizontally in every direction as well as vertically in both directions taking into account all members of the community . . ."[4] In Africa, this community also included the space which the family occupied, for in traditional African societies, the people are tied to the land on which they live because it is the concrete expression of both the past and the present. This land (space) provides the people with the roots of their existence. If people with such psychological ties to the land are separated from it, this can bring disaster to both the family and community life.[5] It is this philosophy, which sees man as being a part of nature — God, the earth, the family, the land — that is the guiding principle of the African and black American family which includes unity, cooperation and mutual responsibility.[6] However, in blacks this tie to the land has been transferred to the family, since blacks generally have not been permitted to own land and thus develop close feeling for it. Thus, although there is diversity in black American families, one is still able to find this African feeling for one another in black families. For all black families in America have a common sense of "peoplehood" in the sense that they have had to help each other in the struggle against oppression since arriving in America. The black American family, then, has its roots in West Africa.

In West Africa, the concept of a family is not limited to the biological parents. It includes the parents, grandparents, children, grandchildren, uncles, aunts, cousins, the rest of the relatives — both living and dead. This type of family unit gives security of all — young and old. In such a society there is no need for orphanages for the young or homes for the aged. Care for all lies in the hands of the community. The securities that the Ashanti extended family offers to its members are numerous.

> Dependence in a crisis is not upon bank accounts. A man does not carry his wealth in his wallet. Instead, the security of the dependent person rests in the respectful hands of other persons, particularly his relatives to whom he has been and will be throughout his life bound by ties of kinship and of reciprocal rights and obligations to service and cooperation. The person who has no family ties faces difficulties as great as those faced by the elderly widows of the Western world, but

such persons are few in number in Ashanti. The orphans, the aged, the sick, the widowed go home to their families. It is as simple, as effective, as reassuring as that. They go home to their families.[7]

The significance of the extended family as it relates to the Ashanti is inescapable, particularly if one realized that in Africa, due to malnutrition, lack of preventive medicine, etc., it is likely that parents, children, or the aged might at any time become unable to provide for themselves or even die. Thus, the extended family acts as a guardian.

The Afro-American extended family tends to follow the pattern of African extended families and includes *all* of the relatives, both legal and biological. The black family is not to be confused with that concept of family which limits it to only the biological parents. The extended family in black America, as in Africa, has given black people much security in times of need.

During slavery, for example, when either or both parents were sold, the grandmothers or other older relatives helped raise the children. Every family member felt more secure because he or she could rely on one another for moral support. As mentioned earlier, the extended family's value to the family of a deceased person was immeasurable. The early migration of blacks from the South to the North was made easier by the fact that some family members would get settled and then send for other members who upon arrival would live in the same house in the new area. This gave the newcomers a better chance to become psychologically adapted to their new environment. The extended family, then, has been another aspect of African culture which has been of great help in the survival of black Americans.

Although a number of black marriages can be called monogamous, upon closer examination one will find that a large number of them are common law marriages, variations of the polygamous marriages that are still legally practiced in many West African societies. Polygamy tends to be nature's way of insuring the survival of a species. The founder of Negro History Week, Carter G. Woodson, describes the necessity of polygamy in Africa:

> Polygamy . . . grows out of their peculiar socialistic system. Because of frequent wars so many soldiers are killed off that there are more women than men. Polygamy is practiced, then, because of the benefit resulting to the state in the production of sufficient able-bodied men to protect it. Polygamy in Africa, moreover, renders impossible spinsterhood and prostitution, which exist among the so-called civilized people. The Africans practice openly what Europeans and Americans practice clandestinely.[8]

The above can easily be applied to many Afro-American families by substituting common-law marriages for polygamous ones in order to understand how nature assures the survival of black Americans. For just as in Africa, there are forces in America which tend to assure that black women outnumber black men, due to imprisonment, lynchings, lack of proper medical care, disease, job discrimination, suicide and desertion.[9] Polygamy, then, guarantees the survival of black people, since the more children are born, the greater is the chance that some will survive. Many never reach adolescence due to malnutrition, diseases, accidents and other causes.

If one considers that every child in the black community belongs to the entire black community, then it will be easier to grasp the importance black Americans give to black children. How often has one heard that black women have too many illegitimate babies? How often has one heard that black women should be forced to practice birth control? What such questions overlook is the fact that in the black community there is no such thing as an illegitimate child. The children are loved and cared for by the entire community. It is everyone's job to protect the children. And the children, in turn, feel that the whole community is their parents. The following describes the feelings of both the Afro-Americans and African communities toward children:

> Children cast off as orphans must be provided for; illegitimate offspring, human beings in spite of their parents' misfortune, must be cared for; the burdens of the unfortunate in the struggle of life must be borne by others even when other-

wise encumbered. God made them as he made others, and they are entitled to the consideration due human beings. Africans built their social order on these principles, and they are still dominant even among the impecunious Negroes in America.[10]

This points out why many black Americans and Africans love their children, whether they are "legitimate" or not. "A child is conceived. What do we do about taking care of it? Who can help? Who has the most to offer? These are the questions; not what will the neighbors think? How will the family be embarrassed? How can we make the situation respectable?"[11] To the African and American, the child is a member of the group and must be cared for by all.

Another reason why Africans and black Americans love to have children is that the more children one has. the longer one lives. That is, in many African societies it is believed that as long as there is someone alive to remember the parents, the parents are considered to be alive. This concept is known as the "living dead," for the dead are remembered by the living.[12] Among black Americans the concept of the "living dead" is known as one's soul continuation through the offspring. Similarly, in the case of the Africans and the Afro-Americans, children are a very important part of each group. Both societies are concerned with preparing their children to face a hostile environment.

In many African tribes; initiation rites are performed on children in order to prepare them for adult life. Between the ages of four and seven, boys and girls undergo circumcisions and clitoridectomies respectively. "The cutting of the skin from the sexual organs symbolizes and dramatizes separation from childhood."[13] These operations are quite painful, "but the children are encouraged to endure it without crying or shouting and those who manage to go through it bravely are highly praised by the community."[14] These operations are useful, for they are the beginning of preparing the children for difficulties and sufferings of later life. "Endurance of physical and emotional pain is a great virtue among Akamba people, as indeed it is among other Africans, since life in Africa is surrounded by much pain from one source or another."[15] Thus, African children are prepared to live in an unfriendly environment.

In black American communities, one finds that black parents, particularly mothers, have had the burden of socializing their children to live with the dangers of their environment. The methods (initiations) are different from those used by Africans to indoctrinate their children, but the goals are the same: to assure survival of the children.

During slavery in America, the black mother was the person who had to condition the children to accept their position in life, for she knew what would happen to them if they rebelled. Black mothers during slavery "traditionally had to establish control over their children, particularly the males, because any show of aggression toward whites might cost them their lives."[16] And there are black families who have forced their children "to accept beatings in order to 'take it' without crumbling."[17] The historical experience of black Americans is full of such examples.

Richard Wright, the black author, was raised by parents whose task was to harden Richard for a very hostile environment. His autobiography, *Black Boy*, the story of his early years, is full of examples of painful experiences forced upon him by his mother in order to teach him to survive in his environment. One night, for example, when she had sent him out to buy groceries, a street gang beat him, took his money and chased him home. His mother would not let him in. She gave him more money and a "long, heavy stick." Then she told him to fight and locked him out of the house. So Richard beat off the gang and went home with the groceries.[18] His "parents, grandparents, uncles, aunts created a bleak authoritarian environment. And when he refused to fall into the miserable mold, they cut him off, isolated him."[19] Modern psychologists would probably say that raising a male in such an atmosphere would emasculate him. But Afro-Americans will recognize that Wright's parents were conditioning "their child for a world which would recognize him only as a black boy; a world which could murder a Negro businessman, as Uncle Hoskins was murdered, simply for being too successful, and which could run a boy off a job, as would happen to Richard himself for wanting to learn a trade."[20] It was this kind of social conditioning that helped southern blacks keep their cool after one of them had been murdered by a mob.

One of the most brutal lynchings in history occurred in the deep South in 1934, a lynching that involved national advertising via newspapers and radio for spectators.[21] After the victim had been killed, the Negroes in the town were as passive as ever. Why? It was because they knew that any sign of hostility on their part would have meant the killing of many more Negroes and the physical destruction of the black community. This can be best explained by the fact that the Negroes had been conditioned by the black community to take such things in stride. A black psychologist pointed out how both Afro-Americans and Africans deal with their hostile environments:

> They recognize very early that they exist in an environment which is sometimes both complicated and hostile. They may not be able to verbalize it, but they have already mastered what existential psychologists state to be the basic human condition; namely that in this life, pain and struggle are unavoidable and that a complete sense of one's identity can only be achieved by both recognizing and directly confronting an unkind and alien existence.[22]

Black children grow up to understand that, by teaching them to deal with the harsh world in which they live, their parents have given them security. They come to have great respect for old black people — the parents, grandparents, and all old people in the black community.

It is a known fact that black communities have great respect for old people. One reason for this respect, as mentioned earlier, is to be found in the West African belief that old people are "almost dead" and should be treated as dead ancestors who have the power to "watch over and either help or hurt their living relatives."[23] Another reason is that in an oral culture it was they who helped pass the knowledge from generation to generation, thereby gaining respect from the community. They may explain why this African survival, respect for old people, had and still has a great force in the black American community. Several examples of how black and white Americans treat their elders might help illustrate this point.

This writer was born in the South, where every child was taught to respect old people. One day on a bus in San Francisco, California, a young lady approached this writer and said, "Sir, I want to congratulate you on what you did on the bus last month." Shocked by her remark, the author replied, "What did I do?" She replied, "You got up and gave an old woman your seat on the bus." "Oh" was the reply, for I had done only what I had been conditioned to do.

There was a recent case of a thirty-five-year-old black man who returned to school to pursue a career in medicine. Many black publications carried stories about his determination. This was a big thing in the black community, but would have been looked upon with indifference in the Anglo community.

In another instance, this writer attended a commencement recently during which a sixty-year-old white male received his B.A. degree. This writer was so thrilled that he almost screamed. But he realized, after observing the passive reaction of the audience, that this was a modern culture which worships youth and pushes old people aside. Had this person been a black, he would have been given the "key to the community."

Some black females — particularly in the American South — will give any older black person the right to discipline youngsters. In this American South, for example, it is not unusual for any old person of the black community to whip a young person for doing wrong. And the youngster's parents, upon hearing about the beating, will usually beat the youngster again. Many black parents feel that old people would not have whipped the youngster had he or she not done wrong. Respect for the elders, then, is one cultural factor that appears to differentiate large sections of black America from many sections of white America.

It can be seen in retrospect that African religious and family survivals in black America have played important roles in helping blacks to adapt to the horrible conditions of slavery and racism. During slavery it was the extended family which provided warmth and security for each black person. Because slave families could be broken up at any time, it was important for the children left behind to know that they could be raised by the grandparents, the uncles, the aunts, sisters and brothers, or cousins, etc., if the mother and father were sold. This type of situation made black American slave families stick together for they realized that the children, the adults, and the elders had to support one another. The extended family was what gave black Americans the strength to endure all kinds of hardships during slavery and afterwards. For they knew that such a family offered much protection and security from the blows of their life in America. The family, then, was a very important survival mechanism.

THE IMPACT OF AFRICAN SURVIVALS ON CONTEMPORARY BLACK AMERICAN FAMILIES

The extended family still assures its members that none of them will be uncared for in case of a catastrophe. If illness causes some parents not to be able to take care of their children, the family will come to their aid. Should the parents die, relatives will gladly provide for the offspring.

The impact of the extended family can be better understood if one can imagine such a family moving from the South to the Northeast. Once they arrive in the new location, every member will help the others get adjusted to the new environment. They help one another financially, psychologically, and socially. And usually they will send for other relatives whom they will help in a like manner. The extended family can be said to consist of members who basically see themselves as one. It is usually from such families that large numbers of common-law marriages originate.

Common-law marriages are beneficial to Afro-Americans for several reasons. They enable black American women, who outnumber black males, to share the males, thus preventing spinsterhood among black females. They also assure the physical survival of black people, particularly in those parts of America where black people have little or no contact with other ethnic groups. Common-law unions, unlike legal ones, do not force the couple to remain together, provided both persons are self-supporting during the seven-year period. Because this kind of arrangement is accepted by large sections of the American black community, there is less guilt feeling among the common-law partners than among common-law partners in the society at large and less guilt among their offspring as well. What has surprised many people is the love shown in the Afro-American community for children born in and out of wedlock.

It has been said historically that children are the backbone of every group or nation. Children of today are the adults of tomorrow. Without children a nation or group can be put in danger. Turkey, for example, in the early twentieth century, after having a program of limited population growth, had to institute a pronatalist policy to increase her population because she feared the military strength of her neighbors.[24] Saudi Arabia recently passed a law which would sentence anyone up to six months in jail for smuggling contraceptives into the country. The government agreed to pay a woman $75.00 for getting married and an additional sum of money for having children.[25] The reason for such a govermental policy is that Saudi Arabia is trying to industrialize, a fact which necessitates an increase in the population growth. Such a policy is not needed for black Americans because historically speaking, black people in America have large families as a duty to God and to their group.

Many black Americans have expressed an unwillingness to use contraceptives because they feel that God put people on earth to replenish the earth. To be childless, unless there are good reasons, such as medical ones, would be a sin. "The Bible says, 'Be fruitful and multiply, and fill the earth!' There is no command to choose family size but to have plenty of children."[26] Pope Pius XII stated very clearly that just because a couple did not feel like having children did not free them from the responsibility of having children. He further stated that "The survival of the species ... depends on people's having children, get in there and have them even if you don't want them ..."[27] Many black Americans believe that by having many children the parents are prolonging their lives and are assuring the survival of the species. This concept of having many children has several positive effects on the black American community.

By having many children, black people are offsetting the high mortality rate among black infants in contemporary America which exists in spite of advancements in medicine. For during the last two decades, the infant mortality rate for black Americans has been approximately double the rate for whites. So blacks still have a difficult time entering the world and an easier time departing. For example, among black Americans, the average life span is 69.3 years for females and 61.2 years for males. For whites the figures are 75.6 years for females and 68.3 years for males.[28] The fact that most black people love to have many children helps to replenish Americans. Also having many children can be of financial help to many black families.

In many parts of black America — the South and some urban ghettoes — children are a financial asset rather than a liability as they are in many parts of middle class America. Contrary to popular belief about black Americans and welfare, a large number of black American young people help support their families by working on farms in the South and by working at various jobs in the rest of the nation. Some black children are old-age social security for their parents, for as stated previously, a large number of black Americans do not live long enough to be eligible for social security benefits. So asking many black Americans to have small families or to have only one child is like asking them to tear up their social security cards. Thus, large numbers of children can not only be a financial asset to black Americans but a political blessing as well.[29] However, much as they are loved and needed, these children must deal with the very difficult environment created by racism and their parents must equip them to cope with it.

The socialization processes that black parents put their children through have the functional value of increasing the chances that black children will survive. It is because of this training that many black youth are able to cope with the seemingly overwhelming difficulties of their lives. One only has to read the newspapers or watch television to see how brave black youth have been while being attacked by white youth and sometimes white adults simply because the black youths were trying to integrate schools for the purpose of quality education. The childrens' initiation teaches black youth to keep cool under pressure. This preparation for life also teaches blacks to have respect for law and authority, which is contrary to the way in which the mass media has tried to portray blacks as having little or no respect for law and authority. During this training period black youth are also taught how to be patient and adaptable. They develop "the kind of mental toughness and survival skills, in terms of coping with life, which make them in many ways superior to their white age mates who are growing up in the material affluence of Little League suburbia."[30] Black gangs also serve as training grounds for black survival. There is a story of a black youth who, before being allowed to join a gang, has to be beaten many times with a whip without making a sound. The new gang member said after the beating, "Out of the hate of that initiation was born a strange kind of affection that binds a boy to a gang."[31] Such an initiation many times also binds a black youth to his family. The most important value of childhood initiation in black America is that it assures that large numbers of Afro-American children will learn to live in an existential society which has always excluded black Americans in varying degrees. Black youth must be prepared to live in such a system. One might say that black children learn early who they are and where they are. Just as highly valued by the black community as children are the senior black people.

Black elders in contemporary black America serve many functions. They transmit history and culture of black people to the young. For the elders have the insight and prudence of age. The elders can be utilized as baby sitters in case the children's parents have to work. In cases of sickness or death the elders can give help in caring for the children. By allowing black elders to be a part of the family, it serves to help the elders emotionally because they are interacting with people of various ages. This makes the elder feel that he is a part of the family. In a sense, one can say that black grandparents act as advisors and overseers not only for their own children, but for anyone in the extended family. This creates a tendency for black children to grow up respecting old folks in general — particularly black folks, for the black children have the experience of seeing that old people have much to offer society. Old black people have also been instrumental in helping black Americans of all ages to adapt to a very hostile, racist and competitive society.

The black people in America have proven by their ability to have survived the evils of slavery and racism in America that there is something unique in them which permitted such endurance. One black writer attempts to point out the nature of the American Negro and his adaptability:

> The American Negro is a prime example of the survival of the fittest, and it is enlightening to contrast his position today with that of the American Indian. He has been the outstanding example of American conservatism: adjustable, resourceful, adaptable, patient, restrained, and not given to gambling away what advantages he has in quixotic adventures. This has been the despair of the reformers, who have tried to lead up on the mountain and who have promised him eternal salvation. Through the succeeding uproars and upheavals that have attended our national development, the Negro has adjusted himself to every change with the basic aim of survival and advancement. Had he taken the advice of the minority firebrands in his midst, he would have risked extermination. The ability to conserve, consolidate, and change when expedient is the hallmark of individuality and group intelligence. It is why the Negro will always be here. As the law, history, and literature show, no other element of the population has had such a profound effect on our national life. They have less reason than others to harbor any feelings of inferiority although naturally they suffer from frustration.[32]

CONCLUSION

The Negro, then, by being so adjustable and adaptable has been able to survive for many years in America. Were it not for his ability to adapt constantly, he would have been exterminated long ago. No other ethnic group in America has had to endure what he has had to undergo. It is very likely that he was conditioned to being adaptable in West Africa where members of a tribe might be captured many times and forced to learn the customs of the conquering tribe or tribes. He likewise has been forced into multiple life-styles in America for his own survival. Thus, the American Negro's survival in America can be summed up by stating that he survived because he has the ability to adapt; and this ability had come down through the generations of blacks in America from the first slaves brought from West Africa where adaptability is one of the prime requirements of life.

REFERENCES

1. Melville J. Herskovits, *The Myth of the Negro Past,* Boston: Beacon Press, 1970, 270.
2. Jacob Drackler, *African Heritage,* London: Collier MacMillan, 1969.
3. Herskovits, *op. cit.,* 153; John S. Mbiti, *African Religions and Philosophy,* New York: Doubleday, 1969, 19.
4. Wade W. Nobles, Africanity: Its Role in Black Families, *The Black Scholar,* 1974, 12-13.
5. Mbiti, *op. cit.,* 34-35.
6. Nobles, *op. cit.*
7. Robert R. Lystod, *The Ashanti: A Proud People,* New York: Greenwood, 1968, 44-45. There is ample data to prove that black Americans are the descendants of the Ashanti tribe from the Gold Coast (now Ghana). See Leonard Barrett, *Soul Force: African Heritage in Afro-American Religion,* New York: Doubleday, 1974, 13-14. Also see Elizabeth Donnan, *Documents Illustrative of the History of the Slave Trade to America,* vol. IV, Washington, D. C.: Carnegie Institute of Washington, 1935, 188, 508. Philip C. Curtain, *The Atlantic Slave Trade: A Census,* Wisconsin: University of Wisconsin Press, 1969.
8. Carter G. Woodson, *The Negro in Our History,* Washington, D. C.: The Associated Publishers, 1962, 29.
9. In many American states there are laws which make it impossible for poor families to receive aid for dependent children unless the father leaves home, thus helping to increase the ratio of black women to black men.
10. Woodson, *op. cit.,* 174.
11. Carlene Young, ed., *Black Experience: Analysis and Synthesis,* San

Rafael, Cal.: Leswing Press, 1972, 7.

12. Mbiti, *op. cit.*, 175.

13.-17. are missing in the journal.

18. Richard Wright, *Black Boy*, New York: Harper & Row, 1945, 24.

19. *Ibid.*

20. *Ibid.*

21. Adam Clayton Powell, Jr., *Marching Blacks: The Rise of the Common Man*, New York: Dial Press, 1945, 75.

22. Joseph White, Toward a Black Psychology, in Reginald Jones, ed., *Black Psychology*, New York: Harper & Row, 1972, 44.

23. James Haskins, *Witchcraft, Mysticism and Magic in the Black World*, New York: Doubleday, 1974, 90-91.

24. J. Mayone Stycon, The Potential Role of Turkish Leaders' Opinions in a Program of Family Planning, *Journal of Public Opinion Quarterly*, 1965, 1:120-135.

25. Lloyd Shearer, Wanted: More Babies, *Sacramento Bee* Parade Section, September 7, 1975, 7.

26. Edward Pohlman, *How to Kill Population*, Philadelphia: Westminster Press, 1971, 51-52.

27. *Ibid.*

28. Socio-Economic Status of Blacks, *Ebony*, September, 1975.

29. Black Mayors, *Ebony*, November, 1975, 164. The importance of black voters can be seen in how white southern politician identifications of blacks change as the black vote increases. When blacks were 5% of the registered vote, they were called "niggers." Blacks were called "nigras" when they were 15% of the registered voters. When 40% of the blacks had registered, they were called "Negroes." And when blacks were 50% of the voters, white southern politicians called them "our Black brothers." See Charles S. Bullock, III, and Harrell R. Rodgers, Jr., *Racial Equality in America: In Search of an Unfulfilled Goal*, Cal.: Goodyear, 1975, 172-173.

30. Joseph White, *op. cit.*, 44. Also see Alvin F. Poussaint, A Negro Psychiatrist Explains the Negro Psyche, in Young, *op. cit.*, 196. This article explains how a Negro psychiatrist had to allow himself to be humiliated by a white southern policeman in front of other Negroes during a Civil Rights movement in Mississippi to avoid being killed. His childhood conditioning probably had much to do with enabling him to cope with this situation.

31. Tom Skinner, *Black and Free*, Michigan: Zondervan Books, 1971, 36-37.

32. George Schuyler, *Black and Conservative*, New York: Arlington House, 1971, 2.

Chapter 4

SOCIAL-PSYCHOLOGICAL CHARACTERISTICS OF ACHIEVING BLACK CHILDREN*

BARBARA J. SHADE

DECADE after decade, the issue of black achievement has been raised. Over these years social researchers have verified that, on the average, black children seem to be at a lower scholastic achievement level than the average white child, if you define achievement as scores on standardized achievement tests.[1] Inasmuch as these findings are incongruent with America's ideal image of itself and its people, they inevitably set off a series of attacks and treatises which seek to establish blame for this failure.

To a large extent, social science has been able to alleviate any social guilt that might be generated by placing the blame for these difficulties on blacks themselves. Poor showing on achievement tests has been attributed to inadequate socialization practices by black families,[2] matriarchial homes and absent fathers, who are equated with inferior child-rearing practices,[3] and inherent intellectual inferiority of the children.[4] As more attention has been given to the relationship traits and achievement, blacks have been labeled as having personality deficits that mitigate against their achievement.[5] These approaches to the problem have resulted in the assumption that poor achievement is the by-product of racial group deficiencies.

Besides leading to false assumptions, these efforts to focus on individuals having difficulty ignore the large segment of black children who are successful and do perform according to "white" standards. As Solomon[6] points out, such an oversight

*From Barbara J. Shade, Social Psychological Characteristics of Achieving Black Children, *Negro Educational Review*, 29:80-86, 1978. Reprinted by permission.

does little to propose solutions and is basically unproductive. A much more helpful approach is one which elucidates the factors that seem to generate success. From this knowledge base, then, blacks would be able to find their own ways of helping their children perform at their maximum level. Identifying the factors that seemed to influence the academic success of black children in elementary and secondary schools became the objective of this review.

Academic success can be defined in many different ways. For some investigators it is equated with a student's grade-point average; to others, achievement represents the scores on an intelligence test; others see it as favorable teacher evaluations; and others specify that achievement is represented by scores on standardized achievement tests. The use of standardized tests to measure the achievement of black children has been criticized profusely.[7] As noted by many investigators, the standardization samples used on the tests are generally inadequate and fail to include a black population. In addition, little, if any, consideration was given to the varying experiential life-styles and perceptions of blacks and other minorities in the development and selection of test questions.

In spite of these difficulties, the concept of academic achievement chosen as a basis in this review was that of scores on standardized tests. Unlike many behavioral scientists, the reviewer did not assume that all blacks are unable to perform on these tests. Instead, it was recognized that many black youth are quite capable of performing more than adequately on standardized measures. To accentuate this point, the studies chosen were limited to those which included black children between the ages of five and eighteen who had obtained acceptable scores on these tests. Other measures such as grade-point averages, intelligence quotients, and teacher evaluations may have been accompanying factors.

Proponents of the deficit theory of black achievement have concentrated their attention on five basic variables: family status, structure and interaction, sex differences, teacher-pupil interactions, personality characteristics, and intellectual performance patterns. Similar categories were adopted in this review to examine the elements affecting black children's success.

FAMILY STATUS, STRUCTURE, AND INTERACTION

Black achievers, for the most part, come from families whose occupational level might be categorized as upper-lower class and above.[8] While it is not surprising to find many achievers within the middle socioeconomic class range, it is interesting to note the type of families who produce black achievers within the lower socioeconomic class. For the most part, these families appear to be what Hannerz[9] classifies as *mainstreamers*. Both the mothers and fathers in this group are largely clerical, semi-skilled, or skilled workers, although their income level may be relatively low. Their most important characteristic, however, is their orientation toward the world, which seems to resemble that of families whose occupation and income place them at a higher level in the social hierarchy. It appears, thus, that the real difference between achievers and nonachievers is not the occupation and income of the family, but the difference in the family perceptions of the world.

Coleman,[10] Solomon[11] and Greenberg and Davidson[12] also seem to ignore socioeconomic status as a major determinant of achievement. They suggest that it is really the interaction between the parent and the child that is more important to the child's success than the family socioeconomic status. Examination of the interaction process of the families of achievers found that black children who do well in school and on achievement tests have parents or guardians who engage in academically supportive behaviors. The most common of these parental behaviors are:

1. The maintenance of a quality of communication that tends to stimulate the child's problem solving ability, independence, and productivity;[13]
2. The expression of warmth, interest, affection, and encouragement;[14]
3. The establishment of close family ties;[15]
4. The maintenance of some structure and order for the child;[16]

5. The establishment of goals of performance;[17]
6. The use of control mechanisms that include moderate amounts of praise and blame, moderate amounts of punishment, and no authoritarian tactics;[18]
7. The giving of assistance when requested or when the need is perceived.[19]

Not only is good parent-child interaction seen as more important to achievement than the family socioeconomic status, it is also seen as more important than family structure. The concept of father absence has been emphasized a great deal, particularly in the relationship to achievement. Yet most recent findings seem to discount the idea that father absence is a significant variable affecting the achievement of black children.[20] In fact, some father relationships were found to be somewhat detrimental, particularly when the father is highly authoritative in his approach to children.[21]

SEX DIFFERENCES

Although the findings have been refuted in a recent study by Edwards,[22] most of the information to date indicates that the greatest proportion of academic achievers among blacks are females. While it is generally noted that there is little difference between the males and females in intelligence, girls have been found to be identified as gifted at a 2:1 ratio,[23] are seen as superior in language usage and science,[24] and are better at word discrimination tasks than black males.[25] Other investigators found that black girls manifested more of the personality traits that have been identified as important to achievement. The girls are found to be higher in need for achievement[26] and also demonstrate more of a willingness to assume responsibility for their learning in a school situation than males.[27] They also are more likely to be self-assertive and individualistic.[28]

TEACHER-PUPIL INTERACTION

One of the most baffling characteristics of black achievers is their apparent ability to induce negative reactions from their teachers. Although black girls do seem to obtain a more favorable response from teachers than do black males,[29] in general black achievers, regardless of sex, are found to be the objects of rejection. In fact, Rubovitz and Maehr[30] found that black gifted achievers receive less attention, are least praised and most criticized in a classroom, even when compared to their nonachieving and nongifted black counterparts. Obviously, this creates a problem for the students. If black students are to perform adequately, they respond best to teachers who are warm, interested, child-oriented[31] and have high expectations of the students.[32]

PERSONALITY CHARACTERISTICS

The personality of an individual is seen as the most important antecedent to achievement, perhaps because it epitomizes the integration of all of the other factors into an interactional response to the environment.[33] Black students who do well in achievement areas seem to have numerous personal characteristics in common. In general, black achievers seem to demonstrate a need to be cautious, controlled, less trusting, and constricting in their approach to their environment. At the same time they are also highly original and creative in their ideas and tend to be very shrewd and manipulative of the situations in which they find themselves.[34] They also appear willing to conform to adult demands and manifest more of a need for conformity than independence as they seem to have very positive views of authority figures.[35]

Black achievers are goal-oriented and exploring,[36] possess greater self-confidence and a more positive self-concept than black nonachievers;[37] and are more internally controlled. They perceive themselves as in control of both their overall destiny as well as their learning situation.[38] Like other achievers, they manifest high levels of aspiration and perceive that they will accomplish their goals.[39]

INTELLECTUAL PERFORMANCE

One of the most common characteristics of black achievers is that they are highly capable people with academic promise who score high on the traditional measures of intelligence.[40] In terms of their specific intellectual skills, the black high achiever seems to excell in cognitive functioning and is especially capable in the areas of memory, verbal ability, analytical or organizational abilities, and convergent thinking.[41] Ames[42] and Greenberg and Alshan[43] also noted that this group of students made fewer perceptual errors than nonachievers.

This high level of cognitive functioning places a large number of black achievers among the intellectually gifted. Jenkins[44] concluded from his study of intellectually superior black youth that there is a proportional representation of black gifted as defined by standardized measures at every age and grade level. In fact, he found that the proportion of high IQ blacks approaches or exceeds the normal proportion in the white population. Although she did not merely limit the sample to highly intelligent blacks, Ames[45] found that about 33 percent of the school population in a northeastern city demonstrated high academic promise. Black achievers, then, seem to be of high intellectual potential and should be found throughout the population.

SUMMARY AND CONCLUSIONS

While family income may make some differences, the most significant variance between black achievers and nonachievers is the behavior of the parents or guardians. Like the teachers, parents of achievers tend to be warm, accepting, supportive, and at the same time, demanding of a better than average performance from their children. In addition, the family sets the stage and provides the environment in which the child can develop the various personality traits that have been identified as important to achievement.

Within the confines of personality, the need for black achievers to be more cautious, constricted, and shrewd while staying within the boundaries of conformity seems to stand out as being somewhat different from achievers of other ethnic groups. This would seem to indicate that, while wary of the opposition they must face, black achievers manage to find acceptable ways of confronting and using the situations they encounter to their best advantage.

One area over which neither the individual nor the family has control is the behavior of the teachers with whom they come in contact. The individuals in these roles seem to perpetuate the differential treatment between the sexes which then leads to a sexual imbalance among black achievers in favor of black females. But a more critical situation is generated by the apparent ostracism of the black intellectually superior student by teachers. It appears that having black students who are not deficient and who do not fit the stereotype is not a particularly welcomed situation. If this is the case, perhaps Coleman[47] was correct when he proposed that the real difficulty in improving black achievement rests in the improvement of teacher behavior rather than the physical plants and other factors on which much attention has been focused.

REFERENCES

1. Doxey Wilkerson, Racial Differences in Scholastic Achievement, *Journal of Negro Education*, 1934; 3:453-477; J. J. Coleman, *Equality of Educational Opportunity*, Washington, D. C.: U. S. Department of Health, Education and Welfare, 1966.

2. D. C. McClelland, *The Achieving Society*, Princeton: Van Nostrand, 1961; Irwin Katz, A Critique of Personality Approaches to Negro Performance, with Research Suggestions, *Journal of Social Issues*, 1969, 25:13-27.

3. D. P. Moynihan, *The Negro Family*, Washington, D. C.: U. S. Department of Labor, 1965; McClelland, *ibid*.

4. Arthur Jensen, How Much Can We Boost IQ and Scholastic Achievement? *Harvard Educational Review*, 1969, 34:1-128; Audrey M. Shuey, *The Testing of Negro Intelligence*, New York: Social Science Press, 1966.

5. Katz, *loc. cit.*; McClelland, *loc, cit.*; Coleman, *loc. cit.*

6. Daniel Solomon, Daniel Scheinfeld, Jay G. Hirsch, and John Jackson, Early Grade School Performance of Inner City Negro High School Higher Achievers, Low Achievers, and Drop Outs, *Developmental Psychology*, 1971, 4:482.

7. Ronald J. Samuda, *Psychological Testing of American Minorities: Issues and Consequences*, New York: Dodd, Mead, 1975.

8. Raymond Schultz, Comparison of Negro Students Ranking High With Those Ranking Low in Educational Achievement, *Journal of Educational Sociology*, 1958, 31:265-270; Alwin Coleman, The Disadvantaged Child Who is Successful in High School, *Educational Forum*, 1969, 95-97.

9. Ulf Hannerz, *Soulside: Inquiries Into Ghetto Culture*, New York: Columbia University Press, 1969.

10. A. Coleman, *op. cit.*

11. Solomon et al., *op. cit.*

12. Judith Greenberg and Helen H. Davidson, Home Background and School Achievement of Black Urban Ghetto Children, *American Journal of Orthopsychiatry*, 1972, 42:803-810.

13. Diana T. Slaughter, Maternal Antecedents of the Academic Behaviors of Afro American Head Start Children, *Educational Horizons*, 1969, 24-28.

14. Daniel Solomon, Kevin Houlihan, Thomas Busse, and Robert Parelius, Parent Behavior and Child Academic Achievement, Achievement Striving and Related Personality Characteristics, *Genetic Psychology Monographs*, 1971, 83:173-273.

15. Bernard Mackler, Blacks Who Are Academically Successful, *Urban Education*, 1970, 5:210-237.

16. H. Davidson and J. Greenberg, *School Achievers From a Deprived Background*, New York: Associated Educational Services, 1967.

17. Diane Slaughter, *op cit.*; Joseph Veroff, Sheila Feld, and Gerald Gurin, Achievement Motivation and Religious Background, *American Sociological Review*, 1962, 27:205-217.

18. Greenberg and Davidson, *op. cit.*

19. A. Coleman, *op. cit.*

20. William R. Morrow, Family Relations of Bright High-Achieving and Underachieving High School Boys, *Child Development*, 1961, 32:501-510; Daniel Solomon, Jay Hirsch, Daniel Scheinfeld, and John Jackson, Family Characteristics and Elementary School Achievement in an Urban Ghetto, *Journal of Consulting and Clinical Psychology*, 1972, 39:462-466.

21. Daniel Solomon, The Generality of Children's Achievement Reading Behavior, *Journal of Genetic Psychology*, 1969, 109-125.

22. Ozzie Edwards, Cohort and Sex Changes in Black Educational Achievement, *Sociology and Social Research*, 1975, 54:110-120.

23. M. D. Jenkins, A Sociopsychological Study of Negro Children of Superior Intelligence, *Journal of Negro Education*, 1936, 5:175-190.

24. Guy Ferrell, Comparative Study of Sex Differences in School Achievement of White and Negro Children, *Journal of Educational Research*, 1949, 43:117-121.

25. Charles Asbury, Sociological Factors Related to Discrepant Achievement of White and Black First Graders, *Journal of Experimental Education*,

1973, 42:6-10.

26. Ann D. Mingione, Need for Achievement in Negro and White Children, *Journal of Consulting Psychology,* 1965, 29:108-111.
27. Daniel Solomon, Kevin A. Houlihan, and Robert Parelius, Intellectual Achievement Responsibility in Negro and White Children, *Psychological Reports,* 1969, 24:479-483.
28. Diane Baumrind, An Exploratory Study of Socialization Effects on Black Children, *Child Development,* 1972, 43:261-267.
29. E. H. Henderson and B. H. Lang, Personal-Social Correlates of Academic Success Among Disadvantaged School Beginners, *Journal of School Psychology,* 1971, 9:101-113.
30. Pamela Rubovit et al., Pygmalion Black and White, *Journal of Personality and Social Psychology,* 1973, 25:210-218.
31. Nancy St. John, Thirty-Six Teachers: Their Characteristics and Outcomes for Black and White Pupils, *American Educational Research Journal,* 1971, 8:635-647; Daniel, *op. cit.;* Solomon, *op. cit.*
32. Fred Guggenheim, Self-Esteem and Achievement Expectations for White and Negro Children, *Journal of Projective Techniques and Personality Assessment,* 1969, 33:63-71.
33. McClelland, *op. cit.;* B. C. Rosen, Race, Ethnicity, and the Achievement Syndrome, *American Sociological Review,* 1959, 24:47-60; Henry A. Alker and Jonathan Wohl, Personality and Achievement in a Suburban and Inner City School, *Journal of Social Issues,* 1972, 28:101-113.
34. H. Davidson and J. Greenberg, *op. cit.;* Barbara J. Shade, Personality Characteristics of Black Achieving Children, unpublished manuscript, 1976.
35. Edgar G. Epps, Correlates of Academic Achievement Among Northern and Southern Urban Negro Students, *Journal of Social Issues,* 1969, 25:55-72; Alker and Wohl, *op. cit.*
36. Henderson and Lang, *op. cit.*
37. Mackler, *op. cit.*
38. *Ibid.;* Coleman, *op. cit.*
39. Edmund V. Mech, Achievement Motivation Patterns Among Low Income Anglo American, Mexican American and Negro Youth, *Proceedings, Eightieth Annual Convention,* American Psychological Association, 1972, 279-280.
40. Martin D. Jenkins, Intellectually Superior Negro Youth: Problems and Needs, *Journal of Negro Education,* 1950, 19:322-332.
41. Davidson and Greenberg, *op. cit.*
42. Louise Bates Ames, Academic Promise in Negro Primary School Pupils, *Journal of Learning Disabilities,* 1968, 1:16-23.
43. Judith W. Greenberg and Leonard M. Alshan, Perceptual Motor Functioning and School Achievement in Lower Class Black Children, *Perceptual and Motor Skills,* 1974, 38:60-62.

44. Jenkins, *op. cit.*
45. Ames, *op. cit.*
46. Coleman, *op. cit.*

CHAPTER 5

THE EMERGENCE OF A BLACK PERSPECTIVE IN COUNSELING*

GERALD GREGORY JACKSON

SCHOLARLY concern with the process of counseling the black client can be traced readily to the 1940s when, for example, workers in the field were disturbed and uncertain about specific aspects of counseling black youth and adults (Williams, 1949). Specifically, need was expressed for special information in counseling such youth. Today, concerned counselors have expressed a similar need for special techniques to use with minorities or asked if it is better for minorities to be counselors to other minorities, since racial and ethnic barriers are so threatening and difficult to penetrate (Vontress, 1973). The difference today, however, is that the volume of data on counseling blacks is greater, as is the tolerance for discussion of those related issues, such as racism. This increase in attention was predicted by one researcher who found three studies on the subject at the time of his review but asserted that in the ensuing years considerably more research would be reported (Island, 1969). The plethora of publications since the initial review tends to confirm the prediction. Ironically though, while the quantity and quality of articles waxed, the number of reviews remained conspicuously low. To illustrate, using the term "review of the literature" in the most liberal sense, only six such "reviews" could be uncovered (Island, 1969; Sattler, 1970; McGrew, 1971; Banks, 1971; Carkhuff, 1972; Denmark & Trachtman, 1973). This finding is particularly striking when one considers both the attacks on the profession in terms of the practices of its professionals toward black clients (Williams, 1949; Barney & Hall, 1965; Washington

---

*From Gerald Gregory Jackson, The Emergence of a Black Perspective in Counseling. *Journal of Negro Education*, 46:230-253, 1977. Reprinted by permission.

& Anderson, 1974) and black professionals (Jones, M. C. & Jones, M. H.; Smith, 1970; Smith, 1971a; Daley, 1972) and the perennial admonishments by black people that they are not receiving adequate services (Himes, 1948; Manley & Himes, 1948; Russell, 1949; Waters, 1953; Brazziel, 1958; Hypps, 1959; Record, 1966; Russell, 1970; Tolson, 1972).

As limited as the number of reviews may be, the genuine need is not for still another summation of contemporary publications but, more importantly, a synthesis of the emerging black perspective in counseling. Briefly stated, this outlook is derived from a sense of black culture and focuses on means of liberating black people. This acknowledgment and ensuing description does not suggest, however, that a concern by black professionals with their profession has not been historically manifested; this viewpoint suggests a new genre of expression, one that emerged from the civil rights throes of the 1960s which exposed many of the shibboleths of the profession. For example, one long-standing barrier to innovation was the notion that everyone should be regarded as the same. More specifically, the individuality of the counselor should not affect the techniques used and the psychosociological background of the client, though probably different, should not affect the techniques which he will use or his role (Trueblood, 1960). Under the aegis of this notion, which has been referred to ironically as the doctrine of color-blindness (Fibush, 1965), consideration of the differential services rendered to black clients, problems basic to blacks because of racial discrimination and changes in the training of personnel based upon the preceding were kept at an ineffectual minimum.

Conversely, the black perspective demands that the construction of counseling theories take into account the factor of culture (Stikes, 1972) and that the ultimate objective of counseling entail more than the development of academic skills. Counseling, from this point of view, should give instruction in black ideology and cultural identity which embraces the social and political realities involved in existing symbiotically with the larger culture (Toldson & Pasteur, 1972). Any other posture, it is viewed, is merely another means of perpetuating the slavery of both blacks and whites — blacks to their victimized status, and whites to their illusions of superiority (Barnes, 1972). Similarly, training institutions located at colleges and universities, it was felt, should transfer experiential learning activities from their academic settings to indigenous community centers, street academies, or store front schools so that students can gain practical skills in assisting black clients (Smith, 1971b). To grasp the meaning of the roles, techniques, and stances advocated by this new perspective, one has to be cognizant of the historical struggle preceding its development, and its clash with traditional outlooks.

STRUGGLE FOR POSITIVE RECOGNITION

Tolson's (1972) charge, "We try so hard not to see black or poor that we end up seeing nothing," suggests that recognition of the black client and professional may apparently be the crux of the problem, but upon closer inspection it is evidently only a symptom. Acts, for example, that are now a part of history cogently demonstrate how both groups were dissected from the benefits to be accrued American citizens. Frank Parsons, one of the founders of the guidance movement, who was paradoxically concerned with matching people with their appropriate job, favored European immigrants, over native born blacks, in allocating his services (Smith, 1971b). Similarly, black professionals found little kinship with the professional organization of the American Personnel and Guidance Association until the inception of the National Defense Act and its training institutes. Moreover, black professionals were denied a modicum of political prominence in the professional organization until the 1970s, after over twenty years of its existence as a body (Daley, 1972). These forms of discrimination could not have transpired without acknowledgment of a separate racial group and as a consequence, support the contention that black people were not only seen but viewed in a negative light.

This negative perception of black people is largely the result of the conceptual framework employed by the vast majority of professional counselors who unwittingly subscribe to the deficit hypothesis (Hayes and Banks, 1972). To elaborate, rather than searching in the environment for causal explanations of observed behavior, it is postulated that black people have underlying deficiencies which are attributable to genetic and/or social pathology, which in the context of this reality, limit the probability of achieving successful academic and/or social adjustment. The implications for practitioners are facile; rather than critically observing their own behavior, the assumption of the hypothesis eliminates such a need and minimizes the likelihood of counselors considering important psychosocial factors which determine black behavior.

More importantly, since the onus of the problem is on the client, the professional's mission is oppressively one of getting the client to adjust to the status quo, while the behavior of those in power and the role they perform in creating and maintaining psychologically oppressive environments, in which blacks must function, are ignored.

In short, professionals alternately espouse the doctrine of color-blindness on the one hand, but practice discrimination on the other because acknowledgment of the latter implicitly demands affirmation of racial difference and discrimination which is too painful for many of them to bear. Clearly, it is the recognition of their passivity in the face of manifestations of racism, coupled with the guise of the notion of a melting pot, which instinctively encouraged them to adhere to certain reactionary principles.

To illustrate, Williams (1949), in reaction to the cry for special information in counseling blacks, responded that there was no need for special information. Deceptively for some, Rousseve (1965) added that while the environment of blacks and whites can be differentiated because of racist patterns still prevalent in America, no essential distinction exists as far as behavioral or adjustive processes are concerned. Myopically, educators have interpreted such statements as meaning that the white middle-class can therefore serve as a model. Frequently overlooked or repressed is the condition of racism resulting from skin color differences. Williams added, for example, that while blacks have the same basic needs, the frustrations, defeats, and conflicts are intensified and faced more frequently because of their color. She observed that in counseling black students, counselors too often, either directly or indirectly, have discouraged vocational interests and choices; and she added that counseling for maximum adjustment does not attempt to adjust them to accept barriers of the status quo but prepares them to cope with the barriers, find ways around them, and even to find ways to master techniques for removing them. This belief that black clients should be assisted in learning how to negotiate in all senses of the term is one of the pillars of the black perspective which is frequently minimized in the general literature and often overlooked in counseling contacts with such individuals.

To return again to the significance of color, Boykins (1959) asserted that to counsel the black college student effectively, one had to proceed on the assumption that the personality development of the youth was affected both by participation in the culture of the larger society and by membership in the caste to which blacks in the United States are subjected by their minority position and status. Being a black, she noted, had many implications for ego development that were not inherent in lower class membership. Here again is another important point which is frequently misconstrued by researchers and professionals in their haste to disregard how black people are treated because of their color. Lumping black with lower-class whites is a more convenient and face-saving alternative than understanding and dealing with the American contradiction of discrimination.

More recently, Siegel (1970) expressed the view that in counseling the nonwhite student today, counselors must be aware of that student's identity because in her estimation, there lies the key to a proper approach to him, that is, does he see himself as a Negro American or an American Negro, colored person, or black man? White counselors in particular it has been shown are uniquely vulnerable in this regard (Vontress, 1971; Jackson & Kirschner, 1973); and Cross (1971) postulated five identifiable psychological stages black people undergo in moving from a self-perception of Negro to a more liberated one of black. Yet, the professional band continues to play the tune of "see no evil."

It is apparent from the references alluded to that the case for viewing blacks in unique ways is not a recent issue and the same holds true for proposals to correct the problems engendered by the profession. Trueblood (1960), as others have similarly reported, felt that a counselor should explore the personality adjustment of the black student and the possible influence that being black, with the attendant social, educational, and economic restrictions has on his personality adjustment. He based his belief on the idea that there are possible problems of behavior and attitude which are related to the fact that the student is black. Where he, in addition, digressed appreciably from conventional wisdom was in his view that while the process or techniques employed in assisting the student remained basically the same as those used for other population groups, the role of the counselor must be affected by his special knowledge of the student's needs. This special knowledge, he felt, could be gained only by studying the psychological and sociological background of blacks. Presumably, such a professional understanding would be gained in graduate training where, theoretically, the opportunities are given and the insights gained. Yet, those who are trained in counseling, those who teach it, and those who write it, do not have the instinctive, internalized knowledge of the ghetto culture, nor has a realistic opportunity to learn been provided them (Jones, M. C. & Jones, M. H., 1970). The student of counselor who wished such knowledge had to find his own way of acquiring it, which took unusual determination and initiative.

To illustrate; Mickelson and Stevic (1967) also felt that counselor educators were not meeting the special needs of trainees in preparing them for work with the disadvantaged. They even conceded that many times the fault may reside within the counselor; however, in the opinion of these authors, "in all too many cases the root of the problem may well be traced to the preparation program of the counselor" (p. 77).

Similarly, the Lewises (1970) noted that present programs of counselor education did not provide the basis for inner-city counselors to understand their students and their culture, or provide them with knowledge of the processes of social change and their potential contribution.

Finally, Boxley and Wagner in their 1971 publication of a survey of APA approved psychology training programs reported that while many of the schools responding indicated an interest in recruiting more minority students, the available sites (clinics and counseling centers) were centered on the white middle-class client; and minority faculty members at these schools were underrepresented. In their replicative study reported in 1973, they found no significant changes in the representation of minority group faculty, significant changes in the representation of minority peoples in the graduate student population but training programs which remained limited in breadth. Proposals to correct this deficit in training have been largely ignored.

Vontress (1969a) for one, proposed preprofessional training, which was undergirded in anthropology, sociology, and psychology, and the removal of counselor training from educational settings. He saw it within the purview of training programs to also provide opportunities for trainees to explore their feelings about the culturally different, live in the ghetto, and have a representative from the community be employed by the training institute to help counselors relate to the culturally different (Vontress, 1969b).

Rousseve (1965) proposed that such trainees be exposed more extensively to updated scientific findings in cultural anthropology and related fields as these findings relate to intergroup prejudice and discrimination. Moreover, he felt that they should be required to sample and analyze some of the recent literary expressions of minority group authors.

In spite of these proposals, training programs in general showed little imagination in practice or in developing attitudes toward the preparation of counselors to work in settings focused primarily on urban blacks (Smith, 1971a). Even those programs, however, which have been designed, in theory at least, with the preceding recommendations in mind still err because the black perspective demands even greater allegiance. A brief description of some of these programs will illustrate the significant difference between the two points of view. Mickelson and Stevic (1970) recommended that counselor educators think beyond the rather traditional approach which had been taken in preparation programs and think in terms of a two-year integrated program. The first year of such a program would entail an introduction to the various theoretical, cultural, and philosophical foundations of the profession. The second year would involve placement in a ghetto school or in a federally sponsored program such as the Neighborhood Youth Corps. In addition, the second year would include courses in black sociology and psychology and seminars which would bring in prominent local black leaders and students at the university. This curriculum they believed would enable counselors to be of service to teachers which would further the rights of the pupil since the counselor would be promoting appropriate classroom behavior and understanding. They concluded that counselor educators could continue to ignore the need, but if they did others would institute programs to replace the school counselor "who is now charged with various guidance and counseling responsibilities, but who because of lack of preparation and/or commitment had fallen far short of the goal of providing assistance to all youth (p. 77)."

The Lewises (1970) proposed that students be paried with an experienced counselor and placed full-time for a year in an inner-city school. During this stay he would be expected to provide direct counseling with students, attempt to involve the community in the operation of the school and the school in the operation of the community and spend a good deal of time working in a consultative capacity with teachers. Didactic course work was viewed as a bridge between theory and practice and included courses designed to enhance the trainees' awareness of the school's total milieu and the sociology of the school and the community. Their model counselor would be recognized as a consultant and an agent of change; however they envisioned a training program that would specifically prepare the counselor for the role rather than assuming "that he will learn these functions later in some mystic manner" (p. 37).

In terms of criticisms, George Banks (1971), after reviewing the literature in counseling, psychotherapy, testing, information-gathering, social casework, and education regarding the effects of race on the outcome of the interview situation, concluded that the task was no longer to analyze the black man, but to reexamine the training and experiences of those involved in working with blacks. He advocated that professionals should be concerned with selection and training based on the set of facilitative and action-oriented variables found to make a constructive difference in one-to-one relationships in general. One step further, the argument was advanced that even training programs which encouraged the perception of differences still may produce helpers who are a part of the problem rather than the solution. Accordingly, the comprehension of alienation divorced from a black perspective, was deemed insufficient because the propensity of the formidable majority of professionals constrained them to center on what they considered to be problems of personal disorganization within the black client (Banks, W. 1972a), that is, the deficit hypothesis.

More specifically, others cautioned against the use of certain approaches. Counselors were cautioned against subscribing to psychoanalytic models in general and classical psychoanalysis in particular when providing assistance to black counselees (Harper, 1973a). The criticism was that the original theory of Freud was based upon middle and upper-class white Europeans of the 1800s which had little, if anything, to do with a black ghetto child.

In addition, it was viewed as a post-dictive therapeutic approach which explained the why of behavior and not how to get food to quell hunger. As a more appropriate objective, it was felt to be the moral duty of the counselor to recondition the behavior of the counselee in helping him to learn new ways of meeting his needs and new ways of relating to the world, since he had been conditioned not to achieve such an end or even predestined by the dehumanizing conditions into which he is born. In contrast with the psychoanalytical approach, the use of behavioral principles was advanced as being progressive since they went beyond the deficit hypothesis (Hayes & Banks,

1972). Once again, from the black vantage point, it was added that behavioral theory would be useless if the counselor did not understand what constitutes reward or punishment for a black client, or if he failed to perceive the particular environmental conditions that effect a reward or punishment to his client (Banks, 1972a). This is an extremely important consideration, but an even more important one is that the counseler using such an approach should not confine himself to remedying the individual's lack of skill or inappropriate response repertoire because to do so is to inherently accept the notion that the problem is solely within the individual and encourages one to lose sight of the parameters of the problem.

The Alternatives

To counteract the unrelenting negative view of black people, the black perspective reordered some fundamental tenets. First, the locus of problems was shifted from the individual to society. Termed systemic counseling, this model assumed that most of the problems that had heretofore been labeled client problems were in actuality system problems. The role of the counselor in such an arrangement would be to treat the system for its problems which, when appropriate, would ultimately bring about a corresponding change in individuals (Gunnings & Simpkins, 1972). A word of caution must be added because of the tendency of some to use the concept of the culpability of the system as a justification for doing absolutely nothing. They ascribe all problems to the operation of the system and postulate that since they cannot correct the system through their individual assistance they cannot assist the black client (Thomas, 1962). Such an approach is not systemic counseling but systemic racism and should not be confused with the view that blacks are not disadvantaged but are placed in situations where they are at a disadvantage (Simpkins, Gunnings, and Kearney, 1973).

Second, techniques and approaches evolved which were based upon black culture. Mitchell (1971), for one, attacked what he perceived as the traditional posture of counselors who attempt to be nice guys by just listening. He felt that such a stance was not enough because black students needed tools for dealing with their problems. The counseling process itself, in his estimation, should deal with the present as well as with the "hereafter." Those counselors, he charged, who dwelled only on early childhood experience often turned off black students, because the latter do not see how such early experiences are relevant to their current crises. Moreover, the Rogerian trilogy of congruence, empathy, and positive regard had to be combined with definite techniques through which the student could acquire desirable skills or attitudinal change.

Toldson and Pasteur (1972) saw the use of soul music as an appropriate way of achieving positive counseling ends when working with black students. Stikes (1972) advocated the use of modeling and simulation techniques, verbal reinforcement, and contracts as culturally specific counseling devices for assisting black clients. In addition, he felt that advising black students was appropriate because they expected authority figures to do so and did not result in expected dependency, and he suggested the use of the environment as a means of teaching the client appropriate attitudes and skills for dealing with the environment. In line with this approach, the counselor would provide psychologically safe experiences by reducing threat and removing barriers and helping the client understand and actualize his personal perspective in the black social movement. Tolson (1973) analyzed the human potential movement and concluded that all black groups were the most appropriate vehicle for black liberation.

Finally, Edmund Gordon (1970) not only challenged the individual psychological model still regnant today, he proposed as a substitute a developmental-ecological model which incorporates the preceding culturally specific recommendations. His model envisioned a shift from the study of clients to the study of systems, i.e. the family, school, or office, and their development as social processes. Adherents to this model would no longer assess behavioral products, but would instead assess behavioral processes and as a consequence examine the nature of intellectual and social functioning for the individual and describe those functions qualitatively — in short, a movement away from prediction to prescription or from identification and placement in available opportunities to the creation of, and placement in, appropriate situations. In addition, the subscriber would no longer rely upon didactic exhortation, but on discovery and modeling as vehicles for learning and give more attention to the use of naturally occurring or contrived environments to provide interactions supportive of learning and development in specified directions. Gordon further suggests that counseling, which he said should be abandoned as a field, should be shifted from interpretation to environmental orientation as its principle focus. Greater emphasis, he imagined, should be given to consultation. Finally, but not inclusive of all his points, he felt there should be a shift from primary concern with socialization to a major concern with politicalization, that is, systems maneuvering skills which would be skills that were not only essential to adequate concept of self but also to future survival.

Third, the black perspective gave new interpretations of black behavior and posited new images based upon strengths to supplant the old images based upon weakness. To illustrate, while most counselors subscribe to the notion advanced by Freud that a counselor should be a blank screen or a reflector of the client's problems, it was acknowledged finally that such an approach registered to black students as indifference, remoteness, and superiority (Scheffler, 1969). In lieu of the blank screen idea was the acclamation that a willingness to reveal something personal is a key to reaching black students (Lefkowitz & Baker, 1971) and can build strong bonds of trust and rapport (Stikes, 1972). In a similar vein, the notion that black people are somehow innately nonverbal was exposed on a number of fronts. It was found, for example, that they disclosed less than whites to certain target persons (Braithwaite, 1973). More importantly, this reservation to reveal oneself is based upon their minority status (English, 1957) and the need to maintain a facade in order to survive in a land that metes out rewards and punishments according to skin color (Phillips, 1961). Again, failure to recognize the genesis of observed be-

havior is not only an indictment of the training of the professional but the institutions which provide such training and the
profession which proposes inclusion in such programs. What is
suggested, also, is complicity in the scheme where black people
are not viewed in terms of how they are generally mistreated
but in terms of their resistance to becoming totally assimilated
into American society. In short, the phenomena is a classical
instance of the self-fulfilling prophecy (Rosenthal & Jacobson,
1968) in operation by a profession avowing humanistic principles. This ambiguity, as well as other discrepancies, is clearly
seen by adherents of the black perspective and has served as one
of its motivational forces.

Another dimly grasped reality, based upon cultural difference, was the fact that blacks and whites have different ways of
communicating and the implication of this lack of recognition
by the professional. Dr. Scheffler (1969), for example, reported
that her expectation of verbal proficiency was a middle-class
bias rooted in her experience in college and psychiatric settings
where articulateness was often used as a convenient "hallmark
of intelligence or potential" (p. 114). She discovered that ghetto
residents were less fluent than middle-class people in vocabulary and form of middle-class English and were inhibited in
using street language with those in authority, but only because
the precise use of English she was accustomed to was less important to them. More important for communicating was observing gestures, intonations, facial expressions, or a variety of
uses for a single word or phrase. From a black point of view, if
professionals such as Dr. Scheffler had been familiar with the
life-style of inhabitants of the ghetto, they would know also
that ghetto residents, too, give prestige and power to the fast
talker, so that nonverbal really translates to "nonverbal in
white terms" (Sager, Brayboy & Waxenberg, 1972). It is, therefore, as Scheffler indicated, the expectation of a certain way of
being fluent verbally and a lack of cognition of nonverbal
messages which result in the label of "uncommunicative," "silent," or "nonverbal" (Barnes, 1972). The real problem, then,
from the black perspective, is that the so-called nonverbal client
is the one who usually receives the little help from the coun-

selor who, in turn, often gets frustrated and gives up his attempt to establish contact, especially when the lure of heavy case loads can be used as a rationalization (Patterson, 1973).

Another example of the disadvantage of the designation "nonverbal" is the case of the clinical and counseling psychology students who were provided with a practicum experience with black trainees (Payne & Mills, 1970). The graduate students reported that the subjects were "nonverbal," and as a consequence, they discovered that they had to abandon the traditional interviewing format which depended upon high verbal interactions and focus greater attention on the nonverbal cues. Two shortcomings are illustrated by the observations made by students: first, that the subjects were defined as nonverbal as a label when the behavior manifested could merely have been a reflection of the appropriate tact to take under the circumstances and had nothing to do with the subject's verbal proficiency. Second, the assumption by such persons that black clients enjoy such roles as professional examinee and should be cooperative, energetic, and enthusiastic is naive and illustrative of how a well-intentioned learning experience can be undermined by a lack of knowledge of the culture and history of black people.

Beyond the challenges to the old notions held of black people as indolent, recalcitrant, and in general, without singular distinctions, is a new view of them as initiators, problem-solvers, and competent. For instance, in one setting a peer counseling program utilizing disadvantaged high school students found that it bettered classroom skills, improved grades, and raised levels of vocational and educational aspirations among the students (Vriend, 1969). In another case, black students demonstrated competencies in counseling peers in a variety of settings, initiating guidance programs, and assessing how an educational system operates to the detriment of black students (Jackson, 1972a). Critical to the point that black people possess unusual strengths are the reports that black students have been trained to serve in a counseling capacity where professionally trained counselors were found to be inadequate (Sue, 1973); initiated and conducted programs on drug abuse (Jones, 1970);

and conducted programs on career guidance (Amsterdam News, 1972). Finally, a program was developed to convert minority school teachers into qualified school counselors. The program had as one of its premises the fact that skin color, language, or inner-city social origin were advantages in counseling minority students (Lindberg & Wrenn, 1972). It was reported also that one of the indirect benefits of the program was the positive reaction of the inner-city community to it and, as a consequence, a greater support for the total counseling program.

In addition to the struggle for positive recognition is the concomitant struggle to gain personnel who will not only have a black philosophical orientation, but a commitment to the new role carved out of this perspective as well. What follows is a description of the struggle for personnel, followed by a consideration of the roles evolving from the struggles.

STRUGGLE FOR SERVICES

One of the earliest studies on guidance services for black students which reported some of the problems entailed found that black high schools in the southeast region of the United States suffered from: (1) inadequately trained personnel, (2) inadequate facilities, and (3) inadequate programs and personnel (Himes, 1948). It was noted further that, in some instances, the community was an additional hindrance. For example, some officials pointed to parental indifference, poor school-community relations, and lack of cooperation from community leaders. Even though the facilities were manned by black people, which suggests that guidance problems may be independent from the factor of race, racial prejudice was blamed in part for the inadequacies cited. In a similar study, poor training of teachers was cited as the number one cause for the problem in guidance and the conclusion drawn from the data that it was probable that the expansion of guidance was making little positive contribution to the success of the total school program (Manley & Himes, 1948). Guidance programs at black colleges started during the 1940s (Russell, 1949), and a report by Patterson (1947) indicated that black students were in need of this form of assistance since the close guidance relationship between student and faculty was no longer a significant practice. A study of black rural high school students found the guidance services were inadequate and the recommendation made that more attention should be devoted to this area (Waters, 1953).

Integrated Settings

In a study which focused on the relative guidance services given in a segregated surrounding, white schools had greater services (Brazziel, 1958). It has been noted similarly that even in cities where black students are not segregated on the basis of race, they are still under-serviced (Hypps, 1959). To amplify, in a study conducted in an integrated high school which sought to determine if students felt black youth were discriminated against in educational counseling (Barney & Hall, 1965), no statistical difference was found. However, a review of individual cases revealed that counselors tended to be a little less willing to advise black marginal students to apply for college admission.

Attitudes Toward Services Given

Civil rights organizations frequently saw counselors who indirectly encouraged black students to drop-out or to aspire to low level occupations or to form poor self-images (Record, 1966) as an integral part of the whole apparatus of discrimination. Brazziel (1970) noted that in 1940, 10 percent of black students went to college in comparison to 20 percent for whites. However, in 1969, 20 percent of black students went to college whereas 40 percent of whites did so.

In terms of the black community, Tolson (1972) observed that blacks were angry and impatient with the traditional role of the counselor which was seen as maintaining the status quo rather than improving the condition of any individual or group. She noted that they were becoming increasingly suspicious of counselors and counseling bodies, to the point that suspicion often becomes rejection. In her view, a counselor was good for working with the powerless only when he had proven in their eyes his effectiveness in working toward a real change in their behalf. Corroborating her belief, Russell (1970) interviewed black residents of one community who were unskilled and seasonal workers and found them to be unanimous in their belief that all guidance did for black children was to put them in special classes, punish them for infractions, and get rid of them as soon as possible. Patterson (1973) noted two extreme and inappropriate practices of many counselors. They either encouraged black clients to accept, in the name of reality testing, menial "black" jobs which required little education or, after 1960 and the realization of new opportunities, they encouraged black clients to aspire to any imaginable goal regardless of apparent qualifications or abilities. This erratic behavior on the part of counselors often stems from their inability to sort out inappropriate behavior on the part of the counselee from the inappropriate behavior of society in engendering such behavior. For example, in a training program for drop-outs in which Southern reared females were transplanted from the South to the North and then released to work in northern urban settings, one white employer complained that he was disappointed that prospective candidates from the program would not look him in the eye. He interpreted such behavior as a lack of confidence. The black counselor, on the other hand, informed the employer that the students had been conditioned to respond to whites in power in that manner and that it was his responsibility to give the students the security to be themselves. The counselor went a step further, however, and used behavioral rehearsal and role-playing techniques to assist the students in being more assertive in the job interview situation (Jackson, 1972b). In short, he worked on both aspects of the problem and indicated to the students that they did not have to accept the offer of appointment. This counselor also had some of his clients enroll in a local college even though the program was not designed to have its graduates seek further education (Bates College newspaper, 1969).

Failure in Counselor Orientation

The implications of the preceding are apparent. First, the remarkable number and variety of college placement programs that developed outside the schools, with or without federal support, suggest that there is a crisis in guidance services in the school (Kendrick, 1970). Second, this crisis or failure, from a black perspective, can be traced to the application of traditional middle-class precollege guidance techniques to black youth which are inappropriate (Kadota & Menacker, 1971).

Another means of delimiting the services given to black clients is the traditional way in which counselors arrange to be seen and how they structure such interviews. Irvine (1968), for example, asserted that a counselor interested in serving such individuals may have to "permit himself to establish contacts in what appear to be inappropriate places at inappropriate times with the most inappropriate people" (p. 177). This is a point supported by Mitchell's (1970) observation that, "The counselor must also be willing to leave the security of his office in order to deal with some of the situational factors in white institutions which cause problems for black students. He should be willing to make a personal contact for the student who is overwhelmed by the bureaucracy" (p. 36). Banks (1973) and Gordon (1965) both support this approach to counseling.

In short, the black perspective castigates counselors for administering services solely from their offices (Washington, B., 1970) or waiting for black youth to seek them out first (Kadota & Menacker, 1971; Smith, 1971a; Banks, 1973). Specifically, Brown (1973) observed that a counseling center, staffed primarily by whites, is generally perceived as a potentially hostile agency whose structure and office atmosphere projects to the black student a sense of "going to see the Man." The problem with changing the situation, he indicated, was the tradition in higher education that often blocks the modification of programs and structures even when adult members of ethnic minority groups are involved in establishing the program or designing the structure. In fact, he was struck by his finding that programs set up on college campuses specifically for ethnic minority students have more often than not been structured in almost identical ways to similar programs offered by the institution for the general student body. By traditional he meant being assigned office space, given a desk, and expected to maintain regular posted office hours. As a consequence, he noted: "I have not been surprised that many students will not come for assistance under these conditions even when they are in serious academic or personal difficulty, but I have been bewildered that nonwhite administrators would expect ethnic minority students to feel comfortable and to relate to counselors under these conditions" (p. 169). This point is not difficult to understand, however, if one considers who trained the administrators and the bulk of their staff, and from what framework the institution operates.

Selection of Staff

Another dilemma encountered, then, in the administration of services is the problem of selecting suitable staff. Russell (1970), for example, suggested that the demand for black counselors by black students was the result of the latter's dissatisfaction with the present functioning of guidance which they considered to be "irrelevant" to their needs and an instrument of repression which was controlled by counselors who constituted roadblocks that they had to somehow manage to get around, particularly if their ambitions did not coincide with those which their counselors considered appropriate for them.

Feelings vary, however, on the subject of the significance of the race of the counselor who attempts to counsel blacks. Taylor (1973) expressed a consensus that it is generally undesirable for whites to be involved in mental health research and treatment with black people because of the former's racist proclivities; and, others have concurred. White counselors have been charged with lacking awareness of the problems, feelings, and outlook of blacks (Hypps, 1959; Brown, 1973), the ability to identify with black counselees (Rousseve, 1965), and the inability to assist when the decision entails rejecting society (Kincaid, 1969). Moreover, white counselors have been viewed in general as being discouraged and defeatist (Smith, 1967), and young white females, in particular, as anxiety-ridden when attempting to assist black males of comparable age (Vontress, 1969b). Smith (1971a) saw one of the major problems as that of overcoming a sense of superiority. In terms of student perceptions, Lewis (1969) reported that most black youth doubted the sincerity of a "helping" white counselor. Similarly, Russell (1970) conveyed that black students' belief that racial bias existed in interracial counseling thwarted them from believing that a white counselor could regard them as individuals who possessed the same emotions, aspirations, and potentials as whites. It was observed that a white skin automatically placed one strike against the counselor (Mitchell, 1970).

On the opposite side of the pendulum, it has been stressed that some black counselors who were born and bred in the ghetto have negative attitudes toward relating to black youth (Smith, 1968). In the same vein, one writer speculated that black militant counselors would reject clients who termed themselves colored (Vontress, 1972).

In more specific terms, Hypps (1959) expressed the view that because most black counselors have been limited traditionally in the United States as a consequence of their race in their vocational, social, and political experience, they would not be able to impart the full evaluation of the business, industrial, and political life in a free society to their counselees.

McDaniel (1968) felt that in a black-black relationship there was the persistent danger that the counselor will have difficulty with the counselee because he perceives the counselor as being a person who is a member of the establishment and, as a consequence, a threat to his existence.

McDaniel noted that he found it easier to work with white clients because the prejudiced ones did not seek his assistance, whereas black students did and wondered whether or not he had been a traitor. Personally, he found greater success with juniors and seniors in college because they had the opportunity to observe his behavior and had at least come to the tentative conclusion that maybe he was not an Uncle Tom and, therefore, was able to relate to them in a meaningful way.

Mitchell (1970) saw two distinct problems for the black counselor. First, if he had not examined himself, Mitchell felt, there would be a tendency to project his attitudes and feelings onto other blacks and as a consequence he would be just as "uptight" as the white counselor. Second, if he works in a white institution, he will have to demonstrate his legitimacy to black students who need to feel that he is someone who is honestly interested in them and not an "Uncle Tom" or an unqualified showpiece. Finally, Lindberg and Wrenn reported (1972) that one criticism occasionally registered about minority counselors was that they tended to be militant at times and push minority causes. Interestingly enough though, as counselor educators these authors did not see such behavior as a criticism but rather an indication of success because they wanted their counselors to be in the front line of the current ethnic-social struggles and fully involved with students who were experiencing these struggles.

Research studies conducted on the race of the counselor point to the employment of black counselors to assist black counselees. To illustrate, a number of reports demonstrate either the efficacy of black counselors over white ones (Phillips, 1960; Stranges & Riccio, 1970; Heffernon & Bruehl, 1971; Gardner, 1972; Grantham, 1973) or that black counselees found comparatively less satisfaction with white counselors than white counselees (Burrell & Rayder, 1971; Brown, Frey & Crapo, 1972). In the same vein, trained black adults were preferred over white professional counselors (Carkhuff, 1970) and white counselors were found to have low linguistic compatibility with black students (Schumacher & Banikiotes, 1972). Other studies on the subject found that race was relatively insignificant (Backner, 1970; Barrett & Perlmutter, 1972, Cimbolic, 1972; Cimbolic, 1973) and in only one instance favored white counselors over black ones (Bryson & Cody, 1972).

From the black perspective, the rhetoric on the subject and even the mounting research which favors the employment of black counselors are embellishments of two central concerns. First, as Barnes (1972) has indicated, if we take seriously what we know about the process of psychological identification, we must inevitably conclude that the white counselor contributes to the identity crisis of the black student. In his view, identification in this instance was simultaneously denying self and identifying with the symbol of the oppressive system. A black counselor, on the other hand, who shares a common experience with his counselee and who has not rejected his own personal history, presents an appropriate figure for identification and is most able to inspire a feeling of confidence and a sense of hope in his black counselees. Second, Banks (1971) argued that in light of the black man's struggle to establish that black people can do something for themselves, proving that they can establish an effective helping program for themselves will give them some additional sense of identity and manhood. In a black context then, the encompassing consideration is the general plight of black people and not solely the advancement of one individual who happens to be black.

THE INTERIM

Today, a number of black students are pleading that skin color be noticed and ask that they not be expected to find their heritage in a counter-part of white society (Siegel, 1970). Black professionals, too, have rejected the notion that a student is a student whether he is black, white, red, or polka dot (Banks, 1970). These developments partially account for why the belief that students are students and that all they need is to be listened to, appreciated, guided, given moral and social examples, and given alternatives, has not worked (Charnofsky, 1971). What is posed as a substitute for the doctrine of color-blindness is a view which recognizes that skin color has an enormous consequence in the United States and that if one is defined as black, then such a person's condition is significantly different from that of any white immigrant or native (Tucker, 1973).

Given this perspective, the traditional role of the counselor is no longer acceptable as an aid to black people. In fact, one writer (Adams, 1973) went so far as to suggest that if counselors were to be helpful in the struggle for fundamental change requisite to assist minorities, they would have to abandon the following traditional activities: (1) vocational guidance, because it made an unfair and inadequate job market more acceptable and also helped to fill "manpower" needs of an economy based on exploitation; (2) large-scale achievement and intelligence testing, because it performed a stratification function; (3) crisis intervention counseling, because it served to keep the lip on potentially explosive situations; and, (4) personal adjustment counseling, because it served to convince clients that the source of their alienation was within the self. As an alternative, counselors would use their skills to help people realize the source of their alienation and organize them to take action. A more general consensus seems to be the abandonment of the individualistic orientation of the profession and movement towards the assumption of responsibility for addressing societal issues which bear upon the effectiveness of counseling. To illustrate, Anderson and Love (1973) advocated that counselors help black clients to develop a sense of pride and white clients an increased racial understanding. To bolster this goal, they developed a program of exercises to increase racial awareness by enhancing relations for the school. Similar in thrust, Sedlacek and Brooks (1973a) reported how research could be employed to lessen the practice of institutional racism. Similar to Love and Anderson, these writers also reported a model for solving the problem of racism in educational settings (Sedlacek & Brooks, 1973b). Viewed as a whole, this model can be interpreted as implying two poorly recognized needs: first, that racism does not only exist in the larger society but in the framework of educational settings as well; and second, that it is the responsibility of counselors to not only be cognizant of the phenomena but to actually initiate programs to ameliorate its occurrence. This approach, by the way, is not an autonomous function but is an integral part of the broader role of consultant which Gordon (1970) felt should replace the counseling function. In general, the role of consultant includes work with the faculty (Proctor, 1970), administration, staff, and community (Banks, 1973) and, in effect, catapults the counselor from the role of individual ministration to environmental manipulator (Harper, 1973b). It has been further defined as entailing the demonstration of teachers of the power of their expectations (Coffin, Dietz & Thompson, 1970), the translation of the needs of students to teachers (Bolden, 1970), the presentation of culturally oriented programs in the school (Charnofsky, 1971), and curriculum adviser (Washington, 1968). In terms of the community, this new role includes seeking employment opportunities and financial aid for black students (Trueblood, 1960), introducing the school to the home (Rousseve, 1965), and giving talks at churches, social organizations, and schools (Jones, M. C. & Jones, M. H., 1970).

Another role emanating from the black perspective is that of innovator. Examples of this role would be the work of Tolson and Pasteur (1972) who developed techniques for therapeutic intervention based upon a synthesis of Rogerian principles and black spirituality, and Stikes's (1972) electic use of behavioral and analytical techniques based upon a unified concept of black culture. An additional case of an innovative advance is the movement by black professionals to make the professional association more responsive to the needs of the black client. Jones and Jones (1970) recommended that black counselors form their own association so they would have a forum to exchange methods and ideology regarding the "neglected" client. Historically though, at the 1969 national convention in Las Vegas, a minority caucus presented a resolution to establish a salaried National Office of Non-White Concerns within the executive structure of the American Personnel and Guidance Association (APGA). These caucus members, according to Daley (1972), were: "tired of acquiescence; they were tired of an 'acceptable' existence; they were tired of all the rhetoric about warmth, acceptance, and development of each one's maximum potential" (p. 495). Each year until 1972 when a separate division within APGA was formed, caucuses met and presented grievances. At present the separate division has its own journal which projects the black perspective in counseling, conducts programs related to minority interests both during conventions and throughout the year, and has moved from the smallest division out of eleven to the seventh in size.

Given the historical roots of the black perspective and the continuation of conditions in the environment which gave rise to this outlook, one may infer that in the ensuing years this perspective will probably grow in substance and acquire a firmer shape. Schools employing counselors and counselor educators who train these counselors will have to adjust their policies and procedures to embrace this expanding point of view. In the absence of such resources, counseling may transpire outside of traditional institutions and training relegated to other agents.

REFERENCES

Adams, H. J. The Progressive Heritage of Guidance: A View From the Left. *Personnel and Guidance Journal*, 1973, 50:531-538.

Amsterdam News (N.Y.), "School Program Studies Local Community Role," December 30, 1972, 8.

Anderson, N. J. & Love, B. Psychological Education for Racial Awareness. *Personnel and Guidance Journal*, 1973, 51:666-670.

Backner, B. L. Counseling Black Students: Any Place for Whitey. *Journal of Higher Education*, 1970, 41:630-637.

Banks, G., Berenson, G. G., & Carkhuff, R. R. The Effects of a Counselor Race and Training Upon Counseling Process With Negro Clients in Initial Interviews. *Journal of Clinical Psychology*, 1967, 23:70-72.

Banks, G. P. The Effects of Race on One-to-One Helping Interviews. *Social Service Review*, 1971, 45:137-146.

Banks, W. M. The Changing Attitudes of Black Students. *Personnel and Guidance Journal*, 1970, 48:739-745.

Banks, W. M. The Black Client and the Helping Professional. In Reginald L. Jones (ed.), *Black Psychology*. New York: Harper & Row, 1972 (a).

Banks, W. M. Militant Counselors: Riffraff or Vanguard? *Personnel and Guidance Journal*, 1972, 50:575, 581-584 (b).

Banks, W. M., & Martens, K. Counseling: The Reactionary Profession. *Personnel and Guidance Journal*, 1973, 51:457-462.

Barnes, E. J. Counseling and the Black Student: The Need for a New View. In Reginald L. Jones (ed.), *Black Psychology*. New York: Harper & Row, 1972.

Barney, O. P., & Hall, L. D. A Study in Discrimination. *Personnel and Guidance Journal*, 1965, 43:707-709.

Barrett, F. T., & Perlmutter, F. Black Clients and White Workers: A Report From the Field. *Child Welfare*, 1972, 51:19-24.

Bolden, J. A. Black Students and the School Counselor. *The School*

Counselor, 1970, 17:204-207.

Boxley, R., & Wagner, N. Clinical Psychology Training Programs and Minority Groups: A Survey. *Professional Psychology*, 1973, 4:259-264.

Boykins, L. Personality Aspects of Counseling the Negro College Student. *Quarterly Review of Higher Education Among Negroes*, 1959, 27:64-73.

Braithwaite, R. A. A Paired Study of Self-Disclosure of Black and White Inmates. *Journal of Non-White Concerns*, 1973, 1:87-94.

Brazziel, W. F. Meeting the Psychosocial Crisis of Negro Youth Through a Coordinated Guidance Service. *Journal of Negro Education*, 1958, 27:79-83.

Brazziel, W. F. Getting Black Kids into College. *Personnel and Guidance Journal*, 1970, 48:747-751.

Brown, R. D., Frey, D. H., & Crapo, S. E. Attitudes of Black Junior College Students Towards Counseling Services. *Journal of College Student Personnel*, 1972, 13:420-424.

Brown, R. A. Counseling Blacks: Abstractions and Reality. In Charles F. Warnath (ed.), *New Directions for College Counselors*. San Francisco: Jossey-Bass, 1973.

Bryson, S., & Cody, J. Relationship of Race and Level of Understanding Between Counselor and Client. *Journal of Counseling Psychology*, 1973, 20:495-498.

Burrell, L., & Rayder, N. Black and White Students' Attitudes Toward White Counselors. *Journal of Negro Education*, 1971, 40:48-52.

Carkhuff, R. R. The Development of Effective Courses of Action for Ghetto School Children. *Psychology in the Schools*, 1970, 7:272-274.

Carkhuff, R. R. Black and White in Helping. *Professional Psychology*, 1972, 3:18-22.

Charnofsky, S. Counseling for Power. *Personnel and Guidance Journal*, 1971, 49:351-357.

Cimbolic, P. Counselor Race and Experience Effects on Black Clients. *Journal of Consulting and Clinical Psychology*, 1972, 39:328-332.

Cimbolic, P. T. Group Effects on Black Clients' Perceptions of Counselors. *Journal of College Student Personnel*, 1973, 14:296-302.

Coffin, B., Dietz, S., & Thompson, C. Academic Achievement in a Poverty Area High School: Implications for Counseling. *Journal of Negro Education*, 1971, 40:365-368.

Cross, W. The Negro-to-Black Conversion Experience. *Black World*, 1971, 20:13-27.

Daley, T. T. Life Ain't Been No Crystal Stair. *Personnel and Guidance Journal*, 1972, 50:491-496.

Denmark, F., & Trachtman, J. The Psychologist as Counselor in College "High Risk" Programs. *The Counseling Psychologist*, 1973, 4:87-92.

English, W. H. Minority Group Attitudes of Negroes and Implications for Guidance. *Journal of Negro Education*, 1957, 26:99-107.

Fibush, E. The White Worker and the Negro Client. *Social Casework*, 1965, 36:271-277.

Gardner, W. E. The Differential Effects of Race, Education and Experience. *Journal of Clinical Psychology*, 1972, 28:87-89.

Gordon, J. E. Project Cause, the Federal Anti-Poverty Program, and Some Implications of Sub-professional Training. *American Psychologist*, 1965, 20:334-343.

Gordon, J. E. Counseling the Disadvantaged Boy. In William E. Amos and Jean Dresden Grambs (eds.), *Counseling the Disadvantaged Youth*. New Jersey: Prentice-Hall, 1968.

Gordon, E. W. Perspective on Counseling and Other Approaches to Guided Behavioral Change. *The Counseling Psychologist*, 1970, 2:105-114. (a)

Gordon, E. W. Guidance in an Urban Setting. *ERIC-IRCD Urban Disadvantaged Series*, 1970, 15:1-14. (b)

Grantham, R. J. Effects of Counselor Sex, Race, and Language Style on Black Students in Initial Interviews. *Journal of Counseling Psychology*, 1973, 20:553-559.

Gunnings, T. S., & Simpkins, G. A. Systemic Approach to Counseling Disadvantaged Youth. *Journal of Non-White Concerns*, 1972, 1:4-8.

Haettenschwiller, D. L. Counseling College Students in Special Programs. *Personnel and Guidance Journal*, 1971, 50:29-35.

Hardy, R. E., & Cull, J. G. Verbal Dissimilarity Among Black and White Subjects: A Prime Consideration in Counseling and Communication. *Journal of Negro Education*, 1973, 42:67-70.

Harper, F. D. What Counselors Must Know About the Social Sciences of Black Americans. *Journal of Negro Education*, 1973, 42:109-116. (a)

Harper, F. D. Counseling the Poor Child. *Journal of Non-White Concerns*, 1973, 1:79-84 (b).

Hayes, W. A., & Banks, W. M. The Nigger Box or a Redefinition of the Counselor's Role. In Reginald L. Jones (ed.), *Black Psychology*. New York: Harper & Row, 1972.

Heffernon, A. R., & Bruehl, D. Some Effects of Race of Inexperienced Lay Counselors on Black Junior High School Students. *Journal of School Psychology*, 1971, 9:35-37.

Himes, J. S. Guidance in Negro Secondary Schools in the Southeastern Region. *Journal of Negro Education*, 1948, 17:106-113.

Hypps, I. D. The Role of the School in Juvenile Delinquency Prevention (With Especial Reference to Pupil Personnel Services). *Journal of Negro Education*, 1959, 28:310-328.

Irvine, D. J. Needed for Disadvantaged Youth: An Expanded Concept of Counseling. *School Counselor*, 1968, 15:176-179.

Island, D. Counseling Students with Special Problems. *Review of Educational Research*, 1969, 39:239-250.

Jackson, G. G. Black Youth as Peer Counselors. *Personnel and Guidance Journal*, 1972, 51:280-285. (a)

Jackson, G. G. The Use of Roleplaying in Job Interviews With Job Corps Females. *Journal of Employment Counseling,* 1972, 9:130-139. (b)

Jackson, G. G., & Kirschner, S. A. Racial Self-Designation and Preference for a Counselor. *Journal of Counseling Psychology,* 1973, 20:560-564.

Job Corps Comes to Bates; Girls Discover Passivity. *Bates College Newspaper,* Lewiston, Maine, January 15, 1969, 7.

Johnson, S. D. Presidential Memo. (Association for Non-White Concerns). In *Personnel and Guidance,* December 18, 1973, 1.

Jones, M. H., & Jones, M. C. The Neglected Client. *Black Scholar,* 1970, 1:35-42.

Jones, L. Rap's Her Way Fighting Drugs. *New York Amsterdam News,* June 6, 1970, 183.

Kadota, P., & Menacker, J. Community-Based Guidance for the Disadvantaged. *Personnel and Guidance Journal,* 1971, 50:175-181.

Kendrick, S. S., & Thomas, C. L. Transition from School to College. *Review of Educational Research,* 1970, 40:151-174.

Kincaid, M. Identity and Therapy in the Black Community. *Personnel and Guidance Journal,* 1969, 47:884-890.

Lefkowitz, D., & Baker, J. Black Youth: A Counseling Experience. *School Counselor,* 1971, 18:290-293.

Lewis, S. O. Racism Encountered in Counseling. *Counselor Education and Supervision,* 1969, 9:49-54.

Lewis, M. D., & Lewis, J. A. Relevant Training for Relevant Roles: A Model for Educating Inner-city Counselor. *Counselor Education and Supervision,* 1970, 10:31-38.

Lindberg, R., & Wrenn, C. G. Minority Teachers Become Minority Counselors. *Personnel and Guidance Journal,* 1972, 50:219-222.

Manley, A. E., & Himes, J. S. Guidance: A Critical Problem in Negro Secondary Education. *School Review,* 1948, 56:219-222.

McDaniels, R. Counseling the Disadvantaged Negro. Paper presented at American Personnel and Guidance Association Convention, Monday, April 8, 1968, 1-4.

McGrew, J. M. Counseling the Disadvantaged Child: A Practice in Search of a Rationale. *School Counselor,* 1971, 18:165-176.

Mickelson, D., & Stevic, R. Preparing Counselors to Meet the Needs of Students. *Counselor Education and Supervision,* 1967, 7:76-77.

Mitchell, H. The Black Experience in Higher Education. *Counseling Psychologist,* 1970, 2:30-36.

Patterson, F. D. The Place of Guidance in Education. *Quarterly Review of Higher Education Among Negroes,* 1947, 15:76-81.

Patterson, L. The Strange Verbal World. *Journal of Non-White Concerns,* 1973, 1:95-101.

Payne, P. A., & Mills, R. B. Practicum Placement in a Counseling Employment Agency for Disadvantaged Youth. *Counselor Education and Supervision,* 1970, 9:189-193.

Phillips, W. Counseling Negro Pupils: An Educational Dilemma. *Journal of Negro Education*, 1960, 29:504-508.

Phillips, W. Notes From Readers. *Harvard Educational Review*, 1961, 31:324-326.

Proctor, S. A. Reversing the Spiral Toward Futility. *Personnel and Guidance Journal*, 1970, 48:707-712.

Record, W. Counseling and Color: Crisis and Conscience. *Integrated Education*, 1966, 4:34-41.

Rosenthal, R., & Jacobson, L. F. Teacher Expectations for the Disadvantaged. *Scientific American*, 1968, 19-23.

Rothenberg, L. Relevance is a Many-Splendored Thing. *School Counselor*, 1970, 17:367-369.

Rousseve, R. J. Counselor Education and the Culturally Isolated: An Alliance for Mutual Benefit. *Journal of Negro Education*, 1965, 4:395-403.

Rousseve, R. J. Reason and Reality in Counseling the Student-Client Who is Black. *School Counselor*, 1970, 48:561-567.

Russell, R. D. Guidance Developments in Negro Colleges. *Occupations*, 1949, 27:25-27.

Russell, R. D. Black Perceptions of Guidance. *Personnel and Guidance Journal*, 1970, 48:721-728.

Sager, C. J., Brayboy, T. L., & Waxenberg, B. R. Black Patient-White Therapist. *American Journal of Orthopsychiatry*, 1972, 42:415-423.

Sattler, J. M. Racial Experimenter Effects in Experimentation, Testing, Interviewing, and Psychotherapy. *Psychological Bulletin*, 1970, 73:137-160.

Scheffler, L. M. What 70 SEEK Kids Taught Their Counselor. *New York Times Magazine*, November 16, 1969, 54-55, 109, 110, 112, 114, 116, 119, 120, 122, 126.

Schumacher, L. C., Banikiotes, P. G., & Banikiotes, F. G. Language Compatibility and Minority Group Counseling. *Journal of Counseling Psychology*, 1972, 19:255-256.

Sedlacek, W. E., & Brooks, G. C. Racism and Research: Using Data to Initiate Change. *Personnel and Guidance Journal*, 1973, 52:184-188. (a)

Sedlacek, W. E., & Brooks, G. C. Racism in the Public Schools: A Model for Change. *Journal of Non-White Concerns*, 1973, 1:133-143.

Siegel, B. Counseling the Color-Conscious. *School Counselor*, 1970, 17:168-170.

Simpkins, G., Gunnings, T., & Kearney, A. The Black Six-Hour Retarded Child. *Journal of Non-White Concerns*, 1973, 2:29-34.

Smith, D. H. The White Counselor in the Negro Slum School. *School Counselor*, 1967, 14:268-272.

Smith, P. M. Counselors for Ghetto Youth. *Personnel and Guidance Journal*, 1968, 47:279-281.

Smith, P. M. Alienation or APGA's Black Image. *Personnel and Guidance Journal*, 1970, 18:312.

Smith, P. M. The Role of the Guidance Counselor in the Desegregation Process. *Journal of Negro Education,* 1971, 11:347-351. (a)

Smith, P. M. Black Activists for Liberation, Not Guidance. *Personnel and Guidance Journal,* 1971, 49:721-726. (b)

Smith, P. M. Help: Change the Emphasis. *Journal of Non-White Concerns,* 1973, 2:42-45.

Stikes, C. S. Culturally Specific Counseling: The Black Client. *Journal of Non-White Concerns,* 1972, 1:15-23.

Stranges, R. J., & Riccio, A. C. Counselee Preference for Counselors: Some Implications for Counselor Education. *Counselor Education and Supervision,* 1970, 10:39-45.

Sue, S. Training of "Third-World" Students to Function as Counselors. *Journal of Counseling Psychology,* 1973, 20:73-78.

Taylor, P. Research for Liberation: Shaping a New Black Identity in America. *Black World,* 1973, 22, 7:4-14, 65-72.

Thomas, A. Pseudo-Transference Reactions Due to Cultural Stereotyping. *American Journal of Orthopsychiatry,* 1962, 32:894-900.

Toldson, I. L. The Human Potential Movement and Black Unity: Counseling Blacks in Groups. *Journal of Non-White Concerns,* 1973, 1:69-76.

Toldson, I. L., & Pasteur, A. B. Soul Music: Techniques for Therapeutic Intervention. *Journal of Non-White Concerns,* 1972, 1:31-39.

Tolson, N. Counseling the "Disadvantaged." *Personnel and Guidance Journal,* 1972, 50:735-738.

Trueblood, D. L. The Role of the Counselor in the Guidance of Negro Students. *Harvard Educational Review,* 1960, 30:324-326.

Tucker, S. J. Action Counseling: An Accountability Procedure for Counseling the Oppressed. *Journal of Non-White Concerns,* 1973, 2:35-41.

Vontress, C. E. Counseling Negro Adolescents. *School Counselor,* 1967, 15:86-91.

Vontress, C. E. Counseling Negro Students for College. *Journal of Negro Education,* 1968, 37:37-44.

Vontress, C. E. Cultural Differences: Implications for Counseling. *Journal of Negro Education,* 1969, 37:266-275. (a)

Vontress, C. E. Cultural Barriers in the Counseling Relationship. *Personnel and Guidance Journal,* 1969, 48:11-17. (b)

Vontress, C. E. Racial Differences: Impediments to Rapport. *Journal of Counseling Psychology,* 1971, 18:7-13.

Vontress, C. E. The Black Militant as a Counselor. *Personnel and Guidance Journal,* 1972, 50:574, 576-580.

Vontress, C. E. Counseling the Racial and Ethnic Minorities. *Focus on Guidance,* 1973, 5:1-12.

Vriend, T. High-Performing Inner-City Adolescents Assist Low-Performing Peers in Counseling Groups. *Personnel and Guidance Journal,* 1969, 47:897-904.

Ward, E. J. A Gift from the Ghetto. *Personnel and Guidance Journal*, 1970, 48:753-756.

Washington, B. Perceptions and Possibilities. *Personnel and Guidance Journal*, 1970, 48:757-761.

Washington, K. S. What Counselors Must Know About Black Power. *Personnel and Guidance Journal*, 1968, 47:204-208.

Washington, K. S., & Anderson, N. J. Scarcity of Black Counselors: A Crisis in Urban Education. *Journal of Non-White Concerns*, 1974, 2:99-105.

Waters, E. W. Problems of Rural Negro High School Seniors on the Eastern Shore of Maryland: A Consideration for Guidance. *Journal of Negro Education*, 1953, 22:115-125.

Williams, C. T. Special Consideration in Counseling. *Journal of Educational Sociology*, 1949, 22:608-613.

Williams, R. L., & Kirland, J. The White Counselor and the Black Client. *Counseling Psychologist*, 1971, 4:114-116.

Chapter 6

COUNSELING BLACKS*

EARL B. HIGGINS AND RICHARD W. WARNER

SINCE the creation of the Office of Economic
Opportunity and the advent of desegregation in public education, there has been within the counseling profession a heightened concern with rendering counseling services to minority
groups. This concern has been reflected in the proliferation of
articles written with recommendations for counseling minorities. The entire May 1974 issue of the *Elementary School Guidance and Counseling* journal, for example, was devoted to this
topic; and three issues of the *Personnel and Guidance Journal*
(May 1970, October 1971, February 1973) were devoted to counseling racial and ethnic minorities.

This review was undertaken to examine the research generated by this increased concern. The senior author, himself
black, has been interested in this area because of his involvement in two special projects dealing with training minority
students at the university level; these projects were designed to
retrain black educators in student personnel services. The
junior author, who is not black, has also been involved in these
two projects, particularly as they have related to the providing
of counseling services to minority students. We decided to include in this review any article that had as its subject racial or
ethnic minorities. The paucity of research articles in the literature dealing with counseling any of the other minority groups,
however, caused us to restrict this review to special programs
for blacks. Furthermore, most of the articles we reviewed that
deal with counseling blacks were written as position papers
and are devoid of research. In most cases the authors discuss
characteristics of blacks and make recommendations or sugges-

*From Earl B. Higgins and Richard W. Warner, Counseling Blacks, *Personnel and
Guidance Journal*, 53:382-386, 1975.

tions as to what would be the best approach to use in counseling blacks. Several recurrent themes are presented in the recommendations of these writers. The focus of this review, then, is to see if there is any research to support these recommendations.

In conducting this review, we used the following resources: The ERIC system, several volumes of each of ten specific journals, and several abstracts common to the field. It is unfortunate that at this point much of the interest reported in the literature on counseling blacks, the culturally deprived and the socioeconomically disadvantaged is in the form of subjective thought articles, with very few articles reporting any attempt at objective evaluation.

NEED FOR UNDERSTANDING THE CULTURE

Currently there is a popular belief in the need for the counselor to understand the cultural background of the client (Rosenfeld, 1971). Vontress (1969, 1971), Kincaid (1969), Sikes (1971), and Arbuckle (1972) all pointed out the need for the counselor to understand the cultural background of the black client.

The documented research showing the need for the counselor to understand the cultural background and language differences of the black and/or disadvantaged client is scarce. In one study addressing this concern, Clarke and Walters (1972) surveyed both black and white counselors working with large numbers of black students. Their results indicate the incorrectness of the notion that communication problems between counselors and black students "feel" a need to be less verbal and more action-oriented. Unfortunately, no attempt was made in that study to ascertain how the students felt.

The differences in language are also assumed to be an important factor in the counselor-client relationship, and one study examined that assumption. Schumacher, Banikiotes, and Banikiotes (1972) conducted a study to see how well white counselors understood words frequently used by black students and how well black students understood words often used in counseling sessions by white counselors. The results showed that the linguistic compatibility between black students and white counselors is low. The effect of this incompatibility on counseling outcomes was not reported, and one is left to speculate that this must mean negative results. As can be seen, there is a paucity of research on the effects of understanding the culture and language of black students.

RACIAL DIFFERENCES OF CLIENT AND COUNSELOR

A review of the literature shows a lack of agreement among authors as to whether a racial difference between counselor and client affects the counseling relationship. Some authors maintain that the racial difference alone will cause difficulties for the white counselor and the black client (Kincaid, 1969). Other authors believe that all black clients will perceive white counselors as being alike, that is, as being ineffective (Washington & Anderson, 1974).

The research literature is inconsistent in its findings relative to the effect of racial differences in the counseling relationship. In an experimental study, Wilson (1973) reported that black high school students expressed mixed emotions regarding their attitudes toward white counselors. In another experimental study, Woods (1974) found no significant differences in the counselor-client relationship. Three experimental studies, however, support the notion that black clients respond better to black counselors. Banks (1969) reported data showing that racial similarity has a positive effect on the initial counseling interview. Granthan (1970-71) reported that disadvantaged black university students preferred black counselors to white counselors to a significantly greater degree. Bryson (1973) found that university students favored intraracial counselor and client combinations (black to black and white to white) over the interracial combination in the initial counseling interview. Thus the findings here are mixed, with three studies supporting the view that black clients prefer black counselors and two studies questioning this assumption.

NEED FOR EMPATHY

Empathy has been identified as the single most important dimension in establishing a counseling relationship (Carkhuff, 1969). The review of the literature supports this, especially in counseling with minorities (Vontress, 1967, 1970; Wittmer, 1971). When inexperienced black counselors and experienced white counselors were compared in terms of reports of black students desiring to return to see the counselor, it was the counselor's empathy, positive regard, and genuineness that were the significant factors rather than the counselor's experience (Banks, Berenson & Carkhuff, 1967). There is a general consensus that, despite dissimilarities between client and counselor, high-empathy counselors are more effective than low-empathy counselors (Banks, 1969).

APPROPRIATE APPROACHES FOR COUNSELING BLACKS

A review of the literature as to whether specific techniques and approaches should be used with the black client shows a general consensus favoring action-oriented approaches.

Lefkowitz and Baker (1971) described an experience in counseling black high school students using the "physical action" approach. McGrew (1971) reviewed the literature and found support for Hollingshead and Redlich's (1958) finding that direct approaches are best when working with minorities. The approaches to counseling blacks suggested by Kincaid (1969) are action approaches that are task-oriented. Harper and Stone (1974) have presented the qualities of a good theory for counseling blacks and suggest rational-emotive therapy or reality therapy. The review of the research articles is also consistent in preferring an action-oriented approach for counseling with blacks.

Morgan (1971) reported that the culturally disadvantaged, underachieving youth exposed to behavior theory counseling showed great improvement in grade point average, study habits, attitudes, and self-esteem. Workman (1974) has reported that a behavioristic approach to counseling produced significantly more success than a humanistic approach in achieving the client responses, more client affect references, and greater client receptivity with disadvantaged black clients. Tucker (1973) compared an action-counseling approach with the "traditional" approach and found that the counselees of the action-model approach differed significantly from those of the traditional approach regarding the degree of satisfactory solutions to identified problems. Further, the counselees of the action-model approach saw their counselors as significantly more helpful.

GROUP COUNSELING

Many writers have recommended group counseling with blacks. The efficacy of using this approach, however, is not well documented. Lee (1961) used group counseling with Negro high school freshmen and seniors. The post-test showed a reduction of problems for the group studied, and the conclusion was that group counseling appeared to be an effective approach when counseling with blacks.

Gilliland (1967), using two experimental groups and two control groups, evaluated the outcomes of small group counseling with black high school students. The results showed that group counseling was an invaluable resource in improving scholastic achievement and coping behavior in black adolescents. Williams (1972) used group counseling with black college students and found that this approach effected significant improvement in grade point average. Moates (1970) studied the effects of group counseling on the self-concept, peer acceptance, and grade point average of disadvantaged black junior high school clients. It was concluded that activity group counseling tended to produce positive changes in self-concept and peer acceptance scores; however, no change in grade point averages resulted. None of these studies demonstrated that group procedures were any more effective for black clients than might be expected for white clients.

CONCLUSIONS AND IMPLICATIONS

The research reported here is unfortunately meager. Counselors who are conducting innovative counseling programs with minorities are encouraged to evaluate the outcomes and report them in the literature; it is indeed sad that more research has not been reported in the literature thus far.

Nonetheless, the research that has been reviewed here does seem to point out some considerations to be taken into account when counseling with blacks. The following recommendations are drawn from what is currently presented in the literature and deal with elements important in counseling with blacks. Because of the paucity of research findings, these recommendations should be treated cautiously.

1. Research shows that, when working with blacks, the counselor needs to communicate empathy, especially during the initial stages of the relationship. There is reason to believe that this dimension of the counseling relationship has the potential for overcoming any initial problems encountered between a white counselor and a black client. While all counselors need empathy training, it is particularly important for counselors who are working with black students. The research indicated that white counselors can work effectively with black students if they can function at a high level of empathy.

2. Black counselors are more effective in counseling black students; however, this difference appears to be a function of the counselor's understanding of the culture and language and the counselor's commitment to the black client rather than a function of race itself. Hence there is a real need for all counselors to understand the cultural and language differences in black clients, and inservice training should be undertaken by those counselors involved with black students. It would seem most helpful if this training were conducted by blacks from the community in question.

3. The literature reveals that the action-oriented approach facilitates more positive change than traditional approaches in counseling with black clients. However, employment of any approach should be attempted only after an empathic relation-

ship is established. Further, it is imperative that counselors recognize that, just as all whites are not the same, neither are all blacks the same.

4. A group approach that would establish an empathic relationship in the early stages of the group and move on to appropriate action during the later stages seems most fitting when counseling blacks. Gazda's (1971) *Group Counseling: A Developmental Approach* should be a good reference.

5. What appears to be the most important finding from the research is that those factors that have been shown to be important for any effective counselor are especially true for counselors working with blacks. All good counselors must provide empathic understanding, must understand the language and culture of their clients, and must respect their clients. These factors are true regardless of the race of counselor or client. While recognizing the many special problems facing blacks and other minority groups, in terms of providing good counseling services perhaps we should spend more time finding out the common core of effective counseling than placing emphasis on racial and ethnic differences.

REFERENCES

Arbuckle, D. S. Counseling with Members of Minority Groups. *Counseling and Values*, 1972, 16:239-251.

Banks, G.; Berenson, B. G.; and Carkhuff, R. The Effects of Counselor Race and Training Upon Counseling Process with Negro Clients in Initial Interviews. *Journal of Clinical Psychology*, 1967, 23:70-72.

Banks, W. M. The Effects of Race, Social Class, and Empathy on the Initial Counseling Interview. Unpublished doctoral dissertation, University of Kentucky, 1968.

Bryson, S. The Relationship of Race to Level of Understanding in the Initial Counseling Interview. Unpublished doctoral dissertation, Southern Illinois University, 1972.

Carkhuff, R. R. *Helping and Human Relations*, Vol. 1: *Selection and Training*. New York: Holt, Rinehart & Winston, 1969.

Clarke, J., and Walters, H. Counseling the Culturally Deprived: A Survey of High School Counselors' Opinions and Attitudes. *School Counselor*, 1972, 19:201-209.

Gazda, G. M. *Group Counseling: A Developmental Approach*. Boston: Allyn

& Bacon, 1971.

Gilliland, B. E. An Evaluation of the Effects of Small Group Counseling with Negro Adolescents. Unpublished doctoral dissertation, University of Tennessee, 1966.

Granthan, R. J. The Effect of Counselor Race, Sex, and Language Variables in Counseling Culturally Different Clients. Unpublished doctoral dissertation, State University of New York at Buffalo, 1970.

Harper, F. D., and Stone, W. O. Toward a Theory of Transcendent Counseling with Blacks. *Journal of Non-White Concerns in Personnel and Guidance*, 1974, 2:191-196.

Hollingshead, A. B., and Redlich, F. C. *Social Class and Mental Illness: A Community Study.* New York: Wiley, 1958.

Kincaid, M. Identity and Therapy in the Black Community. *Personnel and Guidance Journal*, 1969, 47:884-890.

Lee, C. A. A Study of the Effects of Counseling in Reducing the Number of Problems Indicated by High School Freshmen and Seniors. Unpublished doctoral dissertation, Indiana University, 1960.

Lefkowitz, D. M., and Baker, J. Black Youth: A Counseling Experience. *School Counselor*, 1971, 18:290-293.

McGrew, J. M. Counseling the Disadvantaged Child: A Practice in Search of a Rationale. *School Counselor*, 1971, 18:165-176.

Moates, H. L. The Effects of Activity Group Counseling on the Self-Concept, Peer Acceptance, and Grade Point Average of Disadvantaged Seventh Grade Negro Boys and Girls. Unpublished doctoral dissertation, Auburn University, 1969.

Morgan, E. Behavior Theory Counseling with Culturally Disadvantaged Under-achieving Youth. Unpublished doctoral dissertation, Columbia University, 1970.

Rosenfeld, G. *"Shut Those Thick Lips!": A Study of Slum School Failure.* New York: Holt, Rinehart & Winston, 1971.

Schumacher, L. C., Banifiofes, P. G., and Banikotes, F. G. Language Compatibility and Minority Group Counseling. *Journal of Counseling Psychology*, 1972, 19:255-256.

Sikes, M. B. Counseling Psychology Curriculum: A New Dimension. *Counseling Psychologist*, 1971, 2:102-104.

Tucker, S. Action Counseling: An Accountability Procedure for Counseling the Oppressed. *Journal of Non-White Concerns in Personnel and Guidance*, 1973, 2:35-41.

Vontress, C. E. Counseling Negro Adolescents. *School Counselor*, 1967, 15:86-90.

———. Cultural Difference Implications for Counseling. *Journal of Negro Education*, 1969, 38:266-275.

———. Counseling Blacks. *Personnel and Guidance Journal*, 1970, 48:713-720.

———— . Racial Differences: Impediments to Rapport. *Journal of Counseling Psychology*, 1971, 18:7-13.

Walker, P. L. The Effects of Two Counseling Strategies With Black Disadvantaged Clients. Unpublished doctoral dissertation, Georgia State University, 1972.

Washington, K. R., and Anderson, N. J. Scarcity of Black Counselors: A Crisis in Urban Education. *Journal of Non-White Concerns in Personnel and Guidance*, 1974, 2:99-106.

Williams, W. C. The Efficacy of Group Counseling on the Academic Performance of Black College Freshman with Low-Predicted Grade Point Averages. Unpublished doctoral dissertation, University of Georgia, 1971.

Wilson, S. M. A Study of the Relative Effectiveness of Black and White Counselors Counseling Black Youth. Unpublished doctoral dissertation, California School of Professional Psychology, 1973.

Wittmer, J. Effective Counseling of Children of Several American Subcultures. *School Counselor*, 1971, 19:49-52.

Woods, E., Jr. Racial Effects of Verbal Conditioning in Counseling Interview. Unpublished doctoral dissertation, University of California, 1973.

Workman, E. L. A Comparison of Behavioristic and Humanistic Treatment Procedures on the Achievement of Success in a Sheltered Workshop. Unpublished doctoral dissertation, University of Southern California, 1973.

Part II. Mexican Americans

INTRODUCTION

SOME counselors are oblivious to the fact that by working with persons whose life-styles differ from their own, they shape and are shaped by this acculturation process. There is the tendency for Anglo counselors to try to inculcate their cultural values in Chicano clients while leaving intact their own life-styles. It is imperative that counselors not define reality according to a monocultural value system. There are ample studies to support the thesis that counselors who are bicultural have less difficulty with Chicano counselees than counselors who are monocultural.

MEXICAN AMERICAN CULTURAL CONDITIONING

Programs that work well for Mexican Americans may not be successful with other Latino persons because of subcultural differences. For example, knowing that a Mexican American child speaks Spanish is an inadequate cultural description. There are qualitative differences between Latinos who are monolingual Spanish or bilingual Spanish-English, with Spanish or English dominant. Furthermore, there are many dialects of Spanish — those brought to the United States by Latino immigrants and several dialects that have developed in this country. Some of the values of Mexican Americans are listed below.

LA RAZA (THE RACE). All Latin Americans are united by cultural and spiritual bonds emanating from God. Because God controls all events, Mexican Americans tend to be more present than future oriented. The influence of the Roman Catholic Church on La Raza is pervasive — Mexican Americans are born, married, work, die, and buried under the aus-

111

pices of religious ceremonies.

FAMILIAL LOYALTY. The familial role is the most important and the family is the second most cherished institution in Mexican American society. A Chicano owes his or her primary loyalty to the family. The worst sin is to violate one's obligations to God and next comes the family.

RESPECT. The oldest male in the household is the family leader. Respect is accorded on the basis of age and sex. The old are accorded more respect than the young and males receive more respect than females. Latino families are based on family solidarity and male superiority.

MACHISMO. Mexican culture prescribes that the male is stronger, more reliable, and more intelligent than females. *Machismo* dictates that the male will show a high degree of individuality outside the family. Weakness in male behavior is looked down on.

COMPADRAZGO. The Mexican American family is widened by the institution of *compadrazgo*, a special ceremonial bond between a child's parents and godparents. Often the bond between *compadres* is as strong as between brothers and sisters.

READINGS

Jack D. Forbes reviews the Mexican heritage of the United States. Although this nation has surpassed Mexico in technological innovations, the Mexican people's marked abilities in the visual arts, music, architecture, and political affairs have made them constant contributers to North American culture. Mexican Americans, Forbes notes, serve as a bridge for the Latin American northward diffusion of valuable Mexican traits.

By examining various patterns of living among Sal si Puedes nuclear and extended family units, Margaret Clark paints a vivid portrait of Mexican American family structure. Although based on a 1955 study, the observations are as appropriate today as during the time of the study.

Bonnie M. Maldonado and William Cross' article focuses on the self-concepts held by Mexican American Students. Utilizing research from several studies of Chicano high school students, Moldonado and Cross categorize and refute the negative stereotyping associated with Mexican Americans. Based upon their description of the self-concepts actually held by Chicano students, they summarize the role and responsibility of counselors in the development of positive self-concepts of Chicano students.

Ignacio Aguilar briefly outlines different cultural values and patterns of behavior — often barriers to assimilation in an alien culture — which characterize Mexican American families. Mr. Aguilar incorporates his personal experiences into the discussion of methods which can be used to more effectively counsel Mexican American families.

David López discusses both positive and negative effects of bilingualism on Chicano home and school interactions. To fully understand the effects of bilingualism on home/school, we must first understand social class variations.

Group facilitators should heed Aurelio Sandoval Ruiz' suggestions for utilizing ethnicity as a positive variable in growth groups. Seven interaction facilitation techniques are presented in hopes of encouraging group facilitators to devise their own techniques to fit specific group situations.

Wayne R. Maes and John R. Rinaldi discuss the relationship between counselors and Chicano students. To illustrate the relationship they use hypothetical examples. But more than problems are discussed, Maes and Rinaldi provide several recommendations for educators who counsel Chicano students.

Chapter 7

THE MEXICAN HERITAGE
OF THE UNITED STATES:
AN HISTORICAL SUMMARY*

JACK D. FORBES

PRIOR to 1821, when the modern Mexican
nation won its independence from Spain, a Mexican was considered to be a person who spoke the Mexican or Aztec language (Nahuatl). In fact, the early Spaniards almost always
referred to the Aztec people as Mexicans. This practice was
continued in modern Mexico where the Nahuatl language is
called "Mexicano" by the common people and where writers
usually speak of the Mexican Empire rather than the Aztec
Empire. The modern people of Mexico, who are said by scholars to be about 80 percent native Indian in their ancestry, are
proud of their descent from the ancient Mexicans and trace the
history of their people back to the builders of the magnificent
cities of Teotihuacan, Monte Alban, and Chichén Itzá.

OUR ANCIENT MEXICAN HERITAGE

The Mexican heritage of the United States commences long
before the time of Christ. About the year 4000 B.C., Indians
living in southern New Mexico learned how to raise corn
(maize) as a result of contacts with Mexico (where that remarkable plant was first domesticated after what must have been a
long and tedious process). Other crops, including squash and
beans, were subsequently borrowed and still later (about A.D.
500) southwestern Indians began to develop the Pueblo Indian
civilization. This advanced way of life, which still flourishes in

*From Jack D. Forbes, *Mexican Americans: A Handbook For Educators.* Berkeley, Far
West Laboratory, 1967. Reprinted by permission.

Arizona and New Mexico, was largely based upon Mexican influences in architecture, pottery making, clothing, religion, and government.

In about A.D. 1000, according to some scholars, a people known as the Hohokam moved from northern Mexico into what is now southern Arizona. They brought many advanced traits with them, including the construction of monumental irrigation systems, stone etching techniques, and very possible, new political concepts. The Hohokams constructed a large center at Snaketown, Arizona, and spread their influence widely, apparently establishing a colony at Flagstaff and trading their pottery as far as the San Fernando Valley in California. During the same general period, Mexican influences seem to have reached the Mississippi Valley, and advanced cultures developed there. The Indians of the southern United States developed a Mexican-style religious and political orientation and constructed small pyramid-temples, whereas the Ohio River Indians built fanciful effigy mounds, sometimes in the shape of serpents.

THE VITALITY OF MEXICAN CIVILIZATION

It is not at all surprising that ancient Mexico had a great impact upon the area of the United States. The Mexican people were extremely creative, industrious, and numerous (perhaps numbering twenty million in central Mexico alone in the 1520s). Great cities such as Teotihuacan were developed very early and at the time of the Spanish conquest Tenochtitlán (Mexico City) was perhaps the largest and certainly the most modern city in the world. In fact, our cities of today are not as well planned and are probably not as well cared for as was Tenochtitlán.

The ancient Mexicans excelled as artists, craftsmen, architects, city planners, engineers, astronomers, statesmen, and warriors. They also developed centers of higher education (called *calmécac* by the Aztecs), wrote excellent poetry, produced many historical and religious works, and were very interested in philosophical questions. One philosopher-king, Nezahualcóyotl, put forth the view that there was only one Creator-God. Mayan scientists developed a calendar which is more accurate than the one we use today.

Mexican traders (*pochteca*) traveled great distances, going as far south as Panama. They helped to spread Mexican culture and also prepared the way for colonists to settle in places such as El Salvador and Nicaragua and for the last Mexican empire (that of the Aztecs) to expand. By the 1520s the Mexican language was the common tongue of the region from north central Mexico to Central America.

THE SPANISH INVASION

In the 1520s the Spaniards commenced their conquest of Mexico. Although the Aztecs were conquered quickly, in spite of a noble defense of Tenochtitlán led by Cuauhtémoc (the present-day national hero of Mexico), the rest of what is now Mexico was subdued only very gradually. In fact, many Indian groups in northern Mexico and in the jungles of Yucatan-Guatemala were never conquered. Also, many of the Mexicans who were subdued never lost their identity, and this explains why at least one tenth of the people of modern Mexico speak native languages, often in addition to *Mexican Spanish.*

The Spanish invasion did not bring an end to the vitality of the Mexican people. Most Spaniards came to rule, not to work, and the magnificent churches, aqueducts, and palaces of the colonial period are essentially the result of native labor and craftsmanship. Educated Mexicans helped to record the history of ancient Mexico and for a brief period a Mexican university, Santa Cruz del Tlaltelolco, flourished, training many persons of native ancestry. The conquering Spaniards, if of high rank, often married native noblewomen, and the common Spaniards married ordinary Indian women, in both cases contributing to the mixture of the Spanish and native Mexican races.

THE HISPANO-MEXICAN NORTHWARD MOVEMENT

The number of Spaniards who came to Mexico was always

very slight, and the growth and expansion of the Spanish Empire depended upon the use of native and mixed-blood (mestizo) servants, settlers, craftsmen, miners, and soldiers (the Tlaxcaltecos, Mexicans of Tlaxcala, were particularly relied upon as colonists and soldiers). The conquest of the north would have been impossible without Mexicans, and every major settlement from Sante Fe, New Mexico, to Saltillo, Coahuila, had its Mexican district (*barrio* or *colonia*). Many of the settlers taken by Diego de Vargas to northern New Mexico in the 1690s were called *"Espanoles Mexicanos,"* that is, "Aztec-Spaniards"; and Juan de Onate, the first Spanish governor of New Mexico, was married to a woman of Aztec royal ancestry and their son, Cristobal de Onate, was the second governor of that province. Every major expedition, including those of Coronado and DeSoto, utilized Mexicans, and in 1769, eight Mexican soldiers were stationed at San Diego, California, by Gaspar de Portolá. The northward movement of Spain into the southwestern United States was, therefore, a Spanish-Mexican affair. It was Spanish-led but depended for its success upon Mexicans and mixed-bloods. In California, for example, well over half of the Spanish-speaking settlers were of Indian or mixed ancestry and the forty-six founders of Los Angeles in 1781 included only two persons called Spaniards, and the wives of these two men were Indian.

THE CREATION OF MODERN MEXICAN CULTURE

Gradually the way of life brought to America by the Europeans became mixed with native Mexican influence, until the life of the common people became a blend of Spanish-Arabic and Indian traits, much as the culture of England after 1066 became a blend of French-Latin and Anglo-Celtic traditions. The Spaniards used the Mexican language for governmental, scholarly, and religious purposes for several generations and many Mexican words, such as *coyote, elote, jicara, tamale, chile, chocolate, jacal, ocelote,* and hundreds of others, became part of Spanish as spoken in Mexico. Roman Catholic religious practice was modified by many Indian customs, and devotion to the Virgin of Guadalupe has had a profound effect upon the Catholic faith.

Meanwhile, the Mexican people intermixed with diverse tribes and eventually began to absorb both the non-Mexican Indian and the Spaniard himself. This process of migration and mixture made possible the creation of the independent Mexican republic in 1821, after a ten-year struggle for freedom.

THE MEXICAN REPUBLIC IN THE NORTH

Independent Mexico was to have a lasting impact upon the southwestern United States. Many Mexican leaders were imbued with new republican and egalitarian ideals, and they sought to implement these reforms. Legislatures and elected local councils were established in California and elsewhere; the Indians and mixed-bloods were granted complete legal equality and full citizenship, and foreigners were encouraged to take up a new life as Mexicans. On the other hand, many persons found it hard to break with the authoritarian legacy of Spain, and republican reforms were often subverted. Foreign settlers did not always choose to become good Mexican citizens, as, for example, the Anglo-Texans who refused to set their slaves free or to obey Mexican land-title and tariff regulations.

The early Mexican governments were often beset by financial difficulties, and progress was difficult in the face of widespread illiteracy and an unequal distribution of wealth and power. Gradually, however, these negative conditions were overcome, and the Mexican people advanced along the road of democracy, albeit with backward steps from time to time.

In what is now the United States, Mexicans were active in the development of new mining regions (gold was discovered in California in 1842, for example), opening up new routes for travelers (as from Santa Fe to Los Angeles via Las Vegas, Nevada), founding schools (some twenty-two teachers were brought to California in the 1830s, and a seminary was established at Santa Ynez), establishing new towns (Sonoma, California, is an example), and setting up printing presses (as in California in 1835). The north was a frontier region and was, therefore, not in the forefront of Mexican cultural progress, but it did benefit from developments originating further south.

MEXICAN MINERS AND COLONISTS IN THE NORTH

Commencing in the 1830s, Mexican settlers began to move northward once again. Some two hundred craftsmen, artisans, and skilled laborers sailed to California in that decade, and soon overland immigrants from Sonora were joining them. Thereafter a steady stream of Sonorans reached California, only to be turned into a flood by the discovery of gold in the Sierra Nevada foothills in 1848. The Sonorans were often experienced miners and their techniques dominated the California gold rush until steam-powered machinery took over at a later date. Chihuahuans and other Mexicans also "rushed" to California by sea and by land, and they, too, exercised an impact upon mining as well as upon commerce.

The United States-Mexican War of 1846-1848 did not alter immediately the character of the Southwest greatly, except in eastern Texas and northern California. The gold rush changed the language of central California after 1852 (when Mexican miners were largely expelled from the Sierra Nevada mines), but Mexicans continued to dominate the life of the region from San Luis Obispo, California, to San Antonio, Texas. Southern California, for example, remained a Spanish-speaking region until the 1870s with Spanish-language and bilingual public schools, Spanish-language newspapers, and Spanish-speaking judges, elected officials, and community leaders. The first Constitution of the State of California, created in part by persons of Mexican background, established California as a bilingual state, and it remained as such until 1878. Similar conditions prevailed in other southwestern regions.

ANGLO-AMERICANS BECOME DOMINANT

Gradually, however, Anglo-Americans from the East who were unsympathetic toward Mexican culture came to dominate the Southwest. Having no roots in the native soil and being unwilling to become assimilated to the region, these new-comers slowly transformed the schools into English-language institutions where no Spanish was taught, constructed build-ings with an "eastern" character, pushed Mexican leaders into the background, and generally caused the Mexican American, as he has come to be termed, to become a forgotten citizen.

By the 1890s, on the other hand, tourists and writers began to rediscover the "Spanish" heritage, and "landmark" clubs com-menced the process of restoring the decaying missions of the Southwest. A "Spanish" cultural revival was thus initiated, and soon it began to influence architectural styles as well as the kind of pageantry which has typified much of the Southwest ever since. Unfortunately, the Mexican Indian aspect of the region's heritage was at first overlooked and the Mexican Amer-ican people benefited but little from the emphasis upon things Spanish.

TWENTIETH-CENTURY MEXICAN "PIONEERS"

In the early 1900s a new group of Mexican immigrants began to enter the United States, attracted by job offers from agricul-tural developers who wished to open up virgin lands in southern California, Colorado, Arizona, and southern Texas. During World War I and the 1920s this movement became a flood which largely overwhelmed the older group of Mexican Americans (except in northern New Mexico and southern Colo-rado) and became ancestral to much of the contemporary Spanish-speaking population in the Southwest.

These hundreds of thousands of new Mexican Americans had to overcome many obstacles as they attempted to improve their life patterns. Anglo-Americans were prejudiced against people who were largely of native American, brown-skinned origin, who were poor, who of necessity lived in substandard or self-constructed homes, who could not speak English, and who were not familiar with the workings of a highly competitive and acquisitive society. Gradually, and in spite of the trauma of the Great Depression (when all sorts of pressures were used to deport Mexican Americans to Mexico), *los de la raza*, as Mexicans in the United States frequently refer to themselves, climbed the economic ladder and established stable, secure communities in the Southwest.

EDUCATIONAL PROGRESS

Educationally, Mexican American progress has been striking in individual cases, but the overall pattern has been slow. Generally speaking, whenever Anglo-Americans gained control over a particular state or region in the Southwest, they chose to import the kinds of public schools developed in the Middle West or East. Hispano-Mexican and bilingual schools were replaced by English-language, Anglo-oriented schools from which Mexican American children were sometimes excluded. After the turn of the century greater numbers of Spanish speaking youth began to attend schools, but the latter were either irrelevant to the background, language, and interests of the pupils (as in New Mexico) or were segregated, marginal elementary schools (as in much of California and Texas). Normally, secondary-level education was not available to Mexican American pupils except in an alien Anglo-dominated school (and even that opportunity was often not present in many rural counties in Texas and elsewhere).

During the post-World War II period, segregated schools for Mexican Americans largely disappeared, except where residential segregation operated to preserve the ethnic school. Greater numbers of Mexican Americans entered high school, and enrollment in college also increased, although slowly. Nevertheless, drop-out rates remain high even today; and it is also true that the typical school serving Mexican Americans make little, if any, concession to the Mexican heritage, the Spanish language, or to the desires of the Mexican American community.

A SIX-THOUSAND-YEAR-OLD HERITAGE

In summary, the Mexican heritage of the United States is very great indeed. For at least six thousand years Mexico has been a center for the dissemination of cultural influences in all directions, and this process continues today. Although the modern United States has outstripped Mexico in technological innovation, the Mexican people's marked ability in the visual arts, music, architecture, and political affairs makes them constant contributors to the heritage of all of North America. The Mexican American people of the United States serve as a bridge for the diffusion northward of valuable Mexican traits, serve as a reservoir for the preservation of the ancient Hispano-Mexican heritage of the Southwest, and participate directly in the daily life of the modern culture of the United States.

Chapter 8

MEXICAN-AMERICAN
FAMILY STRUCTURE*

MARGARET CLARK

MANY households in Sal si Puedes are com-
posed of nuclear or biological families, that is, a couple and
their unmarried children. The nuclear family is considered the
ideal living group; barrio people agree that a married couple
should live in a house of their own if they can afford it. In
reality, however, many households are of types other than the
simple nuclear family. In 1955 a group of fifty Sal si Puedes
homes were found to have the following compositions:

Households	Number
Normal nuclear families (couple and unmarried children)	23
Nuclear families plus unmarried children of one spouse by previous marriage	4
Joint families (two family heads sharing one residence)	9
Extended families (nuclear family plus other dependents)	8
Irregular families (one of spouses absent from the home)	4
Single-person households	2
Total households	50

In addition to the joint families listed above, a number of
nuclear families who were related by kinship were found to

*From Margaret Clark, *Health in the Mexican-American Culture.* Los Angeles,
University of California Press, 1970. Copyright 1959, 1970 by the Regents of the
University of California; reprinted by permission of the University of California Press.

share part of the living quarters of a related family. For example, Domingo and Ana Marquez live with their five unmarried children in a five-room house. Domingo's two married sons and their families live in a small duplex on the rear of the Marquez house lot. Rudolfo, the oldest son, and his wife and their four children live in a two-room apartment on one side of the duplex; Domingo's second son, daughter-in-law, and grandchild occupy a one-room efficiency apartment on the other side of the duplex. All three families, sixteen persons in all, share the bathroom in Domingo's house. Rudolfo's wife does most of her cooking in her own apartment on a two-burner gas hotplate, but she keeps perishable foods in the refrigerator in her mother-in-law's kitchen and sometimes uses Ana's oven for baking. All of Domingo's grandchildren frequently gather in their grandparents' living room in the late afternoon to watch television programs. While the pistol shots of cowboys and rustlers ring out in the Marquez parlor, Domingo and his sons may escape to the comparative quiet of Rudolfo's apartment to listen to the news or the ball game on the radio and Dona Ana chats with her daughters-in-law and rocks her youngest grandchild to sleep on the other side of the duplex. Even though the three nuclear families have separate dwellings, the apartments of the married sons function simply as extensions of the paternal household. The children of the kinship group freely come and go from one house to another, feeling equally at home in all. On a warm midsummer afternoon a grandchild may fall asleep on his grandmother's bed, wake up in time to go bicycle riding with thirteen-year-old uncle, and arrive home in time to eat supper in his aunt's apartment.

Mike, one of Domingo's grandsons, was once taken for a drive through one of San Jose's more fashionable suburbs. He saw the big brick houses, the expanses of lawn, and the high redwood fences. "I sure am glad I don't live here," he asserted; "The houses are so far apart — must be pretty lonesome!"

SPOUSES

Beals has pointed out the following:

One of the very pervasive patterns of Latin American culture is that of male dominance and its concomitants. The father is the head of the family, woman's place is in the home as a wife and mother, and unmarried girls tend to be secluded. . . . Not only does the father have much authority in the family, but the oldest son dominates the younger. . . . Men do not entertain their friends at home but rather meet on the street or plaza, or at clubs, cantinas, restaurants, coffee shops, or pool halls. A dual standard of morality is found in which men are rather expected to have amorous adventures. . . . Women are expected to be homekeepers and to be virtuous or else bad women. . . . In the home, disciplinary control tends to be exerted solely by the father or older brother. The mother frequently does not even attempt control or correction, even to the point of not asking a small boy to close the door.

Although the patriarchal-authoritarian family pattern described above is regarded by many Sal si Puedes people as an ideal, actual family relationships in the barrio are often quite different. Wives, for example, although theoretically subservient to their husbands, sometimes openly defy male authority. Pete told the following story about his wife, Sara: "When I first came to San Jose in 1944, my brother-in-law and I got jobs at a cannery. One day on our way to work we passed by a movie and decided to go in. In those days [during World War II], they had a hard time getting men, so we didn't think that we would get fired. But when we didn't show up at work, the foreman called my wife to ask where we were. And do you know what she did? She took the bus downtown and looked until she found us and told us to go to work — so we left and went to work. I didn't even get to see all the show."

Husbands most frequently control family finances, but in some households wives exert considerable influence over purchases. Ismael and his wife, Paula, owned two cars, an old model sedan and a pickup truck. In 1955 Ismael decided that he wanted to buy a new car. He planned to trade in both his old vehicles on a new automobile and told Paula of his plan. Paula replied that he could buy a new car if he wanted to, but he was not to trade in the pickup, but should keep it for a work car. Ismael argued that he then would not have enough money to make a down payment on the new car and that he wanted to make the purchase immediately. Paula flatly vetoed her husband's plan and instructed him to save the additional money he needed and postpone buying a new car until he had accumulated enough capital. Ismael finally agreed to Paula's plan, and they remained a two-car family. "My wife has always been bossy," Ismael said with a grin, "It's worse than being in the army!"

One of Paula's neighbors, Carmen, on the other hand, has very little to say about how family money is spent. Carmen's married daughter reported the following incident: During the summer of 1955, Carmen and her four younger children contracted with a San Jose grower to pick prunes. Carmen's husband, José, had a nonagricultural job and so was not a part of the prune-picking crew. At the end of the prune season, Carmen received a check from the grower which was $150.00 less than the amount that Carmen expected to be paid. Carmen had kept records of all the boxes of prunes that her family had picked each day, and she added up these figures again and again, but her records still showed that she was $150.00 short. Carmen asked José about the descrepancy, and he told her that she must have made a mistake. She finally went to see the prune grower to ask him to make up the difference in pay, and discovered that José and his brother had gotten a series of advance payments on the labor contract (the grower had receipts to show that the funds had been disbursed) for exactly the amount that the final check was short. But José and his brother are fond of drinking, and Carmen discovered that they had spent the entire $150.00 drinking and having a good time while Carmen and her children were picking prunes.

Carmen was placed in an embarrassing situation because her husband had lied to her and told her he knew nothing about the money. She had taken him at his word and had spread the story all over the barrio of how she had been cheated by the prune grower. When Carmen finally discovered the truth, she was ashamed to admit to anyone except her daughter what had actually happened. She told her friends and neighbors simply that the matter had been settled. For weeks Carmen was furious with José, not so much for spending the money as for placing her in a ridiculous light. Finally, though, she recovered her good spirits and with a sigh of resignation commented to her daughter, "That's just the way men are."

As more barrio wives seek temporary or full-time employment outside the home, more women take an active part in planning family financial expenditures and regulating family activities. Fidel's wife, Luisa, commented, "The men are not the only important ones in the way that families live; the women have a lot to do with it. In the homes of our people, the wives and mothers are the ones who really keep the old customs and old ways alive. I think the reason that our people here in San Jose get along so well with the Anglos is because so many of us work in the canneries with Anglo women. The main reason that our people want to learn the American ways is because the women are always meeting American women at their jobs."

The change toward a more equal relationship between spouses is not always apparent to Anglo observers, however. It is true that many Sal si Puedes wives are devoted to their husbands and are frequently dependent on them in many respects. But the affection and dependency that wives feel toward their husbands find at least some counterpart in the attitudes of men toward their wives.

Although many men in the barrio follow the Mexican pattern of meeting their friends outside the home in cantinas and restaurants, there are some who invite their male friends to their homes for a bottle of beer or a game of cards. When a husband and his friends are talking in the house, however, wives and children usually discreetly retire to another part of the house in deference to the man's desire for privacy. It is expected that husbands may have flirtations with women other than their wives, and few wives express much concern about their husbands' extramarital activities as long as they are "not serious" and are handled with discretion. Men, on the other hand, are often inordinately jealous of their wives, even sometimes threatening them with violence if their suspicions are aroused.

Spouses in Sal si Puedes seldom display signs of affection for each other in public. Public demonstrations of marital devotion are generally considered bad form. On one occasion Ismael and his wife, Paula, were taking a Sunday afternoon drive in the country near San Jose. Suddenly Ismael said, "Here, mother, hold my hand — I have something that I forgot to tell you." He went on to report that the previous day his truck had turned over and that he had been trapped inside the cab for four hours. Ismael said, "I forgot all about telling you until just now." Paula's only remark to her husband was, "So you forgot to tell me, huh?" The next day, however, Paula confided to a friend, "I had to take aspirins and go to bed after we got home; I was really nervous after what Ismael told me — but don't let him know what I told you. He's spoiled enough already."

PARENTS AND CHILDREN

Although many of the aspects of parent-child relationships have been presented in the discussion of childhood and adolescent activities, it should be emphasized that in almost every Sal si Puedes family both fathers and mothers express deep affection and concern for their children. However, outward displays of sentiment on the part of parents are usually confined to very young children. Esteban, who in everyday life is somewhat formal and abrupt with his eight-year-old son, described his feelings for the boy in this way: "Last year my wife and I decided to take a trip to Tijuana. We were gone just a few days, but we had a miserable time because we both cried and cried all the time because we didn't have Davey with us. You should have seen me — man, I was really chicken!"

Both mothers and fathers have a good deal of authority over preadolescent children. While the father is away at work, the mother is the authority in the family. Mothers may punish very small children, but avoid administering physical punishment to older ones if possible. Even though mothers seldom administer physical punishment, children are strictly under her orders. If a mother reports to her husband that a child should be disciplined, the father nearly always unquestioningly administers the punishment posthaste. Later he may or he may not ask to be told the reason for it. Some women complain that they are unable to control their children properly because the father may work until late in the evening, returning home only after the children are in bed for the night. "The kids have the idea they can get by with anything," Marta reported. "Pete [her husband] usually stops on his way home from work and drinks beer with his friends, and all the time I'm waiting for him to come home so he can spank the kids. But when their father gets home too late, they are already asleep and I can't wake them up for a spanking. Then when morning comes and I tell Pete what the kids have done, he usually says, 'Well, it's too late to do anything about it now.'"

Some fathers are harsh disciplinarians, others tend to be more permissive with their children. This contrast was illustrated by Alfonso's comments about his compadre's behavior toward his sons: "Esteban is always afraid that his oldest boy is getting to be a problem child because the boy's teacher at school has a hard time controlling him. But I think the main problem is the way that Esteban handles the boy. Esteban is afraid that the boy will grow up to be a delinquent, and his idea of how to avoid it is to be as tough on the kid as he can. He's so afraid the kid will be spoiled that he goes overboard the other way."

Sal si Puedes fathers are generally loved and respected by their children. Ramón emphasized the importance of a father in a family: "Fathers can either make or break their kids. They can encourage them to stay in school, or if they're not the right kind of guys they can let their kids run wild. If there's no father around the house, there is no respect for the family, especially if there are girls. Everybody is coming around doing wrong things and the whole family goes mad. The same thing happens if the husband is a drunkard and doesn't ever stay at home with his family."

The oldest son of a family, especially after he reaches adolescence, may have considerable authority. Joe told the following story about his own family: "We always had trouble at home about dating. My older sister wanted to go out on dates, but my mother wouldn't let her go. She finally told my mother that she was going anyway, and she did go out. Then mother called her cheap, said she was no good, and gave her a beating. After this trouble had gone on for a while, my oldest brother, who was a year younger than my sister, decided to step in. He stood up for my sister, and told our mother that he thought his sister should be allowed to go out on dates since it was the custom here and it didn't mean anything except having a good time. Finally my father agreed that my brother was right, and then my mother accepted the idea. Mother didn't say anything else to my sister after that; even a mother won't dispute her oldest son."

The influence that an oldest son may have even over his father is illustrated in a story that Pio told:

> I've been noticing a big change in Pete lately. It began about three or four weeks ago when Pete had an argument with his oldest son, Danny [fifteen years of age]. Danny asked his father one evening for some money to take to school. He needed it for some sort of class collection. Pete told him he couldn't have the money, that they didn't have money to throw away on things like that. Danny got real mad and told his father, "You won't let me have money for school, but you've got plenty of money to go out and get drunk on and raise hell with your buddies!" I guess Danny really gave his old man an argument, told him he was just a drunk and didn't care anything about the family. Pete took that pretty hard, and he didn't try to punish Danny for getting out of line.
>
> After that, Pio reported, Pete stopped bringing home a bottle of wine every night and stopped going out to the bars so much. I guess he just needed something like his oldest son calling him a drunk to wake him up.

BROTHERS AND SISTERS

"It's a sad thing," said Paula, "when a child has no brothers or sisters. You can't keep a child like that at home — he is always leaving the house to try to find some other kids to play with. Large families are much nicer because even though they fight all the time when they're growing up, when they get older they love each other."

Parents encourage older siblings to develop a sense of responsibility toward younger children in the family. An older child has authority over a younger one, but he is also held responsible by his parents for seeing that the younger child is protected from harm and kept out of mischief. An older child may be punished if a younger brother or sister who is in his care misbehaves.

Because older children have authority over younger ones, an older sibling, particularly an older brother, may be feared by his juniors. Marta reported, "My daughter Betty [aged eleven] has the job of washing the dishes for the family. Sometimes she doesn't want to do it, but when her oldest brother, Danny, is around she goes ahead and washes them. She knows she's got a little stepfather. Danny is mean to her if she doesn't do right. He's pretty mean to all the kids, and they really work when he is around." The term little "stepfather" *(padrastrito)* is frequently applied to an older brother in Sal si Puedes.

When thirteen-year-old Mike was arrested for petty theft and was in juvenile hall in San Jose, "He just kept crying and crying and nobody could make him stop," his mother said. "That was because Mike knew that his brother [aged fifteen] was going to hit him for getting in trouble with the juvenile. He was really scared."

In spite of the authoritarian relationship between older and younger siblings, brothers and sisters are usually proud of each other and indirectly demonstrate their feelings of affection. Rosa, for example, told the story of how she had postponed her marriage for several years after her mother died "because I felt like I had to take care of my younger brothers and sisters. I wanted them to stay in school, and I just couldn't leave them alone." Four-year-old Ricky also expressed pride and affection for a younger sibling, his three-year-old brother: "I got a pretty nice little brother, talks good, knows plenty bad words!"

EXTENDED FAMILIES

Barrio people frequently have many relatives outside the nuclear family living in the San Jose area. Alicia and Esteban, for
example, who have only one child of their own, are members of
a kinship group of 205 persons living in Santa Clara County.
Of these, 130 are Alicia's relatives and 75 are Esteban's. The
couple visits frequently with about two-thirds of the members
of this extended kinship group and sees the others at least two
or three times a year. Alicia is in contact at least once a week,
either by personal visit or by telephone conversation, with more
than sixty relatives besides her husband and child.

Relations between grandparents and grandchildren are particularly close. Grandchildren respect their grandparents and
are generally less formal with them than they are with their
own parents. Often grandparents joke and play with their
grandchildren, and demonstrations of affection are more frequent on the part of grandparents than parents. Grandmothers
fondle their grandchildren and praise them in public; mothers
ordinarily do not behave this way toward their own children.

Fourteen-year-old Tony and his family live in a house a few
doors from Tony's grandparents. Tony's grandfather frequently
asks Tony's father to send the boy over to help with some task.
The father then sends Tony over to work. "I used to go over
there almost every day," Tony reported. "I would work around
the garden or on the house, clean the yard, or go with my
grandfather somewhere in the car. Working for my grandfather
is different from working for somebody else. If it gets real hot,
he tells me to get in the shade or to rest for a while. My grandfather doesn't pay me, but when he gets his wages he tells my
grandmother to buy me a shirt or a pair of pants. If I want to
go somewhere, I can usually get the money from my grandfather, and sometimes he brings me a present. Sometimes when
I'm working on my bike, my grandfather comes over to keep
me company. Once I lived with my grandparents for a year,
and my grandmother is just like another mother."

Relations with aunts and uncles tend to be somewhat formal
and very respectful. "Cousins can always joke and have fun

together. I think it's bad that some of the younger people have begun to take their own cousins as compadres. This isn't so good because they are used to being very informal with each other and joking, arguing, or even fighting with each other. Sometimes they forget that their cousin is also their compadre or comadre and they must be very respectful toward each other."

Children are often sent to live with aunts, uncles, or grandparents for several months, or even a year, at a time. Teresa reported that her twelve-year-old daughter had been away from home for several weeks. "My daughter-in-law got lonesome with only a small baby around the house, and she wanted to keep the girl for a month or two for company."

Children live and mature in a wide circle of kinsmen. When a child feels mistreated at home, there are grandparents to comfort and console him; aunts may help him to resolve conflicts with his parents; uncles bring presents or give him a little extra spending money; cousins can always be found to share in a game or an outing; childhood secrets can be shared with older sisters; and a little boy who has a big brother need not fear the neighborhood bully. It is the rare person, whether young or old, who feels lonely in Sal si Puedes.

COMPADRAZGO

Compadrazgo, or the compadre system, is an artificial kinship complex based on various Catholic rituals and the subsequently formed relationship between a child's parents and his godparents. At the time of Catholic baptism, for example, a godfather (*padrino*) and a godmother (*madrina*) are chosen to sponsor the child for this sacrament. The godparents thus enter into a special social and religious relationship not only with their new godchild (*ahijado*) but also with the child's parents, who become their compadres. Thus when Mike and Elvira Chavez asked Juan and Lola Martinez to serve as godparents at the baptism of the new Chavez baby, the two couples became compadres or "coparents" and thus assumed certain social and economic obligations toward each other.

Compadrazgo is a significant social institution throughout the Catholic folk cultures of southern Europe and Latin America. God-parenthood extends the size of the adult group from which a child can expect help and support; and compadrazgo links adults with one another "in bonds of mutual respect and trust . . . or, at the least, it solemnizes and sanctifies a relation of intimacy and trust that has already come into existence through . . . friendship" (39).

The compadre system is one of the strongest Mexican culture patterns found in Sal si Puedes; it plays a major role in fostering and maintaining the social stability of the community by creating new ties in the network of social relationships which bind group members together.

In Sal si Puedes four types of godparents are recognized for the following sacraments: baptism, first communion, confirmation, and marriage. Baptismal godparents are considered the most important. Their religious function is to make sure that the godchild receives proper Catholic religious instruction and all the sacraments. Their social obligations to the child are to see that he does not lack the necessities of life and to supply goods and money, if the parents are unable to provide them, for the child's rearing. In Sal si Puedes, however, these obligations are more ideal than real.

Baptismal godparents, as well as other kinds of godparents, are expected to give their godchild gifts at Christmas, on his birthday, at the time of his marriage, and at the time of his confirmation. They are expected to give advice and administer discipline to the child whenever they deem it necessary, with or without the invitation of the parents. It is generally agreed in Sal si Puedes that a child is more likely to heed advice from a godparent than from his own parents. Although godparents are supposed ideally to administer religious instruction, very few in Sal si Puedes exercise this function.

Relations Between Compadres

The relationship between compadres is a warm and friendly one, but it is believed that compadres should not tease or joke with each other. Above all they should not argue or fight. Marta commented, "My third son is going to take his first communion next month. I don't have a padrino for him yet. I'd like to get Ismael, but he's always teasing me and telling me jokes, so I guess I'll have to get somebody else for the padrino."

Compadres are considered as close as blood relatives and any sort of sexual relationship between them is strictly forbidden. As Rosa said, "Even if the woman's husband died and her compadre's wife died, they could never marry or have anything to do with each other — it would be just as bad as marrying your brother." This prohibition, however, does not extend to the compadre's relatives, even those of his nuclear family.

Compadres visit each other frequently, usually several times a week, and assist each other with labor whenever an extra pair of hands is needed. Irene stated, "I'm really lucky to have one of my comadres living right across the street from me. It gives me someone to visit and to go with me when I want to go out. I wouldn't feel right about asking just anybody to go somewhere with me, but I know I can always ask my comadre."

Two women who are comadres often give each other small presents — a dish of some delicacy which one has prepared, a potted plant, a bit of embroidery or crocheted lace. If one needs to borrow a cup of flour or a few beans, the person to ask is, naturally, a comadre. A woman will not hesitate to leave her husband and children to prepare their own dinner in order to go to the aid of a comadre who needs help. When Paula's comadre, who lives in Hayward (about twenty-five miles from San Jose), was expecting her last baby, Paula left her own family for two weeks to care for her comadre during her confinement.

Men render whatever financial help they can to their compadres who are having economic problems. Pete said, "I sure would like to get my compadre Chavez in the plant where I work; he hasn't got a job right now."

Esteban's story illustrates the fact that a man may feel obligated to help a compadre even if the compadre has relatives who are in a position to come to his aid: "I have always felt like being a compadre was a serious thing and placed me under obligation to do the best I could. Take my compadre Raphael, for example. I was the godfather at his son's wedding. Now Raphael is old and has lost his wife. He lives on a little pension. He has two stepsons living, but those guys don't take their responsibilities seriously, and they didn't ask Raphael to come and live with them after their mother died. So my wife and I talked it over and decided to ask Raphael to come and live with us. He's an old man and he gets pretty lonesome without any family around. I wouldn't have felt right if I hadn't asked him to leave here — after all, he is my compadre."

Social Functions of the Compadre System

Compadrazgo in Sal si Puedes serves three main social functions: it formalizes friendship and extends the size of the kinship group, it enhances neighborhood solidarity, and if compadres are also members of the extended family it strengthens kinship ties.

During 1954 and 1955, Elvira became very friendly with another woman of the barrio, Manuela. Manuela lived across the street from Elvira's mother; she and Elvira both were members of the Sociedad Guadalupana (Altar Society), and both had children of about the same ages. During the summer of 1955, two of Elvira's children were to take their first communion, and Elvira asked Manuela to sponsor her daughter and Manuela's husband to act as communion godfather for her son. Thus the couple became Elvira's compadres, but not through the same child. "I'm real happy," Elvira remarked; "Manuela and I have been such good friends the last couple of years. Now I know that we will always be friends no matter what happens." The compadre system served to formalize friendship and to create a permanent bond between people who wanted to retain that friendship.

The role of compadrazgo in neighborhood solidarity is illustrated by the experience of Pete and Marta. In the winter of 1954, this couple and their children moved from a nearby barrio to Sal si Puedes. After they had lived in their present home for about six months, Marta had a new baby. She asked her new neighbors to the east to serve as baptismal godparents for the child and thus entered into a compadre relationship with them. A few months later the family's eleven-year-old daughter was to be confirmed in the Catholic Church. Pete and Marta decided to ask another neighbor, the woman whose house was next door to theirs on the west, to sponsor the girl for her confirmation. Thus, within a year Pete and Marta had set up close relations with two families living adjacent to them. "Now that I have comadres living nearby," Marta explained, "I really feel at home in this house."

There is a tendency in Sal si Puedes for people to select at least a few of their compadres from among their own relatives. Since Mexican-American families in the barrio are large and since each older child may have several godparents, a single individual may have as many as eight or ten compadres living in his immediate neighborhood; of these, most are usually non-relatives but are generally related to him in some way. Frequently a child's uncle or aunt is asked to become the child's godparent; thus brothers and sisters may also be compadres. Cousins are frequently chosen also.

Rose emphasized the function of the compadre system in family solidarity: "I think having relatives as compadres is a pretty good thing sometimes because it makes distant relatives like aunts, uncles, and cousins seem much closer, and it keeps the family from drifting apart."

REFERENCE

Beals, Ralph. *Culture Patterns of Mexican-American Life.* Proceedings of the Fifth Annual Conference, Southwestern Conference on the Education of Spanish Speaking People. Los Angeles, 1951, 5-13.

Chapter 9

TODAY'S CHICANO REFUTES THE STEREOTYPE*

BONNIE M. MALDONADO AND WILLIAM C. CROSS

RAMON and Linda attend high school in Grant County, New Mexico. Ramon, a twelfth-grader, is a sturdy, dark-haired boy with flashing white teeth. Linda, an eleventh-grader, is petite, brunette, brown-eyed. Ramon's father is a mine foreman, Linda's a ranch worker. Both Ramon and Linda are second-generation Mexican-Americans. And both have brown skin — Ramon's perhaps a shade darker than Linda's.

As Mexican-Americans, Ramon and Linda are members of the second largest minority group in the United States. Historical, cultural, linguistic, and physical characteristics set these group members apart from the Anglo community, particularly in the Southwest where discrimination due to differences in ethnic background and skin color has been high. Here also the traditional folk culture concept of the Mexican-American has flourished.

THE FOLK CULTURE CONCEPT

According to Grebler et al. (1970), the traditional folk culture concept is based on a declining, often rurally-oriented fraction of the entire Mexican-American population (Burma, 1970). Grebler et al. (1970) have described the Mexican-American who would fit the folk culture concept as being poor and proud. He cherishes a value orientation which emphasizes interpersonal relations rather than ideas, abstractions, or material possessions. He resents success, assimilation, and personal advance-

---

*From Bonnie M. Maldonado and William Cross, Today's Chicano Refutes the Stereotype, *College Student Journal*, *11*:146-152, 1977.

ment. He is very protective of his "Spanish" culture, he is Catholic, and he often has an extended family. He is easily identifiable by his Spanish surname, his inadequate or accented English, his lack of employable skills and social graces acceptable to the dominant group; his dress, mannerisms, and food habits.

Additionally, the poor Mexican American is often of a somewhat darker Mexican-American (Grebler et al.). Indeed, nothing marks the individual's group identity more visibly or more permanently than skin color. Dark skin has traditionally served as the mark of inferiority, as in the Negro slave (Isaacs, 1968), and brown-skinned persons have tacitly been recognized as subordinate to the whites. The minority group child soon learns the negative value placed on dark skin by contemporary American society, and the darker Mexican-American is a constant reminder to himself of the stigma of his ethnic background and accompanying feelings of inferiority (Daniels and Kitano, 1970). Some have fled the barrios, rejected Spanish names and accents, and have even powdered their necks to look lighter-skinned (Steiner, 1970). However, ethnic differences cannot be made to vanish by any process of Americanization, and attempts to reduce the Mexican-American's ethnic group identity have resulted in poor psychological adjustments (Coleman, 1966; Derbyshire, 1968; Jessor et al., 1968; Ramirez, 1969).

Groups who appear different will be thought and made to feel different. The "in" group typifies the "out" group by skin color, facial features and expressions, speech and mannerisms, names, and even places of residence, among other things (Allport, 1958). The Anglo tends to be prejudiced against people with such differences. The minority group child sees himself as he believes he is seen and soon accepts as his own the values, norms, and ideals of the dominant group, finding himself a part of what has been neglected (Douglass, 1960) and therefore undesirable. Thus, the Anglo's prejudices are reflected in the self-depreciated stereotypes of the Mexican-American as emotional, proud and authoritarian, materialistic but unambitious, poor and of a low social class, mistrusted and lazy, with small concern for education (Dworkin, 1970; Grebler et al., 1970).

SEX ROLES. Besides being stereotyped in the minority group role, the Mexican-American female has had to contend with sex-role differences. According to the folk culture concept, the roles of the males and females have been rigidly prescribed in the Mexican-American family. The males were expected to demonstrate superiority and masculinity by sexual and physical prowess; the females were expected to submit to male superiority, confining their interests to home and family (Barnes, 1969; Moore, 1970; Rubel, 1970). Children were taught respectfulness and obedience, with household chores assigned to the girls and outdoor chores to the boys, as part of the sex roles (Heller, 1966).

SOCIOECONOMIC STATUS. An almost inevitable accompaniment to the Mexican-American's status is the problem of socioeconomic standing. Since position on the American socioeconomic scale is determined largely by the educational and occupational background of the male parent, Mexican-Americans tend to make a poor showing, especially in the Southwest, on nearly every measure of social and economic position. The educational gap of Mexican-Americans is well known, and associated with this is an unfavorable occupational structure and a low average income. Under the criterion of $3,000.00 per family per year, the poverty group of Mexican-Americans has been found to include 35 percent of all families, more than twice the rate for Anglos (Grebler et al., 1970). Mexican-Americans have traditionally held inferior jobs in practically all major occupations, with poor wages, low social status, depressed self-esteem, and lack of opportunity for betterment (Grebler et al., 1970). These factors have increased prejudice against them because it seems that prejudice increases as socioeconomic level decreases (Ainsworth, 1969; Barnes, 1969; Burma, 1970; Moreno, 1967).

SELF-CONCEPT. Daniels and Kitano have stressed that members of groups discriminated against, no matter what their social class position, will manifest the traits of self-doubt, self-hate, and negative self-concept. According to the literature, the Mexican-American of low socioeconomic status has developed a highly negative self-concept, as reflected in the depreciated self-stereotypes mentioned earlier. Yet the self-concept is important as the core of systematic behavior (Lecky, 1951), and as the individual sees himself, so does he act. The need for a positive self-image is apparent, for the school child as well as for the adult. For the Mexican-American child, his negative self-concept results in educational lag, failure, and dropout only too often and too soon. Self-derogation has been seen by many educators as characteristic of a disproportionate number of Mexican-American students (Carter, 1970). Valdes (1969) attributed the development of defeatism in the Mexican-American child to the ethnic caste system based on myth and unequal opportunity.

We know that a positive self-image is prerequisite to academic achievement (Anderson and Johnson, 1971; Gillman, 1969; Kubinec, 1970). Education should help the student build a positive self-image, and it has failed when the pupil becomes defensive with feelings of inadequacy and incompetence. Aragon (1969) saw the Mexican-American child entering school with an infinitely better view of himself than he takes with him when he leaves. The school is thus seen as the culprit in reducing the barrio child's self-image (Steiner, 1970).

If all this is true, it offers ample justification for researching the self-concept of the Mexican-American adolescent, such as Ramon and Linda, who are nearing the end of their school experience. We may then ask: How do Ramon and Linda really perceive themselves? Is Ramon's consciousness of his skin color detrimental to his self-image? Does Linda's skin color affect her both as a minority group member and a female?

THE REFUTATION

An attempt to answer these questions was made through a study of Mexican-American high school students in New Mexico during 1971-1972. Grand County, the site of the study in southern New Mexico, is remote from large urban areas and has been called one of the "worst pockets of discrimination in the state" (J. Aragon, personal communication, 1969). Additionally, the area population of about 36,000 falls chiefly into the low socioeconomic group since the principal income producing activities are mining and ranching.

In Grant County are two major high schools, Silver High and Cobre High. At the time of the study, 46 percent of Silver High, and 66 percent of Cobre High students were Mexican-American. From the populations of these two schools, 174 students (82 boys and 92 girls, grades 10 through 12) were selected on the basis of Mexican-American ethnicity and low socioeconomic status.

The Tennessee Self Concept Scale (TSCS) was utilized to measure student self-concept. An appended questionnaire provided information as to sex, group membership, and socioeconomic status. Student identification of ethnicity was validated by school counselors and school records. Scores on Hollingshead's Two-Factor Index of Social Position determined that 39 percent and 61 percent of the participants fell into the two lowest socioeconomic classes, 4 and 5, respectively. Skin color was determined by student self-rating, investigator observation, and ratings of three judges of 37 millimeter color transparencies of each subject's hand and arm, according to a scale of light, medium, or dark. These data were subjected to suitable statistical treatment to determine significant differences.

The two major findings of the study were unexpected and rather surprising. These were: (a) the male and female low socioeconomic Mexican-American subjects did *not* differ significantly with regard to overall level of self-esteem; and (b) the group did *not* differ significantly from the norm group on the overall Total Positive TSCS score. The overall Total Positive TSCS score for the group was 332.37 and that for the norm group was 345.57 (Fitts, 1965).

The sex variable affected four TSCS scores: Self-Satisfaction, Physical Self, Variability, and Defensive Positive. The variable of skin color affected three TSCS scores: Self-Criticism, Total Conflict, and Physical Self.

The Defensive Positive and Self-Criticism scores indicate defensive behavior, isolating those individuals who are being defensive as they describe themselves and those who deliberately try to present a favorable picture of themselves.

The Total Conflict and Variability scores indicate the amount or lack of conflict between one area of self-perception and another. Total Conflict scores for both sexes increased as skin color was perceived darker, indicating greater conflict and confusion in the self-images of individuals with darker skin color. Girls scored significantly higher than boys on the Variability measure, showing a greater lack of unity in self-concept.

For the Self-Satisfaction measure, boys scored higher than girls except for the medium skin color group in which male and female scores were almost identical. This indicates that boys with light or dark skin saw themselves more favorably than girls with light or dark skin.

The Physical Self measure, the only one to be affected by both independent variables of sex and skin color, showed higher scores for males than for females. For both sexes, the lowest scores were found for those of dark skin color. Evidently the males were not as self-conscious nor as critical of their appearance as the females; all subjects who perceived their skin color as dark did not view their appearance as favorably as their peers with light or medium skin color.

Both the Self-Satisfaction and Physical Self measure are related to the individual's degree of acceptance of his appearance. They convey the subject's perception of what he is, how he feels about himself, and what he does.

The study's results are perplexing in that they both uphold and refute results of other studies of Mexican American self-perception.

SOCIOECONOMIC STATUS. The group on the whole did not exhibit the sense of inferiority and worthlessness to the extent generally attributed to their low socioeconomic level. Nor did they manifest the characteristic of the disadvantaged . . . high degree of self-hate often reported as characteristic of the disadvantaged (Banks and Grambs, 1972), although there was evidence of some negative feelings toward themselves. Thus, any stigma connected with the Mexican-American minority group in a low socioeconomic class was not reflected in this group's overall self-esteem.

SEX ROLES. Failure to find significant differences in perceptions of sex roles supports the doubt that the folk culture concept of sex roles characterizes the contemporary Mexican-American adolescent expressed by Grebler (1967) and Moore (1970), among others. On the other hand, Rosenkrantz et al. (1968) have reported that the sex-role stereotypes continue to be clearly defined and agreed to by both college men and women, implying that women tend to continue to hold negative values of their relative worth to men.

The reasons for this failure to find sex-role differences can only be speculated upon. True, the legal status of women has changed in recent years in many respects. It is true also that educational and occupational opportunities are opening up for women. As early as 1967, Grebler reported that the average years of education for both Mexican-American males and females was about the same.

It may be that exposure, via newspapers, television, radio, and movies, to the movement for opportunity and equal rights for women has modified the contemporary Mexican-American adolescent's concept of the sex role. But vestigial remainders of the sex-role in the folk culture concept continue, as witnessed by differences found on the Self-Satisfaction, Physical Self, Variability, and Defensive score of the TSCS.

SKIN COLOR. Some internalization of negative attitudes was indicated by the lower self-concepts of the darker-skinner subjects and lack of self-acceptance by female subjects of skin color. This may be interpreted as meaning that the subjects perceived light skin color desirable, and thus reflected the perceptions of the majority group. This interpretation supports the views of other researchers (Proshansky and Newton, 1968; Valdes, 1969) that minority group members still find light skin desirable.

For today's youth, the color of skin seems to be decreasing in importance. Television depicts youth of all races mingling in social activities. Newspapers and periodicals report interracial marriages. Within the worlds of education, recreation, entertainment, and sports, the Negro, the Japanese, the Native American Indian, and the Mexican American are claiming their identities through individual excellence.

Even the Anglo youth prizes a deeply tanned skin, probably because at one time a deep tan was the mark of the affluent Anglo who could afford to spend summer and winter vacations on the beaches and ski slopes. In the Southwest, where year-long outdoor living is possible, a brown skin may be natural or acquired. May we not then say that Brown is Beautiful, too, to express pride in the ethnicity, culture, and heritage of the Mexican-American?

SELF-CONCEPT. The fact that the overall self-concept score for the minority group was only slightly lower than that for the norm was perhaps the most unexpected finding of all, particularly so when we remember that the study site was characterized as one of the worst pockets of discrimination in New Mexico. It should be noted that in both high schools and the populations were chiefly Mexican-American, thus making the "dominant" group the Mexican-American group and the "minority" group the Anglos. It seems that the usual distinction of the dominant group as Anglo and the minority group as Mexican-American was here reversed. Here also, exposure via communication media to the separatist movements of the 1960s and early 1970s — for Indians, for example — may have influenced the overall self-concept of the Mexican-American group.

It may be concluded that the Mexican-American group in this study had reasonably adequate self-concepts. This conclusion supports Cooper (1972) and others who have reported that the self-concept of the Mexican-American subject was not significantly different from that of the Indian, Negro, or Anglo. This should be a cause of concern for those educators who regard the low self-concept of the Mexican-American as the principal reason for poor performance in Southwestern schools as compared to that of other ethnic groups.

EMERGENCE OF THE CHICANO

In contrast to the traditional negative self-concept of the Mexican-American, a new cultural pride and an increase in self-esteem are appearing (Haddox, 1970; Palomares, 1971;

Steiner, 1970). The roots of this new cultural pride appear in the concept of La Raza. Moore (1970) said that La Raza does not refer to race at all but to a vague concept of ethnic identity, a compelling feeling of belonging, and that it offers positive identity to the Mexican-American. Beyond the family and the community, La Raza is a broader symbol of cohesion and identification (Luebben, 1970).

Zirkel (1970) saw the cultural pride movements of minority groups as a means of turning disadvantages into advantages, or negative self-concepts into positive self-concepts. Katz (1969) said that ethnic group membership may depress or enhance. The self-concept of the disadvantaged child would seem to depend largely on society's and education's efforts to remove segregation and alleviate poverty.

The younger Mexican-American, who often refers to himself as the Chicano, is impatient with the identity crisis. Steiner (1970) sees this as typical of the Chicano. Typical of the Chicano, too, is his awareness of the need for Mexican-Americans to retain their cultural uniqueness and not attempt to identify with the Anglo group.

A major change appears to be taking place in the life of the young Mexican-American — the Chicano. The days of segregated swimming pools and schools are usually known to him only through his parents. He is less ashamed of his ethnic ancestry than his father, and cultural marginality and overt discrimination do not affect him to the extent they affected the older generation.

All this is partly due to the growth of studies in Chicano history and culture, and to the development of a new body of literature dealing with the literary, social, and political aspects of his people. The chicano's battle has been partly won for him by his elders, and he has been encouraged by the successes of other minority group movements.

However, for the most part, the new image of the young Chicano is a product of his own awareness (Haddox, 1970).

Apparently the schools have not failed in helping the Mexican-American child to the extent with which they were previously credited. Some problems have been eliminated —

special problems still exist, the education lag being one. In fact, it may be that new and unpredictable problems will arise.

In helping the Mexican-American readjust psychologically, the counselor must remember that toleration is a two-way street. While the Mexican-American is rightfully entitled to pride in his historical, cultural, and racial heritage, the Anglo is rightfully entitled to his. The Mexican-American may still retain the right to question Anglo values and norms, but not to blindly accept them. This entails the need for judgments based on facts, not on hatred or bitterness. The Mexican-American must learn who he is, why he is, and how he is. Self-understanding and self-acceptance are the keys to a positive self-concept.

The Mexican-American child must be made to feel that he is an individual and that the individual is important. We should judge and be judged as human beings, not simply as members of this group or that group, not as white-skinned, black-skinned, or brown-skinned.

REFERENCES

Ainsworth, C. L. *Teachers and Counselors for Mexican-American Children.* Austin, Texas: Southwest Educational Development Corporation, 1969.

Allport, G. W. *The Nature of Prejudice.* Garden City, New York: Doubleday-Anchor, 1958.

Anderson, J. G., and Johnson, W. H. Stability and Change Among Three Generations of Mexican-Americans: Factors Affecting Achievement. *American Educational Journal,* 1971, 31:285-309.

Aragon, J. A. Culture and the Mexican-American. Speech given at the Cultural Awareness Center, Santa Fe, New Mexico, February, 1969.

Banks, J. A. and Grambs, J. D. *Black Self-Concept.* New York: McGraw-Hill, 1972.

Barnes, R. *Conflicts of Cultural Transition.* Davis: University of California, Department of Applied Behavioral Sciences, 1969.

Burma, J. H. A Comparison of the Mexican-American Subculture with the Oscar Lewis Culture of Poverty Model. In J. H. Burma (ed.), *Mexican-Americans in the United States.* Cambridge: Schenkman, 1970.

Carter, T. P. *Mexican-Americans in School: A History of Educational Neglect.* New York: College Entrance Examination Board, 1970.

Coleman, J. S. *Equality of Educational Opportunity.* Washington, D.C.: U.

S. Department of Health, Education and Welfare, Office of Education, 1966.

Cooper, J. G. Perception of Self and Others as Related to Ethnic Group Membership. Paper presented at the annual meeting of the American Educational Research Association, Chicago, April, 1972. (Mimeo.)

Daniels, R., and Kitano, H. *American Racism: Exploration of the Nature of Prejudice*. Englewood Cliffs, New Jersey: Prentice-Hall, 1970.

Derbyshire, R. L. Adolescent Identity Crisis in Urban Mexican-Americans in East Los Angeles. In J. H. Burma (ed.), *Minority group adolescents in the United States*, Cambridge: Schenkman, 1970.

Douglass, J. H. *The Effects of Minority Status on Children: Survey Papers*. Washington, D.C.: 1960 White House Conference on Children and Youth, 1960.

Dworkin, A. G. Stereotypes and Self-images Held by Native-born and Foreign-born Mexican Americans. In J. H. Burma (ed.), *Mexican-Americans in the United States*. Cambridge: Schenkman, 1970.

Fitts, W. H. *Tennessee Self Concept Scale*. Nashville, Tennessee: Counselor Recordings and Tests, 1965.

Gillman, G. B. The Relationship Between Self-concept, Intellectual Ability, Achievement, and Manifest Anxiety Among Select Groups of Spanish-Surname Migrant Students in New Mexico. Unpublished doctoral dissertation, University of New Mexico, 1969.

Grebler, L. *The Schooling Gap: Signs of Progress*. Mexican-American Study Project, Advance Report No. 7. Los Angeles: University of California, 1967.

Haddox, J. *Los Chicanos: An Awakening People*, El Paso, Texas: Western Press, 1970.

Heller, C. S. *Mexican-American Youth*. New York: Random House, 1966.

Isaacs, H. R. Group Identity and Political Change: The role of Color and Physical Characteristics. In J. H. Franklin (ed.), *Color and Race*. Boston: Beacon Press, 1968.

Jessor, R., Graves, T. D., Hanson, R. C., and Jessor, S. L. *Society, Personality, and Deviant Behavior: A Study of a Tri-ethnic Community*. New York: Holt, Rinehart & Winston, 1968.

Katz, I. A. Catalog of Personality Approaches to Negro Performance with Research Suggestions. *Journal of Social Issues*, 1969, 30:13-28.

Kubinec, M. The Relative Efficiency of Various Dimensions of the Self-concept in Predicting Academic Achievement. *American Educational Research Journal*, 1970, 7:321-336.

Lecky, P. *Self-consistency*. New York: Island Press, 1951.

Luebben, R. A. Spanish-Americans of the Upper Rio Grande Drainage. In J. H. Burma (ed.), *Mexican-Americans in the United States*. Cambridge: Schenkman, 1970.

Moore, J. W. *Mexican-Americans*. Englewood Cliffs, New Jersey: Prentice-Hall, 1970.

Moreno, E. View from the Margin. *Claremont Reading Conference Yearbook,* 1967, 31:88-100.

Palomares, U. H. Nuestros sentimientos son Iguales, la differencia en la experiencia. *Personnel and Guidance Journal,* 1971, 50(2):137-144.

Proshansky, H., and Newton, P. The Nature and Meaning of Negro Self-identity. In M. Deutsch, I. Katz, and A. Jensen (eds.), *Social Class, Race, and Psychological Development.* New York: Holt, Rinehart & Winston, 1968.

Ramirez, M. Identification with Mexican-American Values and Psychological Adjustment in Mexican-American Adolescents. *International Journal of Social Psychiatry,* 1969, 11: 151-156.

Rosenkrantz, P., Bee, H., Vogel, S., Boverman, I., and Boverman, D. Sex-role Stereotypes and Self Concepts in College Students. *Journal of Consulting and Clinical Psychology,* 1968, 32:287-295.

Ruebel, A. J. The Family. In J. H. Burma (ed.), *Mexican-Americans in the United States.* Cambridge: Schenkman, 1970.

Steiner, S. *La Raza: The Mexican-Americans.* New York: Harper & Row, 1970.

Valdes, D. T. U. S. Hispano. *Social Education,* 1969, 33:56-62.

Zirkel, P. A. Self-concept and the Disadvantages of Ethnic Group Membership and Mixture. *Review of Educational Research,* 1971, 41:211-225.

Chapter 10

INITIAL CONTACTS WITH
MEXICAN-AMERICAN FAMILIES*

IGNACIO AGUILAR

SCHOOLS of social work have, for the most part, been oblivious to the need for adapting methods of practice to minority groups. Rather they teach practice derived from a generic method that is dictated primarily by the majority. Yet much social work practice is carried out in the United States with minority groups and, too often, social workers apply it by a blanket method supposedly effective with all people.

Each minority group has its own problems and personality — derived from long-existing cultural and moral values, language, patterns of behavior, socioeconomic conditions, ethnic background, and many other factors. Social work practice in a minority community shows that besides the variations that must be made in the generic method to suit individuals, certain adaptations should be made in applying social work methods to the specific minority group.

During ten years' experience in a California community made up mainly of Mexican-Americans, the author learned from the people in the community how to adapt some of the key concepts and techniques of social work to the needs and the life-style of Mexican-Americans and how to avoid some common obstacles to the development of goodwill.

This article briefly outlines different cultural values and patterns of behavior — and barriers to assimilation in an alien society — which the social worker should consider in making initial contacts with Mexican-American families. How social work method was adapted in this initial contact phase in order

*From Ignacio Aguilar, Initial Contacts with Mexican-American Families, *Social Work*, *17*:66-70, 1972. Copyright 1972 by the National Association For Social Workers, Inc. Reprinted by permission.

to provide effective counseling is illustrated by a case example of work with a family in the author's community.

INITIAL CONTACT

There is no doubt that one of the most important and difficult processes in social work is the beginning phase, that is, starting to work with a client. Green and Maloney describe this phase as one in which

> ... emotional interaction takes place. The worker focuses on an emotional engagement with a purpose, explores the possibilities of person(s), agency and worker finding a realistic *common purpose*. On the other hand, the client(s) naturally and rightly questions moving into a relationship with the worker.[1]

Since the first encounter determines the dynamics of the relationship and the kind and quality of the interaction between worker and client, a correct start is vital.

Awareness of differences, an understanding of why the differences exist, and experience in dealing with people of the specific minority group — all these are important to the social worker in establishing feelings of friendliness and confidence from the outset. Without them, a worker can unknowingly arouse antagonism or cause the client to withdraw in fear or confusion.

PATTERNS OF LIVING

The social worker in a Mexican-American community finds that his ways of work are strongly influenced by the people's patterns of living, which differ in many respects from those people having a Protestant Anglo-Saxon background. Consideration of concepts, attitudes, and patterns of behavior that are likely to have a marked effect on the beginning stages of social work method can help to assure that vital correct start.

THE LEISURELY OPENING. When Mexican-Americans meet to negotiate or arrange affairs, the first step is to set the climate or *ambiente*. A preliminary period of warm, informal, personal conversation precedes the discussion of the concerns that brought them together. Jumping into the middle of serious and controversial affairs — as many persons in the United States are inclined to do — seems confusing and even discourteous to most Mexican-Americans.

LANGUAGE. Language is of course one of the main problems in working with non-English speaking people. How can a social worker help people if he cannot communicate with them? How can a common purpose be established if that purpose cannot be discussed? How can a worker start where his clients are and proceed at a pace comfortable to them when he cannot even start at all? Obviously, for any social worker in a Spanish-speaking community, fluency in the language is a tremendous asset, and for those dealing directly with clients it is a necessity — both for communicating and establishing rapport.

ATTITUDE TOWARD THE LAW. Having to deal with the law is considered shameful by the average Mexican-American family, and the family members are disinclined to accept it as a common practice. The social worker needs to reassure his clients that dealing with the law offers them an honorable way of protecting their interests and legal rights. He will also have to explain their relation to such persons as probation officers and the police and tell them about legal services available to them. Knowledge of the basic elements of the Mexican system of law, as well as the system in the United States, will enable him to interpret these subjects more intelligibly to his clients.

INFLUENCE OF RELIGION. Religion plays an important role in the Mexican-American home and shapes the lives of the entire family. As Heller notes:

> Some observers have reported that the church continues to exercise a strong influence in the Mexican-American community. For example, Broom and Shevky contend that "the church is the principal agency of cultural conservatism for Mexicans in the United States and reinforces the separateness of the group." They specify that they have in mind not only the parish organization of the Catholic Church but also the Protestant Missions "with their functional sectarian attri-

butes." There seems to be little doubt that the "religious factor" (to use Professor Lenski's phrase) plays an important role in the rate of acculturation of Mexican Americans.[2]

ROLE OF THE MALE. The concept of the male in society and in the family is important to the understanding of the person of Mexican ancestry. It is not only a concept of philosophy, it is a way of life, quite different from the "American way of life." Paz describes the *macho* concept as follows:

> The ideal manliness is never to "crack," never to back down. . . . Our masculine integrity is as much endangered by kindness as it is by hostility. Any opening of our defenses is a lessening of our manliness. . . . The Mexican macho — the male — is a hermetic being, closed up in himself, capable of guarding both himself and whatever has been confided to him.[3]

The traditional role of the husband and father in the Mexican-American family is explained by Heller, as follows:

> According to the traditional norms the husband is regarded as the authoritarian and patriarchal figure who is both the head and the master of the family, and the mother as the affectional figure in the family.[4]

THE EXTENDED FAMILY. To Mexican-Americans the extended family is of great significance in their pattern of living; they take it for granted that in time of trouble that they can always count on the family to help out. Again quoting Heller:

> Not only in size, but also in organization the Mexican American family displays an unusual persistence of traditional forms. It continues to be an extended type of family with strong ties spread through a number of generations in a large web of kinships. These ties impose obligations of mutual aid, respect and affection.[5]

BARRIERS TO COOPERATION

The social worker dealing with Mexican-Americans may well find that there are certain obstacles to be overcome before he can gain his clients' confidence and they can work together smoothly and effectively in endeavoring to solve problems.

These obstacles may involve attitudes of other people with whom the Mexican-Americans associate or they may be related primarily to the clients' own attitudes.

PREJUDICE. Unfortunately, in many sections of the United States Mexican-Americans — especially the families of poor and unskilled workers — are likely to encounter prejudice. This can occur within the community at large, can reach out to the children in school, and can even be found among persons in the helping professions.

Unfriendly or antagonistic feelings conveyed by insensitive people in positions of authority hinder the progress of such families in becoming assimilated and assuming responsibility. These families with limited financial resources and limited knowledge of English are likely to become the target of prejudiced individuals reluctant to help those who do not fit readily into the mold of middle-class American society. Too often, help is not offered at all. Or it may be offered in such a way that acceptance requires departure from familiar behavioral patterns. Indeed, prejudice in its purest and ugliest manifestations becomes one of the most common problems the minorities face in their encounters with helping professionals. It can also be one of the social worker's greatest obstacles to building confidence.

THE STRANGE SYSTEM. It is hard for the parents in a Mexican-American family to understand the "system" with which they have to deal as they endeavor to cope with their problems. It becomes in their minds a kind of hydra-headed creature, with authorities cropping up from all sides to make demands upon them and press in on their privacy. Yet these families have to learn how to deal with the system if they are to become active partners in the process of being helped. They have to learn how to exercise their rights and to assert their self-worth and esteem as human beings in a society they do not understand. As Hollis notes:

> This emphasis upon the innate worth of the individual is an extremely important, fundamental characteristic of casework. It is the ingredient that makes it possible to establish the relationship of trust that is so essential to effective treatment.

From it grow the two essential characteristics of the case-worker's attitude toward his client: acceptance and belief in self-determination.[6]

For truly effective social work practice with minority groups, the social worker must learn as well as the client. Much more needs to be done in the way of teaching the uniqueness of the cultures of these groups to social workers and others in the helping professions if they are to provide worthwhile assistance to those who need the most help.

The following case illustration presents only the beginning stages in working with a typical family in a Mexican-American community in California. With further involvement, all other orthodox social work methods had to be modified somewhat in order to help the family fully.

CASE ILLUSTRATION

Family X is made up of the parents and three children: a girl six years old and two boys, aged seven and sixteen. Mr. and Mrs. X were legally married at one time, but because of serious marital problems and pressures from Mrs. X's family were divorced three years ago. However, they managed to resolve their problems and came together again; the church never considered them divorced. The family lives in a small house in the back of a large empty lot that has not been taken care of properly. Weeds have taken over the majority of the land, so that they conceal the house.

The probation department referred Family X to the community center because neither the father nor the mother were able to communicate in English. The probation officer explained that this family needed counseling and also "someone who could speak their language." The parents were unable to control their sixteen-year-old son, Freddy, who had been placed on probation for running away from home regularly.

Mrs. X had been told to call the center for an appointment. This might have been sufficient to start the helping process for an Anglo-Saxon Protestant family; for a Mexican-American family it was not. Not only was it difficult for the family to

overcome the shame of having to deal with the law, but Mr. X
— who made all the decisions — had been disregarded by the
probation officer. It was decided that establishing contact was
up to the center, on the assumption that this would be difficult
or impossible for Mrs. X.

Establishing Contact

The director of the community center called Mrs. X, identifying himself in Spanish as a social worker who knew that her
son had been in some trouble, and explained that the center
was a voluntary not a governmental agency. It was suggested
that Mrs. X ask her husband if he could come with her to the
center. She agreed to do so and to call back later in the evening
when her husband came home from work, adding, "It is good
to talk to someone who can speak Spanish." The fact that Mrs.
X had been asked to consult her husband about a conference for
the two of them put her in a situation in which she did not
have to decide on her own. Her husband was now involved in
the decision-making.

A few days later Mr. and Mrs. X came to the center for the
interview. True to Latin custom, the first hour was leisurely,
the talk mainly about familiar things that they could comfort-
ably share with the worker. Conversation centered about
Mexico, where they had lived until about two years before.
They shared information about their respective families and
mentioned how difficult it was for them to get used to the
American way of life. Here they had no close relatives nearby to
whom they could turn when problems arose. It was discon-
certing for them to have to bother people outside the family.

Alien Surroundings

It was no wonder that Mr. and Mrs X were having a hard
time, not only with their son, but with the society surrounding
them, which was completely alien to them and highly threatening to their way of life. In their own little house at the end of
the big lot, hidden by the growing weeds, they had found an

island isolated from the outside world — up to the time that their son had gotten into trouble. But then they had to face the world, and it was difficult to understand and more difficult to be understood.

They were not pressed to talk about their son's situation in detail. They decided to come back the following day to talk about this problem after the probation officer had come to see them.

The purposes in mind for this first interview were accomplished: to meet Mr. and Mrs. X personally and to establish a comfortable relationship that would lead to a partnership once they were able to share their problems with the social worker. The next step would be to share a common purpose, in this case, helping Freddy.

Mr. X was included in the helping process from the beginning. Had he been left out, it would have meant that Mrs. X was assuming an improper role, that Mr. X was being put down by her, and that his role as head of the household plus his *macho* role were being jeopardized.

The following day Mr. and Mrs. X came a little late to the meeting and were reluctant to talk about their conference with the probation officer. Mr. X just kept silent, looking down, Mrs. X, red-eyed, finally said, "I am very ashamed. You should have heard what the probation officer said about us. He blamed us for all the troubles with Freddy and said that if we were not able to speak English we should go back to Mexico. Perhaps worst of all, our daughter heard all of this because she had to translate for us."

It was suggested that they arrange to meet the probation officer the next time at the center; there the social worker could translate for them and make the necessary interpretations. Thus the harmful effect of the probation officer's prejudices against them would be minimized. Mr. and Mrs. X were assured that they had certain legal and moral rights that had to be respected — among them the right to be treated as human beings. Major differences between the systems of law in the United States and Mexico were explained, as were the functions of the probation department and the role of its officers.

Mr. and Mrs. X then seemed somewhat relieved and looked less tense and fearful. Mrs. X thanked the social worker and, looking at her husband, said: "We are not ignorant and dumb. We just did not understand anything about what was happening."

This family is not unusual. Nor are its problems. Many families in minority communities are facing problems like these every day. The situations can be far more critical when compounded by illness and poverty. Preparing the social worker in advance to serve such families effectively — rather than leaving it up to him to learn on the job from the community — offers a challenge to the schools of social work.

REFERENCES

1. Rose Green and Sara Maloney, Characteristics of Movement in Phases of the Social Work Relationship, unpublished paper, University of Southern California, Los Angeles, 1963 (mimeographed).
2. Celia S. Heller, *Mexican American Youth: Forgotten Youth at the Crossroads*, New York: Random House, 1966, 19.
3. Octavio Paz, *The Labyrinth of Solitude*, Lysander Kamp, trans., New York: Grove Press, 1962, 29-31.
4. Heller, *op. cit.*, 34.
5. *Ibid.*
6. Florence Hollis, *Casework: Psychosocial Therapy*, New York: Random House, 1964, 12.

Chapter 11

THE SOCIAL CONSEQUENCES
OF CHICANO HOME/SCHOOL
BILINGUALISM*

DAVID E. LÓPEZ

THE consequences of bilingualism have been the subject of considerable research and controversy. Most research has focused on home/school (H/S) bilingualism — reared in one language, usually of a low status ethnic group, and schooled in another, usually the socially dominant language — and until recently the predominant view has been that bilingualism is more bad than good (some major reviews of this literature are found in: Arsenia, 1937; Darcy, 1953; Haugen, 1956; Arizona State University, 1960; Peal and Lambert, 1962; MacNamara, 1966). But several studies have also shown that bilingualism does not necessarily retard learning, and may even stimulate intellectual development (Arsenian, 1937; Peal and Lambert, 1962; Balkan, 1970; Mackey, 1972; Lambert and Tucker, 1972). The sociological implication is that the apparent negative effects of bilingualism spring more from variable extrinsic social forces, such as how others react to and discriminate against bilinguals, than from psycholinguistic factors intrinsic to bilingualism.

Substandard verbal test performance by H/S bilingual children is widely if not universally documented (Darcy, 1946; 1953; Anastasi and Cordova, 1953; Jones, 1959). But there have been virtually no studies of subsequent effects. The considerably disadvantaged status of Chicanos and other groups with high degrees of bilingualism has commonly led to the presumption that these groups suffer from a lasting language

*From David E. López, The Social Consequences of Chicano Home/School Bilingualism, *Social Problems*, 24:234-246, 1976. Copyright 1976 by the Society For the Study of Social Problems. Reprinted by permission.

handicap, e.g. U. S. Department of Health, Education and Welfare, 1974. But this view has never been substantiated for Chicanos or other bilinguals. The belief is bolstered by misleading impressionistic evidence (poor, and frequently immigrant, Chicanos speak Spanish, Q.E.D.) and by published reports showing negative associations between social status and some measure of connection with the Spanish language (U. S. Department of Health, Education and Welfare, 1974:61; Grebler et al., 1970:424-426; U. S. Bureau of the Census, 1971:10-12; 1973a:20-27). But these reports include large proportions of Mexican immigrants who rank low on indicators of social status and, since they were raised in Mexico, were hardly subject to home/school bilingualism. Moreover, the reports usually relate status to current language. Given the possibility that upward mobility is accompanied by language apostasy (Barker, 1947; Penalosa and McDonagh, 1966), this relation further serves to make Spanish look bad.* This paper briefly reassesses previous research on the effects of bilingualism and introduces new data to test whether or not childhood bilingualism has any lasting consequences on the educational, occupational and income attainments of Chicanos. The paper also assesses the relative importance of extrinsic as opposed to intrinsic causation in these effects to understand whether or not language factors are involved, as disabilities or through discrimination, in the considerable socioeconomic gap between Chicanos and Anglos (Duncan and Duncan, 1968; Grebler et al., 1970:143-149, 181-194; Poston and Alvirez, 1973; Garcia, 1975).

To sociologists the long-run effects of H/S bilingualism are more important and more interesting than school test perfor-

---

*"Chicano" includes all U.S. residents of Mexican or Southwest Hispanic descent or origin. The subject of this paper dictated that only those raised in the United States be considered. About three-quarters of all adult Chicanos raised in the United States were brought up primarily in Spanish (U.S. Bureau of the Census, 1971). But few speak only Spanish — more native Chicanos are monolingual in English than in Spanish — simply because in school and various other social settings they have been obliged to perform in English. Spanish has been maintained in second and third generation homes, and by middle and working-class Chicanos as well as among the very poor. These Chicano subgroups also have considerable proportions of English monolingual homes, providing natural control groups, though previous researchers were not always aware of them.

mance. One need not be an educational psychologist — and indeed it may help not to be — to know that children who do not speak much English will not do so well on tests in English. Moreover, relationships on this level imply little about future lives. Two decades ago a major linguistic student of bilingualism suggested that the great concern for relations between bilingualism and cognitive ability was socially beside the point because, since the latter had so little to do with ultimate social position, any slight reduction in bilingualism would be immaterial in the long run (Haugen, 1956:83). Subsequent research has confirmed that test scores are poor independent predictors of socioeconomic status (Jencks, 1972:220-221, 350). Yet bilingualism is socially relevant. A corollary of the hypothesis of extrinsic causation is that bilingualism may be detrimental even in situations where intellectual function is unimportant.

DATA AND METHODS

Data for this paper came from a 1973 survey of 1,129 Chicano households in the Los Angeles area (weighted to give a representative sample). Los Angeles is by far the largest Chicano metropolis. It offers a more congenial socioeconomic environment than most of the Southwest, and for this reason is extremely diverse in the social origins of its Chicano population. Only United States-raised men aged twenty-five to forty-four are included in this analysis. When possible results are reported separately for ten-year cohorts. But even in the twenty-year band, age is unrelated to occupational status and income, and only mildly associated with Spanish upbringing (r = .20) and schooling (r = .19) . . . not enough materially to confound the analysis. For regression analysis, language of upbringing is dichotomized 1/0, Spanish (or H/S bilingualism) and English, respectively. Education, occupation, and income are measured in ordinary ways: years, Duncan scores, and dollars. Results are presented in a simplified Blau and Duncan (1967) path model, with language added in. Correlational results are supported by the analysis of sub-group means, but space limitations required that most of this be omitted.

The logic of this study is internal analysis. Chicano is compared to Chicano, rather than Chicano to Anglo, thus avoiding a host of complicating differences that can only imperfectly be "controlled" experimentally or statistically. At the same time the principal research question is how far H/S bilingualism explains Anglo-Chicano inequalities. If no effects of H/S bilingualism appear, then it is fair to conclude that language handicaps (intrinsic or extrinsic) play no part in the social lives of Chicanos raised in the United States. Causal complexes cannot simply be broken down into discrete additive factors. But the attempt made in this paper to understand and directly assess one factor in the Anglo-Chicano disparity is preferable to arbitrarily labeling residual differences left after the most obvious controls as "discrimination" or "cultural differences," depending on one's point of view.

THE BILINGUAL STIGMA

A review of the sociolinguistics and educational psychology of bilingualism (necessarily excluded here . . . see López, 1975) indicates that the only necessary difference between monolinguals and bilinguals is that the latter speak a second language. In addition sociolinguists have shown that the home/school bilingual's sound and syntax in either language is affected by the other. This phenomenon, unfortunately labeled by Uriel Weinreich (1953) as "interference," does not necessarily impair expression but it does make the bilingual a language nonconformist and allows others to identify him or her with a particular ethnic group (Bossard, 1945; Haugen, 1956). When that ethnic identification is prestigious the accent can be an advantage. When it is with a despised lower-class ethnic group it elicits conscious and unconscious prejudice, discrimination, and hostility. Like color and other aspects of personal appearance and style, it is a sign of ethnicity. Not bilingualism in itself, but the identity it conveys produces the social consequences of being bilingual.

The voluminous psychological literature on bilingualism

contributes little to the understanding of its social consequences. Some of the earliest work showed that bilingualism
sometimes depressed IQ scores and other times did not, e.g.
Saer, 1923. But rather than investigating the factors that made
for this circumstantial variation, and whether or not low-
scoring bilinguals were handicapped for life, psychologists
have instead sought to isolate "pure" bilingualism among
young children. What this has really amounted to is surrounding bilinguals with *favorable* circumstances, and it is
hardly surprising that in such experiments bilingual children
do as well as monolinguals, though never really better (Arsenian, 1937; Levinson, 1959; Peal and Lambert, 1962; Mackey,
1972; Lambert and Tucker, 1972). These favorable circumstances include good schools, no ethnic stigma and middle-
class or above status . . . usually all three. The problem is that
Chicanos and other large home/school bilingual populations
are stigmatized, lower-class, and attend poor schools. Bilingual
instruction in an upper-class Swiss or German school is not
bilingualism in the barrio.

Arsenian's (1937) data on Italian and Jewish children in New
York provides evidence of the stigma effect in schools. Among
the Jewish children, where Jewish teachers predominate (according to informal sources), bilingualism had no effect on IQ
tests scores or teacher evaluations. Among the Italian children,
who had few if any Italian teachers, bilinguals did moderately
worse on the tests and, significantly, were far behind in the
evaluations of their teachers. The social status and scholastic
difficulties of Italians earlier in this century were not unlike
those of Chicanos today. Then, as now, even well-meaning and
sympathetic teachers with a patronizing missionary zeal felt
they should suppress the native language for the children's own
good. But outsiders tend to see low-status ethnic groups as
homogeneous, so that while they may have thought they were
punishing Italianisms among linguistically homogeneous
children, in fact they were really punishing those from Italian-
speaking homes, and rewarding those from ethnically Italian
but English-speaking homes. The greater effect on teacher evaluations than on outsider-administered tests strongly supports

an extrinsic explanation of the scholastic effects of bilingualism.

Published reminiscences (Bossard, 1945; Haugen, 1972:308-319) and casual interviews indicate that middle-class bilingual children identified with a stigmatized group have resources to overcome initial learning handicaps and discrimination and sometimes even turn bilingualism to advantage. Their resources include the usual class advantages. But the maintenance of a literate ethnic tradition at home (usually requiring language maintenance as well) may provide a further advantage. Perhaps this complementary literate tradition rather than any difference in "values" explains the high educational attainments of middle-class (at least in culture), second-generation Americans.

The hypothesis of extrinsic causation and ethnic stigma explains the varying findings of educational psychologists better than any intrinsic psychological theory of bilingualism. It also leads to explicit predictions about the social consequences of H/S bilingualism. Lower-class minority children should suffer most in schools, with their emphasis on language conformity and middle-class comportment, and their lack of ethnicity. But later, when lower-class bilinguals confront the blue-collar job market to which their poor schooling channels them they may not be particularly discriminated against for language nonconformity and the ethnicity it symbolizes. On the other hand, middle-class children may have the resources to overcome initial handicaps and stigma and do at least average in school. But if they maintain language nonconformity (and according to linguists they do to at least some degree) they may later suffer from direct discrimination in the white-collar job market where language conformity is highly valued and lower-class stigmatized ethnicity is out of place.

ALTERNATIVE MODELS OF BILINGUALISM AND STATUS ATTAINMENT

The lack of previous findings makes it prudent to consider the various ways home/school bilingualism might affect social attainments. These can be summarized by four alternative models, each implying a particular set of relations and nonrelations testable against social life cycle data.

The Class Correlate Model

If H/S bilingualism appears to have negative effects only because Spanish-speaking homes tend also to be low status ones, then one can conclude that H/S bilingualism plays no independent part in Chicano status attainment. For this to be true the association between Spanish and low status homes has to be strong enough or the controlling for the latter reduces all partial effects of the former to zero.

The Cumulative Effects Model

Various studies have shown that Chicanos, like blacks, suffer in comparison to Anglos at each point in the attainment chain. If the intrinsic and extrinsic effects of home/school bilingualism continue to handicap, then among Chicanos those raised in Spanish should attain lower levels of education, occupational status, and income, and the attainment differentials should not be "explained" by previous factors along the line — producing the following set of relations: negative associations of Spanish upbringing with educational, occupational, and income attainments; with occupation when education is controlled; and with income even when both education and occupation are controlled. In the path model relating these variables there would be direct effects of language on each succeeding attainment, as well as indirect effects from language all the way to income. In this model and those that follow, language effects must of course remain when parental status is considered.

The Mediating Factor Model

While Chicano attainment patterns roughly follow the model for blacks, in the sense that background and mediating factors do not fully explain their lower occupational and income attainments, education is usually a more powerful explanatory factor for Chicanos than for blacks. If education is the crucial mediating variable between home/school bilingualism and income, then the subsequent effects of language would disappear when education controls are introduced. In a path model there would be no direct effect from language to income, but rather all the former's effect on the latter would be indirect through education. There are two variants within this general model, according to where occupation fits in. A direct relation between language and occupation means that language of upbringing has no further effect. The absence of such a direct relation supports the great emphasis on education and schooling. Either mediating factor model requires that there be zero-order correlations of upbringing language with education, occupation and income, and that these associations not disappear when parental status is controlled.

The Balanced Effects Model

Any explanation of a negative relation between H/S bilingualism and income should conform to one of the models above. Logically there are other possibilities, for example no path through education and occupation but rather only a direct relation with income. But the limited amount known about the effects of home/school bilingualism strongly suggests that its relation to education is the one most likely to appear. However, there is a fourth interesting possibility. Home/school bilingualism may depress educational attainment but have no long-run negative correlation with or effects on ultimate attainments. But there then emerges a curious implication: since education is associated positively with subsequent attainments, the direct effects between Spanish upbringing and these attainments must be positive. The quantitative logic, which path analysis graphically portrays, is inexorable: a negative path between uncorrelated variables must be balanced by a positive path. In other words, the negative effects on education of rearing in Spanish may be counterbalanced by other positive effects.

Of the four alternatives the mediating factor model emphasizing education is best supported by what is known about Chicano status attainment and also by the theory of extrinsic causation. Cumulative effects are also possible. But the evidence of, in comparison to blacks, less direct discrimination against Chicanos (Pinkney, 1963), and the greater salience of education (Grebler et al., 1970:194; Poston and Alvirez, 1973; Williams et al., 1973; Garcia, 1975), combined with the fact that most Chicanos are in the manual work force, and so less subject to language discrimination, all suggest that the mediating factor model is the more likely. None of the other alternatives is supported by previous findings. One monograph on bilingual Chicano children asserts that bilingualism's apparent effects are really class effects, but the book provides no substantiating evidence (Arizona State University, 1960).

CLASS VARIATION

If middle-class Chicano children can overcome whatever debilitating effects rearing in Spanish has among the poor then their educational attainments would be no different from English-speaking middle-class Chicanos. On the other hand, if they maintain the language style that continues to identify them as "Mexican," and if, as the extrinsic theory predicts, this stigma is a greater hindrance in the white-collar job market, then their bilingual origins should have negative direct effects on their ultimate occupational and income levels. The clearest way to assess class variation is to replicate the language-attainment model for groups divided according to class origins. A distinct pattern of relations among those raised middle class will not greatly affect the overall results because the vast majority of the sample was not raised with (and has not attained) middle-class status.

RESULTS

In contrast to the standard status attainment model (Blau and Duncan, 1967:169-170), education has an independent effect on

TABLE 11-I

INTERCORRELATIONS, MEANS AND STANDARD DEVIATIONS
OF HOME/SCHOOL BILINGUALISM AND STATUS VARIABLES, BY
AGE-GROUPS, FOR U.S. RAISED CHICANO MEN IN LOS ANGELES

25-44	1	2	3	4	5	mean	s.d.
1		-.02	-.24	-.08	0	.70	.40
2			.16	.38	.15	22.6	19.1
3				.41	.34	11.3	2.5
4	N=238				.44	32.3	20.3
5						10144	4723

25-34	1	2	3	4	5	mean	s.d.
1		-.05	-.32	-.22	-.01	.60	.49
2			.06	.23	.05	21.5	17.8
3				.34	.23	11.7	2.2
4	N=138				.51	32.0	19.5
5						10160	4973

35-44	1	2	3	4	5	mean	s.d.
1		-.01	-.08	.07	.02	.80	.40
2			.28	.54	.26	23.9	20.3
3				.48	.47	10.9	2.7
4	N=100				.37	32.5	21.2
5						10127	4447

1. Home/school bilingualism (Spanish at home)
2. Father's occupational status
3. Education
4. Occupational status
5. Income

occupational attainment no greater than that of father's status
and the effect of father's status is mostly direct, not indirect
through schooling. An indication that home/school bilingualism is of fundamental importance for understanding these differences comes from viewing English and Spanish-raised
Chicanos separately. For the latter the standardized regression

coefficient from education to occupation (with father's occupation also in the equation) is only .29. But among English-raised Chicanos it is .65, comparable to the national average.

Despite the distinctive pattern and the apparent importance of language, the first conclusion from our Los Angeles data is that home/school bilingualism has no massive lasting net effects. Educational attainment is clearly affected, and there are interesting interactions and patterns that allow one to choose from among the alternative models. But if enduring effects on occupational and income status are the criteria, then H/S bilingualism ranks well down the list of important factors in Chicano status attainment. On the other hand, if its effects are not spectacular neither are they just artifacts of social class.* In fact H/S bilingualism and father's occupational status are essentially uncorrelated in the wide or narrow age bands.

Education, Occupation and Income Separately

Table 11-I provides the intercorrelations, means and standard deviations for the entire sample and also the ten-year cohorts. Since home/school bilingualism and father's status are unrelated the zero-order correlations between these independent variables and the three attainment measures indicate the total effects of the former on the latter. Home/school bilingualism has its clearest effect exactly where one might expect, on educational attainment. In every case H/S bilingualism has a negative effect on schooling. The considerably greater effect among younger men may be due to a variety of factors, such as more accurate reporting for them, declining discrimination against English-speaking Chicanos, and the greater language heterogeneity among younger men. These and other complications cannot be easily differentiated so the relation of language and

---

*The language effects are not explained away by either generational or rural/urban upbringing variation. The pattern of balanced effects is actually *stronger* among third and subsequent generations. English upbringing and urbanness are strongly related but only about half of those raised lower class and in Spanish were also rural. When rural-urban upbringing is included in the basic path model it has the expected effect on education (beta = −.10) but no other significant effects, and the effect of H/S bilingualism on years of schooling is reduced only slightly, from .23 to .20.

occupation in both cohorts combined is probably the best estimate of the true effect. There is also a considerable negative relation with occupational level among younger men. But in the older cohort, which may better represent ultimate occupational attainment, the relation is actually mildly in favor of H/S bilingualism. Here again the potential complications of interpreting age cohort differences makes the total sample the most prudent data for generalization. Finally, income is clearly uncorrelated with H/S bilingualism in all three groups.

Table 11-II

DIRECT AND INDIRECT EFFECTS* OF HOME/SCHOOL
BILINGUALISM AND FATHER'S OCCUPATION ON EDUCATION,
OCCUPATION, AND INCOME FOR LOS ANGELES CHICANO MEN

	Education		Occupation		Income	
	direct	indirect	direct	indirect	direct	indirect
25-44 (N=238)						
Home/School						
Bilingualism	-.23	-	.01	.08	.08	-.07
Father's						
Occupation	.15	-	.33	.06	-.03	.18
25-34 (N=138)						
HS	-.32	-	-.12	-.09	.14	-.14
Fa Occ	.04	-	.20	.01	-.07	.12
35-44 (N=100)						
HS	-.08	-	.10	-.03	.04	-.02
Fa Occ	.28	-	.43	.10	.08	.18

Notes: *Only the forward (causal) indirect effects are considered. Total effects are the algebraic sum of direct and indirect effects and, since home/school bilingualism and father's occupation are essentially uncorrelated, they are nearly identical to the zero-order correlations in Table 11-I. For calculation of this table all coefficients, significant or not, were included.

Bilingualism in the Context of Status Attainment

Looking at home/school bilingualism in the context of a

path diagram allows one to distinguish its direct and indirect effects, and also to assess its importance in comparison with other factors. Figure 11-I shows graphically what the pattern of correlations implied: H/S bilingualism has a definite depressing effect on educational attainment, but this is balanced by a mild positive direct effect on income. Table 11-II summarizes the direct and indirect effects of language and class of upbringing for all three age groupings. For the older cohort there are two balancing positive effects and the stronger one is to occupation. Among younger men there is only one balancing direct effect, a strong .14 to income, and there is a definite negative direct effect to occupation — probably a life cycle rather than historical difference. The same negative aspects of home/school bilingualism that curtailed their schooling also hinder their early occupational attainment. The important point is that in either age group H/S bilingualism's negative effect on schooling is balanced by subsequent positive direct effects resulting in no net relation between it and income attainment, and even the net relation with occupational attainment is ambiguous. The long-run net insignificance of H/S bilingualism is supported in various other ways. Its inclusion or exclusion in the basic path model of attainments changes the other coefficients hardly at all; nor does it account for much additional variance after education. Table 11-II shows that its total (direct plus indirect) effects on occupation and income are distinctly less than the lasting effects of father's status.*

Class Variation

That bilingualism might have different consequences in different class contexts was tested in two ways: mean attainments were compared by language and class of upbringing (tables omitted) and the path model of Figure 11-1 was replicated for

---

*For readers unfamiliar with path analysis I should point out that total effects are simply the sum of all paths leading from one variable to another, and each path is computed by multiplying the coefficients along the path. The term net effect is sometimes used as a synonym for direct effect, or standardized regression coefficient (beta). This partial relation sense of net applies to a single regression equation, but not to a path model the point of which is to assess the total or net direct and indirect effects.

FIGURE 1

HOME/SCHOOL BILINGUALISM IN THE CONTEXT OF STATUS ATTAINMENT
LOS ANGELES CHICANO MEN, 25-44. 1973.

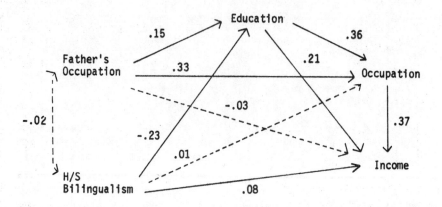

Note: Solid lines indicate effects based on regression coefficients
greater than twice the standard error.

Figure 11-1. Home/School bilingualism in the context of status attainment.
Los Angeles Chicano men, 25-44, 1973.

separate class origin groups (summarized in Table 11-III). Any
reasonable definition of middle-class status produced groups
too small for separate analysis of the ten-year cohorts, but for
reasons already discussed the full sample is probably the best
data. Using subgroup means or path coefficients, the hypothesis of varying effects is not only confirmed, it is clear that
the pattern of effects actually reverses between lower-class and
middle-class Chicanos. Within the lower class those Chicanos
reared in English have a clear two-year schooling advantage.
But among those raised in the middle-class the advantage shifts
to those reared in Spanish, who average about a year more of
schooling than English monolinguals. Table 11-III shows that
among lower-class Chicanos the basic model of Figure 11-1 is
intensified, with direct home/school bilingualism effects of
−.34 and +.17 to education and income, respectively. Among
middle-class-raised Chicanos the same effects are +.17 and −.16.

The total effect on income is mildly positive (+.08) for lower-class origins and mildly negative·(−.06) for middle-class origins. The pattern among those with working-class origins is less clear; the only strong direct effect is the negative one on schooling (−.20), and the total effect on income is somewhat negative.

Table 11-III

DIRECT AND INDIRECT EFFECTS OF HOME/SCHOOL
BILINGUALISM AND FATHER'S OCCUPATION
BY CLASS OF UPBRINGING FOR
LOS ANGELES CHICANO MEN, 25-44

	Education		Occupation		Income	
	direct	indirect	direct	indirect	direct	indirect
Lower Class (N=113)						
Home/School Bilingualism	−.34*	-	−.05	−.07	.17	−.09
Father's Occupation	−.14	-	.08	−.03	−.05	.00
Working Class (N=97)						
HS	−.20	-	.05	−.08	−.02	−.06
Fa Occ	−.03	-	.26	−.01	−.12	.08
Middle Class (N=35)						
HS	.17	-	.02	.09	−.16	.10
Fa Occ	−.07	-	−.28	−.04	−.29	−.10

Notes: *Despite the truncated variance, father's occupation was left in the equations to avoid inflating the effects of language. The simple correlations with education were virtually identical: -.34, -.20, .18

**Lower Class = Duncan status scores 0-12; Working Class = 13-50; Middle Class = 51-99.

DISCUSSION

Clearly the model of balanced effects is best supported, but in neither theoretical nor practical terms does this mean that H/S bilingualism makes no difference. For the Chicano majority (only about 15 percent of the sample were brought up middle class, and two-thirds of the rest were raised primarily in Spanish) home/school bilingualism does have negative educational consequences, consequences possibly underestimated by our results for two reasons: the difference is often between finishing high school or not, and the quality of schooling received by H/S bilinguals is probably also worse. H/S bilingualism is as important as parental status in determining educational attainment among Chicanos. The mean difference between H/S bilinguals and English monolingual Chicanos is 1.3 years, about the same as the difference between lower-class and middle-class Chicanos (tables omitted); the effect on education in a regression (Figure 11-1 and Table 11-II) is actually greater. Further analysis shows that the place of education in the status attainment cycles of English- and Spanish-raised Chicanos is quite different. Family status has no clear impact on years of schooling for the former, but makes a considerable difference (beta = .31) among the latter. This is direct support for the hypothesized importance of resources (class, individual or school, but we can vary only the first) in determining whether or not bilingualism will be a scholastic handicap. The greater subsequent effect of education for those raised in English (mentioned at the beginning of the presentation of results) indicates that education plays its usual key role in status attainment for English raised Chicanos, but not for the home/school bilinguals.

Home/school bilingualism does account for a considerable portion of the Chicano/Anglo schooling gap. The magnitude of that gap for native-born Chicanos aged twenty-five to forty-four is not more than two years (U. S. Bureau of the Census, 1973b) — just about the advantage of English among lower-class Chicanos. The rather good showing of English-speaking lower-class Chicanos (who average over twelve years of schooling) shows that this is not just an additive "class effect" but rather a genuine interaction. What may be an advantage in the middle class is clearly a disadvantage among the poor.

Whether the great gap between poor and middle-class bilingual Chicano children comes from actual cognitive disadvantages and advantages of bilingualism in the two circumstances, or to differential treatment by teachers and others cannot be convincingly answered here. But if status and wealth are regarded as extrinsic factors, then in this sense the disadvantage of Chicano H/S bilingualism is distinctly extrinsic.

I predicted that H/S bilingualism would have no direct negative effects after schooling for the blue-collar Chicano majority. But how could it have positive effects? It is tempting to speculate that the greater flexibility and nonverbal intelligence that some researchers (Darcy, 1946; Leopold, 1949; Balkan, 1970) have found in bilinguals really pays off on the job — not in schools with their emphasis on conformity rather than productivity and creativity. But speculation about the social consequences of psychological mechanisms must be left for bilingual social psychologists. A more mundane sociological explanation can be based on that attribute that most clearly sets bilinguals off from monolinguals, that they are able to function in two languages. Speaking Spanish does not help at school (including Spanish classes according to considerable impressionistic evidence); but then it does not in most jobs either, whether blue or white collar. But competence in two languages could increase one's access to job information and number of contacts. The business of getting jobs is often a question of personal contacts, both close and casual (Bott, 1957:124-125; Granovetter, 1973). The close contacts, with family and good friends, would not seem affected by language. But the network of casual relations that may in fact be the more important (Granovetter, 1973) could be enriched for Chicanos who function well in Spanish.

Preliminary field investigation indicates that mutual aid among Chicanos is very real, if not so organized as among some European and Asian immigrant groups. An effective Chicano ethnic job network exists, not so much for jobs within the community, but rather knowledge about and connections to jobs (mostly manual and often well-paying "dirty work") in the general economy. Fogel argued, and partially demonstrated, that Chicano community-dependent jobs tend to produce lower incomes (in Grebler et al., 1970:234-239), but this applies only to occupations that are actually within the community. On laborer and other manual occupational levels Fogel found that Chicanos do quite well in comparison to their competition, and it is on these levels that the Chicano ethnic job network seems to function best. Access to this network cannot immediately alter occupational level, but it can guide one to better paying jobs within a particular level. That the indirect positive effect goes to income rather than occupation supports this view. On the other hand, among older men only, it goes more to occupation, suggesting that continuous access to the network does improve job status in the long run.

Why does it help to be bilingual? In part it might be the simple capacity to communicate with Spanish as well as English speakers. But Chicano bilingualism, in both its Spanish and its English style, is a badge of ethnic group identification, not just a stigma to outsiders. It is very much a bond that strengthens the ties of Chicano to Chicano. Indeed, Chicanos often test each other (not necessarily consciously) on lingual criteria, especially if the other is in some ways marginal in other aspects of ethnicity. I suggest, then, that H/S bilingualism provides positive direct effects because it is a sociometric resource, giving better access to an ethnic job network in which knowing Spanish widens and strengthens one's network of contact, without reducing the flow of help or information from other sources transmitted through English.

The reversals of effects for middle-class Chicanos can in each case be explained by aspects of the theory of extrinsic effects. Class resources explain how H/S bilinguals can overcome early learning difficulties and reach parity with English-speaking Chicanos. The scholastic advantage of a literate ethnic tradition explains how they might excel. The data indicating their superiority are far from conclusive.* But from even the most

---

*Among women home/school bilingualism has a corresponding strong negative effect and that effect intensifies among those raised lower class. However, H/S bilinguals show no educational superiority among middle-class women, although among those whose parents were also born in the United States they do as well as those raised in English.

cautious perspective one can conclude that H/S bilingualism is not as great an educational disadvantage for Chicanos brought up middle-class. They may be subjected to discrimination in school, but school attainment is not just a question of discrimination. Conscious as well as unintended aspects of home environments also make some difference. The Los Angeles data, combined with impressionistic evidence for Chicanos and others, suggest that ethnic language maintenance may be an educational advantage under middle-class circumstances.

The subsequent negative class interaction is also best explained by two components, both part of the revised extrinsic theory. First, the ethnic job network does not serve middle-class Chicanos, both because middle-class job recruitment and requirements are more bureaucratic and, perhaps most important, there are so few Chicanos already on middle-class levels to provide contacts. This satisfactorily explains their lack of advantage. Their actual disadvantage in comparison to equally schooled English monolingual Chicanos is best explained by direct job discrimination against H/S bilinguals for their lack of language conformity and their persistent signs of inappropriate ethnicity. Siegel (1970:739-741) demonstrated that middle-class blacks suffer from more direct income discrimination than lower-class ones. He offers no explanation, but surely at least part of it is the inappropriateness of their ethnicity in so much of the national middle class. Presumably very dark or otherwise very "ethnic" blacks suffer even more, though research along these lines is strangely undeveloped. Whether or not middle-class Chicanos as a whole suffer from the same relative disadvantage as middle-class blacks, it does seem true that among middle-class Chicanos the more ethnic are at a disadvantage.

CONCLUSIONS AND IMPLICATIONS

The fundamental hypothesis of this paper, that home/school bilingualism has no necessary positive or negative effects on attainments, is confirmed. Only when it interacts with group and individual status does bilingualism have any social consequences. Positive (in-group solidarity, access to speakers of two

languages, a literate ethnic tradition, verbal flexibility) or negative (identification with a stigmatized ethnic group, noncon-
forming speech, early learning difficulties), these consequences
are all only potentials, and their activation depends on circumstances. In the ordinary additive sense the effects of
bilingualism are not "explained" by class variation, and yet
they exist only in particular class and social context environments.

My predictions about where the negative effects occur are
also confirmed, thereby lending support for the ethnic stigma
hypothesis. The principal unexpected finding is the positive
value of Spanish in the blue collar job market, accounted for by
extending the group identification argument. Bilingual speech
style conveys Chicano ethnicity to the in-group as well as the
out-group and seems to support the existence of an effective
ethnic job network among Chicanos.

On the practical level the findings have two implications.
The negative economic value of language ethnicity for white-
collar Chicanos is evidence that direct job discrimination does
indeed exist on this level against Chicanos. The salience of this
discrimination has been minimal, but as more Chicanos
qualify and seek to enter the middle class the importance of
direct discrimination may actually increase. The negative effect
on education has a much greater practical impact. Intergenerational language shift among Chicanos is more rapid than commonly supposed, particularly in urban areas, but a large
proportion of the Chicano population will continue to grow
up poor and speaking mostly Spanish at home. That their
bilingualism can be a positive resource after school, and that
middle-class children can overcome bilingualism's scholastic
disadvantage should not obscure the very real negative effect on
educational attainment for the vast majority of bilingual Chicanos. We do not know the patterns of language effects for
European and Asian immigrant groups, though impressionistic evidence suggests they are similar to the Chicano pattern.
Language solidarity and ethnic solidarity generally are particularly valuable for Chicanos and other groups that cannot easily
shed other indicators of their ethnicity. They can use ethnic

solidarity to counteract the negative externally-imposed consequences of their ethnic stigma. But the Chicano climb out of poverty would be more rapid if schools and bilingual children got along better.

REFERENCES

Anastasi, Anne, and Cordova, Fernando. Some Effects of Bilingualism Upon the Intelligence Test Performance of Puerto Rican Children in New York. *Journal of Educational Psychology*, 1953, 44:1-19.

Arizona State University College of Education. *Investigation of Mental and Pseudo Mental Retardation in Relation to Bilingual and Sub-cultural Factors.* Tempe: Arizona State University, 1960.

Arsenian, Seth. *Bilingualism and Mental Development.* New York: Teachers College, 1937.

Balkan, Lewis. *Les Effets du Bilinguisme Français-Anglais sur les Aptitudes Intellectuelles.* Brussels: AIMAV, 1970.

Barker, George. Social Functions of Language in a Mexican-American Community. *Acta Americana*, 1947, 5:185-202.

Blau, Peter, and Duncan, Otis D. *The American Occupational Structure.* New York: Wiley, 1967.

Bossard, James H. The Bilingual as a Person. *American Sociological Review*, 1945, 10:699-709.

Bott, Elizabeth. *Family and Social Network.* London: Tavistock, 1957.

Browing, Harley L., Lopreato, Sally C., and Poston, Dudley L. Income and Veteran Status: Variations Among Mexican Americans, Blacks and Anglos. *American Sociological Review*, 1973, 38:74-84.

Carter, Thomas P. *Mexican-Americans in School: A History of Neglect.* New York: CEEB, 1970.

Cicourel, Aaron. *Language Use and School Performance.* New York: Academic Press, 1974.

Cornejo, Richard. *A Synthesis of Theories and Research on the Effects of Teaching in First and Second Languages.* Austin: National Educational Laboratory, 1974.

Gumperz, John. On the Communication Competence of Bilinguals: Some Hypotheses and Suggestions and Further Research. *Language in Society*, 1972, 1:143-154.

Haugen, Einer. *Bilingualism in the Americas: A Bibliography and Research Guide.* Alabama: University of Alabama Press, 1956.

Hickey, Tom. Bilingualism and the Measurement of Intelligence and Verbal Learning Ability. *Exceptional Children*, 1972, 39:24-28.

Jencks, Christopher. *Inequality.* New York: Harper & Row, 1972.

Jones, W. R. *Bilingualism and Intelligence.* Cardiff: University of Wales Press, 1959.

Kjolseth, Rolf. "Bilingual Education Programs in the United States: For Assimilation or Pluralism?" In Paul Turner (ed.), *Bilingualism in the Southwest.* Tuscon: University of Arizona Press, 1973.

Labov, W. The Logic of Nonstandard English. In Paolo Gigioli (ed.), *Language and Social Context.* Middlesex: Penguin, 1972.

Lambert, Wallace, and Tucker, Richard. *Bilingual Education of Children: The St. Lambert Experiment.* Rowley, Mass.

Leopold, W. F. *Speech Development of a Bilingual Child.* Evanston: Northwestern University Press, 1949.

Levinson, Boris. A Comparison of the Performance of Bilingual and Monolingual Native Born Jewish Preschool Children of Traditional Parentage on Four Intelligence Tests. *Journal of Clinical Psychology,* 1959, 15:74-76.

López, David E. Home/School Bilingualism and Status Attainment: A Review of the Literature and a Fresh Look at the Chicano Case. University of California of Los Angeles, Department of Sociology. Unpublished, 1975.

Mackey, W. F. *Bilingual Education in a Binational School.* Rowley, Mass.: Newbury House, 1972.

MacNamara, John. *Bilingualism and Primary: A Study of the Irish Experience.* Edinburgh: Edinburgh University Press.

Mittlebach, Frank, and Moore, Joan. Ethnic Endogamy — The Case of the Mexican-Americans. *American Journal of Sociology,* 1968, 74:50-62.

Pearl, Elizabeth, and Lambert, Wallace. The Relation of Bilingualism to Intelligence. *Psychological Monographs: General and Applied,* 1962, 76:1-23.

Penalosa, Fernado, and McDonagh, Edward. Social Mobility in a Mexican-American Community. *Social Forces,* 1966, 44:353-359.

Pinkney, Alphonso. Prejudice Toward Mexican and Negro Americans: A Comparison. *Phylon,* 1963, 24:353-369.

Poston, Dudley, and Alvirez, David. On the Cost of Being a Mexican-American Worker. *Social Science Quarterly,* 1973, 53:697-709.

Saer, D. J. The Effects of Bilingualism on Intelligence. *British Journal of Psychology,* 1923, 14:25-38.

Siegel, Paul. On the Cost of Being a Negro. In Edward Laumann, Paul Siegel, and Robert Hodge (eds.). *The Logic and Social Hierarchies.* Chicago: Markham, 1970.

Tireman, L. S. *Teaching Spanish-Speaking Children.* Albuquerque: University of New Mexico, 1951.

U. S. Bureau of the Census. *Current Population Reports. Series P-20, no. 312. Persons of Spanish Origin in the United States: November 1969.* Washington, D. C.: U. S. Government Printing Office, 1971.

_____ . *Current Population Reports. Series P-20, no. 250. Persons of Spanish Origin in the United States: March 1972 and 1971.* Washington, D. C.: U. S. Government Printing Office, 1973a.

———. *1970 Census of Population. P C (2)-1D. Subject Reports. Persons of Spanish Surname.* Washington, D. C.: U. S. Government Printing Office, 1953b.

U. S. Department of Health, Education, and Welfare. *A Study of Selected Socio-Economic Characteristics of Ethnic Minorities Based on the 1970 Census. Volume I: Americans of Spanish Origin.* Washington, D. C.: HEW, 1974.

Vasquez, Jo Ann. Will Bilingual Curricula Solve the Problem of the Low Achieving Mexican-American Student? *The Bilingual Review,* 1974, 1:237-243.

Weinreich, Uriel. *Languages in Contact: Findings and Problems.* The Hague: Mouton, 1953.

Williams, J. Allen; Beeson, Peter; and Johnson, David. Some Factors Associated with Income Among Mexican Americans. *Social Science Quarterly,* 1973, 53:710-715.

Chapter 12

CHICANO GROUP CATALYSTS*

AURELIANO SANDOVAL RUIZ

FOR the most part, ethnicity has been disregarded by growth group facilitators. This is unfortunate, since culture and language play significant roles in the counseling group process. To demonstrate how ethnicity can be incorporated into growth groups, I have developed seven Chicano group catalysts, or interaction facilitation techniques (Bates & Johnson, 1972, p. 107).

A colleague and I first used the Chicano group catalyst (CGC) when we co-led two Chicano growth groups during the 1974 winter and spring quarters at California State Polytechnic University — Pomona (CSPUP). Each group consisted of eight Chicano students and had equal numbers of men and women. The CGC has also been tried out recently with high school students, with Neighborhood Youth Corps students, with program coordinators, and in other school settings.

It is important to understand the prerequisites and purposes of the CGC. First, the group facilitator should have the proper academic training in group leadership and counseling. Second, this person must be bilingual, speaking Spanish and English. This requirement is essential for optimum communication, since it minimizes the risk of communication breakdown. Bilingualism also allows group members to work through an impasse by permitting them to revert to their primary language, which often is Spanish. Furthermore, it broadens the availability of emotional responses from group members, as the counselor can encourage them to use either language in expressing feelings. Third, the facilitator must be bicultural, having undergone Chicano experiences and being aware of the dynamics of those experiences. Biculturalism is necessary for a complete understanding of Chicano perspectives and language in a cultural context. It also leads to greater insight into the client's frame of reference; the facilitation of counseling processes; and the establishment of rapport, empathy, and trust. Goldstein (1974, p. 89) has stressed that the practitioner "must be cognizant that the target behaviors are not in contradiction to the cultural system within which he is working," and biculturalism facilitates this as well.

THE TECHNIQUES

The seven interaction facilitation techniques have several purposes: (1) to deal with "unfinished business" and resolve it; (b) to enable people to reclaim and integrate those parts of themselves they have ignored, denied, or repressed, so that they can become more holistic; (c) to validate group ethnicity and cohesion; (d) to clarify values; (e) to tap potential and enhance growth; (f) to facilitate the self-actualization of group members; (g) to provide alternatives to "forced" assimilation. The CGCs described below appear in the order of recommended use.

Una Palabra

Spanish is the native language of the Chicano community, and the speaking of Spanish is an emotionally loaded issue. Chicanos either are able to speak Spanish fluently and consider it a strength; are able to speak Spanish but feel embarrassed and ashamed to do so; were once able to speak Spanish but no longer can; or are unable to speak Spanish. The members of the last three categories have expressed, in a group setting, feelings of inadequacy, rejection, hurt, and nonacceptance for not speaking Spanish.

The "Una Palabra" (a word) technique provides a vehicle through which group members can deal with their positive and negative feelings associated with the speaking of Spanish. The group facilitator models by verbalizing a word or phrase in

Spanish and revealing feelings associated with speaking Spanish. The group members are given an opportunity to provide feedback, express their emotional reactions, and point out action alternatives. Each member is then given a turn to repeat the modeled procedure.

The use of this catalyst has resulted in group members expressing greater group cohesion, increased feelings of acceptance, and alternatives for future action.

Reclaim Your Nombre

"Reclaim Your Nombre" (name) was developed in order to increase acceptance of self, identity, and ethnicity. This interaction technique is especially meaningful for those group members whose real names have been changed by others; Vicente, Marcos, Marta, Francisco, and Enrique, for example, became Bert, Skip, Martie, Franky, and Hank, respectively. It is also helpful for those who have had their names mispronounced.

In this procedure, group members are offered the opportunity to state their real names and pronounce them correctly. They can also express and deal with feelings related to their names.

Color

American society has perpetuated the belief that "white is right" at the expense of people with different skin colors — brown, black, red, and yellow (Bunton & Weissback, 1974; Cota-Robles de Suárez, 1971). In light of this fact, skin color is both a significant and a complex issue for Chicanos. Groups can make use of this issue by focusing on skin color gradations and on feelings associated with skin color.

Chicanos vary in skin color from *güeros* (light-complexioned) to medium brown to *morenos* (dark-complexioned). The majority of Chicanos have medium-brown skin. Because of this skin-color range, one may expect to find differing experiences among the Chicanos. Facilitators can introduce the issue of skin color by sharing with the group their feelings about their own skin color and then asking each group member to do likewise.

The use of skin color as a group catalyst has resulted in group members expressing not only positive feelings regarding skin color but also negative ones, many due to painful emotional experiences they have undergone because of the color of their skin. For example, Chicanos who are *morenos* have sometimes expressed feelings of pride at looking so indio (Indian) but have also expressed feelings of hurt, rejection, and nonbelonging for being *prieto* (dark) or *negro* (black). Chicanos who are *güeros* have expressed guilt ("I was favored over my sister because of my lighter skin, and I don't feel good about that"), resentment and rejection ("I wish I were darker and accepted by other Chicanos"), satisfaction ("I know that I'm *güero*; however, I'm still a Chicano"). Chicanos with medium-brown skin have expressed a multitude of feelings, ranging from positive to ambivalent to negative ("I was ashamed of my parents when they came to school. This brought me to the realization that I too was brown — which I didn't like.")

Sonidos

The "Sonidos" (sounds) catalyst is essentially a nonverbal exercise designed to increase listening skills and to serve as a vehicle for nonverbal communication between two people from the group. Each group member is asked to select a Chicano musical instrument, such as a *güiro* (a grooved gourd), a tambourine, maracas, or bongos. Group members are then asked to "get in tune with" their instrument through personification, fantasy, and so on, and to listen to the various sounds it produces. After a ten-minute period, group members are asked to pair off — but they are not allowed to speak to each other. They must now communicate with each other only through their instruments. After another ten minutes or so, they are asked to reconvene as a group and discuss their feelings concerning the exercise.

El Grito

"El Grito" provides the group members with an opportunity to express joy, happiness, and ecstasy in a natural and acceptable Chicano manner. Even though this catalyst is similar to Otto's group yell (1973, pp. 203-206), it has its own uniqueness and Chicano flavor.

The group facilitator begins the session by informing the group members that they will be listening to a mariachi album — preferably one that contains *gritos* (yells) and heavy sounds — and that during its playing or after it is over they should stand up and let out their own distinct *gritos*. A discussion follows in which group members can express how they are feeling.

Chicano Handclap

The "Chicano Handclap" apparently originated during the late sixties out of the intense and active political involvement of many Chicanos. It is a cohesive device that has resulted in catharsis, ethnic solidarity, and group identification. This interaction technique is based on the premise that physical release will help trigger emotional release. The "Chicano Handclap" begins softly with a slow and steady beat, gradually increases in tempo and loudness, and then tapers off. The handclapping can also be accompanied by foot tapping.

The group simultaneously begins the clapping, accompanying it with the verbalization of the emotions they are experiencing. After the clapping is over, an opportunity is provided for the expression and discussion of feelings.

Journey to Aztlán

Aztlán has traditionally been defined in geographic historical terms; it is the southwestern United States and northern Mexico area, in which the Aztecs are said to have originated. Currently the term has philosophical, sociopsychological, and political connotations, primarily in the sense of self-determination. This catalyst is a guided fantasy that allows group members to use their imagination, spontaneity, and creativity. It generates much information about values and beliefs and may result in meaningful experiences.

The group facilitator begins by briefly explaining Aztlán. Group members are asked to close their eyes and imagine that they are climbing a steep, rugged, massive mountain that appears almost overwhelming. After a long pause, they are then asked to imagine that they have reached the top of the mountain and are looking down at the valley of Aztlán. After some time has expired, they are asked to open their eyes when they are finished with the fantasy. They are now allowed to tell the group what they saw and felt in the valley of Aztlán.

SOME RESULTS

At the conclusion of each Chicano growth group held at CSPUP, the participants were asked as a group and individually to evaluate the effectiveness of the CGC. Their feedback indicated that there was increased acceptance of group ethnicity, skin color, name, language, and Chicano cultural factors; that unfinished business was dealt with and in some cases resolved; that potentials were discovered, acknowledged, and tapped. Further, the participants communicated a feeling that the CGC focused on cultural and linguistic areas that needed to be dealt with and probably would not have been dealt with elsewhere. They also expressed satisfaction in having bilingual group facilitators who possessed an understanding of the Chicano cultural experience.

To provide a specific illustration of observed outcomes, the case of Elena, a group member, is presented here. Initially Elena reacted strongly when "Una Palabra" was introduced into the group. This catalyst called to mind painful memories of her early school experiences, when she had been told that if she spoke Spanish she would be punished, would become confused in her thoughts, and would be crippled linguistically because of an awful accent. Through the use of empathy and support from the group, Elena was later able to speak Spanish freely and feel good about it. "El Grito" and the "Chicano Handclap" allowed Elena to exhibit more emotion. "Journey to Aztlán" helped her in overcoming obstacles, formulating strategies, and clarifying goals. Elena underwent numerous other behavioral changes that stemmed from the CGC. By realizing that others in the group shared similar experiences and feelings, she became less alienated. She formed new friendships, and her school attendance and performance improved. Furthermore, her need to act "phony" diminished and her defenses were lowered, resulting in her accepting herself more as a person and as a Chicano.

CONCLUDING COMMENTS

With minor substitutions or modifications, counselors can make use of some of these catalysts with other cultural groups. For instance, blacks, Puerto Ricans, Native Americans, Asians, and others can easily utilize the skin color catalyst. And the *sonidos* catalyst has universal applicability. Hopefully, counselors will begin developing additional group catalysts geared for Chicanos as well as for other cultural groups. I believe that the development and application of such group catalysts will enhance the counseling process for all.

REFERENCES

Bates, M. M., and Johnson, C. D. *Group Leadership: A Manual for Group Counseling Leaders.* Denver: Love, 1972.

Bunton, P. C., and Weissback, T. A. Attitudes Toward Blackness of Black Preschool Children Attending Community-Controlled or Public Schools. *Journal of Social Psychology*, 1974, 92:53-59.

Cota-Robles de Suárez, C. Skin Color as a Factor for Racial Identification and Preference of Young Chicano Children. *Aztlán*, 1971, 2:107-150.

Goldstein, G. S. Behavior Modification: Some Cultural Factors. *Psychological Record*, 1974, 24:89-91.

Otto, H. A. *Group Methods to Actualize Human Potential.* Beverly Hills, Cal.: Holistic Press, 1973.

Chapter 13

COUNSELING THE CHICANO CHILD*

WAYNE R. MAES AND JOHN R. RINALDI

COMENZEMOS can una descripción breve de la familia Romero y de los ninos Carmen y Jesús. Let's begin with a description of the Romero family and of the children, Carmen and Jesús.

The family is the place to begin because it is the center of the Chicano culture. *Chicano*, a word commonly used only recently, denotes a resident of the United States who is of Mexican descent and often also of Spanish descent. Such people are sometimes referred to as Spanish-Americans or Mexican-Americans.

The Romeros are in every sense of the word a family. They spend a great deal of time together working, playing, worshipping, and just plain talking. Mr. Juan Romero is a plasterer, as were his father and grandfather. He is a fine craftsman and makes a livable wage. Jesús, who is seven, already is dirtying himself in sand and cement at his father's work site at every chance he gets on weekends or when there is no school. He really prefers the slap and scrape of the trowel and the clean, damp, sweet smell of the plaster to the classroom. School is a hassle. Jesús reads just well enough to make it in his second grade class, and his math isn't much better. The teacher prods and pushes a lot, and Jesús doesn't openly resist, but inside he resents it. "What's school got to do with plastering anyway," he thinks. Worse yet is social studies. There are all of those embarrassing questions with hard-to-understand words. Besides, the teacher says he must learn to pronounce words correctly. She doesn't make much allowance for the fact that he

*From Wayne R. Maes and John R. Rinaldi, Counseling the Chicano Child, *Elementary School Guidance and Counseling*, 8:278-284, 1974. Copyright 1974 by the American Personnel and Guidance Association. Reprinted by permission.

heard and spoke mostly Spanish for the first five years of his life.

Carmen is twelve, the oldest child, and she likes boys. She gets by in school and is a good help to her mother around the house and with her baby sister. But she thinks of boys. Like her mother before her, and generations before that, she will marry, keep house, and raise children.

Mrs. Maria Romero is an affable sort. She is kind but firm with her children, keeps a neat house, and prepares tasty, nourishing food. She is accustomed to having neighbors in and out of the house, and her parents and Juan's parents, along with uncles, aunts, cousins, nephews, and nieces, come by frequently. It's nice to have friends and relatives near at hand. There is a warm, comforting feeling about it, even though there are occasional spats.

Juan, Maria, the children, and their relatives find it a bit easier to deal with the prejudicial behavior in the larger culture when they have each other. Nevertheless, it galls them to be prevented full access to social and economic resources because of what are thought to be quirks of speech or because of skin color. It can make one very bitter.

Whatever unfairness Jesús feels at school, he responds to in the typical way he usually handles his fear and embarrassment. He becomes combative with his male classmates or does things that are risky. He has been acting this way more often lately, and he resists his mother's embraces whereas he once liked to cuddle. These are the beginnings of what is often referred to in Chicano culture as "machismo." Its counterpart in Anglo culture is described in Adler's concept of the "masculine protest."

This is the Romero family. While there is obviously wide diversity among Chicano families, the Romeros are fairly representative. They provide a picture of a warm, cooperative, interdependent family. They are a family to some extent caught between what they know and value — the Chicano culture — and the broader American culture. Jesús and Carmen face, even more than their parents ever have or will, the challenge of guarding the values of their heritage while learning to gain greater access to the social and economic advantages available.

Even our rather superficial acquaintance with the Romero family and with Jesús and Carmen helps us identify some priorities for providing assistance as counselors. The four most important are (a) language and cognitive skill development, (b) expansion of career choice options, (c) personal respect and pride in the Chicano culture, and (d) personal value exploration.

LANGUAGE AND COGNITIVE SKILL DEVELOPMENT. Underprivileged Chicanos do not score as well on standardized intelligence tests as do the test norm groups. This is due primarily to lower verbal scores (Mercer, 1971). What can be done to help? Some promising breakthroughs are occurring in teaching cognitive skills to young minority children (Blank & Solomon, 1968). Dramatic gains — an average of 14.5 IQ points — for a group of preschoolers after three months of tutoring were highly encouraging. The counselor's role in this regard may include design and implementation of programs that teach cognitive skill development. The counselor can use this opportunity to build cooperative relations with the principal and teachers. While team teaching and tutorial work should be limited so as to allow time for numerous other counselor activities, they can be excellent ways of becoming better acquainted and assisting children and teachers.

An excellent preschool program (Right-to-Read) utilizing parents as tutors has been used in the La Luz Elementary School in Albuquerque. Parents are trained as tutors to assist the child in reading and reading readiness activities. An interesting by-product of this program is the sense of satisfaction and self-fulfillment of the tutors and the more positive attitude toward the school on the part of the parents whose children were tutored. The initiation of such a program provides an excellent entrée for the counselor to be involved in along with the principal and/or curriculum specialists in the community by training and supervising the work of the parent tutors.

Upper elementary grade children can serve as tutors for their peers and for the lower grade children. Such a program can be of direct benefit to the student-tutors in a program designed to improve their ability to help. Selective attention skills, listening skills, and questioning strategies may be taught, and the children may be provided supervision in their tutoring (Gumaer, 1973).

There are also numerous small group activities that the counselor can employ to facilitate language and cognitive development. Dora Macias and Dorothy Crouch, who counsel Chicano children in the El Paso Public Schools, have found the following procedures to be effective:

1. Use newspaper cartoons or magazine pictures that illustrate sharing, good manners, etc. The students paste them on tag board or paper and discuss the situations with the counselor facilitating the discussion.

2. Using magazine pictures displaying various emotions and moods in people, have the students discuss the pictures and situations which they have experienced which prompted similar emotions.

EXPANSION OF CAREER CHOICE OPTIONS. Jesús' and Carmen's career choices were restricted to plastering and being a housewife. The counselor can design programs to make the child aware of careers with which he or she has had very little experience. Community workers might be invited to the school, and visits to work sites might be arranged. Activities can be planned which expose children to many options for women beyond being housewives and options for men in the sciences and other professions. Chicano role models in these new career option areas are essential.

SELF-RESPECT AND PRIDE IN CHICANO CULTURE. This is as often achieved in subtle ways as it is in direct ways. Respected, effective Chicano teachers and counselors in their daily work can convey a sense of pride in self and culture. This can have a positive impact on the children. Assisting children in language and cognitive development has its payoff in more successful achievement, a strong influence on self-acceptance. Chicano community leaders can be invited to the school (for example, in relation to career exploration) and share with the children their success and achievement. The integration of Chicano culture into social studies units can help give children a sense of pride in their food, music, and customs and an opportunity to share these with those less familiar with the Chicano culture.

EXPLORATION AND CLARIFICATION OF PERSONAL VALUES. Dora Macias and Dorothy Crouch have found unfinished stories depicting home or school situations to be useful in stimulating discussion among Chicano children. These stories may be read to the children, and the children may be directed to the question, "What should he do now?" Or, paper sacks can be used to make puppets representing different members of the family. These can be used to dramatize the roles and feelings of family members. Such techniques surface important values and attitudes. For example, the almost unquestioning obedience to parents and authority is commonly brought up. The counselor can skillfully assist the children to examine courses of action that are based on overly selfish desires by the child as well as those based on arbitrary or overly stringent demands by parents and others. This conflict between what "I want" and parents or the church demand is frequent. The objective is to help the child be aware of and employ intelligent solutions which represent enlightened self-interest and a concern for others. Such discussions may be quite sensitive and should be handled carefully. For example, certain courses of action may be contrary to what children learn at home (questioning authority and making a rational decision), and the task will be to help the children be aware of these new alternatives without undermining affection and respect for parents.

CHARACTERISTICS OF THE COUNSELOR

Who can do the work of the counselor with Chicano children? Not every counselor! Children like Jesús and Carmen require some unique attributes on the part of the helper.

BILINGUALISM. In working with Chicano children, particularly during early elementary school, the ability to speak Spanish and English fluently is at least highly desirable and probably necessary. Parent contacts are often impossible without fluency in Spanish or a translator (a second best option of questionable value). Spanish is necessary to have full range of discussion with the children, not to mention its rapport-building benefits.

CULTURAL AWARENESS. In order to better understand the values, goals, and behavior of the Chicano child, the counselor should have extensive first-hand experience with and an understanding of Chicano religion, history, art, music, dance, and literature. Experiencing and understanding the cultural script of the Chicano is as important as individual life scripts are in the counseling process.

COUNSELING REPERTOIRE. The counselor needs more than traditional individual and group counseling relationship skills in his repertoire. Language is often not the most expedient vehicle for change. Behavior modification and Adlerian techniques which influence the environment so as to change it and to face the child with the consequences of his behavior are often more effective. Influencing the environment extends to the family. Since the family is of utmost importance to the child, the counselor must work with the family in effecting change. Finally, the counselor must function as a consultant to teachers and principals to influence the educational setting to be more responsive to the child's language, culture, and psychosocial needs.

THE PERSON OF THE COUNSELOR. The counselor should possess helping characteristics such as empathy, warmth, positive regard, congruence, and authenticity. The question is often raised, "Must the counselor be Chicano?" The answer has to be "No." Unique people can defy all conventional standards. However, the above-mentioned characteristics are usually essential to highly effective work and are not often possessed by persons other than Chicanos.

The counselor of Chicano children such as Jesús and Carmen is first and foremost a counselor of children whose motivation, learning styles, and basic satisfiers are like those of the children of the world. But the counselor of Chicanitos (Chicano children) is more. Standing at the interface of two cultures, the counselor must assist the Chicanito to partake fully of the social and economic resources of the larger culture without sacrificing what is unique and valued in the Chicano culture. The sensitive counselor knows the economic and social necessity of assimilation in the larger culture, while at the same time realizing the danger of loss of personal identity in "selling out" one's heritage and folkways in order to gain the fruits of participation. The counselor's task is to open up more options in the life of the Chicanito as the child grows toward adulthood. These expanded options usually require impacting the people and institutions surrounding the child as well as enhancing the child's skills and attitudes so he can take advantage of opportunities. Both are formidable tasks for the counselor, whose day-to-day efforts sometimes seem to pale into insignificance. But, a stone thrown into a pool does cause ever expanding concentric ripples which go on and on.

REFERENCES

Blank, M. and Solomon, F. A. A Tutorial Language Program to Develop Abstract Thinking in Socially Disadvantaged Pre-school Children. *Child Development*, 1968, 39:379-389.

Gumaer, J. Peer-facilitated Groups. *Elementary School Guidance and Counseling*, 1973, 8:4-11.

Mercer, J. R. Institutionalized Anglocentrism: Labeling Mental Retardates in the Public Schools. In P. Orleans and W. Ellis (eds.), *Race, Change and Urban Society*. Volume 5, Urban Affairs Annual Reviews. Beverly Hills, Calif.: Sage Publications, 1971, 311-338.

Part III. Puerto Ricans

INTRODUCTION

COUNSELORS would do well to remember that test scores are imperfect measurement tools. For example, a large number of Puerto Rican students are mistakenly labeled "educable mentally retarded" and placed in special classes, not because of their abilities, but on the basis of test scores. The problem of language as an impediment in testing has been voluminously documented. Contrary to popular opinion, Puerto Ricans place a high value on education.

PUERTO RICAN CULTURAL CONDITIONING

The continuous movement from the island to the United States has become a way of life for many Puerto Ricans; but they are reluctant to adopt American life-styles. The following characteristics typify Puerto Rican culture.

SENSE OF DIGNITY. *Respeto* demands that proper attention be given to culturally prescribed rituals, shaking hands and standing up to greet and say good-by to people. A sense of dignity is present in all important interpersonal relationships.

PERSONALISMO. Personal contact is established by Puerto Ricans before beginning a business relationship. It is important to exchange personal life data before talking business.

INDIVIDUALISM. High value is placed on safeguarding against group pressure to violate the integrity of the individual. This makes it difficult for Puerto Ricans to accept the concept of teamwork in which the individual relinquishes his or her individuality to conform to group norms.

CLEANLINESS. Great emphasis is placed on being clean and well dressed. To Puerto Ricans, looking good or well includes wearing bright colors and, frequently, styles rich in ornament.

EDUCATION. Puerto Ricans are obsessed by education. However the large number of school failures in this country creates dissonance between the aspiration and the levels of achievement.

FEAR OF AGGRESSION. Puerto Rican children are discouraged from fighting, even in self-defense. A Puerto Rican idiom describes this condition: juegos de mano, juegos de villano (pushing or shoving, even in play, makes one a villain). Survival in slum neighborhoods forces many Puerto Rican children to be villains.

ATAGUES. This is a form of hysteria characterized by hyperkinetic seizures brought on by acute tension and anxiety. The atague is called the Puerto Rican syndrome. It is not a terminal mental disorder but, instead, a culturally expected reaction to situations of stress.

COMPADRAZGO AND MACHISMO are operative in Puerto Rican culture in basically the same manner as in Mexican American culture. (See Part II.)

READINGS

Manuel Maldonado-Denis summarizes the first three centuries of Spanish domination of Puerto Rico. By gaining an appreciation for the history of this ethnically diverse nation we also gain an appreciation for their quest for independence. Furthermore, we realize that Mexican history is not Puerto Rican history and, relatedly, Mexican culture while similar is not Puerto Rican culture.

The Ríos family, their friends and neighbors reflect many of the characteristics of island and American Puerto Rican families. Oscar Lewis succinctly describes the life-styles of low-income Puerto Rican families — their dreams, aspirations, and realities.

Spiritualism plays an influential role in the lives of countless Puerto Ricans and Mexican Americans. Thus it is a spiritual medium and not a professional helper who is sought out for assistance. Melvin Delgado shows how supernatural beliefs and their related practices are culturally functional. Professional helpers are given eight recommendations for understanding and treating Puerto Rican clients.

Sonia Badillo Ghali focuses on the values and traits that are characteristic of Puerto Ricans. Special attention is paid to practical suggestions for helping Puerto Rican students.

Clara Rodriquez points out the educational problems of Puerto Rican students who are fluent in Spanish but not English. In addition to language difficulties, the tracking system which places Puerto Rican students "where they belong" does little to make them functional members of society.

Edward W. Christensen maintains that for Puerto Ricans transition from one culture to another has produced a condition of marginality which is stressful and often results in mental breakdowns. This article centers on Puerto Rican attitudes toward mental health as well as specific skills needed to assess, engage, and treat the Puerto Rican client.

Chapter 14

PUERTO RICO, PUERTO PROBE: THE FIRST THREE CENTURIES OF SPANISH DOMINATION*

MANUEL MALDONADO-DENIS

What centuries ago was Puerto Rico, Should now be called
Puerto Probe; For whoever seeks gold, silver, or copper there,
Will surely find damned little.

Manuel Del Palacio
Spanish Poet of the Nineteenth Century

WHEN Christopher Columbus set foot on Borinquén† on November 19, 1493, he found an island with exuberant vegetation, a beautiful bay, and an indigenous population later calculated to be approximately 50,000 by Salvador Brau and some 70,000 by Ricardo Alegría.[1] That the aborigines populating our territory during that period were in a state of civilization inferior to that of the most advanced indigenous cultures of the New World is demonstrated by the fact that "no West Indian cultural group knew the architectural use of stone, nor how to work metals, and therefore monumental construction and the technique and richness of gold and silver work were skills alien to all of them."[2] Possessing a rudimentary social organization, the native inhabitants of Puerto Rico belonged to the cultural group of the Tainos. Their origin was South American Aruacan. They had a fundamentally agrarian culture with their economy based primarily on the cultivation of yucca and the manufacture of cassave.

---

*From *Puerto Rico: A Socio-historic Interpretation*, by Manuel Maldonado-Denis, translated by Elena Vialo. Copyright © 1972 by Manuel Maldonado-Denis. Copyright © by Random House, Inc. Reprinted by permission of Random House, Inc.
†Borinquén was the original Taino name for Puerto Rico.

Once colonization began, a regime based on the exploitation of the indigenous population was not long in coming. Bent on the exploitation of Puerto Rico's meager gold resources, the Spaniards made the Indians their principal instrument of labor. A European population that in 1510 did not exceed three hundred people immediately converted the Indian into the object of merciless exploitation. With the characteristic brutality of the colonizer, the Spanish colonist imposed on the Indians the iniquitous and painful condition of being strangers on their own soil. In regard to the Spaniards, Brau says: "Received as guests, they made themselves absolute lords. To the cordiality of feeling with which they had been greeted on their arrival, they responded by taking possession of the land, which, after all, being virgin and exceedingly fertile would have provided sufficient food for all; but with the possession of the land came the thirst for gold, and with it the forced labor of the natives, disturbance of their family life, alteration of their simple customs, scorn for their beliefs — the loss, in short, of all that which constituted the human personality in its exercise of the free functions granted it by the Supreme Creator."[3] The result of these acts was a sudden decline in the native population. There occurred what Pichardo Moya calls "the early extinction of the West Indians," due primarily "to the clash with the new civilization and the cruelty of the conquest."[4] But it did not happen without the natives first rebelling against the colonizers, with whom they engaged in bloody battles before giving up, overwhelmed by a technology more advanced than their own. The insurrections led by the chieftains Gueybaná and Guarionex in defense of their legitimate rights deserve special mention. Although their rebellions were crushed, they established as of that moment that the native inhabitants of Borinquén were not in the least docile.

The extinction of the natives around the middle of the sixteenth century made the introduction of a new type of labor — that of black slaves — indispensable. With the depletion of the Puerto Rican gold deposits and the discovery of rich beds of the precious metal in Perú and México, the economy of Puerto Rico came to depend primarily on the cultivation of sugar cane and the creation of sugar refineries. Black slavery was adopted as the mode of production. As a matter of fact, in the instructions given by Ferdinand and Isabella to the governor of the Indies, Nicolás de Ovando, on September 16, 1501, "the entrance of black slaves into the overseas colonies was authorized for the first time in American history."[5]

The substitution of black for Indian labor established the slave system of production in Puerto Rico. Social classes were soon structured on the principle of the master-slave relationship. It was not until 1873 that slavery was abolished in Puerto Rico. From 1501 to 1873 was a period of penury for the black slave, while during this period the slave-owning minority sought by all means possible to perpetuate the regime of privilege which guaranteed them the forced labor of large contingents of workers.

Thus does Brother Inigo Abbad y Lasierra, the first historian of Puerto Rico — writing in his *Historia geográfica, civil y natural de la isla de San Juan Bautista de Puerto Rico* in 1796 — describe the situation of the blacks under the slave system of production:

> Some of the blacks on this island were brought from the African coasts, others are creoles, descendants of the former, without any racial mixture: the first are all sold as slaves; in the second group there are many free men; when all is said and done there is nothing more ignominious on this island than to be a black or one of their descendants: a white insults any of them with impunity and in the most contemptible terms; some masters treat them with despicable-harshness, getting pleasure out of keeping the tyrant's rod always raised and thereby causing disloyalty, desertion, and suicide; others regard them with excessive esteem and affection, making them tools of luxury and vanity, employing them only in domestic service; but even these blacks eventually suffer the harshness of slavery when their master dies and they are passed on to another, or because he has become fond of something else. Then a narrow, miserable hut serves him as a dwelling, his bed is a cot of cords or slats, more appropriate for torturing the body than for resting it; the coarse cloth which covers part of his bare body neither defends him from the heat of day nor from the harmful night dew; the food that

is given him — cassava, sweet potatoes, bananas and such things — scarcely suffices to sustain his wretched existence; deprived of everything, he is condemned to continuous labor, always subject to experiencing the cruelty of his greedy or fierce master.[6]

From this description one can see what the condition of a black slave was a little less than a century before his emancipation.

After the slave, the next instrument of labor was the free day laborer. The economic situation was such that even for the landowner it entailed great hardship. Let's take a look at some figures. The first census undertaken in Puerto Rico (1530) showed the following balance: whites, 369; free "protected" Indians,* 473; Indian slaves, 675; black African slaves: males 1,168; females, 355. Total, 3,040 inhabitants.[7] With the discovery of gold in Perú, the colony ran the risk of becoming almost totally depopulated, and the governor had to take drastic measures to prevent any future exodus. Confronted with Spain's commercial monopoly, obligated to trade only through the port of Seville, deprived of rich gold deposits, and subject to the implacable onslaught of hurricanes, the island was practically abandoned to its fate by the colonial power.

Twenty years after colonization had begun, says Brau, "the gold was giving out in the mines; two cyclones in one year razed the countryside, leveled the huts, and destroyed livestock and cultivated fields; misery was devastating the country and panic was invading the spirits of the people."[8]

In 1582, a military garrison was established at El Morro, thus converting Puerto Rico into a military base. In 1586, the so-called Mexican allowance was set up to provide the island with an annual sum from the treasury of México. During the sixteenth and seventeenth centuries the isolation and economic indigence of Puerto Rico did not prevent the English as well as the Dutch from attempting to take over the island, although

---

*The "indio encomendado" was free largely in a euphemistic sense, as he was entrusted for his welfare to a Spanish colonist, who was also responsible for his religious and secular education. He was often, as a matter of fact, used as a laborer by his "protector." (Translator's note)

both failed. Contraband flourished as a means of avoiding the Spanish commercial monopoly. In 1673 a tax list of San Juan revealed the following figures: 820 whites, 667 slaves, 304 free mulattoes. Total: 1,791 inhabitants. The population was so small that the governor found it necessary to ask the mother country for a shipment of white people to the island.

By this time the Spanish Empire was already in open decadence. While capitalism and the bourgeoisie had already appeared as historical forces in England, France, Holland, and Belgium, Spain remained on the margin of capitalist development and consequently on the margin of the economic development which with the passing of time would make of Europe the world center of the capitalist system. Referring to the Spanish Empire and the causes of its early decadence, Brenan informs us:

> Too easily and with excessive rapidity Spain went through an immense inheritance without possessing sufficient economic or cultural preparation; and this acted like a drug. Spanish pride, belief in miracles, scorn for work, impatience, and a taste for destruction, although they already existed in Castilla, received a powerful impulse at that time. From 1580 on, the few woolen mills which existed in the country disappeared, and the Spanish became a nation of people living on a fixed income, a nation of gentlemen who lived in parasitic dependence on the gold and silver which came to them from the Indies and from the industry of the Netherlands.[9]

This mentality of a people living off others, maintained by the shipment of wealth from colonies to the mother country, would allow Spain to watch the rest of the world plunge into an intense economic activity that would undermine the foundations of the *ancien régime* of Europe and would profoundly affect reactionary Spain, the standard-bearer of Catholicism and of the Counter Reformation.

The eighteenth century was the century of two great revolutions: that of the United States (1776) and that of France (1789). This century saw the germination and growth of the forces which in the nineteenth century would give the final checkmate to the Spanish Empire in America. For Puerto Rico, the eighteenth century was characterized by a long period of peace during which, in the words of Tomás Blanco, "the foundations of Puerto Rican society were laid down."[10] San Juan became the second stronghold of America: commerce was liberalized, the cultivation of coffee was introduced, smuggling was intensified, and the population increased considerably. According to O'Reilly's Memorandum of 1765, the total population was figured at 44,883, with 5,037 slaves. By 1776 it had increased to 70,000, by 1786 to 96,000, 1796 to 133,000 and in 1800 the island had to reckon with 155,426 inhabitants.[11]

In the work previously cited, Brother Iñigo Abbad verifies that at this time (1782) the Puerto Rican economy revolved around sugar cane, cotton, tobacco, and coffee.[12] The economic and political frameworks were the same. All power resided in the governor of the island, "from whom come all the orders, as the military and political governor, and as superintendent of the branches of the public treasury and the royal vice-patronate. He may intervene in the affairs of parishes, in the accounts of personal income, factories, and churches; he disposes of troops and militia for defense, reviews them, arbitrates in their disputes, presides over the commissions of the public treasury, and is the superior judge over all the justices on the island."[13] In short, all authority — political and economic as well as military — was concentrated in the hands of the governor. This condition of centralized authority would characterize Spanish colonialism throughout the years of its existence. In fact, militarism and authoritarianism would march hand in hand in the government of the colony until almost the last moment.

In *Insularismo*, Pedreira calls the first three centuries of Spanish domination a period of "formation and passive accumulation" in the development of our nation.[14] As a matter of fact, the sixteenth, seventeenth, and eighteenth centuries were a period of gestation for our nation; they were the stages during which preparation for the future of our nation were made. The very nature of the works published on our island — like the *Historia* of Abbad — testify to the fact that something called Puerto Rico was taking shape. Actually, Abbad himself tells us that by then "they give the name of creole indistinctly to everyone born on the island, no matter what race or mixture he comes from. The Europeans are called whites or, to use their own expression, *"men of the other band."*[15] Here is the distinction between the creole and the European, the native son and the foreigner, the Puerto Rican and the "man of the other band." The Puerto Rican is already taking his first steps.

REFERENCES

1. Concerning this matter, see the note of Dr. Isabel Guitiérrez del Arroyo in her annotated edition of Salvador Brau, *La Colonización de Puerto Rico*, San Juan: Institute de Cultura Puertorrigueña, 1966, 134, note 62. This book by Brau was originally published in 1907.
2. Felipe Pichado Moya, *Los aborígenes de las Antillas*, Mexico: Fondo de Cultura Economia, 1956, 12. See also in this regard the *Relación* of Brother Ramón Pané about antiquities of Indians (1505), published as a fragment in E. Fernández Méndez, ed., *Crónicas de Puerto Rico*, San Juan: 1957, vol. a.
3. Brau, *op. cit.*, 141.
4. *Ibid.*, 28.
5. Luis M. Díaz Soler, *La esclavitud negra en Puerto Rico*, Rio Piedras: Editorial Universitaria, 1965, 20. "In regard to the slave trade," says Díaz Soler, "a *license* was an authorization by the king to transport slaves for the purpose of increasing the population, supplying the work force necessary for mining and agricultural development and providing overseas subjects with servants." *Ibid.*, 27.
6. I refer here to the edition put out by the Editorial Universitaria de la Universidad de Puerto Rico (1959) with a preliminary study by Dr. Isabel Gutiérrez del Arroyo.
7. Salvador Brau, *Historia de Puerto Rico*, San Juan: Editorial Coquí, 1966, 70-71. This book was originally published in 1904.
8. Brau, *La colonización*, 395.
9. Gerald Brenan, *El laberinto español*, Paris: Ediciones Ruedo Ibérico, 1962, 11.
10. Tomás Blanco, *Prontuario histórico de Puerto Rico*, San Juan: Biblioteca de Autores Puertorrigueños, 1935, 43.
11. *Ibid.*, 48-49.
12. *Ibid.*, 161.
13. *Ibid.*, 146.
14. Antonio S. Pedreira, *Insolarismo*, 2nd ed., San Juan: Biblioteca de Autores Puertorrigueños, 1942, 15. .
15. *Ibid.*, 181.

Chapter 15

THE RÍOS FAMILY*

OSCAR LEWIS

THE Ríos Family presented in this volume consists of five households, a mother and two married daughters in Puerto Rico, and a married son and daughter in New York City. The mother, Fernanda Fuentes, a Negro woman of forty, is now living with her sixth husband in La Esmeralda, a San Juan slum. Her children — Soledad, twenty-five; Felícita, twenty-three; Simplicio, twenty-one; and Cruz, nineteen — were born to Fernanda while she was living in free union with her first husband, Cristóbal Ríos, a light-skinned Puerto Rican.

In addition to the five major characters, I have included the views of the spouses, of two young grandchildren, ages seven and nine, of a maternal aunt, and of a close friend of the family. In all, sixteen Puerto Ricans, ranging in ages from seven to sixty-four and representing four generations, tell their life stories and those of their parents and grandparents.† This gives the reader a historical depth of well over one hundred years, reveals the patterns of change and stability over many generations, and provides some contrasts between rural and urban family patterns.

Although I call this book a family study, the number of people involved is greater than the population of some village communities described in anthropological monographs. Nineteen related households, eleven in San Juan and eight in New York City, with a total population of fifty-five individuals,

*From *La Vida*, by Oscar Lewis. Copyright © 1965, 1966 by Oscar Lewis. Reprinted by permission from Random House, Inc., and Martin Secker & Warburg Ltd.
†I have also studied the life history of Fernanda's great-aunt Funeraria (age eighty), a country woman, and the only surviving family member of her generation. Because of space limitation, however, I have not included her story. Funeraria's story takes us back two generations, to her grandfather, and thereby gives us the perspective of seven generations.

were studied in preparing this volume. The book also includes data on twelve other households. In all, over three hundred individuals appear in these pages.

The organization of the book reflects the actual movement of Puerto Ricans back and forth between San Juan and New York. Part I begins with the mother, Fernanda, in San Juan; Part II moves to New York for a view of Soledad, the eldest daughter; Part III shifts back to San Juan with Felicita; Part IV returns to New York for a view of the son, Simplicio; and Part V is again set in San Juan with the youngest daughter, Cruz. The book ends with an epilogue by Cruz, who describes her move from the slum La Esmeralda to a beautiful public housing project, and tells of her experiences and problems of adjustment in her new environment.

Perhaps the most important methodological innovation in this volume as compared to my earlier studies, *Five Families, The Children of Sánchez,* and *Pedro Martínez,* is the much broader canvas of the family portrait, the intensification of the technique whereby individuals and incidents are seen from multiple points of view, and the combination of multiple biographies with observed typical days. The biographies provide a subjective view of each of the characters, whereas the days give us a more objective account of their actual behavior. The two types of data supplement each other and set up a counterpoint which makes for a more balanced picture. On the whole, the observed days give a greater sense of vividness and warmer glimpses of these people than do their own autobiographies. And because the days include a description not only of the people but also of the setting, of the domestic routines and material possessions, the reader gets a more integrated view of their lives.

In the selection of the Ríos family there was an inadvertent but fortunate convergence of two independent sampling procedures. Three households of the Ríos family were part of a sample of thirty-two families which we selected for study in La Esmeralda slum. Shortly after we began to work with the Ríos family, Dr. Rosa C. Marín of the School of Social Work, University of Puerto Rico, invited me to do an independent study of some of her 225 low-income, multiple-problem families which had been carefully selected from the rolls of social agencies for her Family-Centered Treatment, Research and Demonstration Project. I agreed to study ten of her sample families in La Esmeralda, and was introduced to each of them by a social worker. Cruz Rios and her children, whom we had already been studying for about a week, was one of the ten families.

The Rios family, their friends and neighbors, reflect many of the characteristics of the subculture of poverty, characteristics which are widespread in Puerto Rico but which are by no means exclusively Puerto Rican. They are also found among urban slum dwellers in many parts of the world. Indeed, the Rios family is not presented here as a typical Puerto Rican family but rather as representative of one style of life in a Puerto Rican slum. The frequency distribution of this style of life cannot be determined until we have many comparable studies from other slums in Puerto Rico and elsewhere.

The language used by the Rios family in this volume, as well as that used by the other families of our study, is simple, direct, and earthy. There is relatively little use of metaphor or analogy except that contained in some of the popular proverbs. And while the language is strong and vivid, it never reaches the poetic levels of the language of the Mexicans I have studied. Most of the linguistic creativity in the San Juan slums seems inspired by bodily functions, primarily anal and genital. The description of the most intimate sexual scenes is so matter-of-fact that it soon loses the quality of obscenity and one comes to accept it as an instrinsic part of their everyday life.

The people in this book, like most of the other Puerto Rican slum dwellers I have studied, show a great zest for life, especially for sex, and a need for excitement, new experiences, and adventures. Theirs is an expressive style of life. They value acting out more than thinking out, self-expression more than self-constraint, pleasure more than productivity, spending more than saving, personal loyalty more than impersonal justice. They are fun-loving and enjoy parties, dancing, and music. They cannot be alone; they have an almost insatiable need for sociability and interaction. They are not apathetic, isolated, withdrawn, or melancholy. Compared with the low-income Mexicans I have studied, they seem less reserved, less depressive, less controlled, and less stable.

The Rios family is closer to the expression of an unbridled id than any other people I have studied. They have an almost complete absence of internal conflict and of a sense of guilt. They tend to accept themselves as they are and do not indulge in soul-searching or introspection. The leading characters in *The Children of Sanchez* seem mild, repressed, and almost middle-class by comparison.

In the Rios family, uncontrolled rage, aggression, violence and even bloodshed are not uncommon; their extreme impulsivity affects the whole tenor of their lives. There is an overwhelming preoccupation with sex, the most frequent cause of quarrels. Sex is used to satisfy a great variety of needs — for children, for pleasure, for money, for revenge, for love, to express *machismo* (manliness), and to compensate for all the emptiness in their lives. Even family unity, one of the most sacred values in this family-oriented culture, is sometimes threatened by the danger of seduction by stepfathers, the sexual rivalry between sisters, between mother and daughters, and occasionally even between grandmothers and granddaughters. There is a remarkable frankness and openness about sex, and little effort is made to hide the facts of life from children. Although the children in the Rios family have many problems, they do not suffer from parental secrecy and dishonesty about sex. The male children are erotically stimulated by their mothers and by other members of the family, who take pride in the child's every erection as an indication of his virility and *machismo*. Masturbation is generally not punished. In the Rios family early sexual experience for boys and girls is accepted as almost inevitable, even though ideally mothers are supposed to keep their young daughters under control.

The women in this book show more aggressiveness and a greater violence of language and behavior than the men. The women are more demanding and less giving and have much less of a martyr complex than the Mexican women I have studied. In the Rios family it is the women who take the initiative in breaking up the marriages. They call the police during family quarrels and take their husbands into court for nonsupport of the children. Indeed, a great deal of the aggressiveness of the women is directed against men. The women continually deprecate them and characterize them as inconsiderate, irresponsible, untrustworthy, and exploitative. The women teach children to depend upon the mother and to distrust men.

The failure of the women in the Rios family to accept the traditionally submissive role of women in Puerto Rican society creates tensions and problems in their marital relations, especially in the case of Fernanda and her daughters, because of the bizarre ways in which they express their independence. Their behavior is caused by a deep ambivalence about their role as women, by their occupational history, and by their experience as heads of matrilocal households, a common occurrence in the culture of poverty. It also reflects the general trend toward the greater freedom and independence of women which has accompanied the increasing urbanization, industrialization, and Americanization of Puerto Rico.

On the whole, the men seem to be more passive, dependent, and depressed than the women. It is the men who often express greater interest in having a stable family life and who resist their wives' attempts to separate. This role reversal cannot entirely be explained by the fact that some of these men have married women who have been "in the life" — that is, prostitutes. Many of the men who did not marry this type of woman also showed the same pattern of dependency.

Compared to the lower-class Mexican men, the Puerto Rican men in this volume were less stable, less responsible, and except when goaded, less concerned with *machismo*. In Mexico, although the men were more controlled, their quarrels more often led to killings, usually by shooting or stabbing. The intention was to destroy. In Puerto Rico the men were more explosive but they generally limited themselves to cutting the face of their opponent with a Gem razor. The intention was to disfigure and to demean.

The remarkable stability in some of the behavior patterns of the Rios family over four generations, which span a period of rapid change in Puerto Rican society, suggests that we are dealing with a tenacious cultural pattern. This can be seen clearly in the high incidence of early marriages, of free unions, of multiple spouses, and of illegitimate children. For example, Fernanda's maternal great-grandfather had children with six women — one a legal wife, three wives in free union, and two concubines. Fernanda's maternal aunt Amparo has had six husbands, all in free union, and thirteen children by four of them. Fernanda herself has had six husbands, with children by two of them. Her daughter Soledad has had six husbands in free union and four children. Another daughter, Felícita, has had five children by three men; and the youngest daughter, Cruz, had had three husbands by the time she was seventeen. This marriage pattern is not peculiar to the Ríos family. It is also true of many of the other characters in this book. For example, Soledad's present husband Benedicto has had six wives, five of them in free union, with children by three of them; Flora, Simplicio's wife, has had four husbands, all in free union. In summary, the five major characters, Fernanda and her children, have had a total of twenty marriages, seventeen of which were consensual and three legal. This is a large number when one considers that Fernanda's children were twenty-five years or younger. The nine secondary adult characters who tell their life stories have had a total of twenty-seven marriages, twenty-four in free union and three legal marriages. If we include twelve additional characters mentioned in the life stories, we find that twenty-six adults have had a total of eighty-nine unions, seventy-six of which were consensual and thirteen legal.

The history of the Ríos family, as well as other data, suggests that the pattern of free unions and multiple spouses was not limited to the poor. It has been a widespread pattern among wealthy rural families; Fernanda's great-grandfather, a well-to-do landowner, is a case in point. This illustrates a general proposition which has impressed me in Puerto Rico and elsewhere, namely, the remarkable similarities between some aspects of the lives of the very poor and of the very rich.

In writing about multiproblem families like the Ríos family, social scientists often stress the instability, the lack of organization, lack of direction, and lack of order. Certainly there are many contradictory attitudes and inconsistencies expressed in these autobiographies. Nevertheless, it seems to me that their behavior is clearly patterned and reasonably predictable. Indeed, one is often struck by the inexorable repetitiousness and the iron entrenchment of their behavior patterns.

It has been my experience over many years that the psychiatrists, clinical psychologists, and social workers who have read the autobiographies and psychological tests of the people I have studied, have often found more negative elements and pathology than I am willing to grant. This has also been the case with the present volume. Their findings may reflect some bias inherent in the tests themselves, but perhaps more important, it seems to me, is the failure to see these people within the context of the culture of poverty.

It is true that the Ríos family, like so many slum families, has a history of psychopathology which goes back a few generations. Fernanda's maternal grandmother, Clotilde, was described by her relatives as having been strange and difficult. After the death of one of her children her behavior became bizarre and she reportedly was "crazy" for some time. Fernanda's uncle had an episode of mental illness which was attributed to sorcery, and her cousin Adela "went crazy" for a period of two years. Fernanda's daughter, Soledad, has had a number of epileptic-type hysterical seizures, commonly known as the "Puerto Rican syndrome," and has been hospitalized several times for this. Another daughter, Felícita, has also had one or two seizures of a milder nature. There was a very high incidence of asthma in the Ríos family, especially among Fernanda's children and grandchildren. There was also a high incidence of asthma in our larger sample of a hundred families. In all my years of travel and research I have never seen as much asthma as in Puerto Rico. In Mexico I rarely found it.*

---

*Another striking difference between Puerto Rico and Mexico is the attitude toward the giving away and the adoption of children. In Mexico City slums I found a great reluctance on the part of mothers to give away a child or to adopt a child from a

The Rios family would probably be classified as a multi-problem family by most social workers, but it is by no means an extreme example nor is it the worst I have encountered in the Puerto Rican slums. None of the major characters are drug addicts, alcoholics, professional thieves or criminal types. Most of them work for a living and are self-supporting. Only two of the nine households, represented by the sixteen individuals who tell their life stories, were on relief. On the whole, there is remarkable little delinquency and relatively little involvement with gangs or gangsters. Despite the many violent incidents that occur, there have been no murders or suicides.

In spite of the presence of considerable pathology, I am impressed by the strengths in this family. I am impressed by their fortitude, vitality, resilience, and ability to cope with problems which would paralyze many middle-class individuals. It takes a great deal of staying power to live in their harsh and brutal-izing environment. They are a tough people, but they have their own sense of dignity and morality and they are capable of kindness, generosity, and compassion. They share food and clothing, help each other in misfortune, take in the homeless, and cure the ill. Money and material possessions, although important, do not motivate their major decisions. Their deepest need is for love, and their life is a relentless search for it.

Unfortunately, because of their own negative self-image, the

---

neighbor. Even the sacred obligations of the *compadrazgo* system, which include the adoption of orphan children, are rarely honored. In most cases an orphan in a Mexican slum goes to live with a relative. In Puerto Rico, however, there is a much greater readiness to give children away and there are always women available who want to accept them. A sharp distinction is made between formal adoption and informal non-legal adoption. The latter is more common. Children who are adopted informally are called *hijos de crianza* (foster children). Adult Puerto Ricans never think of this custom of giving away a child as abandonment, but studies suggest that some children feel it as such.

Hijos de crianza were present in a large percentage of our sample families. It is not only childless women who adopt *hijos de crianza*. Often women with five or six children of their own will take in another child. The custom is widespread in Puerto Rico on all class levels, but I found it especially common in the slums. This system gives the woman a certain amount of freedom and mobility. Many young mothers have been able to go to New York by giving their children away to a neighbor or relative as *hijos de crianza*. Often a *compadrazgo* relationship is established between the donor mother and the receiving mother, who become *comadres*.

Rios family do not always present themselves in the best light. Even in the recorded days, their particular style of communication and the crudeness of their language make them appear less attractive than they really are. When Cruz screams at her three-year-old daughter, "I'll pull out your lungs through your mouth!" and the child continues to disobey without apparent fear, it suggests that perhaps the child is quite secure in her mother's love. When Felicita sings a "dirty" song to her children instead of a traditional lullaby, the reader may be so disconcerted by the sexual imagery that he forgets the healthier aspects of the scene, children dancing and clapping happily to their mother's music. And if the children's hurts go unattended, it is equally true that in the long run their mother's lack of concern is not entirely inappropriate in an environment where toughness is necessary for survival. Soledad may seem like a harsh, cruel, inconsistent mother by middle-class standards, but one should also note how much time, energy, and attention she gives to her children and how hard she tries to live up to her own ideal of a good mother. With much effort she has managed to provide them with a home, food and clothing, even with toys. She has not abandoned them, nor permitted anyone to abuse them, and she is devoted to them when they are ill.

Chapter 16

PUERTO RICAN SPIRITUALISM AND THE SOCIAL WORK PROFESSION*

MELVIN DELGADO

PUERTO RICAN spiritualism and other forms of indigenous therapy have received little attention in professional social work journals, although social work intervention plays an influential role in the lives of thousands of Puerto Ricans and Chicanos, two of America's largest Spanish minority groups. The intent of this article is to increase professional awareness of the psychotherapeutic merits of spiritualism in the Puerto Rican community, to compare the role of medium with that of social worker, and to make recommendations for the use of mediums and their techniques as community resources.

SPIRITUALIST BELIEFS

The *Oxford English Dictionary* defines spiritualism as "The belief that the spirits of the dead can hold communication with the living or make their presence known to them in some way, esp., through a 'medium'."[1] Spiritualism is the belief that the visible world is surrounded by an invisible world inhabited by both good and evil spirits who influence human behavior. Spirits fulfill many functions in the visible world. Stanley Fisch notes:

In addition to conferring protection and enabling the medium to function, they can both cause and prevent illness. One's spiritual protection acts as a shield, turning away evil spirits and hexes while at the same time bringing one good

*From Melvin Delgado, Puerto Rican Spiritualism and the Social Work Profession. *Social Casework*, 58:451-458, 1977. Copyright 1977 by the Family Service Association of America. Reprinted by permission.

luck. If one loses spiritual protection . . . one can become ill. The illness may be manifested by such signs as pain, lethargy, nervousness, and bad luck.[2]

In essence, the role of spirits in determining day-to-day activities is fairly extensive, particularly during periods of crisis when explanations for and causes of misfortune are sought.

SPIRITUALISM AND ROMAN CATHOLICISM

There is little or no incompatibility between religion and a belief in spiritualism. Religious faith, belief in spirits, and superstitious fear are intermingled to the point where no incongruities exist, except in the eyes of the Roman Catholic church and some of its most ardent followers. Historically, the Roman Catholic church has been viewed with suspicion by the lower socioeconomic class. One paradox in Puerto Rican culture is the disparity between formal affiliation with the Roman Catholic church and the meager concern for its dogmas. According to various estimates[3], approximately 85 percent of the Puerto Rican community is Roman Catholic, but only 15 percent are sufficiently devout to follow church mandates and rituals with any regularity.

According to Theodore Brameld, one explanation for the lacuna between affiliation and practice is the clerical reputation of the Roman Catholic church in the Puerto Rican community,

> meaning the close affiliation of a politically minded hierarchy with the colonial role of earlier centuries — a fact true of the other Hispanic cultures. Such a reputation has lingered long and helps to explain the continued support of the Church by the top status level of the population. Also, at least partially, it accounts for a half-conscious suspicion if not an outright hostility with which many people of the lower and even middle-class status tend to look upon the Catholic clergy.[4]

F. F. Merino presents a Freudian interpretation of spiritualism and considers the monolithic power of the Roman Catholic church on the psyche of the Puerto Rican:

Spiritualism, in our group of patients, has also the meaning of valiant unorthodox gesture of rebellion against the monolithic power of the Church, it quite probably represents a largely unconscious resentment of the clerical grasp of the psyche of the Puerto Rican man. The authority of the priest cannot be argued along terrestrial lines, only spiritual ones. Engaging into dealings with spirits, commanding them or propitiating them, casting spells, or learning the art of controlling nature, brings defeat to the churchman and victory to the underdog.[5]

FUNCTION OF SPIRITUALISM

Supernatural beliefs tend to persist when they offer solutions to significant human problems. It is widely recognized that supernatural beliefs and practices are a means of channeling aggression and relieving tension, and there are studies noting that the practice increases during periods of stress and insecurity, such as periods of being uprooted and migrating.[6]

Anthropological and sociological studies indicate that the increased urbanization and the uprooting of people, particularly in developing countries, brings about increased reliance on supernatural beliefs — witchcraft, spiritualism, and so forth — as a means of coping with an ever-changing environment. Puerto Ricans have undergone massive industrialization and urbanization during the past four decades with resultant disorganizational processes of the population. Uprooting has caused a shift from rural to urban areas and mass migration to the United States.

Bronislaw Malinowski makes similar reference to the role of magic and religion in relieving emotional distress:

Both magic and religion arise and function in situations of emotional stress, crises of life, lacunae in important pursuits, death and initiation into tribal mysteries, unhappy love and unsatisfied hate. Both magic and religion open up escapes from such impasses as offer no empirical way out except by ritual and belief into the domain of the supernatural.[7]

S. F. Madel's research on the role of the supernatural forces in four African societies reaches similar conclusions:

> Witchcraft beliefs are causally related to frustrations, anxieties, or other mental stresses as psychopathological symptoms are related to mental disturbances of this nature. The role of witchcraft beliefs is to enable a society to go on functioning in a given manner, fraught with conflicts and contradictions which the society is helpless to resolve; the witchcraft beliefs thus absolve the society from a task apparently too difficult for it, namely, some radical readjustment.[8]

Both Malinowski and Madel refer to the need for the uprooted to turn to supernatural forces, be it religion, magic, witchcraft, spiritualism, and so forth, as a means of channeling frustrations and aggressions that cannot be otherwise satisfactorily resolved.

Spiritualism is an institutionalized outlet for the therapeutic discharge of frustrations and aggressions for many Puerto Ricans. As one Puerto Rican candidly states: "We live here with problems. We eat with problems. We work with problems. We are surrounded by problems."[9] It is characteristic of people to turn to those individuals whom they feel offer the most understandable explanation of their problems.

The presence of what might be termed a spiritualist element in emotional problems among Puerto Ricans demands the adoption of a specific form of therapy that is culturally based and not alien. Such a mode of treatment is available in the Puerto Rican community, just as it is represented in different forms in all ethnic minority communities throughout America. This system of support is parallel to traditional support systems found in this country.

MEDIUMS

In general, Puerto Ricans have negative attitudes toward social workers and other mental health professionals, based upon experiences in seeking assistance from social institutions, for example, clinics, hospitals, courts, and so forth. Beatrice Purdy, Sarah Flores, and Harvey Bluestone note these experiences as important in the development of a negative attitude toward support services:

> Professional mental health workers may be seen by these pa-
> tients as punitive authorities who sit in judgment and at-
> tempt to categorize their patients into slots which are
> reprehensible to them. . . . The medium is able to label the
> problem immediately, provides an acceptable explanation for
> it, and gives the patient concrete, action-oriented treatment.
> Perhaps this is a case of exorcism by action as opposed to
> exorcism by thought and insight.[10]

If a Puerto Rican in need of assistance is offered a choice
between a medium and a social worker, he will probably
choose a medium. Social workers lack the prestige given to
spiritualists whose roles are sanctioned by the entire society to
which they and their clients belong.

One means of judging a medium's power, other than treatment outcome, is by observing the power of diagnosis. Little
verbal interaction is needed to assess the presenting problem
and to develop a treatment plan. In essence, a person possessing
supernatural powers need not rely to any large degree upon
information provided by the client. G. Morris Carstairs, a noted
psychiatrist and social anthropologist, notes a wide lacuna between indigenous therapists and Western psychotherapists. His
research in Sujarupa, India, reveals the difficulty of treating
patients with Western insight-oriented therapy when the etiology of the illness can be traced by the patient to an invasion
by a malign spirit:

> My patients would squat before me, as puzzled as I was,
> trying to reconcile my curious behaviour with their expecta-
> tions of how a true healer should behave. They were espe-
> cially disconcerted when I asked questions about their
> symptoms, or the history of their illness; in their eyes, a
> healer who lacked the ability to know these things by virtue
> of his supernatural gifts, was scarcely likely to be able to
> contend with the spiritual cause of their complaint.[11]

Client Expectations

The dissatisfied Puerto Rican will quickly utilize the services of another spiritualist until one is found who produces satisfactory results. Whether Puerto Ricans seek assistance from traditional sources or other sources, client expectations of what constitutes assistance are very important in the therapeutic relationship. Those whose expectations are not met will be dissatisfied with the service and may seek assistance elsewhere until he or she is satisfied. In essence, a medium must be attuned to the client's expectations if a successful encounter between medium and client is to result.

A number of studies have explored the role of client expectations as a variable in predicting later events in seeking and utilizing mental health services. Henry J. Friedman reports that patient expectancy of reduction in symptom intensity was significantly correlated with reduction in symptom intensity following an evaluation interview.[12] E. H. Uhlenhuth and David B. Duncan[13] examine patient optimism on probable outcome of treatment and discover a positive association with relief of symptom distress.

Ralph W. Hein and Harry Trossman approach the issue from a different perspective and note that those patients who expected an active role in therapy were more likely to continue in treatment as opposed to those who placed complete responsibility in the hands of the therapist.[14] Similar results were obtained by Betty Overall and H. Aronson.[15] Patients of lower socioeconomic backgrounds expected the therapist to assume an active role rather than a passive role. Consequently, if their expectations and perceptions differed after the initial interview, there was a higher probability that they would not return. D. Klein also made similar observations.[16] Patients from lower socioeconomic parents preferred advice-giving counseling to a greater extent than did patients of parents of the upper socioeconomic group.

The client expectations of what constitutes treatment are very influential in determining whether a Puerto Rican client will continue to utilize the services of a particular medium or social worker. The existence of a referral system in the community makes it relatively easy to locate the services of a medium. As Lloyd Rogler and August B. Hollingshead note in their study of mental illness in the Puerto Rican community:

> Spiritualism acquires its leaders through informal primary
> group processes, not professional education and training. A
> person becomes a head medium by establishing a reputation
> for competence in dealing with the supernatural and in ef-
> fecting cures. The reputation develops among a circle of
> friends and associates by word of mouth.[17]

The medium divines his client's history and ascertains the
spiritual protection at the client's disposal through his special
powers. The client may offer an interpretation of his problems
and the medium will often utilize such information to conjure
up a treatment plan. The entire process serves to reassure the
client that he is in competent hands and engenders confidence
and faith.

Language is also a very important factor in achieving a therapeutic cure. The use of the client's native language not only
facilitates verbal communication, but, more important, the
level of vocabulary delineates the client's difficulties (symp-
tomatology) in somatic terms and ascribes the cause of illness
to culturally accepted sources, that is, spirits. Much of the anxiety surrounding illness is its unknown origin.

> What was expected from the healer was reassurance. So long
> as the illness was nameless, patients felt desperately afraid,
> but once its magic origin had been defined and the appro-
> priate measures taken, they could face the outcome calmly.
> The parallel with our own clinical experience is obvious.[18]

The identifying process is relatively easy as long as the medium is able to share the same conceptions of causation as the
client. By attributing mental or physical illness to external
sources, projection is fostered and there is little rejection of the
client and the illness is perceived as less of a threat to the
individual seeking assistance.

Whole-Person Treatment

Mediums treat not only emotionally related problems, but
also physical illnesses. The primary function of therapists in
all cultures is to treat illness, physical or mental. Western-based
culture, however, distinguishes rather sharply between physical

and mental illness and has separate therapists for each. Most other cultures, however, do not make such a sharp distinction. This lack of delineation results in conferring on one individual the power and ability to treat physical as well as mental and social problems.

Mediums are aware of the value of treating the whole person rather than concentrating only on the system involved. This process is accomplished by placing the client's difficulties in the light of spiritual and religious values in the Puerto Rican community and by displaying a tendency to utilize these elements in the curative process.

In Puerto Rican culture, psychological symptoms are often expressed as somatic illness. When such symptoms are noted by medical doctors or nurses, however, little or nothing is done. Conversely, mental health professionals in general have a disdain for treating somatic illnesses; consequently, in order to discourage discussion of somatic complaints, they will often ignore them. Mediums, in turn, take for granted the double meaning of presenting complaints and treat their clients accordingly. As Arthur L. Hall and Peter G. Bourne note:

> Of extreme importance in the functioning of all indigenous therapists in this community [Southern Urban Black] was the lack of a clear distinction between mind and body that existed in the somatic culture. Psychiatric problems were frequently couched in somatic terms and, even when a problem was clearly identified as psychological, herbs or potions were frequently sought as the most appropriate treatment. Similarly, spiritual cures for physical ailments were frequently the treatment of choice.[19]

Differentiation between mind and body does not occur in the Puerto Rican community because treatment encompasses both spheres. It should be noted that the medium's role as a doctor is not dominant and is probably the result of availability of health services and lack of stigma associated with seeking medical attention.

Herbal Medicine

Like medical doctors and psychiatrists, mediums prescribe

medicine which performs an important role in the therapeutic relationship. A medium, unlike his professional counterpart, prescribes herbal medicine. Such medicines are symbolic to Puerto Ricans — tropical herbs elicit memories of life in Puerto Rico. Many Puerto Ricans have a romanticized longing to go back to the less organized and more familial and intimate way of life.

The magical and symbolic connotation of herbs is evident. There may be, however, an empirical basis for using herbs. There is little doubt that certain herbs are effective in curing certain symptoms. Herbal medicine dates back farther than any other form of medicine. Herbal concoctions are not restricted to Puerto Rican culture as evidenced by their widespread use in cultures found in Asia, South America, and Africa.

Herbal concoctions are an integral part of the Puerto Rican culture and the formulas are passed from generation to generation. Herbal medicine can be obtained in local *botanicas*. These shops, owned and run by community residents, supply a variety of herbs used in dealing with spirits and the ills they engender. *Botanicas* also provide prayer books, candles, ointments, medicated hot baths, and other spiritually related paraphernalia.

SOCIAL WORK AND SPIRITUALISM

It is interesting to note that at the turn of this century a group of mediums in Puerto Rico advocated the acceptance of spiritualism as a branch of psychiatry:

> At a spiritualist convention held in Mayaguez, Puerto Rico, in April 1903, one of the speakers announced a new basis for modern psychiatry. He claimed that since the phenomena of hypnosis, in which the hypnotist bends to his will the personality of his subject, have been validated and incorporated into medical therapy, the day had come when one should recognize that most mental disorders were produced by the spirits' hypnotic influence on the minds of afflicted persons. Thus spiritualism would become an extension of psychiatry, and its exorcistic rituals would joint the arsenal of psychotherapy.[20]

Much of the confusion surrounding the issue of whether indigenous methods of treating emotional problems can be considered "scientific" and classified under "psychiatry" is the result of the assumption that therapy which is undertaken in an office or professional complex must be scientific; whereas therapy that takes place in an apartment or storefront is magic, and therefore, nonscientific. As E. F. Torrey suggests, the educational level of therapists may have certain limitations in particular settings:

> We confuse the educational level of the practitioner with the therapy; M.D.'s and Ph.D.'s automatically are thought to do scientific things, whereas "uneducated" persons automatically are thought to do magical things. And finally we confuse theories of causation with the therapies; if a person believes a mental disorder is caused by hormonal imbalance or a missing gene, then his therapy is automatically thought to be scientific, whereas if his theory of causation involves evil spirits then his therapy must be magical.[21]

Charles Erasmus notes the similarities between scientific and quasi-religious practitioners in this society:

> The similarity between these two cases and those of psychiatric or religious practitioners in our own society almost tempts a comparison. A large part of the influence of psychoanalytic dogma on the social sciences is undeniably due to a logic that accepts a cure as "scientific" proof of the theoretical postulates underlying the method of treatment. This writer wonders if "magic" in its broadest sense can be completely divorced from "science." Both provide posits for future action, both may include irrelevant correlations, and both may be based on probable knowledge results from frequency interpretations. However, the experiences of the folk cannot provide them with the type or quantity of frequency interpretations that can be derived from laboratory experiences.[22]

One of the few studies ever conducted on Puerto Rican mediums examined the attitudes of mediums toward mental illness and contrasted them with attitudes of community leaders and a cross-section of community residents. The findings suggest that mediums possessed a somewhat broader view of the range of mental illness than the other groups studied. With the exception of the phraseology, mediums approach a psychiatric mode of thinking to a greater degree than community leaders or community residents.[23]

In examining the roles of the Puerto Rican medium and the social work profession, the similarities are striking. Both have a propensity toward task-oriented therapy, place heavy emphasis upon recognizing the impact of environmental factors upon psychic functioning, and utilize similar treatment modalities (individual, family, group). Treatment sessions can range from crisis intervention to long term. The treatment of emotional problems is essentially a social process that may be delineated, for the purposes of analysis, as consisting primarily of three basic interdependent factors; a system of beliefs and concepts, a set of techniques, and a system of social relations.[24]

Social work and other mental health professions can be compared to spiritualism, in that they set out to structure, define, and treat aberrant behavior within a certain set of posits. Treatment, in turn, is based upon the foundation of the defined structure. In the case of spiritualism, the posits are based on a metaphysical foundation.

In the area of treatment, mediums begin by providing private consultations to clients. After a series of these sessions, where diagnostic assessment occurs, recommendations are made for a treatment plan. Usually, treatment entails participation in a group comprising several mediums with varying degrees of abilities, family members of the client, and other individuals seeking treatment.

Mediums, however, are at a distinct advantage when compared with their professional counterparts. Mediums share the same ethnic background, social class, social problems, and often the same residency as their followers. Also, they do not have to maintain case records, fill out bureaucratic agency forms, contend with third party or other funding source restrictions, and, last, do not possess the power to label a client as "crazy." The latter is of great concern for those who utilize mental health services. Probably, however, the most important factor influencing the utilization of mediums over social workers is the authority represented by mediums.

Mediums, as a result of their supernaturally ordained powers, are viewed by their followers as omnipotent. Bolstered by these sanctions, the medium takes an authoritarian attitude toward clients by fostering a passive dependency similar to that found in childhood, thus providing a sense of security and protection. The client's expectations that therapeutic results will occur has been shown by Kenneth Heller and Arnold P. Goldstein to relate positively to the amount of client dependency. There is a significant correlation between a therapist's early expectations of what constitutes therapeutic results and a client's expectation of change — dependency playing a crucial role in both parties' roles and expectations.[25]

When dependency is fostered by the situation and cultural determinants, its therapeutic role is further enhanced. The attitudes toward authority and the relationship with authority figures vary widely among different cultural groups. Jing Hsu and Wen S. Tseng note that attitudes toward authority are a crucial variable in therapeutic outcome:

> Patients who come from a background where authority tends to be autocratic will expect the therapist to be active, instructive, and responsible in the session, while other patients, used to relating with authority in a more equal relationship, expect the therapist not to manipulate them.[26]

Puerto Rican families are patriarchal; the male head of household fulfills a very strong authoritarian role and the female a passive-submissive role.[27] The ramifications of a patriarchal family structure are such that, ". . . great emphasis is placed upon children learning submission and strong obedience to the will and dictates of the father and other authority figures."[28]

Mediums are cognizant of the role of authority and its therapeutic merits and utilize it to the fullest extent in encouraging transference. Social workers, on the other hand, are trained not to foster dependency and are encouraged to develop independent decision-making skills in their clients.

The magical cures mediums can effect places them at an

advantage over social workers. The paraphernalia (prayers, herbs, candles) at the medium's disposal plays a crucial role in bringing about the magical cure. Social workers do not have this arsenal of magical power at their disposal.

The authority and power ascribed to mediums is influential in mitigating symptoms in a relatively short period of time. Mediums can guarantee their work and will quickly assure their client that a cure is forthcoming. Social workers cannot guarantee cures. According to George Devereux, indigenous therapists do not provide psychiatric cures, in the traditional sense, but a kind of "corrective emotional experience," which leads to a repatterning of defenses without real curative insight: ". . . remission without insight, while not a 'cure' because the patient remains vulnerable, is nevertheless a 'social remission' and therefore sufficiently valuable to the patient and community."[29]

In essence, symptom relief is the primary goal of mediums and their followers. Conversely, social workers and other mental health professionals see symptom relief as the secondary goal; the primary goal as basic personality restructuring.

RECOMMENDATIONS AND CONCLUSIONS

The social work profession can utilize sociocultural concepts in treating Puerto Rican clients. The following recommendations are some practice measures which could be extremely helpful in closing the lacuna between social workers and mediums:

1. Gain knowledge of the mental and psychical beliefs and practices of the Puerto Rican community.

2. Bear in mind that there is no division between mind and body among many Puerto Rican clients; attempt to treat the total person rather than the emotional component. The fact that you may be concerned with possible physical concerns and attempt to combine mental and physical concerns will convey a mind-body (holistic) concept to the client.

3. Respect the fact that these beliefs and practices, although perhaps running counter to conventional systems of therapies,

have survived among Puerto Ricans for centuries and may in effect be fulfilling both a medical and psychological role.[30]

4. Once a knowledge base regarding spiritualist beliefs has been obtained, do not hesitate to consider asking a client whether she or he believes in spirits. The fact that the social worker can take this initial important step will serve to legitimize the client's system of beliefs. In turn, it may result in elucidating many important issues that will facilitate treatment.

5. Visit local *botanicas* or other settings in the Puerto Rican community. *Botanicas* can be found throughout the community and many mediums actually practice in storefronts. There is no better way to learn about the Puerto Rican community. It also provides the community with the opportunity of learning about you.

6. If a client believes that spirits are the cause of the presenting problems, attempt to confer with a medium. The possibilities for case consultation are limitless.

7. Note the expectations of you as a therapist and attempt to utilize these expectations in your treatment plan. It may mean the difference between seeing the client again and never again.

8. Seek a more action-oriented treatment plan that brings about modification of behavioral patterns, not just insight.

These recommendations are both practical and within the realm of all social workers, and if implemented, will have far-reaching ramifications regarding treatment of Puerto Rican clients. The need to understand the Puerto Rican culture is self-evident. The social work profession, however, must be prepared to go one step beyond this understanding and attempt to implement innovative approaches. It must be ready to scrutinize its practices and be flexible enough to accommodate differences of opinion and belief if it hopes to have an impact upon the lives of countless numbers of Puerto Ricans in the United States.

REFERENCES

1. *The Compact Edition of the Oxford English Dictionary*, 1st ed., s.v. "spiritualism."

2. Stanley Fisch, Botanicas and Spiritualism in a Metropolis, *Milbank Memorial Fund*, 1968, 41:378.
3. Theodore Brameld, *The Remaking of a Culture: Life and Education in Puerto Rico*, New York: Harper & Brothers, 1959, 106.
4. *Ibid.*, 105.
5. F. F. Merino, Culturally Patterned Behavior Reactions Among Spanish-Speaking Patients of Mt. Sinai Hospital of New York City, *Journal of Mt. Sinai Hospital*, 1959, 26:490.
6. Margaret J. Field, Witchcraft as a Primitive Interpretation of Mental Disorder, *Journal of Mental Science*, 1955, 101:826-833.
7. Bronislaw Malinowski, *Magic, Science and Religion*, Garden City, New York: Doubleday Anchor Book, 1948, 87.
8. S. F. Madel, Witchcraft in Four African Societies: An Essay on Comparison, *American Anthropologist*, 1959, 54:29.
9. Lloyd Rogler, *Migrant in the City: The Life of a Puerto Rican Action Group*, New York: Basic Books, 1972, 106.
10. Beatrice Purdy, Sarah Flores, and Harvey Bluestone, *Mellaril or Medium, Stelazine or Science? A Study of Spiritualism as it Affects Communication, Diagnosis and Treatment of Puerto People, Department of Psychiatry*, Bronx-Lebanon Hospital Center, New York.
11. G. Morris Carstairs, Cultural Elements in the Response to Treatment, in Anthony De Reuck and Ruth Porter, eds., *Transcultural Psychiatry*, Boston: Little, Brown, 1965, 170.
12. Henry J. Friedman, Patient Expectancy and Symptom Reduction, *Archives of General Psychiatry*, 1963, 8:61-67.
13. E. H. Uhlenhuth and David B. Duncan, Subjective Change with Medical Change in Psychoneurotic Outpatients, *Archives of General Psychiatry*, 1968, 23:275-278.
14. Ralph W. Hein and Harry Trossman, Initial Expectations of the Doctor-Patient Interaction as a Factor in Continuance in Psychotherapy, *Psychiatry*, 1960, 23:275-278.
15. Betty Overall and H. Aronson, Expectations of Psychotherapy in Patients of Lower Socioeconomic Class, *American Journal of Orthopsychiatry*, 1963, 33:421-430.
16. D. Klein, Parental Preference for Counseling Approaches as Function of Social Class, *Dissertation Abstracts*, 1967, 28:2141-B.
17. Lloyd Rogler and August B. Hollingshead, *Trapped: Families and Schizophrenia*, New York: John Wiley & Sons, 1965, 247.
18. G. Morris Carstairs, Medicine and Faith in Rural Rejasthan, in Benjamin P. Paul, ed., *Health, Culture and Community*, New York: Russel Sage Foundation, 1955, 120.
19. Arthur C. Hall and Peter G. Bourne, Indigenous Therapists in a Southern Black Urban Community, *Archives of General Psychiatry*, 1973, 28:141.

20. Joseph Bram, Spirits, Medium and Believers in Contemporary Puerto Rico, *Transactions of the New York Academy of Science*, 1958, 20:344.

21. E. F. Torrey, *The Mind Game*, New York: Emerson Hall, 1972, 9.

22. Charles J. Erasmus, Changing Folk Beliefs and the Relativity of Empirical Knowledge, *Southwestern Journal of Anthropology*, 1952, 8:411-412.

23. Isaac Lubchansky, Gladys Egri, and Janet Stokes, Puerto Rican Spiritualists View Mental Illness: The Faith Healer as a Paraprofessional, *American Journal of Psychiatry*, 1970, 127:88-97.

24. Alan Harwood, *Rx: Spiritualist as Needed: A Study of a Puerto Rican Community Mental Health Resource*, New York: John Wiley & Sons, 1976, 34-35.

25. Kenneth Heller and Arnold P. Goldstein, Client Dependency and Therapist Expectancy as Relationship Maintaining Variables in Psychotherapy, *Journal of Consulting Psychology*, 1961, 25:371-375.

26. Jing Hsu and Wen S. Tseng, Intercultural Psychotherapy, *Archives of General Psychiatry*, 1972, 27:702.

27. Kathleen L. Wolf, Growing Up and Its Price in Three Puerto Rican Sub-Cultures, *Psychiatry*, 1952, 15:401-433.

28. Ramon Fernandez-Merina, Edward D. Maldonado-Sierra, and Richard D. Trent, Three Basic Themes in Mexican and Puerto Rican Family Values, *Journal of Social Psychology*, 1958, 48:167.

29. George Devereux, Cultural Thought Models in Primitive and Modern Psychological Theories, *Psychiatry*, 1958, 21:359-374.

30. Clarissa A. Scott, Health and Healing Practices Among Five Ethnic Groups in Miami, Florida, *Public Health Reports*, 1974, 89:531.

Chapter 17

CULTURE SENSITIVITY AND THE PUERTO RICAN CLIENT*

Sonia Badillo Ghali

FOR Puerto Ricans, transition from one culture to another has produced a condition of marginality which is stressful and often conducive to mental breakdown. The traditional family stability and parental authority have been severely challenged by the conditions of life in mainland urban centers. The intent of this article is to discuss the Puerto Rican's attitude and approach toward mental health services, as well as some of the specific skills necessary to assess, engage, treat, and advocate for the Puerto Rican client.

First, however, it is important to note cultural value differences, quality of life and employment opportunities, and the Puerto Rican's attitude and standing in regard to available systems and professional help.

CULTURAL CONFLICTS

The extended family and *compadrazgo* (kinship through godparent roles) have little meaning for the systems that impinge upon the Puerto Rican — public housing, department of social services, child welfare and so forth. A man does not get his *respeto* and *dignidad* in the traditional way in the United States. The *machismo* of the male and the *Marianismo* of the female are roles that are looked down upon. In this society, respect is gained through prosperity and material accomplishment. A Puerto Rican mother concerned about her daughter's virginity will be derogatorily accused of being overprotective

*From Sonia Badillo Ghali, Culture Sensitivity and the Puerto Rican Client, *Social Casework*, 58:459-468, 1977. Copyright 1977 by the Family Service Association of America. Reprinted by permission.

232

and old-fashioned. A young girl growing up in the city will be subjected to a great deal of conflict. For example, in the Puerto Rican world, a very high value is placed on virginity, and, in the outside world, premarital sexual relationships are now accepted. The young Puerto Rican man has little sense of his past and lacks the supportive institutional framework that alone keeps a culture living. What the young man or woman knows of the Puerto Rican tradition is only an adaptation of that culture to slum living and poverty in a foreign setting. Often the reaction to the conflict is resentment toward the group whose characteristics are the alleged cause of rejection by the outside world and a lashing out at the values held most highly by that group. These reactions are often expressed in negative behavior at home and at school and through drug abuse. The Puerto Rican also places a high value on the concept of individualism — safeguarding the inner integrity of the individual against group pressure. This value makes it difficult for the Puerto Rican to relate to the American concept of teamwork. One of the Puerto Rican's greatest fears is that of relinquishing his individuality to conform to the group. He is fatalistic about his destiny, and often responds to crisis with comments like, *"Que sea lo que Dios quiera"* or *"Ay bendito"*: the first, accepting God's will, and the second bemoaning his fate. Submissiveness, deference to others, and passivity are encouraged as the ultimate in civilized behavior, as opposed to the American value on aggressiveness.

QUALITY OF LIFE AND EMPLOYMENT OPPORTUNITIES

According to the report of the United States Commission on Civil Rights, October 1976, the quality of life achieved by the Puerto Ricans (nearly 1.7 million) is inextricably linked with the quality of life in many of America's key urban cities. Thirty-three percent of mainland Puerto Ricans are living below the low income level and are the most economically disadvantaged of the nation's Hispanic cultural groups. According to the report, Puerto Ricans are work-limited largely through lack of skills and because of language difficulties, but those who are qualified for better jobs are victims of discrimination, both on an institutional and individual basis and in both the private and public sectors. There is a definite correlation between the migration from Puerto Rico. Not classed as immigrants because of their citizenship status, for such people migration is, nonetheless, fraught with discriminatory problems: they are not white; they generally do not come on a permanent basis. When the jobs they are mostly engaged in become computerized, when there is inflation, or when there is competition from abroad, for example in the garment industry, they are the first to be fired. On the other hand, they are able to secure fast, low-cost transportation; and they generally have transferability of unemployment insurance and social security credit.

The educational system is not working for Americans, much less for Spanish-speaking youngsters. And the same situation exists in regard to the judicial system. Puerto Rican parents tend to turn to the judges to help them control their children. They need help in seeing the system for what it truly does to their children. Medical programs and mental health programs are also failing the Puerto Ricans.

THE PUERTO RICAN ATTITUDE
TOWARDS SYSTEMS OF HELP

Puerto Ricans will often only make use of social agencies or mental health services as a last resort, although their difficulties frequently include dealing with systems such as welfare, housing, health, judicial, employment, and education; relationship problems within the family, and feelings of depression, nervousness, alienation, or other severe disturbance. Often when a poor Puerto Rican sees a professional worker he is wondering what that person thinks of the poor, of the dark-skinned, of those inarticulate in the English language. Does the professional worker understand how the ghetto has affected him? What it is like to be hungry, humiliated, powerless, and broke? Does he really want to help or just do a job? The middle-class Puerto Rican will wonder if the professional person will attribute all of the usual stereotypes to him or see him as an individual. First, therefore, in seeking help, the Puerto Rican will approach family members, friends, neighbors, shopkeepers, *compadres*, or acquaintances who have some degree of expertise of authority in the area of concern. Second, teachers, clergymen, or educated people who are within his own network or relationships are approached on an informal basis, not as part of an institution. Their mutuality is then explored through the town, the school, and the neighborhood that is common to them; their familial kinship is explored through blood relatives, marriage, *compadrazgo*, mutual acquaintances, and so on.

Another frequent source of help is the spiritualist. (In Spanish Harlem there are a dozen spiritualists in one five-block area.) By this means, many of the previous steps mentioned can be omitted because the spiritualist is often able to tell from the outset the nature of the affliction, explain the cause, and recommend appropriate treatment. Although spiritualists sometimes make appropriate referrals to hospitals or agencies, or even suggest social work intervention, more often they evoke the spirits, the intercession of saints, the application of herbs and potions, the lighting of candles, or the exhortation "to accept this test for spiritual development."

Spiritualist centers hold services several times a week, charge no fee, and are open to the public. They are usually store fronts and named for particular saints. Invariably, candles, statues, books on spiritualism, crosses, and a table and chairs for the principal medium or mediums in development are present. Prayers, chanting, and other rituals take place whereupon the mediums are possessed by spirits and are able to convey messages to the people regarding their problems and the spirits who are trying to communicate with them. While it is impossible to estimate the number of Puerto Ricans who have been to a center or are regular attenders, probably over 90 percent have had contact with someone who has psychic power and has had more than a questioning belief in this phenomenon.

Finally if none of the above sources is able to resolve the

difficulty, the Puerto Rican will seek the social worker's help, so that an authority can be used to effect change. This action can be interpreted by a therapist as manipulation and frequently, to the Puerto Rican's exasperation, questions are turned back to the client. But a Puerto Rican will often not reveal true feelings out of respect for authority. Until *confianza* is established, when two people break down barriers and see themselves in a more familial, trusting relationship, much time is wasted and often treatment is discontinued. If, however, feelings of trust and acceptance are instilled in the Puerto Rican client, he will become ready to share his problems. Establishing this kind of relationship is crucial, and an impersonal institution that requires one to immediately recount one's problems and personal history to a receptionist, an intake worker, a psychologist, a psychiatrist, a social worker, and so on, is demeaning and alien to the culture. Some studies indicate that 65 percent of clients drop out of treatment.[1]

CULTURE SENSITIVITY IN THERAPEUTIC WORK

Because Puerto Ricans continue to turn to spiritualism, where no stigma is attached and the emotions rather than the intellect are related, it is important in therapeutic practice that the worker elicit this part of the client's world and allow or sometimes encourage continuance of faith in the folk healing process while continuing therapy. The client may be hesitant to discuss his belief for fear of being called superstitious or crazy, but if the therapist is natural about it, he will probably succeed in tapping this significant resource.

Often, Puerto Rican Catholics are not regular church goers, attending only on special occasions such as Christmas, Palm Sunday, Easter, or weddings and funerals. But they are very spiritual people and are interested in mysticism. They love processions, rituals, and pageantry and they make promises to God and the saints in return for favors. In view of this leaning, sectarian programs would be wise to make use of traditional saints as decorations in their settings. Celebration of the Three Kings's feast day (the reenactment of the visit to Christ by the

Magi), an important festival, could be observed. Different members of the Puerto Rican family could take part in the cooking, the wrapping of small presents for the children, and so forth. Even nonsectarian agencies could make use of this traditional celebration.

Some Protestantism, imported with the American occupation and to a large extent middle class, exists. Sectarian and fundamentalist groups, for example, the Pentecostal religion, have quite a large following among poor Puerto Ricans throughout the island and in the United States. Clearly, these persons would require a different traditional setting.

For a setting to adequately respond to the needs of the Puerto Rican, Spanish should be spoken by receptionists, workers, and para-professionals. Experts in areas such as housing, education, law, home management, health, and child development who give facts and not just provide cognitive introspection should be included. Home-like waiting rooms where clients can converse while they are waiting and an opportunity to have or purchase Spanish coffee would be helpful.

Home visits and open hours for walk-in clients should be available as well as scheduled appointments. Flexibility in the agency setting is indicated in order to help clients feel comfortable. Puerto Rican professionals and paraprofessionals can assist in making the institutions more culturally sensitive in relation to physical surroundings, in making referrals, and in providing input, such as pointing out significant cultural biases.

Attempts to be culturally sensitive, however, do carry some dangers; one of which involves appropriate and inappropriate roles for professionals and paraprofessionals. The professional must not abdicate his responsibility to the paraprofessional nor merely provide concrete services to the Puerto Rican. Roles should be clearly defined, as each worker has a significant contribution to make which must be recognized and credited. The professional must develop sensitivity both to cultural differences — using the culture on behalf of the clients rather than against them — and to the need to modify techniques when appropriate.

Case Illustration

Mrs. D's mother used to pay for her grandson's boarding school tuition through the rental of part of her large house in Puerto Rico. Following the grandmother's death, Mrs. D flew back to New York City from Puerto Rico, leaving all financial details to be worked out by her uncle because she was too grieved over the death of her mother to attend to these matters. Lacking the house rental income, she was forced to remove her son from the school where he had been doing well. She went to a therapist when her son began to act out after living in a slum area for the first time. The therapist discovered that it was the first time the child had acted out and the behavior was related to the boy's removal from the school where he had been happy. The therapist explored Mrs. D's fantasy and discovered that she had expected her uncle to continue to rent part of the house without her having to ask him; she was very good to him and placed herself in his hands. The therapist encouraged Mrs. D to go to Puerto Rico and confront her uncle with the fact that as the only daughter, the house belonged to her. Nevertheless, the therapist understood why she felt that she would have to wait until her late mother's birthday or anniversary date of death. Dealing with Mrs. D's passive dependency without finding an immediate way to restore the equilibrium would not be helpful. In Puerto Rico, conflict or confrontation with family members must be avoided at all costs; particularly when an elder or money is involved. Recognizing the cultural implications of the situation, the therapist first informed Mrs. D that she was the legal heir, and then encouraged her to take her two children with her in order to gain public opinion on her side and thus pressure the uncle to relent.

The above case illustration[2] describes how understanding and sensitivity to the culture helps to provide an acceptable resolution of a problem. The therapist was able to suggest an acceptable way out for the client. Mrs. D recognized that her uncle would not want to lose favor or standing in the community by depriving a widow and her two children of what is rightly due to them. The therapist understood that his client's going alone to confront the relative would lead to talk that she was only interested in money. His suggestion clearly demonstrates how the culture can be used to effect change.

Another example of this cultural reaction exists in Carlos Buitrago Ortiz's study of a peasant community in Puerto Rico,[3] where a sister is unable to confront her brother about building a house partly on her land. Although several trips are taken from New York City to Puerto Rico by the sister and her husband for this purpose, it would be unthinkable to break a valued relationship over something as insignificant as property. Eventually, two in-laws are pushed into the arena to do the confronting which is seen as more acceptable because it does not directly rock the boat of the brother and sister relationship. Guiding a Puerto Rican toward the heart of a conflict or a confrontation has to be done gently, gradually, and with a great deal of exploration of fantasy; otherwise the client may drop out of treatment for fear of losing favor with the therapist by not following through on a promise. It is more important, therefore, not to overstep the bounds of respect in employing confrontation techniques.

Case Illustration

Another important point to be sensitive to is the Puerto Rican's vulnerability to authority. The following case illustration involves a twenty-three-year-old Puerto Rican woman who was very committed to the value placed on virginity.

> Marta was in group therapy for six months and was beginning to transfer her loyalties to her peer group as well as to the mental health professionals in the clinic. Many of the group members openly mocked Marta's strong belief in virginity and even conveyed the impression that a man who still wanted to marry a virgin had something wrong with him. This reaction had less of an effect on Marta than the implied value judgment of the therapists when they asked the same questions after hearing she had a boyfriend: "Are you having sexual relations with him?" "Why not?" Because of the therapists' authority roles and questions, Marta perceived a message that said, "There's something wrong." A little later, the

therapists and group members were extremely surprised by Marta's unwed pregnancy; so unlike her and so opposite to the strong convictions she had displayed earlier.

In this illustration, the inner controls are not strongly developed, relying as they do on external controls and on following authority's dictum. Here, authority was perceived as changing the rules. While others could hear the question "Why not?" as asking for pros and cons, the Puerto Rican may hear it as "Go ahead." Also, the need to please is stronger in the Puerto Rican because of her traditional role.

The Puerto Rican syndrome has become so well-known that there is a reference to it in Alfred M. Freedman, Harold I. Kaplan, and Benjamin Sadok's *A Comprehensive Textbook on Psychiatry.*[4] Unfortunately, it does not represent the accurate version. Not everyone who experiences *ataques* or the Puerto Rican syndrome is schizophrenic. The *ataques* reaction is a form of hysteria characterized by hyperkinetic seizures as a response to acute tensions and anxiety. It is a culturally expected reaction and an ordinary occurrence. It is most often used as a means to control. It may occur regularly, for example, when a teen-age son gets out of hand or when a husband is going out to drink. As the *ataque* produces less medical intervention (at first it can lead to hospitalization, painful injections, being very sick, and so forth) and as a family becomes more able to communicate openly, they become less frequent. Braulio Montalvo's article[5] contains a case illustration of thirteen-year-old Maria who wore long dresses over her knees. She was asked by her teacher to wear a shorter dress for her part in a school play, to put on lipstick, and to smooth her *sereta* (standing-out hair). Maria became distressed at this request and her teacher contacted Maria's parents, who were quite unresponsive regarding Maria's dramatic talents. They were also unresponsive regarding discussion of Maria's being able to travel to perform with the drama group. When Maria developed vomiting spells and a dramatic convulsive *ataque* three days before the play, the psychiatrist could not explain the nonepileptic seizure through any intrapersonal cues, fears, anger, or inner conflicts. The reason lay hidden until the day of the play when the girl could not perform because she was so weak and hoarse. Over this period, she had become more religious and more conscious of her role as a daughter. Without realizing it, the family members had relayed subtle messages of disapproval immediately after the teacher's visit. The visit had catalyzed the clash, the pulling and counterpulling between school and family. The subculture of a Puerto Rican family was reclaiming one of its members from the school's American subculture. The teacher's miniskirt and her emphasis on Maria's traveling from school to school were definite threats. She had not sensed that the girl's hair and overall appearance were signs in the Pentecostal Puerto Rican church of a humble, unadorned demeanor. Had the teacher been attuned to Puerto Rican sensibility, she would have stressed safety and adult supervision and she would have worn her longest skirt.

ASSESSMENT OF THERAPEUTIC NEED, TREATMENT, AND USE OF AUXILIARY SERVICES

The Puerto Rican's mental health problems will be greatly reduced if he has help in negotiating the systems, in gradually increasing his English vocabulary, in gradually increasing his job skills, in facilitating the obtaining of homemaker service, in obtaining adequate housing, and so forth. This intervention, together with overt demonstration by therapists that the Puerto Rican's color, culture, and values are accepted, will enable clients to feel like partners and will more readily engage them in a therapeutic process of addressing more specific mental health problems. Mental health programs need, therefore, to address themselves not only to being agents of change but also to being coordinators of auxiliary services within their own programs, and if possible, with other programs.

Case Illustration

Juan and Carmen R live in a tenement in the South Bronx. They have five children, three sons born in Puerto Rico and two daughters born in the United States. Juan was previously

employed as a clerk in a New York City grocery store or
bodega. He completed an eighth grade education in a small
interior town in Puerto Rico but was unable to attend high
school in the city because his parents, who had twelve
children, could not afford the necessary shoes, uniforms, and
transportation. Instead, Juan began working full time along-
side his father in the *finca* (farm) of the wealthy L family.
Juan asked God to forgive him for his envious thoughts toward his brother, Jose, who was the godson of Señor L and
had his tuition paid by the wealthy farmer. Juan's own godparents were good to him and remembered all the occasions
and feasts, but they were poor. When Juan was sixteen, his
godfather, Pedro, got him a job on the pineapple farm of the
coastal city of Arecibo. He enjoyed living with Pedro's family.
At age twenty-four he fell in love with Pedro's grand-
daughter, Carmen, who was sixteen, in the tenth grade, and a
virgin. Apart from family gatherings and Sundays in the
plaza, however, he was unable to see her. Finally, he asked
her father for her hand in marriage and the latter consented
because he thought of Juan as a brother. The patron loaned
his *finca* for the wedding and contributed a roasted pig for
the occasion. Over fifty people from infancy to age ninety
were there to celebrate the wedding.

Juan was very proud when his first-born was a son, but his
pride as a man was hurt when Carmen had to return to work
as a seamstress because of the increasing debts. Her family
took care of the baby and fought over who would be the
godparents. By the time a third child was born, a show of
God's blessing, Juan was let go at the pineapple farm and he
and his family moved to San Juan, where his brother, Jose,
got him a job in a supermarket. This job did not last long
and after a long period of unemployment and health problems with the youngest child, Juan moved to New York City
with Carmen's brother, who obtained for him the job in the
bodega.

Carmen was delighted with being reunited with her family,
but when she became pregnant with fourth child, the Rs
moved into their own apartment. Carmen became depressed
because for the first time she was not living with extended
family; because of the stress of the change of culture; because
of her inability to speak English; and because of the deteriora-

tion of the tenement which was impossible to keep sparkling clean. She suffered from headaches, stomach problems, and pains in her chest, but doctors told her these symptoms were due to nerves and her condition was chronic. When she felt better she would raise the volume of the *jibaro* music on the Spanish station and talk to her saints. Finally, Juan sent for Carmen's aunt to come to live with them and her arrival helped Carmen. Carmen accepted Juan's arguments that in America job, schooling, and medical facilities were better than in Puerto Rico. (In some ways the job and medical facilities in Puerto Rico were nonexistent unless one had a car.) The years passed, and Carmen consoled herself that as soon as the children finished their education they would move back to Puerto Rico where Juan could set up a business. As the children grew they adopted the ways of the neighborhood children. They no longer asked for the parents' blessings as they came and left the house; they wanted to go to parties unchaperoned; they sometimes talked back; the girls wanted to wear make-up at age fifteen and dress in nonlady-like clothes. The boys had friends who belonged to gangs and smoked pot, and the parents feared the same would happen to their sons. Juan and Carmen threatened to send them back to Puerto Rico or to a *colegio* (boarding school) if they did not sever these friendships. Another important and traumatic issue that the family was faced with for the first time involved the issue of color. The youngest daughter, Yvette, age twelve, entered junior high school and found herself placed on the black side of the two camps in school. This situation affected the entire family. Carmen reminded her daughter that she was a Puerto Rican and told her to speak Spanish loudly so the school children would not confuse her with the blacks. Inside, Carmen felt guilty that her daughter's dark skin led to problems.

During this very difficult period Juan injured his back while loading merchandise and became permanently disabled. Suddenly, the family had to receive public welfare assistance, and Juan's authority was gradually becoming undermined, particularly as he was no longer the breadwinner. He began to drink. Trips to Puerto Rico, while somewhat supportive, did not provide a solution to the problems the family was undergoing. Finally, Yvette came to the attention of school authorities because of her withdrawn behavior and she was referred to a mental health center.

DYNAMICS OF FAMILY CULTURE

Before discussing treatment in this case it is necessary to understand the dynamics of the family in relation to their culture. Juan's transition from the interior to the coast, to San Juan, and finally, to the mainland for economic purposes reflects a common pattern of Puerto Ricans. By the time of arrival in the United States, they have already experienced upheavals which affect their functioning, and have developed adaptive defenses and behavior often foreign to the culture. (When the Puerto Rican Family Institute in New York City was first established in 1960 by a group of Puerto Rican social workers for the purpose of utilizing well-established Puerto Rican families to serve newly arrived families as "extended family substitutes," it was discovered that the so-called "intact" families were experiencing such culture shock themselves that the program's original objectives had to be modified.)

The manner in which Juan obtained his jobs is not unusual, neither is the relationship of the farm owner with Juan's family. The Puerto Rican's social security consists of maintaining good relationships with extended family, friends, and people with "connections," in order to reap benefits in job or educational opportunities or to receive help with the systems; as stated in Spanish, *se necesita pala.* The wealthy take a paternalistic, benevolent attitude, particularly if the poor are submissive, respectful, and know their place. Having a half dozen or more poor godchildren is a source of pride to the wealthy, and often some of these poor children are raised by them, *hijos de crianza*, in their homes, to be playmates for their own children and to assist in the household duties. The natural parents are very pleased with this arrangement as it ensures greater educational employment and marriage opportunities, as well as an escape from the grinding poverty consistent with large families. It also increases the intimacy of the two families, and the latter basks in the reflected glory of the former.

Carmen's depression and psychosomatic disorders are common to Puerto Ricans who are transposed to a foreign, cold, accelerated culture, without the benefit of the usual supportive, extended family. Puerto Ricans also attach great importance to place of birth, and this family's frequent moves and distance from native town had taken their toll. Because traditionally the Puerto Rican female has few outlets for stress in her long-suffering Marian role, she is much more apt to suffer from psychosomatic disorders and depression. Juan's solution in sending for Carmen's aunt is also not uncommon. The value of family is so important that Puerto Ricans are constantly traveling back and forth to attend christenings, weddings and funerals, and to take care of the newborn or the sick. That the stay may be extended to months or years is not unusual either.

Threatening to send the children to Puerto Rico to be raised by extended family is also a way of dealing with children who are unable to resist the pulls of American society. In Puerto Rico, the alternative is having the nuns or priests raise them in a *colegio* to give them the discipline they need. Many boarding schools take both wealthy and poor children; tuition for the latter being met through scholarships or wealthy friends or relatives. If this course is not open, the children are sent to an orphanage. Puerto Rican parents living in the United States, therefore, often become very rigid and overprotective of their children because of the lack of supports from the outside world and the realistic fears of the crime, drug addiction, different sexual mores, and the different values of slum dwellings. The children rebel at this rigidity, particularly during adolescence when the social relationships are expanded, and they often view their parents as inferior to the American way of life. While Carmen exhorted her daughter to stress her Puerto Ricanness, Yvette had been internalizing the stereotype concept of the Puerto Ricans as dirty, uncultured, involved in muggings, stabbings, and other crimes. Rather than say she was Puerto Rican she said she was Spanish-speaking. She was embarrassed that her parents did not attend Parent-Teacher Association meetings. (Carmen went to the school once but got lost. She did not know the teacher's name and did not speak English; no one could help her.) Yvette also resented having her hair in curls and bows and looking like a little girl; she felt different from everyone else.

Adolescents caught up in a conflict between family and cultural values and the dominant society's expectations frequently reject themselves, become defensive about who they are, and sense that they must apologize for the low esteem in which the group is held. In Puerto Rico, particularly in the small towns, the extended family and family friends go out together for recreational purposes and the split between generations is less emphasized. Storekeepers, teachers, and neighbors are all concerned about everyone's children and provide a deterrent to acting out. In addition, there is much less incompatibility between the expectations of home and family and the larger society; this situation is, however, changing, particularly in the new developments and larger cities. Nonetheless, the Puerto Rican culture relies most strongly on the support of the extended family. Those who migrate are torn from these associations, and it is this disrupted family which is faced with the overwhelming task of easing the acculturation difficulties and the critical confusion of the children.

The issue of color is an enormous factor for Puerto Ricans to contend with upon arrival in the United States. With a white, black, and Indian heritage, there are all shades and colors in the native Puerto Rican. There are numerous categories depending on shades of color, the texture of hair, and features. Cinnamon color is a desired shade to possess. While the higher classes are more snobbish about their whiteness, their attitudes toward their darker brothers never approximate the hostility toward blacks in American society. When Puerto Ricans arrive on the mainland they are judged either white or black for the first time, and, if pronounced black, are attributed all of the racist stereotypes of the black people. Enormous problems of identity and disruption are caused in families, particularly when some are considered white and some black.

Finally, while the disequilibrium caused in the R family by Juan's disability would be similar in any family, the excessive importance attached to fixed and rigid family roles in the

Puerto Rican culture exacerbates the problem. The Puerto Rican family is patriarchal in essence. In theory, the man is the absolute chief and sets the norms for the whole family. He is respected or feared by most members. He is the breadwinner, and his wife is responsible for the care of the children and the housekeeping. As the boys grow, the father becomes closer to them. It is his responsibility to prepare his boys for manhood. The concept of maleness or machismo is very strong and is related to courage, aggressiveness, and sexual prowess. In addition, it is related to the fulfilling of one's own role. In Juan's case, the breadwinner role has been destroyed, the setter of norms has been impaired, and the ability to prove courage, aggressiveness, and sexual prowess hindered by a physical handicap. Juan no longer feels he has the right to *respeto* and *dignidad*. Welfare assistance impingement, as well as the struggles the family is undergoing, reinforce his powerlessness. Drinking is experienced as an escape from the present reality.

Treatment

Clearly, the color issue, culture shock, Juan's disability, and the family crises are important factors in Yvette's problems. In such a case, the author, as a Puerto Rican caseworker, would suggest family therapy in the home and engage auxiliary services.

To implement family therapy in this case, home visits would be made if Juan's disability or other reasons prevented the family's coming to the office. First, the therapist would explore how the family felt about the referral to the clinic and point out the clinic's role and how it could be of service. Intervention in a crisis would undoubtedly be the main advantage. Concrete issues would be addressed immediately to facilitate the engagement process. The author would not accept initial verbal compliance of the contract, because of her belief that she would be viewed as an authority figure not to be openly disagreed with, until a relationship or *confianza* could be established.

The gathering of extensive data on Yvette and setting up of a diagnostic workshop would take place after the family sessions began, to see if they were still warranted. The family crisis, rather than Yvette's withdrawal, should be addressed. Yvette should, however, be seen alone in addition to the family therapy in order to help her make more active use of the family sessions. Carmen's aunt would be included in the sessions, and attempts would be made to assess the different roles of the individual members, particularly in reference to traditional values, Anglo values, and the shifting values of each. The basic family cohesiveness would be relied on heavily at this time. The therapist's role and how he or she is perceived by the family, particularly Juan, would be explored. The author would emphasize her authority role or her maternal role depending on what seemed to work best with this family. She would be prone to provide information about herself, therapeutically guided, and welcome their offer of sharing coffee or a snack with them.

The therapist would address the color issue and reach out to Yvette's siblings to verbalize their difficulties in coping with this discriminatory hostility. Probably, the siblings would be able to express on behalf of Yvette why it was easier to say Spanish-speaking rather than Puerto Rican, contrary to Carmen's advice. Carmen would be helped to deal with her own guilt regarding her dark skin. The ugliness of racism as something external to the family would be pointed out. Self-esteem and pride in their culture should be raised through reminding the family of their heritage and appealing to their sense of patriotism. The Puerto Rican therapist and staff could be seen as role models that counteract against the negative stereotype of the Puerto Rican. The author would also help them see that the status of the Puerto Ricans in this country is no different from other migrant groups who are forced to carve out an existence for themselves and their families against overwhelming odds. Programs like Aspira, an educational Puerto Rican agency for the young, or the Arecibo Social Club, made up of Puerto Ricans from that town, would be used to reinforce their Puerto Rican Pride.

Auxiliary Services

The paraprofessionals and other agency staff, as well as

workers in other programs, would be heavily relied upon to provide their expertise regarding school, job, housing, tutoring, medical areas, and so forth. The therapist's role would be to coordinate these auxiliary services in team meetings on behalf of the family. The role of the church or the spiritualist would also be coordinated in the treatment plan if either or both were significant. Carmen's psychosomatic disorders and depression would be addressed with the understanding that until she had less overall stress and greater outlets, the results would not be great; helping her on this aspect would be on a very gradual basis, especially achieved through the instilling of hope. Without completely toppling the martyr role, it should be constantly reassessed in terms of how far she and Juan are willing to go in establishing more open ways of communicating. Because he has to rely on her more as a result of his disability, the advantage of her becoming less passive might be seen in a better light.

The generation gap would be handled even more gingerly than with an Anglo family. Puerto Ricans are not used to the democratic approach where each side listens and one side attempts to understand the other's perspective. It would be important to bear in mind the need to maintain respect for the father and defer to him in assessing how far to go. Families that Juan admires should be inquired about, and it should be pointed out how they have undergone similar pressures. Their ways of coping could be looked at as additional role models. A main focus of treatment, in addition to help with the acculturation process, would be the building up of the father's role and the provision of insight into how he continues to be the head of the household despite his disability. Rehabilitative job training might possibly restore his breadwinner role. In dealing with Juan's machismo, particularly the sexual aspects, the parents would be seen alone. Such topics need to be handled very delicately; sex is still a taboo subject, and perhaps it might be necessary to schedule individual sessions for the father. Most of all, in work with Juan, the therapist must communicate respect for the man and sensitivity to his vulnerability. Because he is not usually a heavy drinker, his drinking must be seen as a temporary escape mechanism and not dealt with directly. The usual techniques of exploration of fantasy, reflective thinking, ventilation, sustainment, facilitation of communication, softening of rigid roles, and so forth, would be used, but with more emphasis on direct influence particularly at the beginning phase when it is so demanded because of the client's feeling that the therapist has the answers.

IMPLICATIONS

If treatment is successful, the roles will be less rigidly held. The parents will have greater sensitivity to the severe problems their children are facing and hence find ways that will enhance their coping skills. It should be borne in mind that the family has within it the resources and strengths to restore the homeostasis. The therapist and other sensitive professional workers simply help the family to release the energy needed to meet their proper tasks so that the individuals can be free to grow. The family capacity to love, to share, and to be generous and hospitable is the foundation to build on. If at the completion of treatment, the family offers a gift to the therapist, rather than question this action, the author would accept it graciously, recognizing it as a cultural gesture.

REFERENCES

1. Jose Morales—Dorta, *Religion and Psychotherapy*, New York: Vantage Press, 1976.
2. Case illustration provided by Dr. Roberto Reddinger, presented at Seminar on Mental Health for New York University and Columbia University Social Work students of Puerto Rico Project, New York, New York, March 28, 1977.
3. Carlos Buitrago Ortiz, *Esperanza*, Tucson: University of Arizona Press, 1973.
4. Alfred M. Freedman, Harold I. Kaplan, and Benjamin Sadok, *A Comprehensive Textbook on Psychiatry*, Baltimore: Williams and Wilkins, 1975.
5. Braulio Montalvo, Home-School Conflict and the Puerto Rican Child, *Social Casework*, 1974, 55:100-110.

Chapter 18

THE STRUCTURE OF FAILURE II:
A CASE IN POINT*

CLARA RODRIGUEZ

AS a non-English-speaking Puerto Rican child entering the first grade in New York City, I was completely unaware of the situation in which I immediately found myself: a dialectic in which the two polarities were the teacher and myself. A central point of conflict was the teacher's implicit insistence that I (all Puerto Ricans) conform to the norms of white, middle-class America. This dialectic has existed throughout the migration of peoples to this country, legitimized by assimilationist ideology.

But at that early entry point, my only awareness was that the school was antithetical to my way of being; it did not speak my psychic or verbal language — nor did I speak its language. It was only later that I realized it was I who was to be the antithesis in the dialectical relationship between teacher and student. The dynamics that followed between teachers and myself greatly affected my progress and achievement. I sensed throughout my somewhat mediocre public school career that the more I "agreed" with teachers, i.e. the more assimilated I appeared, the greater was my acceptance and "progress." I saw very clearly that those who were the apples of my teachers' eyes, i.e. the "best" students, were generally the least Puerto Rican in language, behavior, and appearance.

This article, then, discusses the historical development of this situation — situation for want of a less loaded word — and how it influences educational policies that very directly affect Puerto Rican students. Assimilationism is underscored here not

---

*From Clara Rodriguez, The Structure of Failure II: A Case in Point. Reprinted From *The Urban Review*, Volume 7, Number 3, July 1974, published by APS Publications, Inc., New York.

because it alone is responsible for the level of achievement of Puerto Rican students, but because it is a tangible, never mentioned factor operative in the process of resistance that informs most relationships between Puerto Rican children and New York City teachers. Teachers, in particular, tend to be unaware that they have an assimilationist ideology and simultaneously are unaware of any alternatives to it.

WHAT THE RECORDS SHOW

Most crucially, the figures show that the more time Puerto Rican children spend in the New York City school system, with notable exceptions, the greater is their failure. Table 18-I shows the proportion of students reading below grade norm in predominantly Puerto Rican schools to be higher in each level than the averages in schools where black or white children predominate, and to increase with age. For instance, 81 percent of eighth grade students in predominantly Puerto Rican schools are reading below their grade norm, compared to figures 73 percent and 35 percent for predominantly black and predominantly white schools, respectively. The effect is not limited to reading grades. See Table 18-II which shows, for arithmetic scores, the same increasing "retardation" with each additional period of schooling.

Furthermore, a large proportion of Puerto Rican students in all grades are termed "English-poor," i.e. speak English hesitantly, with a heavy accent, or speak little or no English. In 1969, these students totaled 104,482 or 9.25 percent of the total (Puerto Rican and non-Puerto Rican) student population (U.S. Commission on Civil Rights of Puerto Ricans, 1972). Of those with English language difficulties, it appears few really do progress once they are beyond the elementary level. Table 18-III shows that the proportion of those with severe language difficulties in high school was 7.7 percent — only slightly lower than the 8.1 percent figure for junior high schools. The proportion of students with moderate language difficulty was actually higher in senior than in junior high schools (16.4% vs. 15.4%).

Although these are not absolute figures collected longitudinally, they do seem to indicate a serious problem of non-learning in the junior high schools. What is not visible in these figures and makes the situation far graver is that a large proportion of second generation Puerto Ricans, while not learning English, lose their proficiency in Spanish; their parents retain at least this (Varo, 1970).

Puerto Rican children drop out at a higher rate than any other group in the country. In 1970-71, only 33 percent of the Puerto Rican students who had been enrolled in the tenth grade in 1967 actually graduated from high school. That is to say, 67 percent dropped out sometime between September 1967 and June 1971. The drop-out rate for black students for the same period was 65 percent, for white students 35 percent. Further analysis reveals that untabulated transfers and migrations tend to make reported drop-out rates for blacks and Puerto Ricans *lower* than actual rates, while making reported rates for whites higher than they really are. Thus, the "holding power" of the schools is less for Puerto Ricans than for any other group (Commission on Civil Rights, 1972).

TABLE 18-I

SECOND, FIFTH AND EIGHTH GRADE READING SCORES
(APRIL, 1969) FOR SELECTED SCHOOLS WITH PREDOMINANTLY
PUERTO RICAN*, BLACK, AND WHITE STUDENTS

Predominantly Puerto Rican Schools	Percent Below Grade Norm	Average Score
2nd Grade	70	2.28
5th Grade	82	4.58
8th Grade	81	6.20
Predominantly Black Schools		
2nd Grade	56	2.59
5th Grade	74	4.78
8th Grade	73	6.75

Predominantly White Schools	Percent Below Grade Norm	Average Score
2nd Grade	22	3.76
5th Grade	34	6.69
8th Grade	35	9.08

*Includes other Spanish surnamed students.
Source: United State Commission on Civil Rights, "Demographic, Social and Economic Characteristics of New York City and the New York Metropolitan Area," Staff Report, February, 1972, pp. 24.

TABLE 18-II.

COMPARISON OF MEAN SCORES ON READING TESTS AND
ARITHMETIC TESTS, NEW YORK CITY — APRII., 1968*

		3rd Grade		8th Grade	
		Reading	Arithmetic	Reading	Arithmetic
Normal (or National) Average		3.7	3.7	8.7	8.7
New York City Mean		3.7	3.6	8.1	7.6
District	Percent Puerto Rican				
15	41	3.1	3.3	6.8	6.5
2	43	3.8	3.7	7.1	6.7
4	44	3.2	3.3	6.7	6.1
1	47	3.0	3.3	7.2	6.9
12	53	3.0	3.1	6.4	6.1
14	59	3.0	3.1	6.8	6.3
7	61	2.8	3.1	6.4	6.0

*Based on Metropolitan Achievement Tests.
Source: Compiled from Table 9-1 and 9-2 in J. Fitzpatrick's *Puerto Rican — Americans*, Englewood Cliffs, New Jersey: Prentice-Hall, Inc., 1971.

TABLE 18-III.

PUERTO RICAN PUBLIC SCHOOL PUPILS HAVING ENGLISH
LANGUAGE DIFFICULTY, BY SCHOOL LEVEL, NEW YORK CITY, 1969.

	Severe Language Difficulty	(in percent) Moderate Language Difficulty	Total
All Schools	12.8	22.6	35.4
Elementary	16.4	26.7	43.1
Junior High	8.1	15.4	23.5
High School	7.7	16.4	24.1
Special Schools	11.4	13.7	25.1

Source: New York City Board of Education, *Survey of Pupils Who Have Difficulty
With The English Language Based on The Annual Census of School Population
Taken October 31, 1969*, September, 1970.

Except for minor variations, the higher the proportions of
blacks and Puerto Ricans in a school, the higher the attrition
rate. As the Commission on Civil Rights of Puerto Ricans
report concludes:

> While these figures only estimate the drop-out differences
> between predominantly white and nonwhite high schools,
> they strongly suggest that the schools are selectively more
> responsive to white students.

Truancy rates, also an indication of "dropping out," tend also
to be higher at schools with a high proportion of Puerto Ricans. According to a *New York Times* study, the following
three high proportions of Puerto Ricans had the following
truancy rates: Benjamin Franklin, 45 percent; Eastern District,
42 percent; Boys High, 40 percent (Jenkins, 1971). Thus, no
matter what measure is used — reading scores, arithmetic
scores, English language proficiency, drop-out or truancy rates
— the achievement of Puerto Rican students in New York City
has been very low.

Finally, and critically, the issues that relate to difficulty with
English involve not 40 or 50 students but more than 100,000

Puerto Rican students; the broader issues of bicultural education involve more than 240,000. More likely these figures will grow, for Puerto Ricans are a very young group. Fully 48 percent of the Puerto Rican population in New York City in 1970 was of school or preschool age (under 19), compared with 42 percent for blacks and 28 percent for whites. At present, there are Puerto Ricans in all of the city's school districts; Puerto Ricans make up at least 22 percent of the total school population in every district in the Bronx and Manhattan, and in all but four in Brooklyn. (In eight districts, Puerto Ricans comprise between 42 and 67 percent of the student body.)

THE DIALECTICS OF TEACHING

Although there have been relatively few studies on the subject, those that have focused on it (Willis, 1960, is one) have been in agreement that negative teacher-student relations have a decided affect on the scholastic adjustment and achievement of Puerto Rican children. A recent proposal for training teachers of Puerto Rican students (no longer so uncharacteristically) recognizes the importance of this factor when it says ". . . teachers who are not especially trained contribute significantly to the conflict in schools with large Puerto Rican enrollments" (Cordasco and Bucchioni, 1972). Many, if not most, teachers are aware of the conflict, the ill-feelings in their classrooms. But relatively few own up to it and fewer still see it related to students' progress. Why is that so? Personal and professional vanity? Intellectual cantankerousness? Tunnel vision? I think the answer lies not so much with any one of these, or for that matter with any simple explanation, as with a process that can be seen best within the framework of a dialectic.

A continuous entry of immigrants to the United States and especially to New York City has made for a continuing encounter within education between immigrant students and more assimilated teachers. Although each immigrant group's historical conditions have varied, their involvement in the basic dialectic has not. While the results of publicly supported schooling have varied over time, the basic dialectical structure has remained the same: assimilated teachers (thesis) teaching unassimilated students (antithesis), producing hyphenated Americans (synthesis).

Moreover, one of the values central to this ideology is that of being and wanting to be a white, middle class American (WMCA). Enlightened educators have ostensibly broadened their criteria in this regard, but there often remains an implicit insistence on the same value, which suggests, in turn a certain negativism — albeit unacknowledged — about those who do not conform to this value. The result is that the free expression of, say, Puerto Rican children as Puerto Ricans is suppressed and those most assimilated or assimilating are sifted out as the brightest, most successful, etc. Those who do not conform drop out or don't "learn."

This assimilationist bias has typified the learning situation of all previous immigrant groups in New York City. Beginning with the forced migration of Africans, through the migrations of Germans, Jews, Italians, etc., to the recent migration of Puerto Ricans, we see that all new groups have had to learn without the aid of their native language and in an atmosphere where their ethnicity was explicitly ignored and, at the same time, deplored. Jews were taught to publicly be non-Jews, yet to remember that they were Jews (Podhoretz, 1968), and the same was true of Italians, Germans, etc. These same "assimilated" ethnics would come to defend the system that had broken them in. They would expect the even newer immigrants to undergo the same painful initiation. Perhaps, more correctly, they would never see or accept an alternative to this method of initiation. In addition, and most important, these former ethnics (Americanizers) would be perceived as "Americans" by the new immigrants, despite the fact that older immigrants may not have seen them to be quite "American." In the minds of the Jews, the Irish were Wasps, and in the minds of Puerto Ricans the Jews were Wasps, or White. In other words, for all intents and purposes, Jewish students by and large saw no difference between Irish-Americans and English-Americans. Similarly, Puerto Rican students have seen no difference between Jewish-Americans and Protestant-Americans. (But in the minds of the Wasps, none of these groups is Wasp).

After the newer ethnics were fully educated, they were, as the

ethnics before them had been, closed to public acknowledge-
ment of even obvious ethnicity. At the same time, they were
privately keyed into ethnic cues: since the whole issue of ethnicity was buried there must have been something wrong with
it. This was the message these "former" ethnics transferred to
all newcomers. The fear of the others' difference as well as the
shame or embarrassment of one's own difference was learned by
the teachers and communicated to the students.

Today, the great majority of teachers still see no alternative
to the English-only system. Puerto Rican children must learn
as they had to. Their problem of ethnicity must be overlooked
— perhaps this way it will go away. Furthermore, to admit to
the necessity, or even desirability, of special programs such as
bicultural education would create an economic threat (real or
imagined) to the teachers' position on the queue. Thus, the
United Federation of Teachers (UFT) argues that there are
many unemployed non-Spanish-speaking teachers. To institute
programs of bilingual education would, in some ways, enlarge
this group of unemployed. (In the 1972 contract negotiations,
the UFT proposed certifying teachers with only six credit hours
of Spanish as bilingual teachers — thereby certifying more
readily non-native speakers. This would have served as a "legitimate" alternative to hiring more Puerto Rican or other
native Spanish-speakers as teachers). Basically, teachers' jobs
would be threatened. Ethnics II would move into the positions
of ethnics I. The fact that children might learn better is irrelevant.

But the present dialectic between students and teachers seems
to be different from that of previous immigrant groups. For any
number of reasons, there seems to be more resistance to assimilate than previously may have been the case. Perhaps most
important among these is the temper of the time. Blacks
touching base with their own deep experience in America have
challenged many of the WMCA values, e.g., styles, esthetic
preferences, linguistic and artistic expression, and made it clear
that these values exclude and degrade nonwhites. In addition to
putting these values in question, blacks have clarified and af-
firmed their identity, their alternative to the WMCA way of life.
Puerto Rican children, often in schools, housing, or play-

ground with black children, have undoubtedly been influenced by these actions and by white reactions (fright). They have been influenced to perceive alternatives to the WMCA way of life, if not to accept the alternative posed by blacks. Furthermore, and perhaps related to the black movement, there has been a more general questioning and critique of the WMCA way of life from other sectors. The diffusion of the drug problem is a manifestation of this change.

There are other factors — inherent to being Puerto Rican — that make the dialectic of today different from that of previous immigrant groups; Puerto Rican racial composition and the social definition of Puerto Ricans as nonwhites; the closeness and constant travel to Puerto Rico; the inherent status of Puerto Ricans as citizens; the colonial relationship of Puerto Rico to the United States. In all probability, these things increase the resistance of Puerto Ricans to the assimilationist ideology.

THE RESPONSE OF THE SYSTEM

As early as twenty years ago, the Board of Education received Ford Foundation support to study the "Puerto Rican problem." The final report of this study recommended proper screening and placement of non-English-speaking children. These recommendations were ignored (Vasquez, 1971). The need for proper screening and placement of Puerto Rican pupils is as great today as it has ever been. In more than 70 percent of Puerto Rican homes the spoken language is usually Spanish (U.S. Dept. of Commerce, 1969).

As of 1970, it was estimated that only one out of four non-English-speaking students received any help at all in English language instruction (Greenspan, 1970). Bad as it is, even this figure hid the reality. In practice, the Board of Education lumped a hodgepodge of programs under the rubric "bilingual," e.g. art classes for English- and non-English-speaking students, programs dealing with the community, etc. Because of this, it was difficult to determine the actual number of students really serviced by legitimate bilingual programs.

A more recent study commissioned by the Board of Education (Jenkins, 1971) described the sad state of Puerto Rican children in the schools and the embarrassingly inadequate measures taken by the Board of Education to meet these needs. The findings were again ignored and the study was not released for more than a year after its completion. In the meantime, more than 100,000 students with English difficulties spent another year in school not learning anywhere near their capacity to do so, or dropped out.

In other words, during the time the bulk of the Puerto Rican community was being educated in the New York City schools (1948-1970), the system was not responding to the special needs of Puerto Rican students. In fact, the system has been rather late in simply recognizing these needs. It was only recently (1972) that a special appropriation of tax levy funds was made for bilingual programs. (It amounted to $6 million in the 1972-73 fiscal year, or about one-third of 1 percent of the total school budget.) Formerly all bilingual programs had been state or federally funded.

Furthermore, to what extent this token monetary input reflects substantive changes, i.e. to what extent the Board of Education has altered its assimilationist stance, it is difficult to say. Of interest, in this respect, is the present debate over whether bilingual programs should be remedial, i.e. teach English only, or whether they should concentrate on producing functional bilinguals. As can be seen, this polemic still centers around the basic issues of assimilation, i.e. whether educators should strive to retain ethnic difference or ignore it. (Both positions insist English should be taught.) This would seem to indicate that despite the growth of programs and the token monetary contribution of the Board of Education to bilingualism, the issues remain the same.

Beyond the need for bilingual/bicultural programs, the school system has been in obvious and desperate need of Spanish speaking teachers, or, at the very least teachers who could teach English as a foreign language. Yet, until very recently, persons who spoke Spanish and were qualified to teach were prevented from teaching if they had a "noticeable accent." (A "noticeable accent," of course, is in the ear of the beholder.

Thus, Irish examiners heard accents from Jewish applicants and Jewish examiners heard Puerto Rican accents.) The Puerto Rican community is replete with examples similar to the following one. I cite it because of its stark discrimination. The top-level Puerto Rican director of a city agency was curious to find out if the Board of Examiners did, in fact, discriminate against Puerto Ricans. Educated in the public schools of New York, he had graduated from Columbia University and had taken his graduate degree from Yale. He took the exam, passed with near perfect scores but was turned down by the board because it thought he had an accent.

Whether this policy on "noticeable accents" has been abandoned is not clear. It appears that some progress has been made towards abandonment, but it is still an "issue" to be dealt with. The official position of the Board of Examiners is that they "require that prospective teachers have the ability to communicate orally, with reasonable clarity and correctness. The emphasis is on clarity of communication. Foreign accents are not a bar to licensure unless understanding is seriously impeded." (Board of Examiners' office). But there still appears to be considerable room for a subjective evaluation of accents. Other factors that are evaluated during the interview and that could possibly be used as biases against the ethnically different are personality, interpersonal relations, and understanding of questions.

Because of the relatively new decentralization policy, district school boards have much greater freedom to hire at the local level. Thus, in many schools can be seen teachers who have "noticeable accents." Such teachers have often been hired through the emergency license route, which is used to circumvent the requirements of regular licensing, e.g. having at least six credits in education, passing a culturally-biased certifying exam, and going through the Board of Examiners. However, this license is valid for only one year, at which time the teacher must go through regular licensing procedures in order to qualify for a permanent license.

In addition, teachers who are licensed to teach in Puerto Rico must get a new license to teach in New York, despite their knowledge of English — a prerequisite to being licensed as a teacher in Puerto Rico. These teachers must undergo the same licensing procedures, including the verbal examination before the Board of Examiners, in order to teach in New York. (For a full appreciation of the double standard applied here, contrast this requirement with the fact that Spanish was not a requirement of the educational curriculum at the city colleges until the 1971-1972 academic year (courses in Puerto Rican history and culture still are not), even though graduates from these colleges staff most of the positions in the New York City school system.)

It is not so remarkable, then, that there were in 1969 fewer than 1,000 bilingual teachers to service the more than 100,000 students termed non-English-speaking. The ratio of Puerto Rican teachers to Puerto Rican students was roughly 1:600; that is, 464 Puerto Rican teachers for 240,746 Puerto Rican students, or 0.8 percent of all teachers. In the same year, in a school system that was then predominantly black and Puerto Rican, there were four Puerto Rican and thirty-seven black principals. The remainder, 95.3 percent, were white. Those areas with heavy concentrations of Puerto Ricans do not fair much better. According to the Civil Rights Commission report:

> The under-representation of Spanish-surnamed faculty is reflected in the districts and high schools with the heaviest concentrations of Puerto Ricans.

It should be said at this point that while the role of teachers in communicating and enforcing the ethnic ideology is an important one, teachers play only a complimentary role in the workings of the institution. They alone cannot be blamed for its failings. I point up their role here because it has too often been omitted in studies of Puerto Ricans in the New York City school system, and because they are the direct enforcers of queue ideology. But guidance counselors, administrative personnel, and even paraprofessionals are also important in this respect. And in the end, everyone's role is to a very great extent determined by the total workings of the institution. Whatever the exact relationships of these components to the total workings of the system, the results are prejudicial to the achievement of Puerto Rican students.

TRACKING

One example of how Puerto Ricans are literally kept in their place at the bottom of the ethnic queue by institutional workings is tracking, or tracting, or whatever euphemism is in use at the moment. This aspect of institutional functioning helps to alleviate the difficulties of coping with the frustrating situation that Puerto Ricans present (because of their "special" needs). Tracks place blacks and Puerto Ricans where they belong: in classes where there is little expectation that they will demand to be taught. The reason there is little expectation is that these classes are considered to be for the stupid or less intelligent. Those within the tracks realize the classes are considered inferior; those who place the students there also realize this.

At the high school level, these tracks are the vocational and special schools, where Puerto Ricans have made up about 30.6 percent and 33.0 percent, respectively, of the enrollment (Langlois, 1967). A much larger proportion of Puerto Rican students were in vocational schools in 1970 than either black or white students (see Table 18-IV). Once placed within these tracks, the students can be forgotten. The burden of teaching them is eased, for the emphasis is on manual work. Custodial care, previously an informal, but oft resorted to technique, is now formalized.

TABLE 18-IV.

PUBLIC HIGH SCHOOL STUDENTS ATTENDING
ACADEMIC AND VOCATIONAL HIGH SCHOOL BY ETHNIC GROUP,
NEW YORK CITY, 1960 AND 1970

	Percent in Academic High School	Percent in Vocational High School	Total
1960			
Puerto Rican	55	45	100
Black	70	30	100
Other	88	12	100

	Percent in Academic High School	Percent in Vocational High School	Total
1970			
Puerto Rican	75	25	100
Black	85	15	100
Other	91	9	100

Source: New York City Board of Education, *Annual Census of School Population*, October, 1960 and 1970.

Even Puerto Rican students in academic high schools have fared poorly. A study of the 1963 graduating class showed that only 20 percent of those in academic high schools received academic diplomas (Puerto Rican Community Development Project, 1964). The remainder received commercial and general diplomas — these were hidden tracks. The commercial diplomas prepared you, albeit inadequately, for a job in an office — these are usually typing jobs or other lower-level jobs. The general diploma prepared you for nothing. It was a very low-grade academic diploma in actual content as well as in sale value. It kept you out of college and in the factory.

Recently, in response to considerable pressures for reform, the Board of Education altered the form of its tracking system. High schools now grant only one diploma; that is, there are no longer academic, commercial, or vocational diplomas. Supposedly, this safeguards graduates from any (further) tracking. However, the various courses of study within the high schools, i.e. academic, commercial, or vocational are largely unchanged. For that matter, the board states (somewhat ambiguously) that it has also done away with "vocational English" or other "modified English" classes. At the same time, however, it states (quite emphatically) that the schools still offer "Regents English, Advanced Placement English, Bilingual English, and Remedial English." The question is, have Puerto Rican students remained in the same tracks despite the policy change? Based on conversations with experts in the field, it appears that the pressures that track Puerto Ricans into dead end courses remain substantially the same, and there are still a disproportionate number of Puerto Rican students graduating from high school with vocational or commercial background.

In fact, rather than doing away with tracking, the school system seems to have found a more sophisticated way of conducting it, if a recent planning meeting to discuss preliminary approval of a site for a mid-Bronx high school is any indication. This high school, which is proposed for a scattered site in an area populated predominantly by blacks and Puerto Ricans, will have eight buildings, each devoted to a subject that is vocationally oriented. For example, the Business Arts Center will teach students to type; the Industrial Training Center will offer carpentry, woodworking and plumbing — areas that tend to have both closed union shops and fewer and fewer jobs; and the Applied Arts Center, which will house a cafeteria and shops open to the public, staffed by students, will provide training for the food service trades, among other things, which now employ (but without the training) the parents of the children the school hopes to educate.

The high school complex will also include a Science building to carry out environmental projects in the community, an English and Social Studies building, a Sports Center, and an Administration and Guidance Center. Each student will have the choice of spending all or most of his time with other students interested in learning to become restaurant workers or traveling a number of blocks to another building where he can socialize with other tradesmen. When (or if) this school is finally constructed some eight years from now, it should effectively eliminate alternate choices for academic study and produce more and more tracked blacks and Puerto Ricans. It will perhaps be considered extreme to imagine an institutional plot going on to carefully place blacks and Puerto Ricans in nonacademic, nondemanding tracks. I would agree but for the fact that I have known too many bright, gifted Puerto Ricans and blacks who have been advised, cajoled, and then forced by guidance counselors and others to think that this is their only alternative, i.e. a vocational or a general diploma. And I have known too many who testify to having had to go to night school for one or two years in order to get their academic credit, so they could then apply to college. (According to a 1972 Board of Education report by Margaret Langlois, a much higher proportion of Puerto Ricans in the eleventh and twelfth grades were enrolled in nonacademic courses in 1970-71 than any other group. The report shows that while other groups have shown decreases of students in general courses between 1970-71, Puerto Ricans continue to show an increase in the number and proportion of twelfth grade students in the general course).

The open admissions policy in the City University system ostensibly does away with this problem, i.e. anyone is admitted regardless of diploma. However, even though students can enter college, how long will they stay if they have not been taught what they need to survive? If open admissions cannot deal with that problem, it is really no solution. In the meantime, Puerto Ricans coming into college as a result of open admissions are coming mainly into the junior, two-year colleges. This is another tracking maneuver. The open admissions policy at the four-year colleges has benefited whites of Italian and Irish descent more than it has blacks and Puerto Ricans. (See "Open Admissions at City College of New York" C. C. N. Y. Alumni Association, Jan. 1973.)

CONCLUSION

What the future holds for the issues discussed here depends both on the extent and nature of the struggle made by Puerto Rican students and the Puerto Rican community to maintain their unique cultural identity and on the pressures brought to bear on them by the assimilationist ideology. The role of teachers (Puerto Rican and others) in enforcing the assimilationist ideology looms large in the weighing of the outcome. Even if all the obstacles are removed (noticeable accents, culturally biased exams, etc.), and more Spanish-speaking adults join the teaching ranks, very little really will have been gained if there is no challenge to the educational philosophy that insists upon making all "the differents" into homogenized Americans. There will be but a repeat of history and its continuing dialectic.

REFERENCES

Alvarado, Anthony. Puerto Rican Children in New York Schools. *New Generation*, 1972, 55:22-25.

Anderson, Theodore, et al. *Bilingual Schooling in the U.S.* Austin, Texas: Southwest Educational Development Laboratories, 1970.

Ascencio-Weber, Daisy. Changes in the Educational Program in P.S. 8, Manhattan, Resulting From the Influx of Puerto Rican Children. Master's thesis, New York University, 1955.

Beaver Bulletin. New York: City College Alumni Association, December 1972.

Bennet, Marion T. *American Immigration Policy.* Washington: Public Affairs Press, 1963.

Cordasco, Francesco, and Bucchioni, Eugene. An Institute for Preparing Teachers of Puerto Rican Students. *School and Society*, 1972, 308-309.

Dentler, Robert A. Equality of Educational Opportunity, *Urban Review*, 1966, 41-50.

Fishman, Joshua. *Language Loyalty in the U.S.* The Hague: Mouton, 1966.

Greenspan, Richard. Analysis of Puerto Rican and Black Employment in the New York City Schools. *Puerto Rican Forum*, New York, 1970.

Higham, John. *Strangers in the Land.* New York: Atheneum, 1966.

Jenkins, Mary. *Bilingual Education in New York City.* New York City Board of Education, Office of Recruitment and Training of Spanish-Speaking Teachers, 1971.

Jones, Maldwyn Allen. *American Immigration.* Chicago: University of Chicago Press, 1960.

Langlois, Margaret. *Special Census of School Population, Classification of Non-English Speaking Pupils.* New York City Board of Education, Educational Program, Research and Statistics Publication, no. 311, PN5394, 1967.

Langlois, Margaret. *Number and Proportion of Pupils by Ethnic Groups Enrolled in Courses Offered by the Public High Schools of New York City in 1970-71.* New York City Board of Education, 1972.

New York Times, various dates.

Podhoretz, Norman. *Making It.* New York: Random House, 1968.

Puerto Rican Community Development Project. New York: Puerto Rican Forum, 1965.

Raisner, et al. *Science Instruction in Spanish for Pupils of Spanish-speaking Background: An experiment in Bilingualism.* U. S. Dept. of Health, Education and Welfare, Project no. 2370, 1967.

Robinson, Gertrude. A Case Study of Puerto Rican Children in Junior High School 65, New York City. Doctoral dissertation, New York University, 1956.

Schwartz, Barbara. Puerto Rican Food Habits and Their Relation To New York Living. Master's thesis, New York University, 1965.

Solomon Miller, Barbara. *Ancestors and Immigrants*. Cambridge, Mass.: Harvard University Press, 1956.

U. S. Commission on Civil Rights, Hearings on Civil Rights of Puerto Ricans. "Demographic, Social and Economic Characteristics of New York City and the New York Metropolitan Area." (Staff report, February, 1972)

U. S. Dept. of Commerce, Bureau of the Census. *Persons of Spanish Origins in the U.S.: October, 1960.* Series no. 213, February 1971, 20.

Varo, Carlos. *Consideraciones Antropologicas y Politicas en Torno A La Ensenanza del "Spanglish" en Nueva York.* Rio Piedras, Puerto Rico: Ediciones Libreria Internacional, 1971.

Vasquez, Hector. Discrimination Against Puerto Rican Professionals and Puerto Rican Pupils in New York City Public Schools. Paper delivered at the Hearings on Minority Hiring Practices of the New York City Board of Education, January 27, 1971.

Willis, Robert M. An analysis of the Adjustment and Scholastic Achievement of 40 Puerto Rican Boys Who Attended Transitional Classes in New York City. Doctoral dissertation, New York University, 1960.

Chapter 19

COUNSELING PUERTO RICANS: SOME CULTURAL CONSIDERATIONS*

Edward W. Christensen

IN recent years the educational world has become increasingly concerned with students whose cultural backgrounds are different from those of the dominant culture in the United States. This concern, though belated and still insufficient, has prompted other helping professions to follow the lead. Thus there has recently been increased publication on counseling members of minority groups, writers advocating giving more attention to the needs of clients who are culturally and ethnically different.

One of the outcomes of the increased attention given minority groups has been a tendency on the part of many to lump all minority individuals together. Thus, although early legislation and educational endeavors were designed to help blacks, American Indians, Mexican-Americans, and Puerto Ricans, they often served only to identify them all as having the same needs and disadvantages. Each group has protested this treatment, and all have insisted that their uniqueness be recognized and preserved. This need to understand the uniqueness of clients from specific cultural and ethnic backgrounds motivated the preparation of this article about counseling Puerto Ricans.

SOME FACTS ABOUT PUERTO RICO

There is a great deal of ignorance among mainland Americans with regard to Puerto Rico. A few years ago, when I was in the United States on sabbatical leave from the University of

*From Edward W. Christensen, Counseling Puerto Ricans: Some Cultural Considerations, *Personnel and Guidance Journal*, 53:349-356, 1975. Copyright 1975 by the American Personnel and Guidance Association. Reprinted by permission.

269

Puerto Rico, I brought my automobile, which had Puerto Rican license plates. A number of people asked if the car had been driven from Puerto Rico! Other typical questions reveal a lack of knowledge concerning this significant group in our society. Mainland Americans have asked: "Aren't all Puerto Ricans dark-skinned?" "Does one need a passport to go there?" "You won't serve me that hot and spicy food, will you?"

Puerto Rico is an island in the Caribbean, about 1,050 miles from Miami and 1,650 miles from New York. The island is about 35 miles by 100 miles and has a population of over 2.8 million. Its population density is greater than that of China, Japan, or India. Puerto Ricans are all American citizens, proclaimed so by the Jones Act of 1917. The population is a mixture of Taino Indians, Africans, and Spaniards, although the Indian influence is much more cultural than biological, as conflicts with the Spaniards practically decimated that group. Skin colors range from as white as any Scandinavian to as black as the darkest African, with all shades and mixtures in between.

It is impossible in this article to clear up all the myths and misunderstandings about Puerto Rico and Puerto Ricans. Indeed, there is currently much study, debate, and conflict regarding many issues of Puerto Rico's culture, identity, and political future. (Readers will find relevant material cited in the list of suggested readings at the end of this article.) These larger issues will not be easily resolved, but the present reality concerning Puerto Ricans is crucial for today's educators and counselors. In order to perform in a helpful and ethical way in assisting clients to grow and make viable decisions, a counselor must recognize personal prejudices and erroneous assumptions.

The problem of understanding Puerto Ricans is confounded by the fact that today there are really two groups of Puerto Ricans. From a crowded island not overly endowed with natural resources beyond its people and its climate, thousands of Puerto Ricans have come to the mainland, especially in the period since World War II. Many have stayed. Scarcely a state is without any Puerto Ricans, and some places, such as New York City, Boston, Hartford (Connecticut), and several areas in New

Jersey, have large numbers of Puerto Ricans. Many have raised families on the mainland, and these second and third generation Puerto Ricans are different in many significant ways from those who were raised on the island.

The mainland-raised Puerto Rican, sometimes called Neo-Rican, is generally English-dominant with respect to language. This Puerto Rican has adapted, as one might expect, to the unique environment of the urban setting but has retained a strong influence from and linkage to a primarily Latin American setting. Thus, having been brought up in another climate, with another language, with different fears and aspirations, and perhaps often with a different reference group, the mainland Puerto Rican is understandably different from the island Puerto Rican. Yet the culturally dominant group in the United States defines all Puerto Ricans in the same way, and the Neo-Rican often suffers from the same prejudices inflicted on the recent arrival from San Juan, Ponce, or Ciales.

In many ways, however, Puerto Ricans from the mainland and those from the island do share common cultural characteristics. As dangerous as generalizations can be, it is important for counselors to consider some of the qualities a Puerto Rican client might possess.

CULTURAL CHARACTERISTICS

There are certain values and traits that are generally agreed on as being linked to the Puerto Rican ethos. Chief among these are *fatalismo, respeto, dignidad, machismo,* and *humanismo* (Hidalgo undated: Wagenheim, 1970). Wells (1972) has added *afecto* to this list. (See the glossary at the end of this article for definitions of Spanish words used.) These cultural attributes are important to any group, and a wise counselor should have some understanding of them. The reader who has difficulty conceptualizing these terms may find it helpful to empathize with what the Puerto Rican experiences on entering an alien culture. The following explanations may help.

There is a certain amount of overlap in the words used above. *Dignidad* and *respeto*, which have to do with the dignity of an individual and respect for those deserving of it, are interrelated concepts. *Machismo*, generally connoting male superiority, is also part and parcel of the other cultural traits. Because these concepts are so central to the Puerto Rican as an individual and as a representative of a culture that is — at least politically — bound to this country, it is very important that the counselor understand how some of these attributes are translated into behaviors. The behaviors discussed apply in some degree to most Puerto Ricans, but in some instances they may be less typical of second-generation Puerto Ricans on the mainland.

Typically the Puerto Rican is highly individualistic, a person who is not used to working in concert with others, following in single file, and, in general, organizing in ways that Anglos would call "efficient." Whether in a traffic jam or a line of patrons in a bank, a Puerto Rican may break line and take a position ahead of others. But the Puerto Rican will also offer another person the same privilege, being much more tolerant than Anglos of this demonstration of individuality.

Another characteristic of Puerto Ricans is their demonstration of love and tolerance for children. It is rare that a baby or tot, taken down any street in Puerto Rico, is not exclaimed over, chucked under the chin, and generally complimented. This love for children is stronger than its stateside equivalent; generally speaking, in fact, the family unit is stronger among Puerto Ricans. Perhaps because of the love for children, illegitimacy is not frowned on or punished among Puerto Ricans. It is not unusual for families to add to their broods with nephews, nieces, godchildren, and even the children of husbands' alliances with mistresses. It is therefore difficult for the Puerto Rican arriving at a mainland school to understand all the fuss about different last names and shades of skin color and all the confusion about birth certificates among siblings.

The characteristic of gregariousness, a trait common to nearly all Puerto Ricans, often dismays many Americans, who view it as excessive when compared with their own culture. The existence of large families and extended families, the *compadrazgo* (godparent) relationship, and life on a crowded island are probably causes as well as effects of this gregariousness.

Puerto Ricans love to talk, discuss, gossip, speculate, and relate. No one needs an excuse to have a fiesta. Music, food, and drink appear instantly if someone comes to visit. Group meetings, even those of the most serious nature, often take on some aspect of a social activity. I remember more than one dull and pedantic committee meeting at the University of Puerto Rico that was saved from being a total loss because refreshments and chatting were an inseparable part of the meetings. A colleague used to reinforce attendance at meetings in her office by furnishing lemon pie and coffee.

Puerto Ricans' hospitality is related to their gregariousness. In the poorest home in a San Juan slum or in a remote mountain shack, a visitor will be offered what there is or what can be sent out for on the spot. And it is not good manners to refuse this hospitality; it is offered from the heart, and refusal is rejection. The visitor in this situation will give more by partaking of the hospitality than by bringing a gift.

As might be deduced from the preceding comments, Puerto Ricans are sensitive. Social intercourse has significant meaning, and Puerto Ricans typically are quite alert to responses they evoke in others and to others' behavior, even behavior of a casual nature. Often Puerto Ricans avoid a straight-out "no" to anyone. Marqués (1967) is among those who have described Puerto Ricans as passively docile, and indeed docility is a noticeable Puerto Rican characteristic. Silén (1971), however, has interpreted this characteristic as actually having aggressive overtones, pointing out that historically this docility was simply a refusal to engage in battles that were impractical. Silén has also reminded us of some of the past and present revolutionary stirrings of the "docile" Puerto Rican. Whichever interpretation is accepted, there is evidence that there has been some change in this behavior, especially among younger Puerto Ricans on the island and those Puerto Ricans who have been raised on the mainland.

PUERTO RICANS ON THE MAINLAND

For most readers of this article, the Puerto Rican living on the mainland is likely to be of greatest interest and relevance.

There are approximately two million Puerto Ricans living in the United States. They come to the mainland primarily for jobs. They generally do not intend to remain here and, as economic conditions for the family improve, increasingly return to the island. In recent years Puerto Rico has made some economic progress and some advances in creating jobs, and thus Puerto Ricans, who typically aspire to live in Puerto Rico, find it increasingly attractive to go back.

This return migration has created some economic, social, and educational problems for Puerto Rico. For example, when younger Puerto Ricans who have been raised in New York City or other areas return to the island, they face certain cultural assimilation problems not at all unlike those their parents faced when they came to the mainland. English-dominant young people must master Spanish for school, work, social life, and participation in family and civic affairs. These youngsters' modes of behavior are often in conflict with the attitudes and values of grandparents, uncles, and the general society. Some efforts are being made to deal with these conflicts, including the establishment of special classes given in English and even the employment of a bilingual counselor or two, but the island's resources are too limited to permit extensive help in this regard. It is fair to say, however, that the Puerto Rican returning to Puerto Rico is treated considerably better than the islander who comes to the United States mainland.

Puerto Ricans coming to the mainland often encounter prejudice. Part of this seems to be due to the fact that they are "foreign"; most Americans — even those whose parents were born in another country — are inclined to be cool, to say the least, toward people different from themselves.

Certainly racism is another significant element in the prejudice against Puerto Ricans. Senior (1965) has reported:

> Census figures show that fewer non-white Puerto Ricans come to the States than whites, in comparison with their proportion of the population, and a special study indicates that a larger percentage of the non-whites return to their original homes after a sojourn on the mainland. (p. 46)

But problems for the Puerto Rican are not limited to prejudice. For those young people newly arrived in the States or born here of Puerto Rican parentage, the generation gap becomes compounded by what Senior has called "second-generationitis." These youngsters must contend not only with the expectancies and pressures of a different and dominant culture but also with conflicts of values representing two different cultures. Mainland Puerto Ricans may not be able to identify completely with the Puerto Rican culture, but neither are they a part of the dominant mainland culture. Social scientists often refer to this situation as the "identity crisis" of the Puerto Rican in the States.

As has been shown in the tragic treatment of blacks in the United States, social and personal prejudice against a group is generally accompanied by a lack of economic opportunities for that group. Puerto Ricans are seldom found in professional or managerial jobs; they are usually working in low-paying, menial occupations, to an even greater degree than blacks. There are many causes for this. The low educational levels of Puerto Ricans on the mainland is undoubtedly a significant factor. Prejudice, suspicion, language difficulties, and the familiar self-fulfilling prophecy of low aspirations leading to lowly positions also play heavy roles in maintaining the Puerto Rican on the bottom rung of the economic and vocational ladder.

PRACTICAL CONSIDERATIONS FOR THE COUNSELOR

The following suggestions offered for counseling Puerto Ricans are based on my eleven years of experience as a counselor in Puerto Rico and on those human relations tenets to which all counselors presumably subscribe. The suggestions may seem simple and obvious to the reader; they are purposely so. They are intended as exhortations for those who are thoughtless, as reminders for those who forget, and as reinforcements for those who truly attempt to accept and understand their clients.

EXAMINE YOUR OWN PREJUDICES. Counselors should consider

their attitudes toward poor, rural, Spanish-speaking, racially mixed, culturally different clients. Knowledge alone cannot overcome prejudice, and an intellectual understanding expressed with emotional distaste will only serve to exacerbate the situation. If a counselor has negative stereotyped feelings about Puerto Ricans, it is not likely that his or her counseling relationships with them will be open and warm.

CALL STUDENTS BY THEIR RIGHT NAMES. In Spanish, people are given two last names. The first last name is from the father's side of the family, the second from the mother's. The American custom is to look for the last word, and this becomes the last name. If this logic is followed with Latins, a student named Angel Rodriguez López gets called Angel López, thus dropping his father's family name. Not only might the father and son be understandably insulted by such cavalier treatment, but the boy's identity — in a real as well as a cultural sense — is in question. For those who fervently desire to maintain their cultural and personal identities without being antagonistic to the larger society, acknowledgment of the correct name can be critical.

Another element in this linguistic area is simply pronouncing names in reasonably accurate ways. Even though other students and staff may pronounce names inaccurately, it would seem that a counselor who espouses the establishment of good relationships might make a special effort in this area. A person's name is that person, and a counselor's mispronouncing it — whether through carelessness or laziness — can easily be construed as the counselor's lack of interest in the client. Counselors can check with a client about pronunciation. (Spanish, incidentally, is much more consistent in pronunciation than English, because each vowel is pronounced the same way in all words.)

WORK WITH THE FAMILY. For the Puerto Rican, the family is much more important than it is for the typical American. If possible, the counselor should deal not only with the young person but also with the family, getting to know them as well as the youngster. If this is not possible, the counselor can at least talk with the client about his or her family. Among Puerto

Ricans, the family and extended family are often sought out for help more readily than is a counselor; research, in fact, indicates that the family is the source of greatest help (Christensen, 1973). The counselor should realize that others are helping and should work with them, understanding that each person has something to offer. Ignoring this fact is equivalent to refusing to recognize that a client is also receiving help from another professional.

REFRAIN FROM USING THE CHILD AS AN INTERPRETER. In cases where a parent knows little English and the child is reasonably bilingual, it is a temptation to rely on the son or daughter to carry a message to the parent. This should be avoided whenever possible. Even though it might be a source of pride for the child, it might place the parent in a dependent position, preventing the parent from entering into the counseling relationship as a full partner. There is an additional concern: the possibility that the child might twist others' statements. Puerto Rican families are close, but a situation in which a parent continually communicates only through the child can alter relationships and create family strains.

UNDERSTAND THAT TO THE PUERTO RICAN YOU ARE THE FOREIGNER. One cannot jump into instant relationships. The counselor must give the client time to know and trust him or her. To facilitate this, the counselor may need to meet the client outside of the school or the counselor's office. The counselor should share and be somewhat self-disclosing, revealing some things about his or her family, ideas, home, and so on, in order to give the client a chance to know the counselor as a person. Counselor self-disclosure can be a sign of trust for any client, but it is even more crucial where some feeling of "foreignness" is present in both counselor and client.

UNDERSTAND THE CONCEPT OF "HIJO DE CRIANZA." This term refers to someone other than the child's parents raising the child — either family members (such as an aunt or a grandmother), extended family members (such as a godparent), or even a friend or neighbor. It also may refer to a family's raising the father's children from another marriage or even from outside a legal union. Counselors must not apply their moral values in such situations. The child is the parents' child through love and acceptance, and exact relationships are not that important.

BE PATIENT. This should be a given for all counselors with all clients, but it is especially true when counselors desire to establish any kind of relationship with clients from a different culture. Puerto Ricans have many obstacles to overcome, some of which are not of their own making. In the counseling relationship, counselors have to overcome some of these same hurdles. Counselors must demonstrate their credibility, honesty, and reliability, just as their Puerto Rican clients must do almost daily in an alien society. The difference is that the counselor is in a more advantageous position, and therefore the counselor's initiative is crucial. The Puerto Rican client may expect the counselor to be prejudiced, arrogant, and lacking in knowledge about Puerto Ricans. The burden is on the counselor to demonstrate that these expectations will not be fulfilled.

THE FRUITS OF LABOR

The counselor who works with Puerto Ricans of any age and in any setting may find some difficulty in doing so. But counselors who are willing to learn will find the effort rewarding. Puerto Rican clients need counselors as much as — or more than — other clients do. Moreover, in the final analysis, we Americans need them also. For they, along with all people of differing ethnic and cultural backgrounds, offer all of us a richness that even a wealthy country cannot afford to be without.

GLOSSARY OF SPANISH TERMS

afecto literally means "affect." Refers to the affective side of life — warmth and demonstrativeness.

compadrazgo refers to the relationship entered into when a person becomes a godfather (*padrino*) or godmother (*madrina*). This person then becomes a *compadre* or *comadre* with the parents of the child and traditionally not only takes on certain responsibilities for the child but also is closely related to the entire family of the other person. In some cases this may also involve even other *compadres*, and then the total relationships derived from this system of *compadrazgo* are complex and far-reaching and form the basis for what sociologists term the extended family, which is so characteristic of many societies.

dignidad dignity, but of special importance in Puerto Rico and closely related to *respeto*. One can oppose another person, but taking away a person's respect or dignity in front of others is about the worst thing one can do.

fatalismo fatalism.

humanismo humanism, especially as contrasted with the more pragmatic set of the typical Anglo.

machismo related to male superiority and, in its original form, implying the innate and biological inferiority of women. Characterized as an overcompensatory reaction to the dependence-aggression conflict, *machismo* is acted out through fighting and sexual conquest.

respeto signifies respect, especially respect for authority, family, and tradition.

REFERENCES

Christensen, E. W. (ed.). *Report of the Task Force for the Study of the Guidance Program of the Puerto Rican Department of Education, Vocational and Technical Education Area.* San Juan, Puerto Rico: College Entrance Examination Board, 1973.

Hildalgo, H. A. The Puerto Rican. In National Rehabilitation Association (ed.), *Ethnic Differences Influencing the Delivery of Rehabilitation Services: The American Indian; The Black; The Mexican American; The Puerto Rican.* Washington, D.C.: National Rehabilitation Association, n.d.

Marques, R. *Ensayos (1953-1966).* San Juan: Puerto Rico: Educational Antillana, 1967.

Senior, C. *The Puerto Rican: Strangers — Then Neighbors.* Chicago: Quadrangle Books, 1965.

Silén, J. A. *We, The Puerto Rican People: A Story of Oppression and Resistance.* New York: Monthly Review Press, 1971.

Wagenheim, K. *Puerto Rico: A Profile*. New York: Praeger, 1970.
Wells, H. *Le modernización de Puerto Rico: Un análisis político de valore y instituciones en proceso de cambio*. San Juan, Puerto Rico: Editorial Universitaria, 1972.

Part IV. American Indians

INTRODUCTION

COUNSELORS frequently find themselves ranked below spiritualists, medicine men, and witches in ethnic minority cultures. The Indian medicine man is a vivid reminder that long before doctors, nurses, social workers, and counselors intruded into their lives Native Americans had folk cures for physical and mental illnesses. Supernatural beliefs still exist in traditional Indian families. Upon reflection it is not more logical to believe in atoms that we cannot see. In many ways, counselors who work with Indians behave like anthropologists — they define Indian ways as being foreign.

AMERICAN INDIAN CULTURAL CONDITIONING

When we understand the differences between Indian and non-Indian culture, we understand the meaning of cultural pluralism.

PRESENT ORIENTED. Indians are taught to live in the present and not to be concerned about what tomorrow will bring. Non-Indians tend to be future oriented, they are constantly destroying the past and building the future.

LACK OF TIME CONSCIOUSNESS. Many Indian tribes have no word or concept for time. Thus the emphasis is placed on doing as opposed to going to do something or being punctual. Unlike non-Indians who rush to meetings in order to be punctual, Indians try to finish current activities. (Blacks and Latinos have similar time consciousness.)

GIVING. The Indian who gives the most to others is respected. Saving money or accumulating goods would historically lend to ostracism in almost all Indian tribes.

RESPECT FOR AGE. Respect among Indians increases as their age does. Indian leadership is seldom given to the young. (All minority groups in this book share a similar respect for age.)

COOPERATION. Indians place great value on working together and sharing resources. Failure to achieve a personal goal is believed to be the result of competition.

HARMONY WITH NATURE. The Indian believes in living in harmony with nature. He or she accepts the world as it is and does not try to destroy it. Along with this belief goes the belief in taking from the environment only what is needed to live.

READINGS

Kathleen Wright provides us with an in-depth historical review of the first truly native Americans. Historically, Indians have been treated as the other Americans — those persons who are not native born white Protestants with Anglo-Saxon names. This article begins with early archaeological studies of periods 10,000 to 25,000 years ago and concludes with Indian conditions in 1763.

Harry Saslow and Mary H. Harrover suggest that the school experiences of Indian youth often conflict with family lifestyles. This results in a decline in school achievement — between the fourth and seventh grade Indian students fall behind their Anglo counterparts.

John G. Red Horse et al. examine the characteristics unique to urban American Indian families. After identifying the important attributes of the American Indian family network, they present a human ecology model for understanding the structure of the Indian family.

Teachers attempting to teach students of another culture should learn all that they possibly can about the students' language, customs, and more. James M. Mahan and Mary K. Criger show how this can be done in relation to Indians. Teachers who acknowledge the need to study native American culture will find this article of much value.

Geraldine Youngman and Margaret Sadongei are aware that working with Indian children may cause a counselor to question his or her own beliefs and values. To effectively counsel Indian students and avoid educationally disastrous behaviors, counselors must first put themselves in the position of their students. The authors look at various counseling situations that must be handled with great skill.

Chapter 20

AMERICAN INDIAN HISTORY*

KATHLEEN WRIGHT

IT seems incongruous to begin a study of minority groups in American history with the first truly native Americans, the Indians. However, in the highly pluralistic society that is the United States today, the American Indian, like other nonwhites, forms a part of the "Other Americans" — those who are not the native-born American white Protestants with Anglo-Saxon names who make up the majority of the population.

Ancestors of today's American Indians probably migrated to North America from Asia some 10,000 to 25,000 years ago. Archaeologists believe that a land bridge between Asia and North America existed during the Ice Age, making possible movement back and forth between the two continents. Even today, the distance across the Bering Strait is only some 50 miles. In their search for new hunting lands, food, warmer climate, or by accident, these early men spread themselves across the land that is now the United States. By the time of Columbus' discovery of the New World, there were at least ten well-defined areas of Indian settlement, five of them within the present area of the United States.

Because the first Americans came out of Asia, it was formerly assumed that all were Mongoloids, related to the present day Mongolians. Now, however, many scientists believe that the very early Asiatics were not all Mongoloid and that other races lived in the region or at least passed through it. The belief that the Indians, too, came from varying origins is reinforced by the variety of physical appearances among them. Some tribes tended to be tall and thin; some were fat; skin color differed;

*From Kathleen Wright, *The Other Americans: Minorities in History,* Los Angeles, Lawrence Publishing Company, 1969.

nearly all had coarse black hair; few were bald. On the Northwest coast the men usually wore mustaches and beards, although most Indians were beardless. Archaeological findings, which are the bases for our rather scanty knowledge of the first Americans, indicate that after their initial entrance to the North American continent, local conditions of climate, soil, etc., tended to make the various groups become specialized in their culture. Those Indians living in the plains areas where the buffalo roamed became hunters, while Indians of the northwestern coastal regions became fishermen. Of course, Indians of all groups might do a little fishing or some hunting, but the local environment tended to create groups which were characterized by specific modes of life.

Certain characteristics, however, were more or less common to all Indians. The names by which we know Indian groups are usually those given them by other Indians or the white man. The name which a tribe took for itself nearly always meant "the men" or "the people." Each tribe held on to its family language, even though it might be far removed geographically from its place of origin. The words might be modified to meet new needs, but the grammatical structure of the parent language was retained. It is this characteristic which has enabled scholars to determine membership in the various language groups. The sign language used by the Indians was a result of living near groups which used different language roots. No North American Indians had achieved a written language by the time of the arrival of the white man, but some of them, notably the Chippewas and the Delawares were moving in that direction.

Whatever their ethnic background, at a very early age the people we have called "Indians" possessed certain skills. 10,000 years ago a group of nomads called by archaeologists the Folsom people left their spear points in the area of what is now Folsom, New Mexico. These people were hunters and the spear was an important weapon for their survival. Their spearheads are some of the best ever found. Today some scientists believe that the Folsom people were of Negro origin. The second oldest group of whom we have evidence have been called the Cochise.

In the later years of their history, about 5,000 years ago, they raised tobacco and corn. They used the spear thrower, or *atlatl*, very much like that used by European cave dwellers. *Atlatl* is an Aztec word, but the spear thrower was also used by Australian aborigines and was not abandoned by American Indians until they began to use the gun introduced by the white man.

Another group, the Algonkins (Algonquin language groups), came to America about 4,500 years ago and continued their migration for some 2,000 years. Examples of their polished stone axes can be traced from the Atlantic across Europe, Asia, and North America. Some scholars believe the Algonkins stem from a dark branch of the white race which originated in Spain. Mongoloid groups came with the Algonkins and after them in successive waves. Some continued to Mexico, others settled in the Mississippi Valley, between the Rocky Mountains and the Pacific Coast, others stopped in Canada, and others, the Eskimos, stopped in the Arctic. All of these diverse groups, mixed even more by intermarriage, are called "Indians." Obviously, it is absurd to consider them a single race as is usually done. They differ from one another in language, customs, and appearance as much, if not more so, than many of the peoples of Europe.

With the arrival of Columbus the first contacts between the Indians and the white man, contacts which were to culminate in the subordination of the indigenous Americans to the conquering Europeans, began. The great discoverer himself expressed in a letter to Queen Isabella an opinion which was to prevail for centuries in the dealings between the two groups. He commented that he believed the Indians would make good "servants." This assumption of the inferiority of the Indian continued to color relationships between him and the white man and much of the history of conflict between the two groups may be traced to it.

One of the first acts of Columbus, and he was followed in this by subsequent explorers, was to enslave some of the natives and take them back to Europe, either as proof of the voyages or to work, or both. The Portuguese explorer Gaspar Corte Real wrote that in 1500 (1501) he kidnapped more than fifty Indians to be sold into slavery. Another early explorer, Verrazano, met friendly Indians as he scouted the coast from North Carolina to Newfoundland and repaid their various acts of kindness by calculated brutality. Word spread so rapidly among the tribes that by the time he reached what later became known as New England, the natives would not permit him or his crew to come ashore. In his work on early American history Parkman describes Verrazano and his men as "kidnappers of children and ravishers of squaws."

In the various skirmishes that ensued as the explorers again and again ravaged the tribes and their lands, the Indians came to understand the nature of the white man's invasion. As tribe after tribe came to the realization that the Europeans had come to enslave and to exploit, the Indians began to fight back. They decimated Ponce de Leon's followers and wiped out nearly half of the followers of Hernando De Soto. Such action on the part of the natives met with equally savage retaliation on the part of the Spaniards. In one senseless show of force, De Soto's men killed a hundred helpless, sleeping warriors in a village as they passed through. Coronado, who began by a more humane treatment of the Indians, in the end hanged the very native who had acted as his guide and brought him safely into the interior of the continent. In spite of this, Coronado left behind a tradition of moderation, while De Soto's legacy was one of pure hatred.

The English colonists who penetrated the American continent farther north than the Spaniards were not much more civilized than their fellow Europeans. Sir Richard Grenville, landing in Virginia in 1585, was warmly received by the natives, but after the theft of a silver cup, he sought to teach the Indians a lesson by burning and plundering their village. When more permanent English settlements were established after 1607, the Indians were helpful in teaching the white men how to raise corn and other crops and how to find food. Had they been hostile, they could easily have wiped out the struggling Jamestown settlement as well as those that came after. The relations of the Indians with the Pilgrim colonists are too well known to require repetition. This friendly spirit, however, was soon dissipated as the number of white men increased.

With greater numbers, greater organization became possible. As the Spaniards and Portuguese had endeavored to enslave the Indians, so the British sought to remove them from the lands.

The English colonists urged the Indians to withdraw farther and farther into the forests to the West. However, the limits of the possibility of movement were very real. The Algonkins, for example, could withdraw from the New England coast only insofar as their movements did not bring them into open conflict with their ancient enemies, the Iroquois, who held the land west of the Hudson. Indian group fought Indian group not only Algonkin against Iroquois but also Algonkin against Algonkin and Iroquois against Iroquois. In such circumstances, it was not difficult for the white man to bribe or hire one group to betray the other.

The Indians suffered many bitter experiences at the hands of the colonists. They were frequently tricked and swindled out of their lands; traders made them drunk in order to take advantage of them; they were easy prey to European diseases such as measles, tuberculosis, smallpox, and the like. In fact, some historians believe that the deadliest weapons of the white man were not his guns with their firepower, but his diseases and his vices.

Conflict between the two groups was intermittent over a period of some 400 years. In battle the Indians were accused of great cruelty and barbaric conduct. While this is true, and not surprising considering that most of the tribes lived at a level of stone-age culture, the warring white men were equally as cruel in their treatment of the Indians. In New England, colonists cut off the hands and heads of Indians they had killed and set them up on poles as warnings to others. Indians retaliated by burning towns and farms and carrying women and children off in captivity. The vicious practice of scalping usually attributed to the Indians was actually not a common practice among the tribes of either the Atlantic or Pacific seaboard, and appeared late among the Plains Indians. Scalping was practiced by white frontiersmen as well as by Indians, and it was the European powers contending with one another for economic advantage who introduced the practice of paying for scalps of the enemy.

The conflicts between white colonists and Indians, though variously named and carried on in different places, are generally referred to as the Indian Wars. One of the first, the Pequot War, broke out in 1636 when a white trader who had mistreated some Indians was murdered by them. The Connecticut colonists attacked a Pequot village and killed 600 Indians. It was an uneven war with all the firepower in the hands of the whites. The chief resource of the Indians was their ability to use guerrilla tactics. Of the Pequots not killed in the fighting, some were enslaved in Massachusetts and Connecticut; others were sent in chains to Bermuda.

The destruction of the Pequots naturally had a depressing effect on the other tribes. For the first time it became evident that the white man would not be easily destroyed. Thus, there began a long period of accommodation to the presence of the white man, a period of some forty years during which the Indians continued to be cheated and driven from their ancestral lands. During this period many Indians were ripe for revenge, but the influence of the aging Massasoit, the Algonkin chief who welcomed the Pilgrims at Plymouth, prevented hostilities from breaking out. In 1660, however, Massasoit was succeeded by his son Philip, sometimes called Metacomet. Under his leadership the Indians hoped to find relief from the encroachments of the white man.

Philip's strategy was to form an alliance with other Indian tribes. In all, some 20,000 Indians faced a numerically superior group of about 35,000 colonists. After a series of humiliating confrontations and the forced signing of several treaties, open warfare broke out in 1675. A long series of encounters between Indians and whites finally culminated in the defeat of King Philip the same year.

During the French and Indian War, 1689-1763, two of the largest groups of Indians found themselves allied on opposite sides, the Iroquois aiding the English, while the Algonkins were allied with the French. Under the leadership of Pontiac, chief of the Ottawas, the tribes of the Great Lakes area were organized to aid the French. They attacked the British in 1763. Many small forts along the Lakes were wiped out, but Pontiac made peace with the English after the signing of the treaty of Paris in 1763. Pontiac's help for the French marked the end of a period in which the Indians had allied themselves with the white man. Henceforth, they would be aligned against the colonists.

Chapter 21

RESEARCH ON PSYCHOSOCIAL ADJUSTMENT OF INDIAN YOUTH*

Harry L. Saslow and Mary J. Harrover

WE have not attempted to present here a comprehensive review of the literature on social and emotional problems of Indian youth. Rather, we have decided to present a point of view, buttressed by some pertinent research, which might serve as an appropriate transition to the paper which follows on preventive programs for American Indians.

Our point is basically a simple one: There is a failure in psychosocial development of Indian youth during the latency and early pubertal years which contributes heavily to the reported incidences of problem behavior and the reported differences between Indian and non-Indian youth. We are referring specifically to what Erikson calls the stage of initiative vs. guilt and the stage of industry vs. inferiority (9). That these stages involve the time span during which youth attend school implicates the school system. Some attempt will be made to point out how school systems fail to provide for these important developmental steps.

EARLY DEVELOPMENT

Child-rearing practices within Indian tribes follow well-defined patterns of socialization to insure conformity of behavior with the ideals of the tribe (6, 8, 9, 18). This early socialization is accomplished primarily within the extended family group, with well-defined and institutionalized roles for the adults involved in the process.

*From Harry L. Saslow and Mary J. Harrover, Research on Psychosocial Adjustment of Indian Youth, *American Journal of Psychiatry, 125*:224-231, 1968. Copyright 1968, the American Psychiatric Association. Reprinted by permission.

291

Dozier, (8), for example, in his study of the Hopi-Tewa describes the socialization process of the child as consisting of a distribution of responsibility among three sets of relatives. The primary relationships involving authority and control are centered in the matrilineal, matrilocal household. The women of the child's lineage have the duty and responsibility of running the household; the mother's brother is charged with primary disciplinary powers. The father and his sisters and brothers have a relationship to the child which is one of mutual aid and affection. The third set of relatives — husbands of the father's sisters — seem to serve as friendly protagonists. These paternal relatives may joke and even engage in physical fights with a boy, who is permitted to retaliate. A girl may engage in loud talk, "pretending to be angry" with her father's sister's husband, but is not permitted to strike him.

The tight community organization, with its viable ceremonial life, enforces social conformity among families. Social control in the village is exercised through gossip, public ridicule, social ostracism, and, at least in the past, by charges of witchcraft.

Dennis (6), in his study of the Hopi child, observed a remarkable uniformity in the behavior of the children in their relationships with age mates and parents. Hopi society seems to be based on a system of reciprocity, with no well-defined economic or social status differences. Social roles are differentiated only by ceremonial positions which carry no authority or power but only the respect of the community. The Hopi approve of the person who is good-natured, a hard worker, and who causes no trouble; the ideal of the "good life" is a state in which the person has peace of mind and only good thoughts, devoid of anxiety and hatred.

The Hopi parents expect the child to perform part of the work of the household within well-defined sex roles, to avoid conflicts, and to respect property rights. The expectation that the child will absorb the religious ideas of the Hopi, so Dennis states, is so assured that it is taken for granted and is not a cause of parental anxiety. As among the Hopi-Tewa, while the parents exercise primary authority and control, the duty of lecturing and punishing the child is the responsibility of the maternal uncles, who are expected to correct the behavior of their sister's children. In addition, the child is taught to believe that the supernaturals are concerned about his behavior. The *kachinas* bring gifts as rewards for good behavior and threaten to take the child away when he is bad.

It was observed that those few cases of deviant behavior among the Hopi children occurred in families which did not conform to community norms and in which child training was inadequate. The Navajo, though a more mobile people than the Hopis and other Pueblos, share with them basic attitudes toward the developing child. In all of these groups, training in the developmental tasks is encouraged and rewarded but not forced; the child is permitted to progress at his own rate.

As Erikson (9) says of the Pine Ridge Sioux, "The developmental principle in this system holds that a child should be permitted to be an individualist while young." There is an acceptance of basic impulses, the infant being nursed when hungry and the toddler allowed to eat and sleep when he chooses. Toilet training is not attempted until the youngster can walk, talk, and understand some words. The child is expected to be trained at about two years of age, and after training, lapses are handled with teasing and ridicule.

Among the Navajo and the Mescalero Apache the delegation of responsibility for the weaned infant to an older sibling seems to have a different quality than among the Pueblos. There is more a cutting off of the maternal relationship and regulation of the child to membership of his sibling group, while his place is usurped by the next born. The Mescalero Apache child, too, pushed away by the mother, is observed to turn from one to the other of adults for attention, and tends to "freeze his emotions" (4). It may be that an early and abrupt psychological weaning of the child in the historically nomadic tribes was an adaptive mechanism.

One can conclude from the studies referred to above that the Indian child from the Southwestern tribes has, at the age of five, a fair degree of social competence within his extended family. Developmental tasks have been accomplished without trauma or anxiety, institutionalized relationships with significant relatives have been established, and an ordered pattern of social interactions is developed. Shortly after the age of two years for the Navajo (18) and considerably later for the Hopi (6), the child is expected to assume prescribed responsibilities in the household economy and is disciplined by the parents for irresponsibility. Emphasis is placed on social behavior, and control is exercised by the reactions of the people in the environment. Leighton comments that control of the individual in Navajo society is achieved primarily by "lateral sanctions" rather than by sanctions from above (18).

The conclusion that early stages of development are reasonably satisfactory in most instances seems warranted. Furthermore, the potential for further growth socially and intellectually can be assessed by examining another line of evidence.

The data for Indian children enrolled in Head Start programs are encouraging. In a study done by Saslow (25) children from Santo Domingo Pueblo enrolled in a Head Start program showed an average increase of 12.5 months of development as measured by the Goodenough Draw-A-Man test during six months of Head Start programming. Unfortunately, there is also evidence to suggest that the Head Start gains may be readily dissipated unless some continuing stimulation is provided.

There is also some indication that traditional classroom approaches make a contribution to the loss of gains. The study by Wolff and Stein (30) is but one of a number of those suggesting that gains are not necessarily maintained. An intriguing study done by Homme (13) with four extremely apathetic children at San Felipe Pueblo showed dramatic improvement in reading readiness, free speech usage, verbal discrimination, and general social behavior in response to programmed learning procedures. Homme also reported that a visit several months after the project ended revealed the children to be as apathetic as they had been before the study began.

ACADEMIC ACHIEVEMENT

Tracking the progress of Indian children through school

yields surprisingly uniform findings. Academic achievement is comparable to the cultural majority for the first few grades of school. Then somewhere between the fourth and seventh grades the achievement scores for Indian children fall below the national norms and actually decline progressively further through high school. This phenomenon has been called the "crossover effect." Essentially this same characterization has been reported by Bryde (3) for the Oglala Sioux, Dick (7) for Indian groups in Arizona, and Coombs and associates (5) for Indian children in six geographical areas. In the Indian research study Zintz (32) tested 657 pupils in five pilot schools enrolling children from Spanish-American, Indian, and Anglo cultures in the third, fourth, fifth, and sixth grades. All ethnic groups were somewhat behind national norms on the Iowa Tests of Basic Skills, but the Anglos remained a constant one-half year below at all levels and the Spanish-American pupils tested one-half year below the national norms in the third and sixth grades and one year below the national median in the fourth and fifth. The Indian population became more educationally retarded as they progressed through elementary school. Retardation was seven months in third grade, eleven months in fourth grade, fourteen months in fifth grade, and fifteen months in sixth grade. Results with the Gilmore Oral Reading Test were similar, showing increasing retardation as a function of increasing grade for Indians but not for others.

According to data supplied by the principal of the Albuquerque Indian School (24), the average grade placement score of the twelfth graders at the school in testing conducted in the spring of 1965 was 9.5, which compares with 9.3 for grade 11, 9.0 for grade 10, and 9.0 for grade 9. These data suggest essentially no improvement in achievement as measured by standardized tests over the last four years of education. However, the average grade placement of the seventh graders is 6.5, suggesting only a half-year of academic retardation compared to two and a half years of retardation in grade 12. The foregoing constitutes only a sampling of evidence to indicate that Indian students (as well as students from other cultural minority, socioeconomically depressed groups) do not seem to prosper in the academic situation, especially from the onset of puberty.

The situation does not improve for those who move on to college. A study conducted at Southern State Teachers College in South Dakota of all Indian students who attended this institution is cited by Wax and associates (29). In some thirty-three years, 112 Indian students had attended, of whom fifty-nine (52 percent) had failed to last three quarters.

Zintz (32) reported on the achievement of Indian students enrolled at the University of New Mexico in the years 1954-58. Of 100 students enrolled in 1954 (all classes), 70 percent were dropped with low grades, 20 percent were still enrolled, and 10 percent had obtained degrees. Of the 30 percent who remained in school or obtained degrees, the majority were at some time placed on probation for inadequate scholarship. Zintz performed a further analysis of the performances of thirty-one New Mexico Indian students enrolled in the fall of 1958. He reported that 84 percent of these students failed to get a "C" average in their first semester.

The explanations for this academic maladaptiveness center around two main sources of difficulty. Educators seem to favor hypotheses emphasizing inadequate early preparation, home backgrounds, parental support, and classroom procedures. Mental health personnel tend to emphasize psychosocial factors. Lately, linguists have entered the picture as well.

Data can be assembled to support all of these positions but, by virtue of our audience, we will consider psychological factors only. However, we believe that health and nutritional personnel and even physical education personnel could also claim that deficiencies in their areas of concentration relate to the comparative malfunctioning of Indians and could find data to substantiate their view.

PSYCHOLOGICAL FACTORS

Bryde (3) administered the Minnesota Multiphasic Personality Inventory to eighth grade students on the Oglala Sioux Reservation and found significant differences between Indian and white students on twenty-six of twenty-eight variables studied.

> On each of these measures, the total Indian group revealed greater personality disruptions and poorer adjustment. Notable among the more meaningful variables were: feelings of rejection, depression, anxiety, and tendencies to withdraw, plus social, self, and emotional alienation.

He reported similar results at other grade levels up to but not including the twelfth grade, where only seven variables significantly differentiated the Indians from the whites. He attributed this difference to differential dropouts: the Indian students were more likely to withdraw without completing high school. Bryde reported a national dropout rate of 60 percent for Indians from eighth to twelfth grade. The national average is 23 percent. In a comparison of eighth-grade Indian students with twelfth-grade Indian students, Bryde reported: "The eighth-grade Indian student in comparison to the twelfth-grade showed themselves significantly different in feelings of powerlessness and external influences, rejection, depression, and alienation."

Also, in analyzing the relationship between the twenty-eight variables examined and achievement, Bryde found twenty-one variables to relate significantly. In summary, he reported: "Notable among these relationships were those with feelings of rejection, depression, paranoid schizophrenia, and emotional and social alienation."

Alienation and Achievement

Spilka and Bryde (28) studied alienation among Oglala Sioux high school students. By alienation, they referred to a general condition in which values, mutually agreed upon goals, and means do not regulate behavior. Associated with this condition are such attributes as powerlessness, normlessness, meaninglessness, social isolation, and self-estrangement.

An analysis of alienation, powerlessness, and normlessness scores for 105 Oglala school children showed that they increased steadily from the ninth through the eleventh grade and then declined for the twelfth grade.

A study by Kerekhoff (15), cited by Spilka and Bryde (28), showed a negative relationship between measures of alienation and achievement motivation among Chippewa school children. Spilka and Bryde, in their study of 105 Oglala children, found that alienation and its components also tended to be negatively and significantly related to achievement scores on the Iowa Tests of Educational Achievement; these relationships increased with grade level, reaching a maximum in the twelfth grade. The authors acknowledge that the relationship found tells nothing about the causative pattern: i.e. does the failure to perform adequately in the academic situation lead to feelings of inadequacy and defeat leading to poor academic performance? They conclude that the pattern of influences may well be mutually supportive and circular.

In another paper Spilka (27) suggests that the school system contributes toward the feelings of alienation by virtue of the abruptness of change in culture that it presents and by its concentration upon the defense of that culture. It is also true that school systems, whether public, private, or federally operated, openly attempt to inculcate the middle-class premise that individuals can change themselves if they really desire to do so. This is an attitude not necessarily shared by their pupils, no matter how well integrated they may be from the standpoint of their own culture. The report by Wax (29) describes the view of the "country" Indian as follows:

> No one "improves" or "betters" himself in the Western sense; if one man or woman is respected more than another, it is because he has "acted" more friendly, generous, considerate, and modest. . . . The essence of what one is does not change through the course of one's life.

Leighton and Kluckhohn (18) described an orientation with similar consequences for the Navajo: "The Navajo tendency . . . is to depend as much upon magical acts and precautions as upon personal ability and effort for both security and success."

Krush and his colleagues (16, 17) administered both the Min-

Man/Nature, Time, and Activity. The findings can be summarized as follows: the academic and dormitory staffs responded in a manner consistent with middle-class American orientations. The students, however, deviated from this norm in a number of respects, with some sex differences occurring.

Boys tended to reach a middle position between girls and the middle-class norms. For example, their preference for Present time was not significantly greater (statistically) than their preference for Future time, though both were significantly more preferred than Past time. This was in contrast to girls, who favored Present time. Both Indian boys and girls deviated from middle-class norms in the Relational category, preferring Collateral activities (nonsignificantly) to Individual and preferring both significantly more than Lineal.

Validation of Krush's last point concerning superficiality of responses is admittedly difficult. It is hypothesized, however, because it seems to be an obvious interpretation of children's behavior in face-to-face situations: that is, they attempt to match their values to the values of the people with whom they are in contact. This resembles the behavior of socially deprived children described by Zigler (31).

This suggestion is certainly consistent with our experience. The students monitor the examiner rather than themselves for cues regarding the adequacy of their responses. It is not as if the student is directly trying to please the authority figure per se, though this may be true frequently, but rather that there is no confidence in the quality of the performance or the capacity of the performer to evaluate his or her own performance.

Some findings illustrating the differing attitudes and values concerning schooling and self come from a preliminary analysis of data collected by one of us (26). Ninth grade boys in the Gallup Junior High School in Gallup, New Mexico, were given a modified version of the Mooney Problem Check List. Three ethnic groups, Spanish-American, Anglo, and Navajo, were compared with respect to their responses to the sixty-one-item questionnaire of potential problems or areas of personal concern.

The Navajo boys could be distinguished from the other two

groups by items which dealt with achievement, interest in present school, and disinterest in the current social scene. For example, Navajo students more frequently checked items such as: "I get too low grades. I want to go to school some other place. I am not good looking." and checked less frequently: "I often feel left out of things. I am not often chosen as a leader." Paxton (22) reported the same kind of results from a Q-sort by students also enrolled in an Indian boarding school.

Acculturation

One factor that would seem to require consideration in examining the behavior of Indian youth is acculturation. Unequivocal studies of this variable are surprisingly difficult to design and carry out. A preliminary study of students selected by the staff of the Albuquerque Indian School as representing high, average, and low levels of adjustment, defined by predicted degree of success in future life activities, showed that students in the best adjusted group seemed to be characterized by strong motivations either toward or away from reservation life. There were two notable examples. In one girl, whose parents enjoyed some social status in the home community on the reservation, the motivation was to attain a reasonable level of education and to return to that area to take her place as a leader armed with additional skills. In the other instance, the girl was highly motivated for an education in order to guarantee that she would not have to return to the reservation but could maintain herself in a larger community and even marry an Indian of another tribe.

Roessell (23) noted that students whose attitudes and beliefs show either a high level of traditionalism or a high level of acculturation achieve at the highest levels in school; those in a culturally intermediate position suffer academically by comparison.

Graves (11) analyzed the drinking behavior of ethnic groups in a single southwestern community. Comparing Indian and Spanish groups matched both for acculturation (number of contacts with people of other groups) and economic access (the fit between their education and employment level), he found that Indians with low levels of acculturation and either high or low access to appropriate employment showed a higher level of drinking behavior than Spanish in the same categories. Both groups were similar when there was a high degree of acculturation and high access (little drinking) and high acculturation and low access (much drinking).

Graves attributed the difference to the stability factor of community life for the low-acculturation Spanish in terms of more intact marriages and high church attendance. This contrasts with the "city" Indian who is less likely, according to the Graves analysis, to have such regulatory influences (or counterpressures) against deviant drinking behavior. Ferguson (10) makes a similar point in attempting to explain drinking behavior among Navajo in the Gallup area. This theory is further supported by the lack of participation among Indians in non-Indian community life and has been documented elsewhere (1, 14, 29).

The exact etiology for the lack of adequate identity in early adolescence is not known. However, there is a growing body of evidence to suggest that self-image, industry, and self-control — important variables in academic achievement — are often lacking in Indians as well as youngsters of other minority groups (2).

CONCLUSIONS

From the foregoing one might postulate that the culture shock of having to renounce, with the beginning of school, much of what has been learned before school undoes the pattern of trust and personal worth developed up to that time. With traditions crumbling, it is even possible to suggest that this pattern might not be well developed. The identities of the children are weakened, and the possibility of diminished initiative is presented, as well as a subsequent breakdown of adequate self-image and competence with which to manifest subsequent achieving behavior.

All of this, coupled with a reality-based lack of economic

access, leads to the sense of hopelessness, reported to be accompanied at times by frustration. Parker (21) has described this in his paper comparing the thematic responses of young people in two Alaskan villages differing greatly in acculturation: "A devalued ethnic self-image and hostility toward Western society emerge from a situation where individuals set new goals which they then perceive cannot be reached."

A recurrent theme voiced by school administrators and teachers in many settings is that all students must be treated the same. School functioning is usually expressed by rules or policies such that behavior which conflicts with these is viewed not as a coping or reactive device, whether appropriate or inappropriate, but as a legal transgression either willfully carried out or done in ignorance. As a consequence, such behavior is handled as though it were an additional problem in education and/or one of discipline.

For example, the student who drinks is educated further about the evils of drink and is assigned extra work so that he will remember and not repeat the offense. There is a minimal attempt to explore the motivation for drinking (or other behaviors), as has been suggested by Ferguson, Levy, and MacGregor (10, 19, 20). Rather, the admonition is to avoid repeating the behavior in the school setting. The situation is exacerbated in a boarding school, where the school setting is a full-time situation and the repressive air (nonrepetition of offense) is carried right through the full day, week, and month.

The premise is that all students are in attendance for the purpose of obtaining an education, though most of the staff privately agree that most are there for other reasons. One of us surveyed students as they emerged from buses at the beginning of the school year (12), and the statement which most clearly indicated a preference for this or any school was made by one student whose father had attended this school and wanted her to do as well.

Interestingly, the project personnel have yet to see an instance of a student dropped for academic reasons; students are sent home for reasons associated with their behavior. Yet with added funds and resources, the bulk of attention has gone into cultural enrichment and tutoring in academic subjects. The combination of this with pressure to minimize dropouts places the staff in a dilemma which is sometimes resolved only by the student's demonstration of his inability to adjust to the school. The school (most schools) tries to treat all the students the same: all students are supposed to behave the same.

Without having definite answers to offer, we would suggest that a case has been made that Indian and other minority groups suffer from identity problems in adolescence which manifest themselves in feelings of low self-worth, alienation, helplessness, etc. Unfortunately, at least for the present, such feelings are not completely at variance with educational and economic reality and this can only serve to support them.

As Bryde (3) suggests:

> Education in harmonizing the Indian and non-Indian value systems must be offered *prior* to the offering of the non-Indian technical, vocational, and liberal education; otherwise these programs (and this could seem to include the war on poverty for Indians) are largely thwarted because of the value conflict.

REFERENCES

1. Benham, W. J., Jr. Characteristics of Programs in Public Schools Serving Students from Reservations in Five Western States. Unpublished doctoral dissertation, University of Oklahoma, 1965.
2. Bloom, B. S., Davis, A., and Hess, R. *Compensatory Education for Cultural Deprivation.* New York: Holt, Rinehart & Winston, 1965.
3. Bryde, J. F. Indian Education and Mental Health. Paper read at a meeting of the Association on American Indian Affairs. New York, New York, November 14-15, 1966.
4. Cobb, J. C., ed. *Emotional Problems of the Indian Students in Boarding Schools and Related Public Schools.* Workshop Proceedings. Albuquerque, 1960.
5. Coombs, L. M., Kron, R. E., Collister, E. G., and Anderson, K. E. *The Indian Child Goes to School.* Washington, D.C.: Bureau of Indian Affairs, 1958.
6. Dennis, W. *The Hopi Child.* New York: John Wiley & Sons, 1940.
7. Dick, W. W., ed. *Report of the Annual Conference of the Co-Ordinating Council for Research in Indian Education.* Phoenix: Arizona State Department of Public Instruction, 1962.

8. Dozier, E. P. *The Hopi-Tewa of Arizona.* Berkeley: University of California Press, 1954.

9. Erikson, E. H. *Childhood and Society.* 2nd ed. New York: W. W. Norton, 1963.

10. Ferguson, F. N. The Peer Group and Navajo Problem Drinking. Paper read at the first annual meeting of the Southern Anthropological Society, New Orleans, 1966.

11. Graves, T. D. Acculturation, Access and Alcohol in a Tri-ethnic Community. *American Anthropologist,* 1967, 69:306-321.

12. Harrover, M. J. Reasons Given for Attending a Federal Boarding School for Indians. Unpublished paper.

13. Homme, L. E. *A System for Teaching English Literacy to Preschool Indian Children.* Pittsburgh: Westinghouse Research Laboratories, 1965.

14. Kelly, R. E., and Cramer, J. O. *American Acculturation in Two Northern Arizona Communities.* Flagstaff: Northern Arizona University Department of Rehabilitation, 1966.

15. Kerekhoff, A. C. Anomie and Achievement Motivation: A Study of Personality Development Within Cultural Disorganization. *Social Forces,* 1959, 37:196-202.

16. Krush, T. P. *Fourth and Fifth Annual Reports of the Mental Health Clinic at the PHS Indian School Health Center.* Flandreau Indian Vocational High School, June, 1961.

17. Kruch, T. P., Sindell, P. S., and Nelle, J. Some Thoughts on the Formation of Personality Disorder: Study of an Indian Boarding School Population. *American Journal of Psychiatry,* 1966, 122, 866-875.

18. Leighton, D., and Kluckhohn. *Children of the People.* Cambridge: Harvard University Press, 1957.

19. Levy, J. E. Navajo Attitudes Toward Mental Illness and Mental Retardation, n.d.

20. MacGregor, G. *Warriors Without Weapons.* Chicago: University of Chicago Press, 1946.

21. Parker, S. Ethnic Identity and Acculturation in Two Eskimo Villages. *American Anthropologist,* 1964, 66:325-340.

22. Paxton, S. G. *A Study of the Composite Self-Concept of the Southwestern Indian Adolescent.* Washington, D.C.: Bureau of Indian Affairs, 1966.

23. Roessell, R. Personal Communication, 1964.

24. Rosenberg, S. Achievement Test Score Results for Albuquerque Indian School Regular Program, 1965.

25. Saslow, H. C. Goodenough Draw-A-Man Test Changes in a Group of Indian Children Enrolled in a Project Head Start Program. Unpublished manuscript, 1966.

26. Saslow, H. L. Problem Check-List Responses of Adolescents in Three Ethnic Groups. Paper read at the Rocky Mountain Psychological

Association, Albuquerque, 1966.
27. Spilka, B. The Sioux Indian School Child: A Tentative Perspective for Education, 1966.
28. Spilka, B., and Bryde, J. F. Alienation and Achievement Among Oglala Sioux Secondary Students, 1966.
29. Wax, M. L., Wax, R. H., and Dumont, R. V., Jr. Formal Education in an American Indian Community. *Social Problems,* 1964, 11. Special Supplement.
30. Wolff, M., and Stein, A. Six Months Later: *A Comparison of Children Who Had Head Start, Summer, 1965, with Their Classmates in Kindergarten.* New York: Yeshiva University, Ferkauf Graduate School, 1966.
31. Zigler, E. Familial Mental Retardation: A Continuing Dilemma. *Science,* 1967, 155:292-298.
32. Zintz, M. V. *The Indian Research Study, Final Report.* Albuquerque: University of New Mexico, College of Education, 1960.

Chapter 22

FAMILY BEHAVIOR OF
URBAN AMERICAN INDIANS*

JOHN G. RED HORSE, RONALD LEWIS
MARVIN FEIT, AND JAMES DECKER

ECOLOGICAL formulas are becoming increasingly popular as protocols for human service models. This trend represents a certain irony in the context of service provision to minority families. The function of American Indian families, for example, has long been disabled by social service personnel who appear insensitive to unique Indian family cultural and structural needs. Removal of children from American Indian families following a variety of social diagnoses is approaching epidemic proportion. William Byler cites that 25 to 35 percent of American Indian children are raised outside their natural family network.[1] If ecological standards are applied, American Indian families appear qualified for endangered species status.

This article examines characteristics unique to American Indian families and attempts to relate these to developing human ecology models in casework. Attention is directed toward extended family networks which represent the interactive field in which caseworkers should conduct transactions.

Irving M. Levine's social conservation model serves as a theoretical orientation. This model assumes that individual mental health is linked to a sense of selfhood which is accomplished through adherence to an historical culture and is transmitted principally through family socialization.[2] Family structure and process, therefore, represent the cornerstone for individual behavior, cultural acquisition, and mental health.

*From John G. Red Horse, Ronald L. Lewis, Marvin Feit, and James Decker, Family Behavior of Urban American Indians, *Social Casework*, 59:67-72, 1978. Copyright 1978 by the Family Service Association of America. Reprinted by permission.

FAMILY STRUCTURE AND CULTURAL BEHAVIOR

American Indian family networks assume a structure which is radically different from other extended family units in Western society. The accepted structural boundary of the European model, for example, is the household. Thus, an extended family is defined as three generations within a single household. American Indian family networks, however, are structurally open and assume a village-type characteristic. Their extension is inclusive of several households representing significant relatives along both vertical and horizontal lines.

Network structure influences individual behavior patterns because family transactions occur within a community milieu. This is important for professionals to understand so that mislabeling may be avoided. Normal behavioral transactions within the network relational field, for example, may appear bizarre to an outside observer.

Case Illustration

The following case illustration provides a typical example of this point.[3]

> A young probationer was under court supervision and had strict orders to remain with responsible adults. His counselor became concerned because the youth appeared to ignore this order. The client moved around frequently and, according to the counselor, stayed overnight with several different young women. The counselor presented this case at a formal staff meeting, and fellow professionals stated their suspicion that the client was either a pusher or a pimp. The frustrating element to the counselor was that the young women knew each other and appeared to enjoy each other's company. Moreover, they were not ashamed to be seen together in public with the client. This behavior prompted the counselor to initiate violation proceedings.

A Minneapolis American Indian professional came upon the case quite by accident. He knew the boy's family well and requested a delay in court proceedings to allow time for a more thorough investigation. It was discovered that the young women were all first cousins to the client. He had not been frivolously "staying overnight with them"; he had been staying with different units of his family. Each female was as a sister. Moreover, each family unit had a responsible and obligated adult available to supervise and to care for the client.

A revocation order in this case would have caused irreparable alienation between the family and human service professionals. The casework decision would have inappropriately punished the youth as well as several members of his family for simply conducting normal family behavior. Moreover, its impact would affect people far beyond the presenting client and those members of his family who were directly responsible for his care. The young man had a characteristically large Indian family network consisting of over 200 people and spanning three generations.

Structural characteristics of American Indian family networks confront human service professionals with judgmental issues beyond that of labeling. Extended family often serves as a major instrument of accountability. Standards and expectations are established which maintain group solidarity through enforcement of values.

Single-parent and single-adult households do appear in American Indian communities. Professionals bound by nuclear family parameters point to this fact in planning service resources. Consequently, they are reluctant to use legitimate aunts, uncles, cousins, and grandparents as alternate or supportive service care givers.

Other Case Illustrations

Nancy, for example, was an eighteen-year-old mother identified as mentally retarded and epileptic by the department of welfare officials. Although retardation was subsequently disproved, the department assumed control and custody of Nancy's infant child. Nancy's parents insisted that the family network was available for assistance, if necessary. The welfare staff, however, considered this offer untenable. The grandparents were deemed senile and unable to care for an infant. They were in their early fifties. The staff ignored the fact that the grandparents had just finished caring for three other young and active grandchildren without dependence on institutional social intervention. Moreover, these children appeared to be well-adjusted. The officials simply insisted in this case that standard placement procedures be followed; a foster home was obtained for Nancy's child.

The placement orders were eventually overruled in Nancy's case, but not without heroic legal intervention. It is unfortunate that such adversary strategies are necessary to prove competencies of natural family networks. Often, as the following case illustrates, family competency and responsibility evolve as a normal process of network accountability.

Anita was the elder within the family. She was a direct descendent of the most renowned chief of her band and enjoyed high status. She lived alone in a trailer. Shortly after her seventieth birthday, she became ill and unable to care either for herself or to perform routine household chores. A social worker arranged for Anita's admission to a rest home.

The family accepted this plan of intervention without comment. Subsequently, however, the situation changed. Anita received regular visits, but these did not satisfy family needs. Anita became lonely for home and the family became lonely for her. A ritual feast was held which Anita attended. Family concerns regarding her absence were expressed and a decision was made that she should remain at home.

The family developed its own helping plan. Each member was given a scheduled time period to provide homemaker services for Anita. Through this shift system, the family network assumed service responsibility. In this case, the family in the immediate vicinity consisted of ten households. Service providers ranged from thirteen-year-old grandchildren to fifty-year-old children.

Family Network Hierarchy

American Indian family network behavior also contributes to a very conservative cultural pattern. A vigorous network is both retained and developed for transmission of cultural attributes. Continually reinforced and enduring relational roles serve to illustrate this behavior.

Grandparents retain official and symbolic leadership in family communities. Both are active processes sanctioned by the children and their parents. Official leadership is characterized by a close proximity of grandparents to family. It is witnessed through the behavior of children who actively seek daily contact with grandparents and by grandparents who monitor parental behavior. In this milieu, grandparents have an official voice in child-rearing methods, and parents seldom overrule corrective measures from their elders. Symbolic leadership is characterized by an incorporation of unrelated elders into the family. This prevails during an absence of a natural grandparent, but it is not necessarily limited to, or dependent on, such an absence. It is witnessed through the behavior of children and parents who select and virtually adopt a grandparent. In this milieu, younger people are seeking social acceptance from an older member of the community. Symbolic grandparents will not invoke strong child-rearing sanctions. Because their acceptance is sought, their norm-setting standards are seldom ignored.

THREE DISTINCT FAMILY PATTERNS

Extended family networks represent a universal pattern among American Indian nations. Data from one American Indian family service program, however, point to significant variability among the networks. Specific family characteristics, therefore, serve as critical information in the development of methodological guidelines for casework practice.

Three distinct family life-style patterns serve for initial identification: (1) a traditional group which overtly adheres to culturally defined styles of living, (2) a nontraditional, bicultural group which appears to have adopted many aspects of non-American Indian styles of living, and (3) a pantraditional group which overtly struggles to redefine and reconfirm previously lost cultural styles of living.[4] Selected behavior variables for each pattern appear in Table 22-I.

Many observers of American Indian life tend to hold biases concerning which pattern is most legitimate or functional in contemporary American society. This judgmental behavior represents a luxury that caseworkers must avoid, because each pattern is legitimate within its own relational field and contributes to a family sense of selfhood.

Many observers assume that different family life-style patterns point to an ongoing erosion of cultural values. Studies suggest, however, that American Indian core values are retained and remain as a constant, regardless of family life-style patterns.[5] Pattern variables, therefore, do not represent valid criteria for measuring "Indian-ness."

The importance of family life-style patterns to human service professionals is that each pattern represents a different interactive field, that is, a different environmental context for social casework. As would be expected, family responses to intervention vary. Traditional families, for example, cannot relate to professionals and prefer to ignore mainstream social methodologies. Generally, these families are very courteous to strangers. They will politely listen to professionals, but seldom respond to any social prescriptions which depart from customary practice.

Conversely, bicultural families are able to relate to professional care givers. They are able to accept and cope with contemporary social prescriptions. Pantraditional families denounce professionals and mainstream social methodologies. They are engaged in attempting to recapture and redefine cultural methodologies.[6]

FAMILY NETWORK DYNAMICS

Diverse family network interlockings have emerged over time as a result of geographic movements and intertribal marriages, and these complexities warrant scholarly investigation. Of critical significance to this discussion, however, is the fact that American Indian relational values have remained intact through the years: Extended family networks remain as a con-

TABLE 22-I

SOME SELECTED VARIABLES OF BEHAVIOR ACCORDING TO FAMILY LIFESTYLE — PATTERNS AMONG MINNEAPOLIS URBAN CHIPPEWAS

Variable of Behavior	Family Life-style Pattern		
	Traditional	Bicultural	Pan Traditional
Language	Ojibway constitutes conversational language of parents and grandparents. Children are bilingual and able to transact family affairs following Indian language.	English constitutes conversational language by parents, grandparents, and children. Grandparents are usually bilingual. Some Indian language is recaptured through formal classes.	Either English or Ojibway constitutes conversational language of parents, grandparents, and children. Indian language is recaptured through formal academic classes.
Religion	Midewiwin remains as the belief system. It retains the characteristics of a very closed system, following family networks.	Anglo belief system prevails; is generally, but not exclusively, Catholicism. Some all-Indian congregations exist with culturally adapted canons.	A modified Indian belief system mixing several traditional forms; i.e. Midewiwin, Native American Church, etc. Unlike closed structure of traditionalists proselytizing strategies are employed.
Family relational field	Extended network	Extended network	Extended network
Social engagement	Some acceptance of dominant society's activities; i.e. bowling, etc. Cultural activities such as feasts, religion and pow wows prevail and take precedence over all others.	Dominant society's activities prevail i.e. bowling, baseball, golf. Relate to non-Indians well. Church activities remain of interest but not necessarily enacted through behavior, e.g. will sit and watch at pow wows and read about religion. Very active in Indian meetings and politics.	Openly eschew activities of dominant society Cultural activities prevail. Those who are not expert try to recapture singing and dancing skills.

stant regardless of family life-style patterns.

Network behavior patterns clearly point to the emergence of a distinct, closed American Indian community. Outsiders, including representatives of agencies providing mandated services, do not gain entrance easily. This attitude has influenced the development of health and welfare services. Ninety percent of the American Indians in Minneapolis responding to questions relating to health needs behavior, for example, indicated a preference for receiving services from American Indian workers.[7] This preference is clearly demonstrated by American Indian clients in the St. Paul-Minneapolis "Twin Cities" metropolitan area of Minnesota who rely upon American Indian service agencies. This contrasts with non-Indian health programs located in the same community, which are continuously involved in strategies to recruit American Indian clients and are unable to serve a representative number.[8]

Outside observers often cite this network behavior as fraught with dangers, because many American Indian service providers are not professionally trained. American Indians, however, have a commendable history in medicine and in community mental health. American Indian families, for example, traditionally organize supportive networks for children through a naming ceremony.[9] This ceremony actually reconfirms the responsibilities of a natural network, that is, aunts, uncles, and cousins. The family emerges as a protective social fabric to provide for the health and welfare of the children. Namesakes provide what professionals define as "substitute services" if parents become incapacitated. Unlike similar religions and cultural rituals, namesakes become the same as parents in the network structure.

American Indian programs in the "Twin Cities" metropolitan area formally incorporate aspects of ethnoscience, such as naming ceremonies, into care-giving strategies. Traditional feasts represent a common activity. Ritual feasts are held according to customary standards, for example, at the seasons' changes or at naming ceremonies. Preventive feasts are conducted to bring a family together whenever danger is imminent. Celebrative feasts are held during special occasions, such

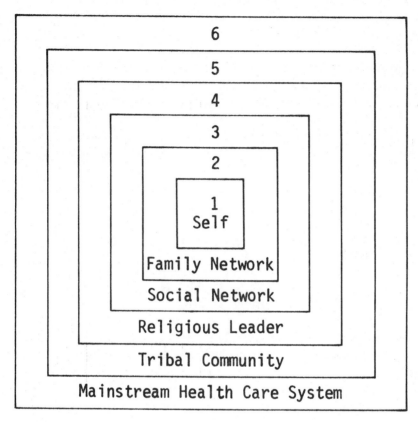

1. **Individual**
2. **Goes to immediate family first**
3. **Goes to extended family (cousins, aunts, uncles) -- social network**
4. **Goes to religious leader**
5. **Goes to tribal council**
6. **Finally goes to formalized health care system**

Figure 22-1. Individual seeking aid — numbered according to order of significance and sequential path followed by urban Indians seeking help.

as Mother's Day observances. American Indian people, of course, feel comfortable in these surroundings. Moreover, they are secure in developing relationships with American Indian service providers who attend the feasts.

Ronald Lewis developed an interesting schematic through a tracking of Indian health behavior in Milwaukee, Wisconsin.[10] Figure 22-1 identifies various resource levels and a sequence of behavior that emerged from his investigation. It confirms network behavior. Its prevailing characteristic is that the mainstream health care system is used only after network resources are exhausted.

CONCLUSION

The objective of this article has been to identify important attributes of American Indian family network structure and cultural behavior and to inform professionals about the importance of culture as a variable in human services, especially as it affects understanding within an interactive field.

Because any health care is dependent upon client utilization, an understanding of American Indian network behavior appears critical to policy development and service planning efforts.

Using Levine's social conservation model, two critical human ecology imperatives emerge: (1) to identify traditional, longstanding cultural attributes, which have contributed to family cohesiveness and individual mental health, and (2) to develop human service systems which reaffirm a sense of family purpose.

An exigency specific to American Indians is that the cultural and structural integrity of extended family networks be revitalized and be supported. The authors believe that the adoption of a social conservation model by the human services would greatly improve service efficiency and, at the same time, vigorously enrich the quality of life of a currently alienated and underserved client population.

REFERENCES

1. William Byler, The Destruction of American Indian Families, in Steve Unger, ed., *The Destruction of American Indian Families*, New York: Association on American Indian Affairs, 1977, 1.

2. Irving M. Levine, Ethnicity and Mental Health: A Social Conservation Approach. Paper presented at the White House Conference on Ethnicity and Mental Health, Washington D.C., June 1976.

3. This case illustration and all subsequent cases are drawn from the files of Ah-be-no-gee, an innovative demonstration program in child abuse and neglect. Ah-be-no-gee is located in Minneapolis, Minnesota, and funded by the National Center for Child Abuse and Neglect, Office of Child Development, U.S. Department of Health, Education, and Welfare.

4. Data on family patterns were drawn from Ah-be-no-gee.

5. See, for example, A. Irving Hallowell, Objibway Personality and Acculturation, in Paul Bohannan and Fred Plog, eds., *Beyond the Frontier*, New York: The Natural History Press, 1967; Thaddeus P. Krush, John W. Bjork, Peter S. Sindell, and Joanna Nelle, Some Thoughts on the Formation of Personality Disorder: Study of an Indian Boarding School Population, in *Hearings Before the Special Subcommittee on Indian Education of the Committee on Labor and Public Welfare, United States Senate — Part 5*, Washington, D.C.: U.S. Government Printing Office, 1969; and Native American Research Group, *Native American Families in the City*, San Francisco: Institute for Scientific Analysis, 1975.

6. Caution must be exercised in appraising the issues of "coping ability" and "openness to mainstream social methodologies." Staff at Ah-be-no-gee, for example, have witnessed an overwhelming preference by American Indians for self-determination and self-governed programs, regardless of differences in family life-style patterns.

7. Willy DeGeyndt, Health Behavior and Health Needs in Urban Indians in Minneapolis, *Health Service Reports*, 1973, 88:360-366.

8. John G. Red Horse and Marvin Feit, Urban Native American Preventive Health Care. Paper presented at the American Public Health Association Meeting, Miami Beach, Florida, October 18-22, 1976.

9. Frances Densmore, *Chippewa Customs*, Minneapolis: Ross & Haines, 1970.

10. Ronald Lewis. But We Have Been Helping Indians for a Long Time..., April 1977. Unpublished research.

Chapter 23

CULTURALLY ORIENTED INSTRUCTION FOR NATIVE AMERICAN STUDENTS*

JAMES MARK MAHAN AND MARY KATHRYN CRIGER

TYPICAL recommendations to pre-service and beginning teachers from supervisors and experienced teachers often include being firm and consistent with discipline, generous with positive reinforcement, stimulating higher order questions, using show and tell activities and extending the school into the community.

But are these supervisory guidelines appropriate for all teachers in all cultural settings? For educators who opt to serve on an Indian reservation these concerns may be secondary or even dysfunctional. Young teachers in Native American communities have to acquaint themselves with a new set of values which should influence their professional behavior. They have to learn as much as possible of the Indian ways so that they can better understand their students and avoid blatant violation of any social norm. Following are some typical guidelines generated by beginning teachers of Native American youth:

A teacher should read about and know in which seasons certain legends and animals can be talked about, and respect any taboo to avoid unnecessary confusion and fear in the classroom. Local supervisory personnel should help teachers discover and understand these cultural conditions and priorities.

The teacher must be very careful not to praise a child highly in class. Light reinforcement is better. Praise should be given in written form, e.g. at the top of a paper, or when nesota Multiphasic Personality Inventory and the California Psychological Inventory to students at the Flandreau Indian Vocational High School. In general, the results paralleled those reviewed above. In discussing their findings, these authors utilized the concept of "psychosocial nomadism." This notion has much in common with alienation. It refers to the adjustment tendencies of young persons who move from one setting to another, thus necessitating the development of new sets of interpersonal relationships. Krush and associates postulated that such people prefer to take the lines of least resistance and tend to back off and avoid stressful situations.

Our own experience confirms the relative high frequency among Indians of shifting from one school to another. This occurs not only by the whim of the student but also upon the recommendation of school personnel. In the latter instance, the recommendation is prompted by a belief that a different setting may have a salutary effect upon behavior. Academic performance may have little bearing upon such a decision.

This is in keeping with another observation of Krush and his associates (16) which has other implications as well. In the time span of 1959-61, 77 percent of the dropouts from that school were included in the category of "poor adjustment to school." This represented such items as failure to return from leave, being away without leave, homesickness, lack of interest, parent's request, etc.

Shifting Standards and Superficiality of Response

Krush and his group (16, 17) presented two additional problems as being relevant for mental conflicts among the students they studied: shifting standards and superficiality of response (the "chameleon" effect). They suggested that there are distinct variations in the value orientations of the students, their relatives, teachers, dormitory personnel, and the administrative staff.

Students and staff at the Flandreau School were given the Kluckhohn Value Orientation Scale. This is a technique which measures value orientation in four dimensions: Relational, the student is alone or at least out of earshot of other students.

Don't assume that the students understand you verbally. Demonstrate by bodily and visual expressions. Allow the students to learn by observation of actions.

Teachers must be careful in the materials they choose. If the only thing available is a basal text, you must be careful to explain things that are not familiar. Hope that you are lucky and have an instructional supervisor with enough cultural knowledge to stock up the curriculum center with appropriate extra learning materials.

Do not expect the children to respond consistently to direct questions. They like to avoid self-centeredness and they may not like numerous questions.

From this small sampling it is obvious that non-Indian teachers serving in Native American settings have many things to contend with in addition to the usual problems of discipline, lesson planning, organization, or allotment of time. Young teachers may indeed be treading on dangerous ground, for who knows what injuries Native American children may suffer at the hands of an inexperienced teacher who does not understand their needs, their language, their gestures, their home life, or the sources of their joy and satisfaction? Obviously, it requires very perceptive and very conscientious young men and women to attempt to teach children of a culture different from their own. They must be willing to work diligently to learn about the culture if they are to be good teachers of its youth. Similarly, all who are responsible for supervising young teachers in these settings must also be continuing students of the local culture and willing to help orient the newcomers to the culture.

PLACEMENT OF NON-INDIAN
TEACHERS ON RESERVATIONS

For the past five years, the Division of Teacher Education at Indiana University has been preparing and placing a few selected, committed student teachers on Indian reservations in the southwest. These student teacher volunteers have been enrolled not only from the Indiana University student body but from other institutions as far away as Maryland, Massachusetts, Oregon, and West Virginia. They are selected on the basis of their interest in and willingness to learn about the Indian culture, their maturity, academic performance, and professional dedication to Indian students. Before arrival on-site the student teachers engage in an intensive preparation program designed to enhance their knowledge of Native American cultures. Native American instructional consultants have major roles in the preparation. Trainees are expected to learn as much as possible about the people, their customs, their language, their institutions, and so on.

Student teaching assignments are for seventeen weeks to allow for a period of adaptation and acceptance. While on-site the student teachers are required to reflect on the life around them and to formulate some guidelines for teaching consonant with the specific Indian culture in which they are working. It is an essential aspect of the project that student teachers serving an ethnic group other than their own have to modify their teaching behaviors/strategies to fit that group. If they are to become truly effective in-service teachers in a minority group setting, then they must continually reassess and redefine their teaching methods to work to the advantage of their students. Through once-a-semester site visits, telephone conversations, letters, and required reports, project staff members maintain direct contact with each group of student teachers and with most of the many young project graduates who are now in-service teachers in various types of schools serving Native American youth.

The following comments were taken from lists of guidelines drawn up by these young teachers as they taught/teach in Native American communities in the Southwest. Their guidelines are not meant, obviously, to be the final word on the cultural values of any specific Indian group. But they are offered as examples of the types of local modifications and considerations teachers and teacher supervisors must contemplate when serving youth of a culture different from their own.

PERCEPTIONS OF PUPIL DIFFERENCES
AND SIMILARITIES

The first impulse of many beginning teachers serving in Native American settings seems to be to say that the Indian children are not any different from children anywhere, that traditional cultural values no longer apply to them. Over a period of time however, non-Indian teachers find that the students are not as Anglicized as they may appear in first encounters. Many of the children come from very traditional families but have learned to vary their behavior with the situation. Thus, they may act one way in the classroom, another way in the dormitory, a different way on the athletic field, and still another way at home. As time passes, the beginning teachers and student teachers become more acquainted with situational variance in student behavior and are able to reconcile apparent contradictions. Many of their comments emphasize this expanded awareness:

A teacher should be aware of the culture, habits, etc., but not expect all children in a setting to do the same things or to believe the same things.

Be prepared for all types of behavior — including some which you saw back home and some which is unique.

You cannot expect to see everything you read or hear. All people are different and perceive differently and no author has described any given community with total accuracy.

Realize that students may appear "modern" in some respects but still be "traditional" in many ways.

Essentially, current and former project participants urge that while it is imperative to be as knowledgeable about the culture as possible, one should still be open-minded and not try to superimpose preconceived notions on the people. Similarly, they repeatedly stress the importance of respect for the people and their beliefs. Inexperienced teachers should be quiet and respectful, not pushy and aggressive. They must remember that they are "foreigners" in the Indian world and study, respect, and accept the beliefs of that world even if they do not fully understand them nor wish to adopt them.

TURN-ABOUT IN MINORITY STATUS

Non-Indian teachers in an Indian world also experience the phenomenon of being members of a minority group and they experience some of the subtle and not-so-subtle implications of that. There is no doubt that minority status is an illuminating experience for those who have never been in this position. They have to learn to "ignore prejudicial remarks" and to "not get upset when they call you names." One young women put it this way, "Be open to prejudices towards your own race and recall them if you ever feel prejudiced towards someone or something else." Beginning teachers learn quickly that they must earn the respect and confidence of the Indian people with whom they are working. "Don't come on too strong," "Don't be too anxious to make your students like you," "Let them move at their own pace," "Respect will come through time," "Listen to what they are saying, and think about how you must sound to them," are frequent comments. Indian students may not be receptive automatically to a new, young non-Indian teacher. That teacher will have to demonstrate in and out of class that he or she merits professional respect. Some group encounter activities and multicultural rap sessions in teacher and supervisor preparation programs are very necessary. A sound understanding (often lacking) of one's own culture and its values will also help immensely.

SPECIAL CLASSROOM CHALLENGES

What are some of the specific problems beginning teachers may encounter in the classroom? What will make the teaching of Native American youth different from the teaching of children back home? The first and most noticeable difference is in the area of language. For the majority of Native American students with whom Indiana University teachers have interacted, English is a second language. Until the time children enter school they may speak their own language exclusively.

Thus, when children enter the first grade they have to learn a new language on top of all the regular material first graders must learn. This creates innumerable problems for the Indian children, often causing them to fall behind in the conventional school curriculum. As many research studies indicate, Indian children tend to hold their own until about the fourth grade and then they begin to fall further and further behind.

Naturally, Indian children as a group are no less intelligent than any other children, but by the fourth grade language in texts begins to get more conceptual and complicated. The children encounter words and concepts which have little experiential meaning to them. What meaning can mortgage, skyscraper, escalator, or marina, have to a child who may never have been off a reservation where subsistence living often prevails and who may have no corresponding concepts in his own language? Children who can carry out the fundamental processes of arithmetic easily enough are likely to become confused when they start encountering mathematical word problems involving interest rates, insurance, supermarkets, etc. So, besides being a problem in itself, language affects every aspect of the child's curriculum, learning, and sense of identity. Young teachers in an Indian setting must learn to deal with all of this effectively. In high school classrooms where they sometimes find students substantially below the academic "norm" they must place much emphasis on making sure students understand the vocabulary and concepts before they discuss issues in any subject area. Some comments from preservice teachers are:

Teachers should work on vocabulary in a unit first, defining words that students may not know.

Teachers should spend time on explicit and precise examples of explanation — especially when talking about abstract ideas.

Constantly check the class to see if they understand the concepts within the words you are saying.

If necessary, repeat questions in a different way: give hints, etc. Translating is hard to do. Wait time is important. If you do not give students time to translate you may never get an answer. Do not talk too much or too fast. We all have to watch ourselves on this.

The list goes on and on. Teachers often discover that they must spend much, much time in developing their own materials to use for specific lessons. They cannot rely on ready-to-use programs packaged for sale in most schools. Neither must they make the mistake of correlating a student's academic ability with his intelligence. As one student teacher said, "The students may be very brilliant but not be able to express themselves in English."

Another of the major complications in the area of language is the fact that the majority of teachers of Indian youth do not know the language of the Indian people with whom they are working. Teacher preparation programs have included little opportunity to study Indian languages, and many young teachers learn the language as they teach the Native American students. This means that student teachers and beginning teachers must have the courage to become struggling learners, while fellow teachers, teacher aides, and pupils teach them vocabulary and sentence structure. While Native American languages are rarely offered in colleges and universities, English as a Second Language (ESL) courses are offered. Teachers and supervisors in Indian communities need ESL skills; such courses could be included in Master's degree programs and school system in-service offerings. To increase professional effectiveness, teachers and supervisors must seriously evaluate and upgrade their ESL knowledge, skills, and techniques.

Another major area of concern is student participation. Traditionally, Indian youths are not aggressive, competitive, or academically ambitious. They tend to remain relatively passive in the classroom. To teachers and students alike it is sometimes a challenge to generate activity and verbal replies in the classroom. Teachers have found that Indian children do not like to have attention drawn to themselves; they do not like to be put on the spot. A sample of related comments are:

> The students do not like to be the focus of attention. Avoid teaching lessons that require the individual children to stand out.
>
> Do not try to hold large group discussions or question-

answer sessions. Work with small groups or individuals.

Do not push a child for an answer. Often he/she knows it but does not want to say it.

Allow children to call out answers from the group and perhaps gradually work up to questioning individuals. Try not to ask for oral readings or reports immediately.

Use student teams as much as possible for motivation and competition.

Do not praise children in front of others directly because most prefer not to appear better than their brothers. Do it individually.

It is also advisable for teachers to become familiar with student ideas of assistance and sharing which are often related to basic cultural values. Some student teachers have noted:

Very few try to outdo the others. Most prefer to remain equal in status.

The students tend not to compete against each other in class as much as Anglos do. After all, isn't the basic goal of education just to learn?

Often I allow my students to help each other on practice exercises. This seems to take some of the pressure off.

The teacher must find a way to motivate the students and use of noncompetitive sub-group methods is often effective.

CULTURAL AND GEOGRAPHICAL FORCES

Other problems are associated with the high rate of absenteeism among Indian students. The Indian groups with whom Indiana University has worked tend not to place a very high value on Anglo-structured schooling. Students may leave school often — simply for long weekends at home, to attend ceremonials, or to help with work at home. Teachers have to learn to understand and cope with student absenteeism:

Because of spotty attendance by some students, the teachers must make a definite attempt to help them make up work missed. You cannot hold absences against a student. If you do he or she will probably quit coming altogether. Be glad that they care enough to come at all.

Teachers should not be discouraged by the absenteeism of the students; many times parents take children out of school for several days for culturally relevant ceremonial occasions.

Be prepared to review often. Give make-up tests, etc.

Don't put your hopes in structured learning sets and prerequisite exercises that must be mastered in an unbroken sequence. Plan how and when you will reteach each unit and have extra sets of materials on file for "make-up."

Try not to be upset when children return late from weekends.

The family I stayed with thought the schoolwork their kids were doing was ridiculous. They let them stay home whenever they wanted to as long as they maintain that more useful learning occurs at home.

Traditionally, Native Americans do not like to operate on a strict time schedule. Some Indian students remain unconcerned about time and this can create problems for teachers regarding assignments:

I try to stick to short-term assignments. However, some long-term assignments and deadlines are necessary because students must learn to cope with the values of the outside world too.

It would be more effective to penalize students for what they have not accomplished assignment-wise than to penalize them for not doing it when you ask.

Children may have trouble switching quickly from the Indian concept of time to the Anglo concept. Make loose schedules and talk about why we need schedules in school.

Many Indian children attend school in a dormitory situation. They live too far from school and/or the roads are often too impassable for them to commute to school daily. Thus, they stay in dormitories during the week to attend school and are usually free to return home on weekends. Dormitory life, especially for small children, cannot replace the warmth and happiness of being a part of the family circle. Many student teachers have tried to ease the feelings of alienation which children may experience by getting involved with them in outside activities and by visiting in the dorms. The children appreciate genuine interest and affection. Many teachers also emphasize the importance of understanding and talking about the students' home life:

> To the students it means a lot if you can speak with them about their homes and weekends there.
>
> Understanding what goes on at home is beneficial and necessary.
>
> Talk about home life, work they do, games they play, etc.
>
> It is important for teachers to learn about activities that take place in the children's homes and try to work them into teaching and counseling. I think this shows the students you really care about them.

Non-Indian teachers in an Indian setting must also take care that they observe the Indian customs as much as possible and try to do nothing in the classroom which would confuse or alienate the children and/or their parents. This has many implications. Since many Indian groups are in transition themselves, what may be offensive to one person may be perfectly acceptable to another. But, in the long run, it seems best for the teacher to be aware of the tribal traditions and customs and to try to avoid violating them. Customs and taboos vary, of course, from one tribe to another; but the following are the kinds of things which teachers should consider:

> It is a tradition not to ask someone his name directly. In order to make a student more comfortable I should learn his name from a friend.
>
> Don't be too casual and don't take things for granted. Inquire before bringing any animals into the classroom. Some animals are not to be touched or looked upon for various reasons.
>
> Some of the people believe in reincarnation. All forms of life are to be treated with respect.
>
> Death is not a subject to be discussed in the classroom.
>
> Do not attempt to plant seeds in the classroom as a science project ... the people of this community believe that the

earth provides enough room for growing things.

When preparing foods in the classroom you should find out the proper way in their culture to prepare and serve them in order to avoid scaring some of the children.

The teacher should not offer the children strings to play with or introduce any activities with strings during the season when string games are not to be played.

Family ties are very strong and the children call their cousins brothers and sisters and this tie is as strong as true sibling ties in the Anglo culture. Respect this custom and do not tell them they are not brothers and sisters.

TOWARD CULTURALLY ORIENTED INSTRUCTION

We have tried in this article to emphasize that anyone attempting to teach children of another culture should be as fully aware as possible of the language, customs, traditions, and taboos of that culture so that he or she can avoid classroom and community misunderstandings and can become an effective teacher. The teacher must not try to force his or her beliefs on the children but should try to teach the children within the richness of their own culture. Hopefully, teacher preparation begins anew for a teacher who accepts a teaching position in an Indian community. Teachers who acknowledge the need to study a Native American culture will welcome assistance from instructional supervisors who have made it their goal to understand, appreciate, and respect that culture and to incorporate it into the school's curriculum.

Chapter 24

COUNSELING THE
AMERICAN INDIAN CHILD*

GERALDINE YOUNGMAN AND MARGARET SADONGEI

"THE Indians are coming!" Or so it might
be said by those who live in large metropolitan areas. The
Indians are moving to the urban areas of the country and are
sitting in the classrooms from kindergarten through college.
Not all have descriptive last names. There are Browns, Smiths,
Gutierrizes, and Johnsons, and they come in various sizes and
colors. They come from various tribes — Apache, Pima, Sioux,
Hopi, Navajo, Kiowa, Papago, and Pueblo. There are approximately 400 recognized tribes in the United States. Some
children are bilingual and, depending on tribal background,
some speak only English. Contrary to popular belief, there are
many different tribal languages. This is why sign language was
developed and is still used by the older members of the various
tribes, particularly the Plains Indians.

Approximately 400,000 Indians are under twenty-one years of
age today. Of these, 75 to 80 percent will obtain their education
on reservations or in the federal boarding schools off reservations. To meet that need, many school systems can be found on
one reservation. There are schools operated by the tribe, by
churches, by public school districts, or by the Bureau of Indian
Affairs. Five percent receive their education from both areas
because of moving from reservations to urban areas and back.
Another 5 percent who are handicapped, deaf, or blind receive
their education through special institutions.

It is now shown that 10 percent of school-age Indian children
are born and reared in cities. These children have never lived

*From Geraldine Youngman and Margaret Sadongei, Counseling the American Indian
Child, *Elementary School Guidance and Counseling*, 8:272-277, 1974. Copyright 1974
by the American Personnel and Guidance Association. Reprinted by permission.

on a reservation but they too bring their cultural differences to the school systems, where many counselors are not fully aware of their needs. Many times it is assumed that the urban influence has made the Indian child like all other urban children, but in reality they tend to have stronger ties to their own tribe, customs, and languages.

Differences exist in languages — a Papago cannot understand a Kiowa — and in customs: Southwest tribes strive to develop a reserved nature while the Plains Indians strive to develop openness and instant acquaintanceship. There are general characteristics among all Indians that are known as "Indian ways." Some of these are tribal loyalty, respect for elders, reticence, humility, avoidance of personal glory and gain, giving and sharing with as many as three generations of relatives, an abiding love for their own land, attribution of human characteristics to animals and nature, and strong spiritual beliefs. These characteristics are often in direct contrast to a school system based on competitiveness not humbleness, scientific research not social acceptance, verbosity not reticence.

Consequently, we often hear the comment, "Well, we don't have any problems with our Indian children. We get along fine." These "good Indians," as they are dubbed by some educators, are those who fit the concept held by the non-Indian society: "All Indian children are slow learners, shy, lack positive identification, are thieves by nature, are undependable, and are potential alcoholics. Indian children who do not care to fit in the mold are labeled incorrigible, hyperactive, brain damaged, and rude.

The Indian child who has been reared with a tribal cultural background faces a difficult task in a non-Indian school, especially if he has no inkling as to what the dominant society expects. He must first learn what is expected and meet those expectations before he can be fully accepted.

One of the most common incidents involving Indian children that confronts teachers and counselors is the taking of things off the teacher's desk. Pencils, markers, tape, etc. from the teacher's desk are often found in an Indian child's desk. When confronted by the teacher, the child will usually admit to taking the objects. In the teacher's eyes the child is a thief, and the child is whisked off to the office.

The Indian child is surprised and hurt when such an act is called stealing, because Indians know that any person of rank and importance *shares!* The child feels that it is his classroom (actually, it is a compliment to the teacher), and, since he has a sense of belonging, he also has the right to use things off the teacher's desk.

Another incident might involve eye contact, which is considered important and necessary in the non-Indian society. But, in the Indian culture it is (depending on the tribe) an act of rudeness. Indian children are taught to see without looking directly at someone.

In the first incident, a counselor can say to the child, "Sharing with mother and other family members is wonderful, but sharing with teacher in school is not possible because she is not family. There are too many other children in the the room to allow taking things without asking permission first." Or, "I know that you did not steal; I know that you really needed the pencil, and I will try to help you get your own."

In the second incident, the counselor might say to a concerned teacher, "These children are taught that to stare or look directly is rude. Try to accept it, but check periodically on attention as you would with any other child. You know, there are many non-Indian children who look but never hear."

In most Indian cultures it is considered ill-mannered to speak of one's accomplishments. Praise is welcome when earned but is always given by someone else. Yet, in classrooms teachers use "self-disclosure" procedures that encourage children to talk about their strengths in front of their classmates. Therefore, most Indian children attempting to meet the teacher's request suffer extreme embarrassment. The child may stand but not talk at all or may tell unbelievable stories. Teachers might suggest a general subject rather than talk about self. The Indian child is often aware of his own capabilities and if he sees the need to excel, he does. Last year in the sixth grade Richard sat in class, not doing anything, just sitting. When the reading specialist tested him, she found him capable of reading at the eighth-grade level. Richard knew he could do the work but he did not see any pressing reason why he should put forth the effort. This year Richard is in the seventh grade, and, through a game, the reading teacher learned how "sharp" he was. The game was fun. Why such an attitude? Perhaps during his first three grades, Richard was told either verbally or nonverbally that he was not teachable or that because he was an Indian he was not quite up to par with non-Indian children.

Indian children are very much involved in decision making at home and are usually given choices. Perhaps they do not always decide wisely, but, nonetheless, they have a part in the decision. Counselors working with Indian children should always present a choice: "Either this or that," "Do you or don't you want to?" For example, in counseling toward more school participation, a counselor could say, "I see that you are a good basketball player; you shoot well and you are fast. We would like to have you join us. Will you play on our team?" It calls for a definite yes or no answer. If the student says no, he will supply the reason.

Indian children are very much aware of nonverbal communication. One of the greatest factors in counseling is the counselor's own individual personality and his perception of people and children around him. If the counselor gives the impression of being busy, communication is broken. The Indian child would not dream of being in the way or taking up anyone's time. The Indian's concept of time is not the number of conferences, the number of minutes, or racing the clock. Rather, it is a relaxed few minutes of listening and talking. This is especially true of Indians who have not spent much time living and working within the urban structure.

As most counselors know, what works for one child may not work for another. This is even more so for Indian children. The key word is patience. Patience and more patience!

The sincerity of a person is a trait that most Indian children are very much aware of. A child brought up in the Indian culture is going to observe how closely the counselor lives with what he says. One of the reasons an Indian is slow to open up is because he is going to watch and observe whether the counselor says one thing and does another. A counselor who shows sincere friendliness, perhaps by visiting the home and developing interest in the entire family, will be more likely to find Indian children confiding in him more often.

Friendly inquisitiveness is considered nosiness by Indians. It can slam doors of communication shut. In counseling a child on being late, one counselor said, "I'm happy you made it to school even though you are late. Do you have to help clean house or wash dishes before you come to school?" (Yes) "Let's find ways to help you get your work done on time." Some choices were given, such as "You could do more work at night; you could talk to your mother to see if you could do more work when you get home from school." The problem was handled without embarrassment to the child or family.

There are no set rules for working with Indian children because of different tribal backgrounds. If there are a large number of Indian children in school, the counselor might find out the tribal background and do some research before approaching the child. Use a slow approach: The first session may be all one sided with the counselor doing the talking, or it might just be a comfortable silent session. Counselors should have open minds and understand the need for patience and time. Keep in mind that the child's response is apt to be slow. The Indian people have a lot to contribute, but they have learned to be careful in dispensing any knowledge.

Working with Indian children who have different beliefs and values may cause a counselor to question his own beliefs and values. For the young Indians who are caught in the middle, with the dominant society urging them to forge ahead and achieve according to certain standards, and the Indian culture saying it is not important to be the "top cheese," there can be paths to tragic ends, which must be carefully avoided. Remember — before coming to any conclusion regarding any Indian child try to put yourself in his mocassins.

Part V. Chinese Americans

INTRODUCTION

SOME of the gains attributed to Asian Americans are illusory. For example, the high median family income for Chinese Americans when compared with non-Asian American families is partially due to the fact that most Chinese American families have more than one wage earner. Nor do most statistics show the higher incidence of poverty for elderly Chinese Americans than elderly Blacks and Chicanos. In summary, there is room for considerable improvement in opportunities for Chinese Americans too.

CHINESE AMERICAN CULTURAL CONDITIONING

Many of the following values which characterize Chinese Americans are applicable to most Asian cultures, especially traditional Japanese American families.

FILIAL PIETY. There is unquestioning respect for and deference to authority. Above all else, there is the expectation that each individual will comply with familial and social authority.

PARENT-CHILD RELATIONSHIP. The child defers to his or her parents, especially in communication, which is one way from parents to children.

SELF-CONTROL. Individual achievement is pursued in order to enhance the family name. Verbal, assertive and individualistic students are called crude and poorly socialized. Strong negative feelings are seldom verbalized.

FATALISM. Resignation and pragmatism is the manner in which Chinese Americans deal with changes in nature and social settings. The often brutal and harsh treatment early Chinese immigrants to this country received was tolerated because

335

of the belief in fatalism.

SOCIAL MILIEU. Chinese Americans are other directed and, therefore, are greatly concerned with how their significant others view and react to them. Social solidarity is highly valued.

INCONSPICUOUSNESS. Chinese Americans are taught to avoid calling attention to themselves. Thus they are likely to be silent and inconspicuous in public settings.

SHAME AND GUILT. Since Chinese Americans are taught to respect authority and maintain filial piety toward their parents and ancestors, a violation of the above norms results in feelings of shame and guilt.

READINGS

Kathleen Wright presents some of the historical events which have been omitted from most histories of the Chinese migration to America. She also discusses the Chinese American's participation in the industrial development of this country. Despite their contributions, various laws were enacted to restrict the freedom of Chinese in America.

Francis L. K. Hsu compares and contrasts Chinese and American families. In China, childhood is a privilege given by parents; and in America it is a right protected by federal, state, and voluntary agencies. The author illustrates the ways in which Chinese and American parents prepare their children for survival.

San Francisco's Chinatown is a microcosm of the Chinese American communities scattered throughout the United States. Ken Huang and Marc Pilisuk amply capture the major social and economic ills that have an impact on student achievements.

Lucie Cheng Hirata examines the triadic relationship between students, parents, and teachers in public schools in Los Angeles Chinatown. Too frequently, counselors fail to appreciate the significance of this triad.

Derald Wing Sue and Stanley Sue summarize values held by Chinese Americans and the counseling conflicts growing out of these values. The authors suggest modifications in counseling approaches so that more Chinese American students will be helped rather than hurt in counseling sessions.

Chapter 25

CHINESE AMERICAN HISTORY*

KATHLEEN WRIGHT

ACCORDING to official records of the pe-
riod, the *Empress of China* was the first of the famous China
Clipper ships to touch China. The *Empress* sailed up the Pearl
River and anchored in Canton in 1784. There is evidence to
show, however, that trade existed between the American colonies and China even before the Revolutionary War. Some historians claim that the tea destroyed at the Boston Tea Party came
from China through the East India Trading Company. This
company, whose ships began moving in Chinese waters as early
as 1620, established a four-way trade system between India,
China, England, and the American colonies. It was not until
1784, however, that regular trading ships from the United
States began plying their course to Canton, the city designated
for such purposes by the Manchu Emperor.

In 1786 President George Washington appointed Major
Samuel Shaw, a Boston merchant who had shared in fitting out
the *Empress of China*, as the first American consul to China.
Major Shaw continued in this post until his death in Canton in
1794. The chief function of his position was to promote closer
cultural and trade relations between the two countries. The
results of this contact can be seen in the historic centers of the
United States today; Williamsburg, Monticello, Mount Vernon
and other sites of colonial America display many examples of
intricate Chinese arts and crafts. Objects in ivory, jade, porce-
lain, lacquer, bronze, copper, and other precious metals and
stones were highly prized by Americans. Although Americans
valued the output of Chinese artisans and artists, few of the
colonists had ever seen a Chinese person. For many years a

---

*From Kathleen Wright, *The Other American: Minorities in History*, Los Angeles,
Lawrence Publishing Company, 1969.

somewhat romantic idea of the inhabitants of the exotic Celestial Kingdom was prevalent in America. Even after Chinese began to emigrate to America in sizeable numbers, this notion continued, often in sharp contrast with the attitude of Americans towards the Oriental immigrant himself.

There is little agreement among historians as to when the first Chinese immigrants came to the United States. Bancroft, the famous nineteenth century historian, claimed that Chinese were shipbuilders in lower California between 1571 and 1748. Other historians believe that as early as 1788 Chinese laborers were employed in parts of the Far West. Still others claim that Chinese settlements preceded those of the Spanish and English. Major Shaw, the first American consul to China, stated that there were Chinese in New England during the later days of the eighteenth century. Official count of Chinese in the United States began to appear in 1830 when three Chinese were noted. In 1840 there were eight, in 1850, 758. Between 1850 and 1860 the number of Chinese immigrants rose considerably. This was the period of the building of the transcontinental railroads and the legalization of "coolie" labor. The census of 1860 recorded 34,933 Chinese located primarily in California. Chinese writers are in accord with these figures. They indicate that large-scale emigration from China began about 1860 with the importation of cheap labor for the railroads into the United States and when the economic, social, and political conditions in China were deteriorating in the last years of the Manchu dynasty. The "coolies" were largely from the poorer class of Chinese society, unskilled and uneducated. They came willingly enough to the Western world in search of economic betterment. Many intended to return to their homeland at a later date.

At the same time that poor laborers were reaching Western shores, Chinese students and intellectuals began coming to the West to find out for themselves the reasons for white dominance. Most of these, of the higher class of Chinese society, came to study. The differences between the two groups of Chinese immigrants were vast, indeed. It is possible that because of the dissimilarity of their aims, intentions with regard to permanence of residence, and centers of interest, these two groups did not meet until long after their arrival and when the Chinese began to disperse throughout the country. Dr. Rose Hum Lee points out that not only did two disparate groups of Chinese come to the United States, but also, two very different groups of Americans went to China. Basically, the latter groups were made up of merchants and diplomats on the one hand; missionaries, welfare workers, and educators on the other. The former, interested primarily in profit, dealt with the sources of power and wealth within China ignoring the "man in the street." The latter group, concerned with the needs of the Chinese masses, saw a very different China.

On the American scene, the average citizen came in contact most frequently with the lower class Chinese laborer. These industrious and hardworking men often succeeded where whites had failed, as for example, in the mining fields. Diggings abandoned by whites as unprofitable were often bought by the more frugal and painstaking Oriental and built into a successful operation. This tendency, together with the Chinese willingness to work for lower wages, soon brought about an insupportable tension between the two groups.

In 1852, at the beginning of the period of "coolie" labor in the United States, Governor John MacDougall spoke to the California legislature and referred to the Chinese as the "most desirable of our adopted citizens." He went so far as to recommend a "system of land grants to induce further immigration and settlement of that race." Extensive use was made of the new immigrants in this period of rapid growth and expansion. Chinese laborers contributed greatly to the building of the Union Pacific, the Northern Pacific, and the Southern Pacific railroads. They reclaimed swamplands, built levees and roads, were engaged in mining, and a wide variety of manufacturing tasks. On the Western frontier Chinese were often employed in jobs commonly reserved to women but which the shortage of women in the mining camps and frontier towns made available to the willing Oriental. Cooking, washing, and gardening were done to a large extent by Chinese workers.

These seemingly ideal conditions, however, did not last long. When the speculative economic system began to fail, unemployment forced whites to compete in the job market with Chinese. Highly visible as they were, the Chinese soon became the object of derision and abuse by the white laboring class, both native born and immigrant. Their industriousness and frugality, born of centuries of struggles for survival, became symbols of hatred to many whites. The shuffling walk, somewhat resembling a dogtrot, which many newly arrived Chinese used, the strange food customs, different clothing, the long queues, and the strange sounding language infuriated white Americans as the Oriental became not a compliant servant but a serious economic threat. Part of this threat was seen in the rapid rise of Chinese immigration rates. By 1870 there were 105,465 Chinese in the United States, most of them in California. Not surprisingly, then, the movement to remove this threat itself arose in the California area. One of the chief agitators for Chinese removal was the "sand lot orator," Denis Kearney, who aroused groups of workingmen in San Francisco with his denunciations of the Chinese and ended each of his rallies with the ringing phrase, "The Chinese must go!"

The economic collapse of 1876 brought near panic to the over-expanded system. Business houses failed, banks and mines were closed, even agriculture suffered from a period of drought. As in so many similar situations, a scapegoat had to be found to assume the blame for the country's disaster. The Chinese were ready victims for such thinking. Chinese were assaulted in the streets, their homes and businesses razed. In San Francisco a Chinese was not safe on the streets; riots and bloodshed prevailed, they were pelted with mud and stones as they walked the streets, and often groups would attack them and cut off their queues. This seemingly prankish gesture was more than a prank to the Oriental, and the presence of the queue seemed to point up the difference between the Chinese and the whites, infuriating the latter. Under these trying circumstances Denis Kearney's Workingman's Party succeeded in electing officials to state and local office and the movement to expel the Chinese intensified. Some Chinese fled the country to return to their homeland; others dispersed from the cities where they were the objects of hatred and violence and moved to sections of the country where the small number of Orientals kept them from attracting notice.

Meanwhile, in California, acts discriminating against the Chinese were passed by the state legislature and by local governments. San Francisco, for example, had an ordinance relating to laundries. The license fees were proportioned as follows: laundries using a one-horse vehicle were obliged to pay $2.00 per quarter for licensing fees; those with two horses, $4.00 per quarter; those using no horses were charged $15.00 per quarter. Since it was the Chinese laundries that commonly used no horse-drawn vehicle, the ordinance was clearly aimed at them. It was declared a misdemeanor for anyone walking on the sidewalks of San Francisco to carry baskets suspended on a pole across the shoulders. This, too, was a common Chinese practice. Along the same line of discriminatory legislation was a California law which required a special county tax on miners. Each miner was obliged to pay a tax of $4.00 per month. Whereas in the case of white miners, the amount was often reduced when the man was obviously unable to pay; this was not done for the Chinese. In fact, the practice became common of charging them only $2.00 if they would pay without receiving a receipt from the tax collector. The regular $4.00 was charged for those insisting on a receipt. Although the receipt was the sole means of proving that the tax had been paid, many Chinese, thinking they were being assisted, paid the smaller sum only to find themselves faced with paying the full amount later when the tax office demanded a receipt and the original collector had absconded with the funds.

These laws and ordinances were indicative of the animosity aroused by the presence of Chinese in the United States, and particularly in California where large numbers of them were situated. As early as 1868 the United States negotiated a treaty with China recognizing the right of immigration of Chinese for "purposes of curiosity, trade, or permanent residence," but expressly restricting the right of naturalization. Both presidential candidates in the election of 1876 included anti-Chinese measures in their platforms. Pressures from various States, in particular California, finally brought about the passage of the

Chinese Exclusion Act in 1882. This Act specifically prohibited the entrance of Chinese laborers. A special provision aimed at those Chinese already within the country, further prohibited any State court from admitting Chinese to citizenship. Originally, the Exclusion Act was to last for ten years. In actuality, the provisions of the Act were continued until 1902. Discussions relative to the renewal of the Exclusion Act during Theodore Roosevelt's administration were indicative of the American attitude of superiority over the Chinese. Roosevelt believed that Chinese, especially Chinese laborers, must at all costs be kept from the United States in order to keep "pure" the American spirit and to protect the American workingman. It seems strange, in retrospect, that the presence of some 100,000 persons of Chinese ancestry should have seemed such an economic threat to the country.

The Knights of Labor picked up the cry of Denis Kearney and his Workingman's Party and "The Chinese Must Go!" became the cry of organized labor. Politicians jumped on the bandwagon and repaid their constituents for their votes by passing legislation detrimental to the Chinese. Excessive taxation was placed on their businesses, they were restricted in certain areas of employment, for example, medicine, teaching, dentistry, mining, railroading, manufacturing, etc. When they tried to fight back, they were driven from the cities or lynched. The contributions of the Chinese to the building of the country, especially the West, were forgotten. It seems ironic to recall that shortly before the passage of the Act prohibiting the immigration of Chinese laborers, the transcontinental railroad was completed, the Western half of it largely by Chinese "coolie" labor.

Chapter 26

PARENTS AND CHILDREN*

FRANCIS L. K. HSU

THE difference between Chinese and American homes reflects their contrasting patterns of behavior in the family. In no other country on earth is there so much attention paid to infancy or so much privilege accorded childhood as in the United States. In contrast, it may be said without exaggeration that China before 1949 was a country in which children came last.

The contrast can be seen in a myriad of ways. Americans are very verbal about their children's rights. There is not only state and federal legislation to protect the young ones, but there are also many voluntary juvenile protective associations to look after their welfare.

In China, parents have had a completely free hand with their children. Popular misconception notwithstanding, infanticide was never an everyday occurrence in China. It was the last resort of poor parents with too many daughters, especially during a famine. Certainly no parents would brag about it. In fact, there are stories about the grief of parents in such a predicament and quite a few jokes on the theme of how some irate parents deal with tactless clods who utter unwelcome expressions about the birth of a daughter.

However, before 1949, infanticide by needy Chinese parents was never cause for public shock or censure. Parents who committed infanticide were seldom punished by the law. It is literally true that from the viewpoint of American children, parents have practically no rights; but from the viewpoint of Chinese parents, children have little reason to expect protection from

*"Parents and Children" From *Americans and Chinese* by Francis L. K. Hsu. Copyright © 1953, 1970 by Francis L. K. Hsu. Reprinted by permission of Doubleday & Company, Inc.

their elders. If an American were to point with justifiable pride to his country's many child protective associations, a Chinese would simply counter with an equally proud boast about his nation's ancient cultural heritage in which Confucian filial piety was the highest ideal.

American parents are so concerned with the welfare of their children, and so determined to do the right thing, that they handsomely support a huge number of child specialists. Chinese parents have taken their children so much for granted that pediatrics as a separate branch of medicine was unknown until modern times. I know of no piece of traditional literature aimed at making the Chinese better parents, and even during the days of the Republic there was hardly any scientific inquiry into what children might think and desire. Articles on how to treat children appeared only sporadically in a few Chinese newspapers and magazines, many of them translations or synopses of material from the West.

But Americans not only study their children's behavior — they glorify it. Chinese did not only take their children for granted — they minimized them. The important thing to Americans is what parents should do for their children; to Chinese, what children should do for their parents.

The extent to which some American parents will go to suit the convenience of their children is exemplified by a mid-Western couple I know. To make their little ones happy, they installed a fancy slide in their living room. Guests entered the apartment by bending under it, and then they attempted to enjoy a conversation within reach of the boisterous sideshow provided by the young ones sliding up and down.

That this is unusual even for the United States is indicated by the fact that this couple felt compelled to justify their action every time they had a visitor and by the fact that their friends remarked about it. No Chinese parents could have kept the respect of the community if they permitted anything remotely resembling this indulgence.

For many centuries Chinese were both entertained and instructed by tales known as "The Twenty-Four Examples of Filial Piety." These tales were so popular that different versions of them are available. Following the traditional approach to literature of writing on some exalted model, the Chinese ancients have handed down to posterity at least two series of "The Twenty-Four Examples of Filial Piety."

These stories were illustrated in paintings, dramatized on the stage, and recited by storytellers in tea houses and market places all over the country. Here is one of these "examples":

A poor man by the name of Kuo and his wife were confronted with a serious problem. His aged mother was sick in bed. She needed both medicine and nourishment which Kuo could ill afford. After consultation between themselves, Kuo and his wife decided that the only way out was to get rid of their three-year-old only son. For Kuo and his wife said to each other, "We have only one mother, but we can always get another child." Thereupon the two went out to the field to dig a pit for the purpose of burying the child alive. But shortly after the man had started to dig he suddenly struck gold. It transpired that the gods were moved by the spirit of their filial piety, and this was their reward. Both the child and the mother were amply provided for and the family thrived happily ever after.

To the Chinese this story dramatized their most important cultural ideal — that support of the parents came before all other obligations and that this obligation must be fulfilled even at the expense of the children.

Economic support is not, however, the only way in which Chinese children are obligated to their parents. The son not only has to follow the Confucian dictum that "parents are always right," but at all times and in all circumstances he must try to satisfy their wishes and look after their safety. If the parents are indisposed, the son should spare no trouble in obtaining a cure for them. Formerly, if a parent was sentenced to prison, the son might arrange to take that parent's place. If the parents were displeased with their daughter-in-law, the good son did not hesitate to think about divorce. In the service of the elders, no effort was too extraordinary or too great. In addition to parents the elders in question could be a man's stepmother or a woman's parents-in-law.

Here again folk tales are useful indications of the actual values. One classical story tells how a man gave up his hard-won official post in order to walk many miles in search of his long-lost mother. Another tells how a youngster of fourteen jumped on and strangled a tiger when the beast was about to devour his father. In a third story, a man cut a piece of flesh from his arm and boiled it in the pot with his father's medicine, believing that the soup would help the elder to recover from his long illness.

In a fourth story a certain Wang Hwa who was married and had a son wanted a father of his own. His real father was presumed to have died during a civil war. He got the idea of buying a father to whom he could be filial. When he met an old man who was searching for his long lost son, Wang made his offer and it was accepted. The newly installed father of Wang was really a rich man in disguise who could not refrain from his extravagant wining and dining. But Wang and his own son, being only of modest means, worked as hard as they could to satisfy the whims of the adopted father. Moved by his adopted son's filial behavior, the old man decided to give Wang all his riches, only to discover later that Wang was his long lost son after all.

Moreover, many Chinese stories did not remain as ideal literature but were sometimes copied to the letter by daughters or sons. In the district histories and genealogical records to be found in every part of the country are many individual biographies of local notables. After a cursory reading of about fifty of them, I obtained at least five instances in which men and women were said to have sliced flesh from their arms to be boiled in the medicine pot of one or another of their parents. One man did this twice during one of his father's illnesses. Because the elder's condition remained serious, the filial son decided to take a more drastic course of action. He cut out a piece of what he thought was his "liver" instead. Both he and his father died shortly afterward. . .

American parents not only wish to help their children according to their own experiences, but also they must try to find out by elaborate research what the youngsters really want, [so that the elders can better satisfy the youngsters' individual predilections]. They feel compelled to reduce even the rudiments of a child's education to a matter of fun. Not long ago I came across two books advertised as *Playbooks That Teach Your Child to Dress* — one for boys and one for girls.

The annual business catering to all infant needs had already reached, in 1951, the colossal figure of five billion dollars. The toy industry alone rose from an annual business of a mere 150 million dollars in 1939 to 750 million dollars in 1951, and to the astronomical high of $2,100,000,000 in 1965.... We may expect that this figure will increase continuously as the child population grows. Certainly the increasing number of commercially profitable events such as local "Baby Week," the acceleration of learning by playing, and the coming and going of fashions in playthings as in other products cannot but spur on the toy industry.

The relationship between Chinese parents and children shows entirely different characteristics. Chinese parents are amused by infantile behavior and youthful exuberance, but the measure of their children's worth is determined primarily by the degree to which they act like adults. Chinese parents are rather proud of a child who acts "older than his age" whereas some American parents might take a similar child to a psychiatrist. Or what Chinese parents consider rowdiness in a child's behavior, American parents might approve of as a sign of initiative.

Take toys again for an example. It is not merely that Chinese children have very few toys; even more interesting is their approach to whatever toys they have. When I was six years of age my mother bought me a cart made of tinfoil. Soldered above the entrance to the cart was an ornamental rectangle. Having seen movable curtains on real carts, I attempted to lower the curtain at the entrance to my toy cart and yanked the stationary ornament out of place. An American mother might have gloated over the creative impulse of her "budding genius," but my mother was very much displeased because she thought me destructive and temperamental. Had I acted the model child that the Chinese mother hoped for by nursing one old toy for a couple of years, an American mother might have worried about the retarded or warped state of my mind.

It is true that a good many things have happened to the Chinese parent-child relationship since 1949. But in order to understand the contrasting life-styles of the two peoples, we must explore the long-standing parent-child bases that have nurtured them. Only then can we evaluate how far more recent developments have or have not altered the picture.

To start with, the average size of the Chinese family is, contrary to popular belief, about five persons. The average number of people in an American family is three. More importantly, when an American speaks of a family he refers to parents and unmarried children; a Chinese includes grandparents and in-laws. Even if Chinese grandparents and in-laws do not live under the same roof, they usually reside in the same village, a neighboring village, or, more rarely, a neighboring district. This is one of the traditional features which the Communist government of China has worked hard to alter by assigning places of work, by stimulating population movement, and by the work-study program and other measures. On the other hand, Americans related by blood or legal bonds usually live so far from one another that this broader group does not come together except on holidays.

These differences mark the point of departure in the early experiences of Chinese and American children. The Chinese child grows up amid continuing or frequent contacts with a number of related individuals besides his own parents and siblings, but his American counterpart grows up in much greater physical isolation. Thus very early in life the former is conditioned to getting along with a wide circle of relatives while the latter is not.

Far more crucial, however, is the manner of interaction between the growing child and individuals other than those belonging to this immediate family. American parents are the sole agents of control over their children until the latter are of age. The grandparents and in-laws do not ordinarily occupy a disciplinary role, whether they live in the same house or not.

Even when grandparents take over during an emergency such as sickness or childbirth, the older people are supposed to do no more than administer things according to the laws laid down by the younger couple, most likely by the younger woman.

Chinese parents have much less exclusive control over their children. In cases where grandparents do not share the same roof with them, during a brief visit the older couple can do almost anything they see fit in regard to the children, even if it means going over the parents' heads. The liberty taken by most Chinese aunts, uncles, and in-laws would cause very severe stress in American families. Furthermore, while an American mother exhibits her displeasure with an overindulgent grandmother and is considered right by others, a Chinese mother doing the same thing would have been an object of censure rather than sympathy.

The inevitable result of the omnipresent and exclusive control of American parents over their children is greater and deeper emotional involvement. The American parent-child relationship is close and exclusive. To the extent that they are the only objects of worship, they also are liable to become the only oppressors. Accordingly, when an American child likes his parents, they are his idols. When he dislikes them, they are his enemies. A conscious or unconscious attachment to one parent at the expense of the other, a situation which gave Freud ground for postulating his famed Oedipus Complex, is the extreme expression of this configuration.

The mutual affection of Chinese parents and children is toned down. Since parental authority varies with circumstances, the parental image in the mind of the growing child must necessarily share the spotlight with men and women held in much higher esteem, such as grandparents, and with those regarded as the equals of the parents, such as uncles and aunts. The feeling toward parents and other adult authority figures being divided and diluted, the child does not develop a paralyzing attachment to, or strong repulsion against, the elders. There is still less reason for the emergency of the Oedipal triangle in which the child is allied to one parent against the other. Consequently, when the Chinese child likes his parents, he fails to idolize them alone; when he dislikes them he still vents his displeasure with great reserve.

These contrasting results flow inevitably from the respective kinship premises of the two cultures. Even though the biological family consists of parents and unmarried children everywhere, according to the American pattern of interaction, it tends to become a collection of isolated dyads; according to its Chinese counterpart, no dyadic relationship is free from the larger network.

This contrast reveals itself with great clarity when pseudo-kinship is involved. The only pseudo-kinship relationship left in the present-day United States is that of godparent and godchild. Our older daughter Eileen's godfather, Mr. L. (an anthropologist and a native American), died in 1953. Some years later my wife and our two daughters paid a social visit to Mrs. L. While the five of us were having dinner, our younger daughter, Penny, then about twelve years old, casually declared to all of us that since Mrs. L. was Eileen's godmother, she was naturally also her godmother. This came to my wife and me as a surprise. Though born, raised, and partially educated in China, I had understood — intellectually at least — the American usage. Eileen was Mr. L.'s goddaughter, and he her godfather. But that relationship had nothing to do with Mrs. L. nor with any of Eileen's family members. Our Evanston-born second daughter, though she had never seen China, had obviously picked up our implicit understandings of Chinese kinship logic. According to that, not only would Mrs. L. be Eileen's godmother and Eileen's sister would be Mr. and Mrs. L.'s second goddaughter, but all of Mr. and Mrs. L.'s children would be both of our daughter's godsiblings.

The beginnings of the contrasts between the two ways of life now become apparent. In America, the child learns to see the world strictly on an individual basis. Even though he did not have a chance to choose his parents, he can choose to prefer one more than the other. Extending from this basic tie outward, the American's relationship with other members of his kin group is strictly dependent upon individual preference. The American "must see early in life that a powerful force composed of many aspects of individual choice-making operates to create, maintain, or cancel out interpersonal relationship." His parents, for their part, have to conduct themselves so that they will not lag in the competition for the affection of their children.

· This, and the fact that most American parents encourage their children very early to do things for themselves — to feed themselves, to make their own decisions — lead the American child to follow his own predilections. He expects *his environment to be sensitive to him.*

The Chinese child learns to see the world in terms of a network of relationships. He not only has to submit to his parents, but he also has little choice of his wider social relationships and what he individually would like to do about them. This, and the fact that Chinese parents are firmly convinced that elders know better and so never feel defensive about it, leads the Chinese child to appreciate the importance of changing circumstances. As to defending themselves, the characteristic advice to Chinese children is — "Don't get into trouble outside, but if there is danger, run home." The Chinese child is obliged to be *sensitive to his environment.*

Though consciously encouraging their children to grow up in some ways, American parents firmly refuse to let the youngsters enter the real world of the adults. They leave their children with sitters when they go to parties. If they entertain at home, they put the youngsters to bed before the guests arrive. Children have no part in parents' regular social activities.

Chinese parents take their children with them not only to wedding feasts, funeral breakfasts, and religious celebrations, but also to purely social or business gatherings. A father in business thinks nothing of bringing his boy of six or seven to an executive conference.

This pattern is still adhered to by the majority of second, third, and even fourth-generation Chinese-Americans in Hawaii. Like their Caucasian neighbors, Chinese organizers in Hawaii also resort to "family" picnics and "family" evenings and even athletics for the purpose of maintaining or increasing club or church enrollment. But unlike their Caucasian neighbors, Chinese parents in Hawaii take their very young children with them on many more occasions — for example, on social and business visits which regularly last until late at night.

A few years ago the idea of "togetherness" between parents and children became fashionable at least in some sections of American society. The central concern was that the parents and children should do things together — such as outings, shows, hobbies, and church activities. Some writers observed that television, for all of its faulty programs, had at least brought members of a family together. However, the fervor for togetherness has since died down, for the togetherness that progressive American parents looked for was a *planned* one — an activity-studded one in which children and their elders had each other but defined the rest of the world as outsiders and gave it no part in that circle of togetherness. So conceived, it was literally a honeymoon between parents and children. It was bound to get on the nerves of all, especially its commander-in-chief, the father. It failed because it was an artificial togetherness, not one nurtured in the American kinship constellation.

Chinese youngsters enter into the adult world unobtrusively in the course of their mental and physical growth. Their own infantile and youthful world is tolerated but never encouraged. On the contrary, they reap more rewards as they participate more and more in adult activities. From as early as they can remember their elders have shared with them a community of interests, except relating to sex; they have participated in real life, not an artificially roped off sector of it.

American parents, except for the very poor, proceed on quite the opposite assumption with their insistence on privacy for all individuals. The business of American parents — social and commercial — is their private reserve, and no trespassing by children is allowed except on those rare and eventful occasions when a explicit invitation is extended. By the same token, parents are also supposed to refrain from entering into the activities of their youngsters.

Not so among the Chinese. Chinese children consider it a matter of course to witness or participate in adult affairs, exactly as Chinese adults have no constraint about joining in their children's activities. This reciprocity goes so far that neither has any reservations about opening letters addressed to the other.

Nothing is more strikingly symbolic of these profound differences than the fact that American children celebrate their birthdays among themselves, their parents being assistants or servants, while Chinese children's birthdays are occasions for adult celebration at which children may be present, as in wedding or funeral feasts, but where they certainly are not the center of attraction.

The line of demarcation between the adult and the child world is drawn in many other ways. For instance, many American parents may be totally divorced from the church, or entertain grave doubts about the existence of God, but they send their children to Sunday schools and help them to pray. American parents struggle in a competitive world where sheer cunning and falsehood are often rewarded and respected, but they feed their children with nursery tales in which the morally good is pitted against the bad, and in the end the good invariably is successful and the bad inevitably punished. When American parents are in serious domestic trouble, they maintain a front of sweetness and light before their children. Even if American parents suffer a major business or personal catastrophe, they feel obliged to turn to one of their children and say, "Honey, everything is going to be all right." This American desire to keep the children's world separate from that of the adults is exemplified also by the practice of delaying transmission of the news to children when their parents have been killed in an accident, or concealing the facts from them when one of the parents goes to jail. Thus, in summary, American parents face the world of reality while many of their children live in the near-ideal unreal realm where the rules of the parental world do not apply, are watered down, or even reversed.

It is this separateness of the children's world that makes the kind of hero found in J. D. Salinger's *The Catcher in the Rye* so meaningful to so many youthful American readers. Here is an adolescent who sees through the invisible walls around him.

He denounces as phonies the people who act according to rules outside that wall, but he feels terribly lonely because most of those inside the wall are working so hard to be content with their place. However, even Holden Caulfield returns to the American fold in the end. He decides not to run away; he goes back to school; and he reflects while his little sister, Phoebe, is on the carousel: "The thing with kids is, if they want to grab for the gold ring, you have to let them do it, and not say anything. If they fall off, they fall off, but it's bad if you say anything to them." (p. 11).

Chinese children share the same world with their parents, and the parents make little effort to hide their problems and real selves from their children. Very early in life, Chinese children learn that reward and punishment are not necessarily consistent with the established rules of conduct, and that justice and love do not always prevail. Yet at the same time they are more likely than American children to become conscious of the power exercised by the environment — they see their parents' faults as well as their virtues. From the beginning, they see their parents as ordinary mortals succeeding at times but failing at others, following inevitably the paths marked by custom and tradition.

American children are not only increasingly convinced of the importance of their individual predilections, but they are equally sure that they can accomplish what they set out to achieve. In the American child's restricted and comforting world, he experiences few irreparable setbacks and knows few situations in which he is entirely frustrated by reality. It is only parents who can impose restrictions that the child may see as barriers to his own advancement.

The Chinese child is not only fully aware that he should obey his parents and other seniors, but even when he succeeds in circumventing them, he still faces the hurdles presented by custom and tradition. Through his active observation of and participation in adult activities, he is already well acquainted with his own shortcomings and the real nature of his society. The foci of attention and power being many, the restrictions imposed upon the individual come not from the parents, but the society at large. Even if he resents these barriers, he can still see no point on which to center his attack, for they are too numerous and too diffuse.

Chapter 27

AT THE THRESHOLD OF THE GOLDEN GATE: SPECIAL PROBLEMS OF A NEGLECTED MINORITY*

KEN HUANG AND MARC PILISUK

DURING the latter half of the nineteenth century, large numbers of Chinese gained passage through the Golden Gate. Although translating, their notion of "gold-digging" in Kum San, or the "Gold Mountain," into a reality has proven as remote as rainbow chasing, this realization has not deterred the Chinese from joining those immigrant millions from all parts of the globe who have come before and after them, seeking the promise of an affluent America.

It must be anti-human nature to dig up one's roots, sever one's ties, abandon a customary way of life, and gamble on a world that is unknown. Hence, immigrants frequently glorify the opportunities of a new world. Upon arrival, however, the feelings of loss can be enormous. Miners have returned from Chicago and Detroit to the familiar surroundings of jobless Appalachia and their kin. Fried's[12] description of "grieving for a lost home" captured the degree of uprootedness and disorientation involved in geographical movement, and Maris[18] stressed the impact of losing familiar places and people. If relocation is painful to contemplate, the forces behind the choice must be either a great lure in the new environment or a great curse in the old. Like other immigrants, the Chinese fled from man-made disasters such as foreign invasions, military upheavals, political oppressions, from natural catastrophes such as drought, flood, earthquake, famine, or simply from harsh, squalid living conditions. For such reasons the war victims, the city dwellers, the nomadic herdsmen, the vast impoverished rural villagers came to America with fervent hope of finding something better.

Unlike the white, European settlers, the Chinese did not come to "discover" an unexploited and unclaimed America. They came when the severe shortage of women on the Pacific Coast created a need for cooks, laundry workers, and houseboys — workers who would be both cheap and docile. They came to sell their labor, toiling for the transcontinental railroad, sweating in the mine or the textile mill or the cigar factory, working in the laundry, and steaming in the kitchen in exchange for the dream that their lot might be better.[20] The dream is not yet realized for a majority of residents of San Francisco's Chinatown. Now, however, there is another dream, even more magnetic than the first; it is to reunite their families.

This desire for family reunion is not unique to immigrants of Chinese descent; what is special about the Chinese is the fact of their forced separations. Many have gone years before getting a glimpse of their loved ones; others have waited a lifetime, only to die with deep regret.

THE PAPER CHILD

The American household has many unwanted children — children of color, with few birthrights. Each group has some distinctive problems relating to its history. The "paper child" phenomenon has long been associated with the Chinese immigrants. The term arises out of the ingenuity of the "unscrupulous" Chinese who attempt to defy the immigration authorities and gain entry to this country by falsifying a relationship to a United States citizen; many, largely mainland Chinese entering from Hong Kong, have no documents of identification. The incidence of this kind of illegal entry is undeniable, but its existence is tied to a century of discriminatory laws directed specifically against the Chinese.

For reasons contrary to their merit, Africans and Chinese were the only peoples America banned from immigration by name and law in the nineteenth century and only the Chinese in the twentieth century.[26] (p. 103)

As a result, the traditionally male-dominated Chinatown not only has "paper children," but "paper families" as well. A lifetime of enforced separation has brought into being families that exist only on official documents.

This inhumane, official discrimination against the Chinese was finally rectified when a new immigration act became fully effective in 1968. But the degree of psychosocial damage to this ethnic community appears beyond reparation. One cannot appreciate the extent of this damage without consideration of the importance of families in traditional China. The family meant not only nurturance, but loyalty, pride, and a sense of continuity of life across generations. Parenting is strict, and respect for the authority of elders almost absolute.[11] *Family* is so enmeshed in the the identity of the Chinese that (quite like the Native American tribes) it resists assimilation even upon threat of exclusion from the promise of society, even upon the threat of destitution or annihilation.

CHINATOWN — WHY?

Chinatown is not an island; like any other neighborhood, its fortunes are determined not only by its own members, but by the attitude and level of support of the larger community.

The reasons for Chinatown's existence cannot be understood without at least brief reference to its history. The genesis of San Francisco's Chinatown as a racial quarter occurred about 1850. Its inception and growth were not based solely on the need for companionship of one's kind, but, more importantly, on the need for survival and self-protection.[15] This was imperative in view of the widespread anti-Chinese movement that followed the arrival of the first Chinese coolies. The Exclusion Act of 1882 and the Quota Act of 1943, aimed at keeping out the Chinese (and, in the process, destroying numerous families), are probably among the important precursors of the current social ills of Chinatown. The Chinese today are no longer subject to head tax, lynching, burning, wanton murder, and other flagrant acts of racial oppression that were once part of their lives in America. But pervasive discriminatory practices — overt and covert — persist. A few lucky Chinese can use San Francisco's Chinatown as a way station to the middle-class Richmond and Sunset districts, but tens of thousands cannot. Their survival depends upon Chinatown, and for them there is no escape.

Chinatown is essential not just to its residents, however, but the rest of the city's well-being as well. It may be an exaggeration to say that Chinatown plus Fisherman's Wharf equals San Francisco — but can one imagine San Francisco without Chinatown? Where could workers with marginal incomes go for a bellyful of tasty meal for $2.00 or the gourmet feast at moderate prices? From Chinatown comes the cheap labor for the city's clothing industry, and to Chinatown flock the visitors who make up the city's vital tourist trade. Yet, the lion's share of the tourist dollars go to the affluent San Franciscans on Nob Hill and in the downtown financial district.

In return for its significant contributions to the larger community, Chinatown receives what can at best be called "benign neglect." Its "paper" attention has been more than needed — a community studied time and time again — but little has been done to change it. What is life like in this peculiar, confined, "sardine can" entity in which 54% of the city's 58,969 Chinese are jammed?[8] It is a

> . . . sweatshop world of long hours, low pay, hard work, and fear. . . . For all its outward ambiance, the largest Chinese enclave outside Asia is one of America's most wretched slums.[7]

The area is a repository for the worst of this nation's social ills: dilapidated housing, overcongestion, high unemployment and underemployment rates, poverty, and poor sanitation; the incidence of tuberculosis among its squalid tenements is more than double that of the rest of San Francisco; the suicide rate is nearly three times the national average. In recent years, its political, young "Red Guard" and outbreaks of violent crime have shattered a long-cherished American image of a "quiet minority."[25]

The composite picture, drawn from a number of observations, is of a reality of sharp contrast to the notion of a "model" minority that can take care of its problems on its own.[22] Such a view serves to mask the covertly racist intent of justifying "cumulative neglect" by the government, and of legitimizing the neglect of those Asian-Americans who cannot take care of themselves. The focus on middle-class Asian-Americans, extolled as tokens of the success of American democracy and free enterprise, has made it easier to blame blacks, Hispanics, and Native Americans, whose poverty is more widely known, for their own failures.[19]

The crux of the problem of the Chinese minority, as it is with all minorities, is racism. They are despised and rejected. Harsh and cruel stereotypes hold the Chinese to be dirty, dull, and cowardly.[16,20] They have been neglected, dispossessed, and exploited. They suffer harsh work conditions so that others, consumers and tourists, can enjoy their shops. They sweat in factories so others may profit. They live in overcrowded and inadequate housing, so others can live with more space. They bicker among themselves, often fueled by outsiders, so that vested economic-political oligarchs can continue to dominate and exploit their community for profit. Those are the generic reasons for the "colonized status" analogy of the color minorities in America — and they apply clearly to Chinatown.[3]

Just as Michael Harrington once looked beyond the circumventing freeways to unmask the invisible poor, it is essential to discover Chinatown through its backstage by stripping the ornate facade and neon attraction of Grant Avenue. Only then is it possible to reveal what life beyond the dark alleys and above the curio shops is all about. The conclusions drawn from studies of what Chinatown is like must take into account the reasons for Chinatown's existence. Valentine's excellent study[24] of the culture of poverty shows the need to distinguish basic cultural patterns from reactive adaptations to forced conditions. "Don't mistake the finger pointing at the moon for the moon," warned a Zen Buddhist:

Any study involving an ethnic minority group is a commentary on the total society ... The minority group is but the finger pointing at the larger society.[13]

A ROOF OVER THEIR HEADS

The most urgently felt need the immigrant family faces is housing. Chances are the immigrant has little choice but to join those in the already overcrowded Chinatown or its spill-over environs. In the conventionally defined Chinatown "core" area, the density per residential acre stands at 912.4, 11.5 times greater than the city average. This is the area dominated by a building height of two to four stories, and its housing stock consists of units of two rooms or less. Many are hotel-type housing. Between one and two-thirds of the housing units are considered substandard, deficient in the amenities that most Americans take for granted. These antiquated buildings with deficient overhead lighting and faulty electrical wiring make such a habitat dreadful. Communal kitchens and community baths have become a way of life. Yet, the rent situation is equally grave. According to the 1970 census,[8] rent in the area has risen 234.4 percent (for under-$150.00-per-month housing) to 824.2 percent (for $150.00-and-above units) since 1960. This far exceeds the rate of increase of household incomes.[21] For this reason, one hears increasingly of "cubicles" or even "bedspace" instead of apartment units or rooms, a condition reminiscent of the slums in Hong Kong.

A vivid description by an elderly woman brings one close to the actual scene.*

In tears, the woman told of her current living situation, while recapitulating her life-long sufferings. She had come to the United States three years prior to this interview (1971) to join the man whom she had married in China forty years ago. Their long separation was largely the result of discriminatory U.S. immigration laws. Banking on the dream of this reunion helped to ease the pain of her lifetime "widowhood."

---

*Case illustrations are drawn from the senior author's three-and-a-half years of experience as a mental health worker in San Francisco's Chinatown; first-person observations are those of the senior author.

Sadly enough, she found him old (twenty-seven years her senior), physically incapacitated, and mentally deranged. He also suffered from a chronic diabetic condition. Living on welfare, the couple paid $60.00 for a tiny room, and shared a communal kitchen and a grossly inadequate toilet facility with some thirty people on the same floor. During certain congested hours of the day, queuing for the single toilet bowl became unavoidable. Often it was impossible for the old man to reach the toilet in time for his needs. My attempt to get them into public housing was a disappointing one. I was able to put them on a priority list only after I had reached a higher authority in charge of public housing. Nine months had slipped by and no progress had been made. When the issue was pressed, I was reminded that there were applicants who have been on the waiting list for over ten years, and the prospects for its easement were extremely remote.

The need for public housing in Chinatown and its vicinity has become so bad that many consider it a joke even to apply. The social worker's advice to those in need has been "to file anyway, but forget that you have for many years to come." The futility affects the service worker's psyche. It breeds a cynicism frequently shared by workers in human services in the ghetto. "What is service when you have nothing to serve with?"

FILLING THE RICE BOWL

Chinatown is an enclave that few of the ill-prepared Chinese immigrants can afford to escape. The immigrants, inclusive of those who have come to join their families, have chosen to adopt this country as their own, but the country has not been ready to accept them. With no alternative, they crowd themselves into the city's 1.9 percent of the acreage for mutual protection and for mere survival.

Unlike ghettoes in Hong Kong, where there is a homogenous grouping of those of low socioeconomic-educational background, the Chinatown ghetto consists of illiterate seamstresses, semi-illiterate dishwashers, as well as college graduates and former professors. There are a substantial number of oldsters, with 34 percent aged fifty-five and over, in the core area.

They eke out an existence on welfare or subsist below welfare standards on social security checks. Equally significant is the number of working poor brushing shoulders with the day population of landlords, mercantile, and suburban Chinese.

To fill the rice bowl is not easy. In getting a job, the Chinatown resident is faced with formidable barriers. A large proportion of the immigrants are not equipped with marketable know-how and skills. Two out of three have little or no English at their command, and almost every other one has less than a grade-school education. Those on the top of the educational ladder find it no easier. Teachers, nurses, and dentists cannot practice for lack of licensed credentials. For sundry jobs, even if it means the acceptance of a descending social ladder, there may be the English deficiency, the lack of work experience in this country the seeker's age of "over-qualification." One of the many personally encountered was an experienced pediatrician whose job-hunting was a fiasco; not even a house-servant's position could be found.

To compete in the open "outside" job market, even without the language problems, involves overcoming the residue of a century of discrimination against Chinese by the government, business, and labor unions. Confrontation tactics and pressures to enforce affirmative action make it possible for some blacks to be integrated into the labor market. Chinese and Asians, although more populous than blacks in San Francisco, remain virtually unseen and totally unrepresented among the hardhats, organized trades, and large employers like the police and municipal railways. Lacking political muscle, they continue to suffer from benign neglect by public and elected officials. In the words of Theodore Chen,[6] they are neither the majority, nor the minority group, and they cannot share in concessions made to the blacks and the browns. .

The Chinatown residents are a "trapped" labor force, caught between high unemployment and underemployment rates. Social and economic exploitation has become the order of the day and night. Working a mandatory ten hours a day, six days a week, yet with a "paper" forty-hour work-week, at minimum wages is commonplace among restaurant workers. Piece work for garment workers makes it necessary for them to work either at a back-breaking speed or to labor fifty to seventy hours a week to net an income sometimes lower than they can obtain on welfare. Many do not have paid vacations, sick leave, holiday benefits, nor are they covered by medical insurance or even unemployment and disability insurance. The bulk of unfair employment practices are left unchallenged since employees are generally reluctant to bring charges against their employers. The cultural dictum holds: "What an ungrateful thing to do to one who gives you a job." Even enlightened employers find it hard to adhere to fair employment practices that include a forty-hour work week and minimum wages if they want to stay in business and lower their costs. And to drive one's employer out of business is, in fact, job-suicide against oneself.

Teaching of English communication skills, along with vocational training for the foreign-born through the Manpower Development and Training Act, has moved toward filling a vital need. Such efforts nevertheless represent drops in the bucket unless training can eventuate in employment.

For the able, willing workers who cannot find jobs the feeling is not the same as for those who denounce work as a way of life and choose to drop out. Among the older generation, a common reaction is to turn the angry feeling inward, resulting in depression and psychosomatic equivalents of depression. Ultimately, the society provides nothing "but a welfare net to catch their fall." Even so, these are the "chosen ones." Hardest hit, of course, are those who fall through a large hole in the "welfare net." These are the middle-aged within the two decades approaching the magic age of sixty-five. They are old, but not old enough for Old Age Assistance; they are disabled, but not disabled enough for Aid to the Totally Disabled; they are young, but not young enough to have children of AFDC range. They fit nowhere in American society. One striking fact is that, with all their sources of despair, alcoholism is rare among Chinese Americans.[9] Gambling, however, is widespread and may be a functional equivalent to problem drinking.[1]

As for the young and the frustrated, they tend to project their angry feelings outward. They blame the society for deserting them and for the lot they are in. They see through the subtle and the not-so-subtle discrimination in "fair" employment and job opportunities. Some feel that unless they, too, adopt the explosive "confrontations" that have gained attention for the blacks and the Chicanos, job equality will pass them by.[21]

The less patient ones feel that even this is too remote. "After all, you can't fight city hall anyway, why bother." So they band together, taking the law into their own hands. And, at gunpoint, each carves out a "rightful turf," and more often than not they work hand in glove with illicit enterprises and alleged police agents. Self-styled extortionists exact tolls from merchants for their protection, and from residents for the living the society owes them.

BITTER-SWEET SECOND HONEYMOON

Having been subjected to a century of discriminatory practices and institutional racism, Chinatown, until recently, had been known as a predominantly one-sex community. A series of exclusionary immigration laws, designed to keep out the Chinese and to deny their naturalization, left Chinese males stranded in this country, unable to bring their families from China. The repeal of the Exclusion Act did not come about until 1943, when China's participation in the Grand Alliance against the Axis powers swung public opinion toward its repeal. It was then that some 5000 Chinese wives of veterans, including American-born Chinese who had served in World War II, were able to enter the United States. The final lap — the discriminatory immigration quota system of 105 per year to which the Chinese were subjected — was not removed until the enactment of a new immigration act of 1965, which became wholly effective as of June 30, 1968.[14]

At this point the hallmark of immigration of families, rather than of individual males, began in the Chinese history of America. It was largely after this date that reunions for thousands of American Chinese families became a reality.

A sizable number of elderly men who had been separated

from their wives ever since their early wedding months, and had never seen their children, were confronted by family for the first time. Naturally, their adjustments have been hard. With two divergent sets of attitudes and customs, crystallized through the span of time and space, the spouses found for themselves nothing in common save the rigidity of their set personality structures.

To many, the second honeymoon has been a curse rather than a blessing, or at best a bittersweet mixture. Health and welfare agencies serving the Chinese community are replete with such case histories, among them the following:

A woman in her mid-fifties was among the first batches of Chinese immigrants arriving in 1967 under the revised immigration law. She came with high hopes of making a bona fide marriage out of a "paper marriage." The strength of family had persisted after twenty-nine years of forced separation! With her were her daughter and the daughter's family. Pulling all their meager resources together, they recreated a three-generation family under the same roof. But, tragically, their physical proximity did not bring the family any closer than had the vast Pacific Ocean. Daily bickering and endless fighting, coupled with the added burden of making ends meet, made life a "living hell." In but a few months the family was broken apart. Deserted, the woman's health precipitously declined physically and emotionally. Care, which depended upon the married daughter, who had young children and who could hardly take care of her own family, was totally inadequate. Following our discovery of the case, and after a stormy five-year course of unsuccessful hip operations, the poor woman became grossly psychotic. Seen in a home visit, she posed rigidly on her bed, with bland countenance and shaky hands. She mumbled a train of sentences that would not stop. Her behavior seemed a clear case of psychosis of traumatic onset. The woman had shown the strength to adapt to years of hardship before rejoining her family in the promised land. Finally, assistance in the form of ATD, surgical operation, and psychiatric attention were forthcoming, but too late. She died two years later, in fear and bitterness.

The case illustrates the thesis suggested earlier of the cause-effect chain deriving from a racist immigration policy. The intensity of stress added to a married couple after twenty-nine years of forced separation cannot be explained by ordinary circumstances.

DOWNFALL OF THE CONFUCIAN FAMILY ORDER

For somewhat younger adults, those with children, especially teenagers, Chinatown holds an entirely different set of problems. The strong multigeneration Chinese family has always required an intense loyalty and obedience from its children. Not since the era of Confucian scholars has respect for the aged and the concept of filial piety been so challenged. These values and traditions meet head on with America's democratic, egalitarian mores, and, perhaps more appropriately, the polarity of adoration of the young. This attitudinal collision becomes inevitable for many when the East meets the West.[11] Chinese youth are bombarded daily by such indoctrination, transmitted through classroom teachers and street philosophers. Even if they are confined to the family's tight-spaced living quarters, they cannot escape the omnipresent, audiovisual electronic tube. The destitute parents fade before the values of equal opportunity that are reinforced, at least verbally, in the peer culture.

It is the unsophisticated patriarch who is most likely to be caught, perplexed and unprepared. He has no innovative way of dealing with the situation save the old tricks that have been passed down to him through generations. So he tightens his grip on the insolent child. Sometimes the teenagers will fight harder. Even worse, for the family, is the decline in respect.

To illustrate, we cite a man whom we shall refer to as C. H. Tan. He was obviously agitated and distraught when he came to the clinic. Asking for help had never been his style. But he had no choice now: his fourteen-year-old son had been murdered in cold blood a few days earlier, and his wife had become acutely psychotic. Emergency psychiatric intervention prevented further deterioration of his wife's condition, and time was a healing partner. The family then declined further assistance. Two months had elapsed when a social worker from another agency called for consultation. A new crisis had developed in this family. At this interview, the man's face was criss-crossed with long scratches marked by finger nails. In spite of these undeniable proofs, the man did his best to deny the urgency of his family situation. The fact that he no longer had the family under his control was most painful for him to face. But what had happened was not unusual. When the grief over the lost child was over, it was time for fixing blame. Years of old grudges were dug up to support each other's charges. The family was divided, with Mr. Tan on one side, his wife and children on the other. While Mr. Tan blamed the lax discipline of the American school for the loss of his truant, unruly son, his wife and children projected all the blame onto Mr. Tan. He was called lazy, selfish, a no-good tyrannical bum. The sad truth was — the survival issue was too much for any and for all of them. Since the family's arrival in the United States, Mr. Tan, without English at his command or skills to market, had not been able to find a job. The burden of his family of seven fell on the shoulders of his wife, who labored tediously as a seamstress. Her $300.00 monthly income necessitated an AFDC supplement. As a man who cannot find work, who is saddled a family that depends upon his wife and welfare, and whose teenage children daily barter for their share of the empty financial pot, he had lost his mandate as a patriarch.

A number of immigrant families have been caught in such a bind, especially those with children involved in delinquency. Usually, a protracted family warfare produces no victor, only losers. While the patriarch loses his children psychologically, if not physically, the rebellious youth may ultimately lose himself to his peers. The youth gang typifies this. The gang leader now takes over the role of the family patriarch. Gang loyalty supplants family solidarity, in a break with 5000 years of tradition.

EMOTIONAL CASUALTIES

The hurdles for the Chinese immigrant to overcome are many. The basic and most pressing is the bread-and-butter issue. To resolve this would mean employment, or mean income of some decency, in order to guarantee food, shelter, clothing, and education for the young. Beyond this there is the hurdle of cultural shock, the ability of the father to provide. For the Chinese, the fullness of one's rice bowl could affect the degree of one's ability to weather such a shock. For instance, a one-time prestigious high school principal in Canton is now working as a janitor. The ability to adapt and adjust under the circumstances he finds himself in may not assure him and his family of much of a living, but it may save his sanity.

For the Chinese American, the concept of success ranks next to family solidarity in self-appraisal. Expectation and aspiration are high since the Chinese seem to put so much premium on success. Success in the present era, as with the *nouveaux riches* all over the world, is measured in terms of the fortune one can accumulate. The road to success for the Chinese is generally paved with self-denial, discipline, hard work (or education), and a bit of parsimony. As one succeeds, his family and kin also expect to share the glory of a child's success and the benefits derived from it. Unfortunately, for each one who has succeeded, scores have not. In a shame-oriented Chinese society,[10] the effects of failure can be disastrous. Many dropouts on the road to success blame themselves for the shame they caused to be bestowed upon their families. The toll of failure is heavy. It affects the young, the old, the middle-aged, and the not-so-old.

A spate of publicity in the news media in recent years spells blood in San Francisco's Chinese community. Since the first gangland-type slaying in April 1969, more "aggressive acts," such as robbery, assault, burglary, and extortion committed by Chinese youth have been recorded. A similar situation prevails in New York's Chinatown. In comparison with other racial and cultural groups, the rate is still relatively low. The change, however, is reflected in a 600 percent increase in arrests and citations of Chinese juveniles in San Francisco during the period 1964-69.[25]

Crime and violence are youthful ways of reacting to failure and disillusionment. These most frequently involve school drop-outs, a product of insurmountable language handicap or academic deficits, and an antiquated school system unresponsive to Chinese language or culture. To this must be added the customary deficits of the ghetto existence: no spending money, no wholesome recreation or outlet, no job, and little energy remaining for love at home. They see no hope now or in the future. Striking out is a form of protest, "righting the wrong," and a plea for societal action.

The elderly Chinese are precluded, by cultural heritage as well as by age, from acting out against others; they, therefore, turn against themselves. The suicide rate in the Chinese community noticeably including the lonely, the sick, the elderly, approximates three times the national average. Undoubtedly many of the functional bachelors or men with "paper families" are among them. Statistical comparison on suicides from 1954-1967 for all Chinese Americans is on a par with that of the city of San Francisco, which has won the dubious distinction of being called the mecca of the suicide-prone.[4]

Between the younger group, who make others liable for their failures, and the relatively older group, who hold themselves responsible, are those who seek escape in unreality. The few available studies concur on the salient feature of a high rate of mental illness coupled with an unusually low rate of utilization of mental health facilities.[15] A study by Stanley Wang, one of the two Chinese-speaking psychiatrists in San Francisco, revealed a disproportionately higher number of psychotics among Chinese admitted to the psychiatric ward in San Francisco General Hospital than among the general population.[21] Over half (54.5%) of these admissions required police intervention and transportation. The evidence tends to support the theory that it takes a real crisis for the Chinese to seek outside help,[5] and psychiatric admissions are used only as the "last resort."* Even so, since 1930 psychiatric admissions for Chinese Americans matched the national figure for all Americans. The rates were highest for males, the aged, and the foreign-born.[2] It

---

*A careful study of utilization rates, completed by Dr. Sanford Tom for the period from July 1, 1965, to June 30, 1966, showed the Chinese in San Francisco's Health District No. IV to constitute 26.6 percent of the population. Their contribution to the utilization rate for mental health facilities amounted to only 7 percent.[21] Similarly, Sue and Sue[23] reported a noticeable underutilization of mental health facilities by Chinese Americans on the college campus.

is important to note the findings that 73 percent of the Chinese patients admitted had a moderate or severe language handicap. This supports our contention concerning the vulnerability of the immigrants because of multiple stress factors. It is also indicative of the gross deficiency in the supply of Cantonese-speaking professionals in mental health.

Compounded by the traditional tendency of not seeking outside help — equated with spreading family disgrace — is the fear of and intolerance toward mental illness. Ignorance and superstition enter here. As leprosy is feared, and the leper rejected, the same formula applies to the mentally ill. At times the psychotic individual is believed to be bewitched and devilish. To cast out the devil, it is essential to cast out the bewitched member — and everything associated with the person.

> Typical of this orientation was a middle-aged woman whose husband had been partially paralyzed for years for no apparent reason. Precipitous to a psychiatric hospitalization were attempts made by the woman to cast herself out of a second-story window. She was commanded to do so by an inner voice in order that the rest of her family might be spared. With psychiatric intervention and as soon as the woman began to show signs of progress, the family (her husband and grown children) became grossly anxious about the prospect of her going home. They pleaded with the Chinese-speaking therapist to send her to Napa State Hospital for good. Meanwhile, they incinerated her clothing and belongings with the idea of cleansing the family of this evil spirit — the children's "bewitched mother!"

Where the traditional Chinese family is strong and its members well provided for, there is both normative pressure and support to maintain the disturbed person in a functional family role. Only a scant few beyond the pale would be so banished. In Chinatown, the stresses are apparently greater and the family support is apparently less than was part of the original cultural pattern. The therapist in cases such as these is often powerless. The deficiency implied here is of course the prerequisite of penetrating the linguistic and cultural barriers. The sad fact is that agencies and institutions, customarily recalcitrant in meeting needs and demands of even the most vocal minorities, do very little for Chinese Americans. The preservation of the existing delivery systems always seems to deserve more bureaucratic attention than services about which the professional feels uncertain.

CONCLUSION

The focus of this chapter is on the Chinese immigrants, without distinction as to whether they were raised in Chinatown or recently arrived. They congregate in an ethnic enclave, Chinatown, at the threshold of the Golden Gate, which denotes the marginality of their stance. Like all others, the desire to better their lot motivates them to migrate. Equal if not stronger motivation, among the more recent immigrants, is to reunite with their families after a long, forced separation.

Though the bulk of this chapter was devoted to the exposition of the major social ills in this Chinese community, the reader is reminded of their interrelatedness to the overriding issue of racial oppression of all minorities of color. Specifically for the Chinese, the long-standing exclusion policy and discriminatory immigration quota have caused disruption of their families. The prolonged involuntary family separation, the existing ghettoized conditions, the cumulative discriminatory effects and governmental neglects, and the influx of separated families and relatives have, in combination, taxed the generally inadequate, insufficient, and frequently fragmented services in the community beyond their capabilities.

The severity of impoverishment in this community is seen in social indices of problems that parallel any ghetto in the country. Suicide rate, tuberculosis, density, substandard housing, unemployment, underemployment, exploitative wages, and unsanitary working conditions have been statistics quoted by social scientists for years. But the government and the general public remain unconcerned. Not until the situation had become so bad that repeated violent crimes and gangland killings captured the headlines of the news media were there signs of public uneasiness. Many were shocked beyond belief at eruptions of protest and crime coming from this traditionally docile, patient, hard-working, and inordinately high-threshold-of-suffering "model minority."

Our hope is that the general concern, once focused upon the symptoms, will change to an examination of causes and remedial steps. The time has come to view these desperate acts of violence and the indicators of social disorder from Chinatown both as a signal of cumulative neglect and a plea for help. To miss this cue would be a gross disservice to the society at large.

Let's be reminded once more of the Zen quotation: "Don't mistake the finger pointing at the moon for the moon." The minority problem is basically the majority problem. The minority is but that finger pointing toward the dominant society and the pathology of its own.

REFERENCES

1. Adler, N., and Coleman, D. Gambling and Alcoholism Symptom Substitution and Functional Equivalents. *Quarterly Journal of Studies on Alcohol*, 1969, 30: 733-736.
2. Berk, B., and Hirata, L. Mental Illness Among the Chinese: Myth or Reality. *Journal of Social Issues*, 1973, 29:149-166.
3. Blaunor, R. Internal Colonialism and Ghetto Revolt. In R. Perrucci and M. Pilisuk, eds., *The Tripple Revolt: Emerging Social Problems in Depth*. Boston: Little, Brown, 1971.
4. Bourne, P. Suicide Among Chinese in San Francisco. *American Journal of Public Health*, 1973, 63:744-750.
5. Cattell, S. *Health, Welfare and Social Organization in Chinatown*. New York City: Community Service Society of New York, 1962.
6. Chen, T. Topical Comment: Silent Minority — The Oriental American's Plight. *Los Angeles Times*, June 8, 1969.
7. Chinaman's Chance. *Time*, September 8, 1967.
8. *Chinatown 1970 Census: Population and Housing Summary and Analysis*. San Francisco Department of City Planning, 1972.
9. Chu, G. Drinking Patterns and Attitudes of Rooming House Chinese in San Francisco: *Quarterly Journal of Studies on Alcohol*, 1972, 33.
10. DeVos, G., and Abbott, K. The Chinese Families in San Francisco. Master of Social Work dissertation, University of California, Berkeley, 1966.
11. Fong, S. Assimilation and Changing Social Roles of Chinese Americans. *Journal of Social Issues*, 1973, 29:115-128.
12. Fried, M. Effects of Social Change on Mental Health. *American Journal of Orthopsychiatry*, 1964, 34:3-28.
13. Fujimoto, I. Don't Mistake the Finger Pointing at the Moon for the

Moon. In *Chinese-Americans: School and Community Problems.* Chicago: Integrated Education Association, 1972.

14. Kroot, C. A Chronology of the Yellow Peril. *San Francisco Bay Guardian,* March 28, 1972.

15. Kung, S. *Chinese in American Life: Some Aspects of Their History, Status, Problems and Contributions.* Seattle: University of Washington Press, 1962.

16. Lyman, S. *The Asian in the West.* Reno, Nevada: Desert Research Institute, 1970.

17. Lin, T. A Study of the Incidence of Mental Disorder in Chinese and Other Cultures. *Psychiatry,* 1953, 16:313-336.

18. Maris, P. *Loss and Change.* New York: Random House, 1974.

19. Murase, K., ed. *Asian American Task Force Report: Problems and Issues in Social Work Education.* New York: Council on Social Work Education, 1973.

20. Paul, R. The Origin of the Chinese Issue. In J. Jakes and F. Jakes, eds., *The Aliens.* New York: Appleton-Century Crofts, 1970.

21. *San Francisco Chinese Community Citizen's Survey and Fact Finding Committee Report,* 1969.

22. Sue, S., and Kitano, H., eds. Asian American: A Success Story. *Journal of Social Issues,* 1973, 29.

23. Sue, S., and Sue, D. Chinese American Personality and Mental Health. *Ameriasia Journal,* 1971, 1:36-49.

24. Valentine, C. *Culture and Poverty.* Chicago: University of Chicago Press, 1968.

25. Wang, L. The Chinese American Student in San Francisco. In *Chinese-Americans: School and Community Problems.* Chicago: Integrated Education Association, 1972.

26. Yee, A. Myopic Perceptions and Textbooks: Chinese-Americans' Search for Identity. *Journal of Social Issues,* 1973, 29:102-103.

Chapter 28

YOUTH, PARENTS, AND TEACHERS IN CHINATOWN: A TRIADIC FRAMEWORK OF MINORITY SOCIALIZATION*

Lucie Cheng Hirata

THIS study integrates two sets of concerns in the socialization of minority children by examining the triadic relationships between minority adults or parents, minority youth or students, and teachers in public schools located in the minority community.

One set of concerns deals with the continuity and discontinuity between the family and the school as agencies of socialization. While the school is seen as an extension of the family in the continuing socialization of the white child, it is more often seen as antithetical to the minority family. A bulk of the literature typically assumes socialization to be a cumulative process for the general population, but as far as the minority population is concerned, disjointedness in the socialization process is more generally assumed. The minority family is often treated as an institution that impedes Americanization, and the school as an agency which "rescues" the child from the remnants of the old country or from the ethnic subculture, and resocializes her/him to conform to the values and norms of white America. The success or failure of the minority child in school is usually attributed to the congruence or conflict of value orientations between the family and the educational institution (Ramirez, 1969), and the level of achievement of a minority people is seen as determined by the degree of cultural congruence between their country of origin and America (Caudill and DeVos, 1956).

*"Youth, Parents and Teachers in Chinatown: A Triadic Framework of Minority Socialization" by Lucie Cheng Hirata is reprinted from *Urban Education* Vol. 10, No. 3 (October 1975) pp. 296-297 by permission of the Publisher, Sage Publications, Inc.

Based on this conception of cultural determinism and the ideology of white supremacy, the schools are given the charge of ridding the minority children of their old values and having them embrace the new ones. The schools are thus seen as factories whose output consists of individuals with certain cognitive skills and white middle America values. Whether the schools should be concerned with turning out a particular type of product or whether they should be factories at all were not seriously challenged until recently (Jencks, 1972; Rist, 1972). As the assimilation perspective wanes and the ideology of cultural pluralism surfaces, the functional relationship between the family and the school becomes problematic. The bilingual-bicultural instructional programs and the alternative schools are two institutional arrangements that testify to the existing concern over the role of public education in the socialization of minority children.

The second set of concerns stems from the question of generational conflict assumed by many to exist between age groups. However, it has been noted that the generation gap does not seem to be distributed evenly throughout society. Those groups that face greater cultural discontinuity tend to experience more generational conflict. Thus, the gap is found to be considerably wider for the white affluent, the black (Brunswick, 1970), and the immigrant populations (Eisenstadt, 1964) than for the majority population. Mead (1969) writes that a parallel can be drawn between immigrant parents and adults in modern society in the sense that rapid social change has diminished the capacity of all. In other words, adults as a whole are experiencing the same cultural shock as do immigrants to a new society. Even though Mead may be overstating the case, it is important to realize that from the viewpoint of the minority youth, not only have the "old" values lost their meaning, the "new" ones that they learn in the schools also do not work. Minority youth may come in conflict with adults in their community, adults in the schools, or both. Therefore, in order to examine the generational gap question among minority populations, we have to allow for a comparison between minority youth, parents, and teachers.

When we read the literature on minority socialization, we see either the first or the second set of concerns expressed, but seldom both. This is partly due to the way sociology as a profession is compartmentalized. Those who are identified as "family sociologists" tend to look only at the relationship between parents and their children; those who are mainly associated with the sociology of education tend to look only at the relationship between teachers and students, or parents and teachers. If youth is part of their study, they are almost always treated as a dependent variable and only in terms of achievement, achievement motivation, or deviance.

A FRAMEWORK

If we consider adults, youth, and public school teachers in an ethnic community as three distinct groups involved in the socialization process, we have a triadic frame within which congruence and conflict, agreement and disagreement, similarities and differences between generations and between majority-minority cultures may be studied simultaneously. In regard to a defined object X — which may be a value, a norm, an attitude, an act or behavior, or a group — the possible relationships between these three groups can be delineated as follows:[1]

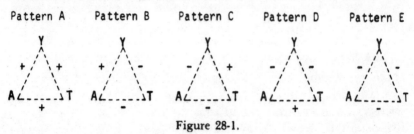

Figure 28-1.

Pattern A: All three groups are in agreement. This pattern would not support either the generational conflict or the cultural conflict hypotheses.

Pattern B: Youth and adults are in agreement, but youth and teachers, adults and teachers are in disagreement. This situation would support the cultural conflict hypothesis.

Pattern C: Youth and adults are in disagreement, adults and teachers are also in disagreement, but youth and teachers agree. This pattern will support the notion of acculturation, or the destruction of minority culture and the existence of generational conflicts within the family.

Pattern D: Youth and adults disagree, youth and teachers also disagree, but adults and teachers agree. This situation would indicate that there is an overall generational gap, the existence of a youth subculture, or adults (minority parents and public school teachers) gang up on the adolescents.

Pattern E: None of the three groups are in agreement. This pattern would indicate conflicts between minority and majority cultures and between generations and the existence of a youth subculture.

If one assumes the perspective of the traditional educator vis-á-vis minority education, one may postulate that the relationship between the three groups begins with Pattern B, goes through C or D, and finally should arrive at the ideal situation of Pattern A. Other views can be advanced. In fact, some studies on adolescents have concluded that major institutions of socialization such as the school and the family are playing a role in encouraging youth to create a "reaction subculture," one that rejects larger societal values and strikes out against them (Cohen, 1955). Since these studies see the family and the school as sharing similar values, they reflect the situation depicted in Pattern D. However, the same argument may apply even if the family and the school do not share similar values. Both the minority and the majority cultures within whose frameworks the minority youth are socialized may be found wanting and rejected by them. In fact, if the purpose of socialization is to teach young people to have the will to transform society, Patterns D and E may indicate how well or poorly the school and the family are doing and thereby have positive rather than negative implications.

The following data derived from a pilot study on socialization in Chinatown are presented as an example simply to illustrate one limited application of the framework, and are not meant to demonstrate conclusive support for any of the patterns discussed above.

SOCIALIZATION IN CHINATOWN: A PILOT STUDY

Los Angeles Chinatown traditionally refers to a five census tract area in the central part of the city. However, since 3,062 or 92 percent of the population in one of the tracts are inmates in an institution and only about 123 Chinese reside in that tract (U. S. Bureau of the Census, 1970; WERC, 1970), it seems more reasonable to exclude the particular tract from demographic and socioeconomic analysis of Chinatown.

According to the 1970 census, the ethnic composition of the Chinatown population is 43 percent Chinese, 45 percent Spanish surname, 8.5 percent other white, 0.3 percent black, and 3.2 percent others. In the decade 1960 to 1970, while the total population in the area has declined from 11,742 to 9,805, the Chinese population has doubled from approximately 2,100 to 4,218 (U. S. Bureau of the Census, 1960, 1970; WERC, 1970). A large portion of the increase can be accounted for by the influx of immigrants from China (including Taiwan) and Hong Kong. While 36 percent of the total population in the area were reported to be foreign born in 1960, about 57 percent were foreign born in 1970. The proportion of foreign born among the Chinese population in this area is estimated to be between 62 percent and 87 percent, much higher than that for the total area population.[2]

The major economic activities in the Chinatown area are connected with tourist-oriented businesses or the garment industry. The 1970 census shows that 28 percent of the population were engaged in manufacturing and 33 percent in retail trade. Among those who were sixteen and over, about 60 percent were employed. Because of the low wages, many families find it necessary for both husband and wife to be employed. In the census category "married females with husband present," 44 percent of the females are in the labor force. Yet the median family income for the Chinatown area is only around $7,100, and 18 percent of all families have incomes below the federal poverty line.

In summer 1971, the Asian American Studies Center at UCLA organized a team of graduate students and members of the Chinatown Neighborhood Youth Corps to conduct interviews with teachers in Chinatown public schools, and Chinese youth and adults who were residents in the Los Angeles Chinatown area. Almost all the interviews with Chinese adults were conducted in Chinese or a combination of Chinese and English, and the rest were conducted in English.

Sampling Procedures

TEACHER SAMPLE. Names of teachers listed in local public school directories and mailing lists were assembled, arranged by grades taught, and alphabetized. For each grade from the fourth grade up, four names were selected randomly to be in the sample. Through this procedure, a total of thirty-six names were obtained and eventually thirty-five teachers were interviewed. Six of the teachers in the sample were American-born Chinese.

THE RESIDENT SAMPLES. Within the Chinatown area only two census tracts have 50 percent or more Chinese in the total tract population. All dwellings in these two tracts were numbered beginning with a random choice, and the residents of every third dwelling were approached. If the residents were non-Chinese, their names were eliminated from the sample. If the residents were Chinese, the pair of interviewers would list all their ages, and ask to interview one married adult (twenty years or older), and/or one young person (twelve to nineteen). As a result, fifty-six adults and thirty-five young persons were interviewed. Among these, sixteen pairs of adults and young persons came from the same families.

Table 28-I presents some demographic characteristics of the three samples. It is evident that while all the teachers were born in the United States, almost all the Chinese adult residents and four-fifths of the youth sample were foreign born. However, a majority of the foreign born have lived in the United States for more than five years. All of the adolescents interviewed were either enrolled in school at the time or had completed a few years of schooling in America. In view of the fact that we were able to conduct all youth interviews in English but had to conduct most of the adult interviews in Chinese, there was at least a built-in difference between these two generations. However, since all the young persons interviewed claimed that they could also speak Chinese, this difference in language facility should not be construed as inability to communicate between the two generations.

FINDINGS

Attitudes toward the family, schooling, and ethnic/racial stratification were selected for comparisons among the three groups of Chinese parents, Chinese youth, and teachers of Chinatown public schools. Since these are three distinct aggregates involved in the socialization process and not individually matched triads, we can only examine and compare the domi-

TABLE 28-I

DEMOGRAPHIC CHARACTERISTICS OF THE THREE SAMPLES

	Teacher	Adult	Youth
Sex:			
Male	17	21	16
Female	18	35	19
Age:			
10-14	--	--	16
15-19	--	--	19
20-24	3	9	--
25-34	15	22	--
35-44	12	9	--
45-55	1	11	--
55-65	4	5	
Nativity:			
Native born	35	3	7
Foreign born	--	53	28
Length of stay in the U.S.:			
3 to 5 years	--	16	7
6 and over.	--	37	21

nant patterns exhibited by these groups.

Sociologists have used attitudes toward filial responsibility as an indicator of family solidarity, particularly in relation to social change (Dinkel, 1944; Wake and Sporakowski, 1972). While traditional family relations are characterized by children's greater willingness to support aged parents and by parents' greater expectation of such support, the importance of filial responsibility is believed to have diminished in contemporary American family relations. Although filial responsibility is a central value in traditional China, many writers have reported a breakdown or substantial modification of the traditional parent-child relationship (Hsu, 1971; Lee, 1960). If we only look at Chinese parents and Chinese youth and find a difference in their attitudes toward filial responsibility, we would not be able to say whether it is a case of generational gap or one of minority-majority cultural conflict unless we also examine the teachers' response. On the other hand, if we find a similarity in attitudes between parents and youth, we cannot conclude that there is a conflict between minority-majority values unless we also examine the teachers' attitudes. This line of argument can be extended to point out similar shortcomings of looking at any two groups in a socialization process which basically involves three distinct aggregates. If our finding shows a greater emphasis of filial responsibility by Chinese adults than by American teachers, then children may show ambivalence, agree with parents, or agree with teachers. However, since Chinese parents and teachers are both adults and thus form an age-group, they may be closer together on this attitude, and children therefore may agree or disagree with the older generation.

Table 28-II shows that as far as filial responsibility is concerned, there is greater agreement between Chinese parents and youth than between Chinese parents and teachers. Instead of being ambivalent, Chinese youth in our sample regardless of native or foreign born overwhelmingly indicated that they believed children should support their aged parents. These responses correspond to our Pattern B. Interestingly, there are

TABLE 28-II

ATTITUDES TOWARD FILIAL RESPONSIBILITY AND EDUCATION

	Teacher	Chinese *Adults*	Chinese *Youth*
Percent agreeing with the statement:	(N=35)	(N=56)	(N=36)
"Children should support their parents when they need it."	58%	94%	97%
"The quality of the schools is not high."	20%	61%	58%
To get ahead it's who you know that counts, not ability or education."	51%	16%	33%

slightly more young persons who agreed with the statement than their parent generation. This somewhat perplexing finding was also reported by Wake and Sporakowski (1972) in their study of Caucasian youth and their parents. Contrary to a commonly held belief, youth do not seem to be "heartless," but rather, at least at that stage of the life cycle, show an unexpected degree of concern for their parents. Chinese parents seemed to be aware of this since 62 percent of the adults interviewed believed that their children would support them in their old age. Given the insecurity of the aged, particularly for the immigrant population, it must be comforting to know that one's children care. Perhaps children themselves realize the lack of adequate public assistance for their aging parents and are willing to assume this responsibility if necessary. Comparatively, the low proportion of teachers who gave an affirmative answer to the statement set them apart from the Chinese resident community. Teachers may see filial responsibility as a remnant of the past and a burden on the younger generation, rather than as a humanistic necessity in an individual-oriented, capitalist society.

The character of the parent-child relationship for our sample is further indicated by the responses to two additional questions: (1) parents were asked if they felt they understood their children, and youth were asked if they thought their parents understood them; and (2) both parents and youth were asked if they got along with their children and parents, respectively. A majority of the parents (77%) claimed that they understood their children well or very well, and 74 percent of the youth sample responded that their parents understood them well or very well. As far as getting along with each other is concerned, 83 percent of the adolescent respondents said that they got along fine with their parents, and 66 percent of the adults responded the same way with regard to their children.

Turning to attitudes toward the school and education in general, we found that a majority of the Chinese respondents, both youth and parents, did not think the schools to be of high quality, whereas only 20 percent of the teachers held the same opinion. On the other hand, more teachers than other groups thought that education was not the most important determinant of upward mobility (Table 28-II). Taken together, the pattern of responses reveals a most significant point. Chinese parents, and to a lesser degree Chinese youth, believe in education as a tool to "get ahead," but are dissatisfied with the particular type of education that takes place in the schools. Teachers, in contrast to the Chinese samples, have great faith in the quality of the schools, but do not think education would help the children very much in "making it." The response patterns began to make more sense when we juxtapose them against the goals of education as they were expressed by the teachers and Chinese parents. Table 28-III shows that while a majority of the parents interviewed emphasized the instrumental function of education, the teachers emphasized the acculturating function over all other functions. Given this difference in expectations, we can understand the corresponding difference in the assessment of the quality of schools. The model that Chinese adults have in mind is essentially that good schools lead to good education which leads to good jobs and a good position in the society; therefore the implication is to improve the quality of the schools and of education. On the other hand, the model that teachers hold is basically that schools and education teach minority children the values of the dominant culture and have very little to do with one's success or failure in society. They feel that the schools are doing fine, but schools and education are more or less irrelevant to the future of their students. By adopting such a view, teachers can claim that the future of Chinese students is beyond their control. Caught in between these two very different views, Chinese youth seem to be in agreement with their parents about the poor quality of the schools, but differ from them in that they do not quite know how much importance they should place on it. To sum up, the dominant responses for these three groups in regard to attitudes toward education can be represented by Pattern B. Perhaps Chinese parents and youth would rather find the "right" values themselves and prefer the teachers to concentrate on how to best develop the basic cognitive skills in their students.

TABLE 28-III

TEACHERS' AND CHINESE ADULTS' EXPECTATIONS
REGARDING EDUCATION

	Teachers (N=35)	Chinese Adults (N=56)
Develop right values and attitudes.	46%	3%
Expand knowledge.	26%	10%
Ability to think for oneself.	17%	20%
Develop skills in order to get a good job.	11%	67%

This preference is not to be construed as meaning Chinese parents are only interested in vocational training for their children. Teachers, Chinese adults, and youth were asked to indicate whether they consider it important to learn American culture, Chinese culture, or both. Their answers were very similar. Seventy percent of teachers, 75 percent of adults, and 83 percent of adolescents claimed that Chinese and American cultures are equally important. However, only 11 percent of the adolescents indicated that their teachers knew something about Chinese culture. The irony is more obvious when we noticed that the only bilingual program in Chinatown public schools taught one single character a week! There were no classes on Chinese history or contemporary Chinese society, and nothing about the Asian American heritage.[3]

The last set of attitudes that we have chosen deals with ethnic stratification. A series of social distance questions were asked during the interviews, and respondents rather than the ethnic groups being ranked were classified according to the pattern of their responses (Table 28-IV).[4] Two types of responses were evident: those that distinguished between ethnic groups and those that did not. Respondents who exhibited the former pattern may be labeled stratifiers, the others nonstratifiers. On this level of classification, we found that while a majority of the Chinese youth were stratifiers, less than half of the Chinese adults and teachers made distinctions among the groups. Children, in this instance, did not fall in between the two aggregates of adults, but rather differed markedly from them. The reason for this difference, if it is real, is unknown, although one may venture some hypotheses. Few sociologists would disagree with the assertion that American society is ethnically stratified. Since any social pattern has to be learned, it is not surprising that the Chinese adults in our sample have not learned it well enough to distinguish between the various ethnic groups that they have been asked to rank. If this explanation seems tenable, one would expect the highest percentage of teachers to be stratifiers. But instead we could see that this was not the case. We feel that it is because either teachers have simultaneously learned not to express discriminatory attitudes in interviews, or they have responded with the ideal dictated by the liberal ideology. In view of the near perfect correlation of the rankings of ethnic groups by the adolescents in our sample, we feel that the relatively high percentage of stratifiers in the youth sample reveals that Chinese children have learned to discriminate among ethnic groups, but have not learned to hide them. In other words, they were "telling it like it is."

Among those who did not stratify other ethnic groups, three distinct patterns could be observed. Those respondents who would accept all other groups equally into their immediate family by marriage which would indicate an eventual racial mix have been classified as assimilationists; those who would accept all other groups as friends and/or as next-door neighbors have been labeled social integrationists; and those that would exclude other groups except their own from their social network altogether have been classified as isolationists. Table 28-IV gives a percentage breakdown of these response patterns.

TABLE 28-IV

TYPES OF ATTITUDES TOWARD RACIAL/ETHNIC GROUPS

	Teacher (N=35)	Chinese *Adults* (N=56)	Chinese *Youth* (N=35)
Stratifiers	41%	34%	61%
Nonstratifiers	59%	66%	39%
Assimilationists	50%	12%	15%
Social integrationists	9%	45%	19%
Isolationists	--	9%	5%

Contrary to the commonly held stereotype of cliquishness of Chinese, few adults or youth interviewed would like to restrict their social network to members of their own group. Considerably more teachers (50%) than Chinese adults (12%) or Chinese youth (15%) favored the assimilationist view. Given that the assimilation perspective has dominated the social sciences and has come to be the ideal for America, it is not surprising that more teachers echoed accordingly.

One may feel that our interpretation is too harsh on the "egalitarian" teachers and too lenient on the "prejudiced" youth. We believe that children are not innately prejudiced, but learn to be so through interaction with others. And teachers are at least partly responsible.

During our interviews in Chinatown, we heard of racial disturbances in some public schools. In response to our questions on the subject, 83 percent of the teachers in our sample indicated that there were racial tensions in their schools, most of which resulted in fights between Mexican and Chinese students. When questioned about the causes of these fights, 52 percent of the teachers blamed them on the Mexican students. Specific responses included: "Mexicans were taught to fight with hands, they are more aggressive," "Mexicans are troublemakers," "they are jealous of the Chinese, racial resentment, that's what it is," and so on. If teachers hold these attitudes, how could we believe that they would willingly have their children marry Mexicans as indicated by their responses to the social distance questions, and how could we expect Chinese children not to be affected by these prejudicial judgments?

If we take into consideration all the patterns of responses, we find that the configuration resembles Pattern E — each group of people has its own dominant response. For the teachers, the favorite response reflects the value of assimilation; for the Chinese adults, it is social integration; and for the Chinese youth, it is neither assimilation nor universal integration, but selective acceptance or stratification.

SUMMARY AND CONCLUSION

This study attempted to develop a framework for the analysis of minority socialization by simultaneously taking into account the questions of generational gap and minority-majority conflict. The similarities and differences of attitudes toward the family, schooling, and ethnic/racial groups as expressed by Chinese adult and youth residents in the Los Angeles Chinatown area and by teachers in public schools located in that community were examined to illustrate a limited application of the framework.

We found that while cultural difference rather than generational difference predominated in attitudes toward supporting aged parents the two variables did not always operate the same way in other areas examined. Although both Chinese parents and Chinese children expressed dissatisfaction with the quality of education and believed that a good education was important to get ahead, they disagreed somewhat on the degree of that importance. The teachers, on the other hand, were convinced of the high quality of the schools, but, ironically, did not think it would make much difference on the upward mobility of the children. Lastly, in terms of attitude toward ethnic/racial groups, each sample exhibited a distinct dominant pattern of response.

While we do not claim that our samples fully represent the public school teachers, Chinese adults, and youth in Chinatown, our findings in general lend credence to what other researchers have reported on minority education (Rist, 1972; Harvard Educational Review, 1973). We do not intend to condemn teachers; what we do want to emphasize is that our public educational institutions have got to be made more responsive to the minority community, since students must solicit the largest input from groups involved in order to develop varied responses to different needs.

REFERENCES

Brunswick, Ann F. What Generation Gap? *Social Problems*, 1970, 17:358-370.

Caudill, W., and DeVos, G. Achievement, Culture and Personality: The Case of the Japanese Americans. *American Anthropologist*, 1956, 58:1102-1125.

Chinese-Americans: School and Community Problems. Chicago: Integrated Education Associates, 1972.

Cohen, K. *Delinquent Boys*. New York: Free Press, 1955.

Davis, K. The Sociology of Parent-Youth Conflict. *American Sociological Review*, 1940, 5:523-536.

Dinkel, R. Attitudes of Children Toward Supporting Aged Parents. *American Sociological Review*, 1944, 9:370-379.

Eisenstadt, S. N. *From Generation to Generation*. New York: Free Press, 1964.

Harvard Educational Review, ed. *Perspectives on Inequality*, 1973.

Hsu, F. L. K. *The Challenge of the American Dream: The Chinese in the United States.* Belmont, Cal.: Wadsworth, 1971.

Jencks, C., et al. *Inequality: A Reassessment of the Effects of Family and Schooling in America.* New York: Basic Books, 1972.

Lee, R. H. *The Chinese in the United States of America.* Hong Kong: Hong Kong University Press, 1960.

Mead, M. The Generation Gap. *Science,* 1969, 164:135.

Ramirez III, M. *Potential Contribution by the Behavioral Sciences to Effective Preparation Programs for Teachers of Mexican-American Children.* Las Cruces: New Mexico State University, 1969.

U. S. Bureau of the Census. *Census of Population and Housing: 1970 Census Tracts — Los Angeles and Long Beach,* 1970.

———— . *Census of Population and Housing 1960 Census Tracts — Los Angeles and Long Beach,* 1960.

Wake, S. B., and Sporakowski. An Intergenerational Comparison of Attitudes Towards Supporting Aged Parent. *Journal of Marriage and the Family,* 1972, 34:42-48.

Weinberg, C. *Education and Social Problems.* New York: Free Press, 1971.

Western Economic Research Company (WERC). *Census Data by Census Tracts.* Los Angeles, 1970.

Chapter 29

COUNSELING CHINESE-AMERICANS*

Derald Wing Sue and Stanley Sue

MANY people believe that the Chinese in America represent a model minority group. Unlike the blacks and Chicanos, the Chinese have tried to function in the existing social structure with a minimum of visible conflict with members of the host society. Historically, they have accepted much prejudice and discrimination without voicing strong public protest (DeVos & Abbott, 1966). Their traditional nonthreatening stance and the public's lack of knowledge about Chinese people have masked their problems of poverty, unemployment, and juvenile delinquency. The notion that Chinese people experience few problems in American society is also shared by many educators, counselors, and mental health workers. The Chinese-Americans' strong emphasis on educational achievement (DeVos & Abbott, 1966), their custom of handling problems within the family, and their limited use of mental health facilities (Kimmich, 1960; Kitano, 1969) have reinforced this misconception.

Since many Chinese-American college students find it difficult to label themselves as having emotional problems, they tend to under-use psychiatric facilities on campuses when they encounter personal problems (Sue & Sue, 1971). Rather, they often seek the less threatening services of campus counseling centers with an educational-vocational orientation, because they feel that less social stigma is involved. It is especially important for guidance workers to understand the Chinese-American students' cultural background and the conflicts they experience. These cultural influences may, in fact, hinder the development of a therapeutic relationship between counselor and client. However, very few counselors know enough about the Chinese-Americans' background to understand their reaction to the counseling-therapy situation. An examination of Chinese culture and family interaction patterns suggests that the counseling situation may cause a great deal of conflict for many Chinese-American students.

CHINESE CULTURE AND PERSONALITY

Although the Chinese family in America is changing, it still retains many of the cultural values from its past (DeVos & Abbott, 1966). The Chinese family is an ancient and complex institution, and the roles of family members have long been rigidly defined. Chinese are taught to obey parents, to respect elders, and to create a good family name by outstanding achievement in some aspect of life, for example, by academic or occupational success. Since misbehaviors (juvenile delinquency, academic failure, and mental disorders) reflect upon the entire family, an individual learns that his behavior has great significance. If the expression of his feelings might disrupt family harmony, he is expected to restrain himself. Indeed, the Chinese culture highly values self-control and inhibition of strong feelings (Abbott, 1970).

Sue and Kirk (1972, in press) found that the personality traits of Chinese-American students reflect this family and cultural background. The investigators studied the entire entering freshman class in the fall of 1966, at the University of California in Berkeley. Chinese-American students seemed to be more conforming to authority, inhibited, and introverted than the general student body. They also tended to be more practical in their approach to tasks and to be less tolerant of ambiguity, preferring to deal with concrete facts and events. Although their quantitative skills appeared high, their verbal scores were lower than that of the general student body, perhaps reflecting a bilingual background and limited communication patterns in the home.

THE ACCULTURATION PROCESS

The Chinese individual in America is in a position of conflict between the pulls of both his cultural background and the Western values he is exposed to in school and by the mass media. American values emphasizing spontaneity, assertiveness, and independence are often at odds with many Chinese values. As Chinese people progressively adopt more of the values and standards of the larger community as their own, the transition is not always smooth. Indeed, culture conflict seems to be an intimate part of the Asian-American experience.

It is our impression that Chinese students do not react in any stereotyped manner to culture conflict (Sue & Sue, 1971), but we have most frequently observed three main types of reaction. Some tend to resist assimilation by maintaining traditional values and by associating predominantly with other Chinese. Others try to become assimilated into the dominant culture by rejecting their Chinese culture. The Asian-American movement on college campuses has attracted yet another group of students by stressing pride in racial identity.

Obviously, each Chinese student does not fall neatly into one of the three groups, and there are quantitative differences in the types of conflicts exhibited in counseling situations, depending upon the cultural orientation of individuals. To illustrate the many conflicts experienced by Chinese-American students in their personal life and in their reactions to counseling, in this article we will use case descriptions of clients we have seen for counseling. We have taken care to insure the anonymity of all case materials.

MAINTAINING TRADITIONAL VALUES

John C. is a twenty-one-year-old student majoring in electrical engineering. He first sought counseling because he was having increasing study problems and was receiving failing grades. These academic difficulties became apparent during the first quarter of his senior year and were accompanied by headaches, indigestion, and insomnia. Since he had been an excellent student in the past, John felt that his lowered academic performance was caused by illness. However, a medical examination failed to reveal any organic disorder.

During the initial interview, John seemed depressed and anxious. He was difficult to counsel because he would respond to inquiries with short but polite statements and would seldom volunteer information about himself. He avoided any statements that involved feelings and presented his problem as a strictly educational one. Although he never expressed it directly, John seemed to doubt the value of counseling and needed much reassurance and feedback about his performance in the interview. In view of John's reluctance to open up, it seemed unwise to probe immediately into areas that aroused much anxiety in him:

As the sessions progressed, John became less anxious and more trusting of the counselor. Much of his earlier difficulties in opening up were caused by his feelings of shame and guilt at having come to a counselor. He was concerned that his family might discover his seeking of help and that it would be a disgrace to them. This anxiety was compounded by his strong feelings of failure in school. However, when the counselor informed him that many Chinese students experienced similar problems and that these sessions were completely confidential, John seemed quite relieved. As he became increasingly able to open up, he revealed problems such as we have found are typical of Chinese students who have strongly internalized traditional cultural values and whose self-worth and identity are defined within the family nexus.

John's parents had always had high expectations of him and constantly pressured him to do well in school. They seemed to equate his personal worth with his ability to obtain good grades. This pressure caused him to spend endless hours studying, and generally he remained isolated from social activities. This isolation did not help him to learn the social skills required in peer relationships. In addition, John's more formalized training was in sharp contrast to the informality and spontaneity demanded in Caucasian interpersonal relationships. Therefore, his circle of friends was small, and he was never really able to enjoy himself with others.

John experienced a lot of conflict, because he was beginning to resent the pressure his parents put on him, and also their demands. For example, they stated that it would be nice if he would help his brothers through school after graduation. This statement aroused a great amount of unexpressed anger in John toward them. He felt unable to lead his own life. Furthermore, his lack of interest in engineering was intensified as graduation approached. He had always harbored secret wishes about becoming an artist but was pressured into engineering by his parents. His deep-seated feelings of anger toward his parents resulted in his passive-aggressive responses of failure in school and in his physical symptoms.

The case of John C. illustrates some of the following conflicts encountered by many Chinese students attempting to maintain traditional Chinese values: (a) there is often a conflict between loyalty to the family and personal desires for independence; (b) the learned patterns of self-restraint and formality in interpersonal relationships often result in a lack of social experience and subsequent feelings of loneliness, and furthermore, they can act as impediments to counseling; (c) the family pressure to achieve academically accentuates feelings of shame and depression when the student fails.

REJECTING CHINESE CUSTOMS

Many Chinese-Americans attempt to become Westernized and reject traditional Chinese customs. Vontress (1970) points out that many blacks develop a hatred of their own group and culture, and many Chinese counselees experience a similar type of conflict, especially in their social life. It is typified in the following counseling interchange.

Counselor: You seem to prefer dating Caucasians . . .

Client: Well . . . It's so stupid for my parents to think that they can keep all their customs and values. I really resent being Chinese and having to date all those Chinese guys. They're so passive, and I can make them do almost anything I want. Others [Chinese] are on a big ego trip and expect me to be passive and do whatever they say. Yes . . . I do prefer Caucasians.

Counselor: Is that an alternative open to you?

Client: Yes ... but my parents would feel hurt ... they'd probably disown me. They keep on telling me to go out with Chinese guys. A few months ago they got me to go out with this guy — I must have been the first girl he ever dated — I wasn't even polite to him.

Counselor: I guess things were doubly bad. You didn't like the guy and you didn't like your parents pushing him on you.

Client: Well ... actually I felt a little sorry for him. I don't like to hurt my parents or those [Chinese] guys but things always work out that way.

The client's last statement reflected some feelings of guilt over her rudeness toward her date. Although she was open and honest, her desire to be independent was confused with a constant rejection of her parents' attempts to influence her life. During a later session, she was able to express her conflict:

Client: I used to think that I was being independent if I went out with guys that my parents disapproved of. But that isn't really being independent. I just did that to spite them. I guess I should feel guilty if I purposely hurt them, but not if I *really* want to do something for myself.

Although the rejection of Chinese culture is often a developmental phase adequately resolved by most Chinese-Americans, many come to look upon Western personality characteristics as more admirable. For example, some Chinese-American girls come to expect the boys they date to behave boldly and aggressively in the Western manner. Weiss (1969) found that many Chinese-American college females were quite vehement in their denunciation of their male counterparts as dating partners. They frequently described the Chinese male as immature, inept, and sexually unattractive. Although the males denied the more derogatory accusations about themselves, they tended to agree that they were more inhibited and unassertive than Caucasians.

THE ASIAN-AMERICAN MOVEMENT

Recently, a growing number of Chinese students on college

campuses throughout the nation are, like the blacks and Chicanos, emphasizing their own heritage, pride, and self-identity. They feel that the role of a conforming "banana" (a derogatory term used to describe a person of Asian ancestry who is "yellow on the outside but white on the inside") is too degrading. In an attempt to gain the self-respect they feel has been denied them by white society, they have banded together in an attempt to reverse the negative trend of bananaism among their own group. This group of individuals seem much more aware of political, economic, and social forces that have shaped their identity. They feel that society is to blame for their present dilemma and are actively challenging the establishment. They are openly suspicious of institutions, such as counseling services, because they view them as agents of the establishment. Very few of the more ethnically conscious and militant Asians will use counseling — because of its identification with the status quo. When they do, they are usually suspicious and hostile toward the counselor. Before counseling can proceed effectively, the counselor will have to deal with certain challenges from these students, such as the following:

> *Client*: First of all . . . I don't believe in psychology. . . . I think it's a lot of bullshit. People in psychology are always trying to adjust people to a sick society, and what is needed is to overthrow this goddamned establishment. . . . I feel the same way about those stupid tests. Cultural bias . . . they aren't applicable to minorities. The only reason I came in here was . . . well, I heard your lecture in Psychology 160 [a lecture on Asian-Americans], and I think I can work with you.

The counselee in this case happened to be hostile and depressed over the recent death of his father. Although he realized he had some need for help, he still did not trust the counseling process.

> *Client*: Psychologists see the problem inside of people when the problem is in society. Don't you think white society has made all minorities feel inferior and degraded?
>
> *Counselor*: I know that. White society has done great harm to minorities.

The client was posing a direct challenge to the counselor. Any defense of white society or explanations of the value of counseling might have aroused greater hostility and mistrust. It would have been extremely difficult to establish rapport without some honest agreement on the racist nature of American society. Later, the counselee revealed that his father had just died. He was beginning to realize that there was no contradiction in viewing society as being racist and in having personal problems.

Often, growing pride in self-identity makes it difficult for students who are having emotional problems to accept their personal difficulties. This is not to say that militance and group pride are signs of maladjustment. On the contrary, the Asian-American movement is a healthy attempt to resolve feelings of inferiority and degradation fostered by discrimination and prejudice.

THE COUNSELING PROCESS AS A SOURCE OF CONFLICT

Chinese students are often caught between the demands of two cultures, but individuals react differently to this conflict. The counseling situation reflects the cultural conflicts encountered by Chinese students in their everyday life.

First, counselors and other mental health professionals are often at a loss to explain why Chinese counselees do not actively participate in the counseling process. Our colleagues have remarked that Chinese students are difficult to counsel because they repress emotional conflicts. These remarks indicate that counselors expect their counselees to exhibit some degree of openness, psychological-mindedness, or sophistication. Such characteristics are often beneficial in counseling. However, openness is quite difficult for many Chinese students who have learned to inhibit emotional expression, and direct or subtle demands by the counselor for openness may be quite threatening to them.

Second, Chinese students frequently find it difficult to admit they have emotional difficulties, because such problems arouse a great deal of shame and a sense of having failed one's family.

Often, Chinese students may indirectly ask for help with personal difficulties by presenting educational problems or somatic complaints. Some investigators (Abbott, 1970; Marsella, Kinzie, & Gordon, 1971) feel that Chinese frequently express psychological distress through indirect routes such as bodily complaints and passive-aggressive responses. Since emotional problems are felt to reflect on family upbringing, somatization could represent a more acceptable means of expressing psychological disturbance. Such was the case of John C.

Third, the counseling or therapy situation is often an ambiguous one. The counselee is encouraged to discuss any problems; the counselor listens and responds. Many Chinese students prefer concrete and well-structured situations, and the well-defined role expectations in the Chinese family are in sharp contrast to the ambiguity of the counseling process.

IMPLICATIONS FOR THE COUNSELING PROCESS

Just as it is unwise to suggest definite guidelines in dealing with all Chinese-Americans in counseling, it seems equally unwise to ignore cultural factors that might affect the counseling process. The counselor's inability to recognize these factors may make the Chinese counselee terminate prematurely. The difficulty in admitting social and emotional problems despite a need for help places the Chinese-American in an intense conflict. A too-confrontive and emotionally intense approach at the onset of counseling can frequently increase the level of shame. The counselor may facilitate counseling by responding to what may be viewed as superficial problems, such as the educational difficulties and somatic complaints that may mask more serious emotional conflicts. The counselee is then in a position to move at his own rate in exploring more threatening material.

In addition, the counselor can often facilitate self-disclosure by referring to psychological material relevant to vocational choice or job demands. For example, test interpretation can be threatening to the Chinese student, especially when psychological problems are involved. Many students are able to talk more freely about their difficulties if test interpretations are related concretely to their vocational future. Therefore, counselors involved in vocational decision-making may be in an advantageous position not shared by other mental health professionals, as the following case illustrates.

Pat H. was a nineteen-year-old pre-pharmacy major who came for vocational counseling. Since he was the eldest of three boys, his parents had high expectations of him. He was expected to set a good example for his younger brothers and enhance the good name of the family. Because his grades were mediocre, he was beginning to doubt his ability to handle pharmacy. However, results of his interest and ability tests and his counselor's impressions supported his choice of the pharmacy major. The counselor felt that his difficulty in courses reflected passive resistance to his parents' high expectations of him being the oldest son.

On his Edwards Personal Preference Schedule, Pat showed high achievement, change, and abasement scores. Earlier attempts to explore his feelings dealing with parental expectations proved fruitless. However, the following transcript demonstrates how testing was used to open up exploration in a nonthreatening manner.

Counselor: Let's explore the meaning of your scores in greater detail as they relate to future vocations. All right?
Client: Okay.
Counselor: Your high score on achievement indicates that whatever you undertake you would like to excel and do well in. For example, if you enter pharmacy, you'd like to do well in that field [*client nods head*]. However, your high change score indicates that you like variety and change. . . . you may tend to get restless at times . . . feel trapped in activities that bore you.
Client: Yeah.
Counselor: Do you see this score [abasement score]?
Client: Yeah, I blew the scale on that one. . . . What is it? [*some anxiety observable*]
Counselor: Well, it indicates you tend to be hard on yourself. . . . For example, if you were to do poorly in pharmacy school . . . you would blame yourself for the failure . . .
Client: Yeah, Yeah . . . I'm always doing that. . . . I feel

that ... it's probably exaggerated.
Counselor: Exaggerated?
Client: I mean ... being the oldest son.
Counselor: What's it like to be the oldest son?
Client: Well ... there's a lot of pressure and you can feel immobilized. Maybe this score [*points to change scale*] is why I feel so restless.

The progression marked a major breakthrough in Pat's case and led to an increasingly personalized discussion.

The difficulty in self-disclosure for Chinese-American students indicates that assurances of confidentiality between counselor and counselee are of utmost importance. A frequent concern of many Chinese-American students is that their friends, and especially their parents, will find out that they are seeing a counselor. For this reason, group counseling or therapy is very threatening. It is difficult enough to share their thoughts with one individual, let alone an entire group. Chinese students frequently refuse to participate in groups, and when in a group, they are often quiet and withdrawn. It may be wise to discuss the issue of confidentiality, the feelings of trust and mistrust in one another, and the cultural barriers in talking about feelings. We have found that many Chinese-American counselees are able to open up and express feelings quite directly once they develop trust of the counselor.

Since many Chinese-American students tend to feel more comfortable in well-structured and unambiguous situations, counseling by providing guidelines in the form of explanations and suggestions may be helpful. Such guidelines might include an explanation of the counseling process. In addition, the Chinese-American's emotional inhibition and lower verbal participation may also indicate the need for a more active approach on the part of the counselor. The following case description is an example of an active structuring of interviews.

Anne W. was quite uncomfortable and anxious during the first interview dealing with vocational counseling. This anxiety seemed more related to the ambiguity of the situation than anything else. She appeared confused about the direction of the counselor's comments and questions. At this point the counselor felt that an explanation of vocational counseling would facilitate the process.

Counselor: Let me take some time to explain to you how we usually proceed in vocational counseling. Vocational counseling is an attempt to understand the whole person. Therefore, we are interested in your interests, likes and dislikes, and specific abilities or skills as they relate to different possible vocations. The first interview is usually an attempt to get to know you . . . especially your past experiences and reactions to different courses you've taken, jobs you've worked at, and so forth. Especially important are the hopes and aspirations that you have. If testing seems indicated, as in your case, you'll be asked to complete a battery of tests. After testing we'll sit down and interpret them together. When we arrive at possible vocations, we'll use the vocational library and find out what these jobs entail in terms of background, training, etc.

Client: Oh! I see . . .

Counselor: That's why we've been exploring your high school experiences. . . . Sometimes the hopes and dreams in your younger years can tell us much about your interests.

After this explanation, Anne participated much more in the interviews.

CULTURE AND COUNSELING

Since guidance workers may lack understanding of cultural influences, they frequently encounter difficulty in working with minority groups. Because there are cultural determinants of behavior, and counseling is essentially a white middle-class activity, it may be necessary to modify counseling approaches. This is especially true in working with many Chinese-American counselees. The suggestions we have offered are primarily directed to the establishment of a working relationship of rapport and trust. Once a strong relationship has been established, the counselor has greater freedom in varying his therapeutic approach. To avoid oversimplification and the creation of an artificial situation, we have purposely kept our discussion of techniques somewhat general. The use of counseling techniques should be evaluated on the basis of the client's needs and their compatibility with the counselor's style and personality. Perhaps the most important tool a counselor could possess is knowledge of the Asian-American experience and its relationship to counseling. The counselor must address himself to problems of guilt and shame and lack of openness in the case of the traditionalist, to problems of independence and self-hate in the marginal man, and to racism in society with the Asian-American.

Finally, a word of caution must be noted. Most Chinese-Americans are able to handle cultural conflicts and adequately resolve them. This article has been mainly concerned with that relatively small number who seek counseling help when they feel that they cannot resolve their conflicts.

REFERENCES

Abbott, K. A. *Harmony and Individualism.* Taipei: Orient Cultural Service, 1970.

DeVos, G., and Abbott, K. The Chinese Family in San Francisco, Unpublished master's thesis, University of California, Berkeley, 1966.

Kimmich, R. A. Ethnic Aspects of Schizophrenia in Hawaii. *Psychiatry,* 1960, 23:97-102.

Kitano, H. H. L. Japanese-American Mental Illness. In S. D. Plog and R. B. Edgerton, eds., *Changing Perspectives in Mental Illness.* New York: Holt, Rinehart & Winston, 1969.

Marsella, A. J., Kinzie, D., and Gordon, P. Depression Patterns Among American College Students of Caucasian, Chinese, and Japanese Ancestry. Paper presented at the Conference on Culture and Mental Health in Asia and the Pacific, March 1971.

Sue, D. S., and Kirk, B. A. Psychological Characteristics of Chinese-American Students. *Journal of Counseling Psychology,* 1972, in press.

Sue, S., and Sue, D. W. Chinese-American Personality and Mental Health. *Ameriasia Journal,* 1971, 1:36-49.

Vontress, C. E. Counseling Blacks. *Personnel and Guidance Journal,* 1970, 48:713-719.

Weiss, M. S. Inter-racial Romance. The Chinese-Caucasian Dating Game. Paper presented at the Southwestern Anthropological Association. Las Vegas, Nevada, April, 1969.

Part VI. Japanese Americans

INTRODUCTION

THE crux of the counselor's dilemma is what to do with students of ethnic minority cultures who, borrowing from cultural anthropology, are like all other persons in some behaviors, like some other persons in other behaviors, and like no other persons in many behaviors. All cultures share the common experiences of birth, helplessness in growing up, and the processes of growing old and dying. Some cultures share similar ways of socializing the young, language, and expectations about authority. However each culture has a unique history and life-style. The more effective counselors know that Japanese Americans, like all ethnic groups, are tripartite in culture.

JAPANESE AMERICAN CULTURAL CONDITIONING

The norm of *enryo* is the most characteristic of Japanese behavior. This concept originally referred to proper role behavior among "inferiors" and "superiors," mainly deference and obsequiousness in order to avoid confusion, embarrassment and anxiety. The blank stare, noncommittal answer, and passive group behavior reflect *enryo*.

Ha zu ka shi (others will laugh at you) is part of the *enryo* syndrome. To publicly make a fool of oneself is to publicly shame one's family. Being reticent in order to avoid embarrassment is seen in classroom and counseling situations. *Hi-ge* or refusing to praise self or family, especially in public, does not prevent Japanese American students in traditional families from being highly competitive. Again like their Asian ancestors, they are taught to do the best they can, no matter what they are doing, but to be humble and self-deprecating if they succeed. This, then, is the quest for personal excellence that seems foreign to most non-Asians.

READINGS

Like her review of Chinese American history, Kathleen Wright presents a detailed study of early Japanese migration to America. Of special interest may be the occupational roles of Japanese Americans during the period of 1840 to 1920.

John W. Connor examines the extent to which Japanese families have retained characteristics associated with the family system in Japan. Although acculturation has taken place, even third generation Japanese American families have retained certain traditional Japanese family values.

Unlike non-Asian American minority groups, Japanese American and Chinese American students generally are high school achievers. Audrey J. Schwartz looks at the cultural values which differentiate white Anglo students from Japanese Americans. The Asian tradition, he concludes, has resulted in culturally advantaged students.

Lawrence Onoda investigates the difference in attitudes toward achievement and personality characteristics of mainland Japanese American Sanseis high and low achievement students. The impact of acculturation as well as Japanese nationalism is examined.

Edward Kaneshige discusses the problems Asian American students encounter when participating in group counseling. The conditions, goals, and techniques of group counseling may *ipso facto* prevent traditional Asian students from being assertive in small group school situations. The nine recommendations made by Kaneshige can, if carefully implemented, improve the counseling process as it pertains to Asian Americans.

Chapter 30

JAPANESE AMERICAN HISTORY*

KATHLEEN WRIGHT

ALTHOUGH there are existing legends which speak of numerous shipping wrecks on the western coast of the United States which may have brought the earliest Japanese to America, and a report from San Francisco of several Japanese reaching that city in 1851, official Japanese immigration began following the treaty negotiated by Commodore Perry in 1854. Townsend Harris, who journeyed to Japan in 1856 on business relative to the Perry Treaty, is credited with opening the doors to Japanese immigration. The first wave of new comers came in response to the demand for cheap labor in the United States.

Prior to the accounts of shipping wrecks which left Japanese stranded on American shores, is the story of the man who may well have been the first Japanese to settle in the United States. In June of 1841 an American whaling vessel commanded by Captain Whitfield of New Bedford came upon a small island. He sent men ashore to see if there were any turtles on the island. Instead, his crewmen found five shipwrecked Japanese almost dead from hunger and exposure. During the next six months, while the Japanese learned something of whaling from their rescuers the ship made its way to Honolulu. There four of the Japanese remained; the fifth, Manjiro Nakahama, a fifteen-year-old boy renamed John Mung by the crew, chose to remain on board the *John Howland* and return to the United States with Whitfield. It was three years later, 1844, when the *John Howland* came into port at New Bedford harbor. Bystanders took little notice of the "Chinese looking fellow" who disembarked with Captain Whitfield. There was no publicity

*From Kathleen Wright, *The Other Americans: Minorities in History*, Los Angeles, Lawrence Publishing Company, 1969.

for the first Japanese who came to American soil.

Manjiro, John Mung, came to the United States at a time when Japan's government was still enforcing the rigid exclusion policy adopted about 1640. He came with the intense curiosity and desire to learn that was to characterize Japanese immigrants for years to come. Adopted as a son by Captain Whitfield, John Mung attended school in New England and learned the trade of a cooper. His schoolmates are said to recall him as an industrious and scholarly student with a special aptitude for mathematics and navigation. In 1857 he completed a translation of Bowditch into Japanese. Although he came to America at his own insistence, Manjiro retained a longing to return to his native land and to see his mother. He sailed to Hawaii on an American ship and reached Japan by whale boat launched off the shores of Okinawa. He was kept prisoner for three years by the Japanese government and not released to carry out the planned visit to his mother until January, 1853. Soon after, he was summoned by his government to Tokyo where Western powers were seeking an entrance into the land. His knowledge of English was used profitably, and when Commodore Perry arrived, he was employed as an interpreter between the Commodore and the shogun.

Manjiro returned to America in 1860 as a government official and again in 1871, en route to Europe to study military science during the Franco-Prussian War. He returned to Japan where he was engaged as a university professor until his death in 1898. By that time, many thousands of his countrymen had migrated to Hawaii and would soon move on to the continental United States as he himself had done some fifty years before.

On the West Coast an incident somewhat similar to the experience of John Mung occurred. A Japanese, Hikozo Hamada, a lad of thirteen, was shipwrecked and brought to San Francisco aboard the *Auckland* in 1851. After a year, he and his shipmates set out for Hong Kong by way of Hawaii. But Japan was still closed to foreigners and foreign ships. After a year of trying to enter his native land, Hikozo returned to San Francisco. There he came to the attention of the Collector of Customs while he was serving as an interpreter. Like Captain Whitfield of New

England, the Customs official offered Hikozo a home while he attended school in America. Hikozo became a Roman Catholic, attended a Roman Catholic school in Baltimore and assumed the Christian name of Joseph. He was introduced to Presidents Pierce and Buchanan, and, at the age of twenty-one, became the first Japanese to gain American citizenship. In 1859 he returned to Japan as an interpreter to the American consul. On a trip to the United States in 1861 he was presented to President Abraham Lincoln and was accredited a representative of the American government to Japan. There, he was offered many positions in the Japanese government, all of which he refused on the grounds that he was an American. While in Japan he wrote several books describing the United States to the Japanese. In 1865 he founded what may well have been the first Japanese newspaper.

Several other Japanese came to America before the large migrations at the end of the century. Among them was Korekiyo Takahashe, later to become Minister of Finance in Japan, and Joseph Niishima, graduate of Amherst and Andover Theological Seminary, and founder of Doshisha, one of Japan's great Christian colleges. The first wave of Japanese immigrants, small though it was, consisted of students rather than laborers, young men eager to learn the ways of the Western world. It was the letters and writings of this group of early Japanese immigrants that inspired the later group, those desiring better economic conditions, to come to America. Official emigration from Japan was not sanctioned until 1886. United States Census figures for 1870 record the total population of Japanese in America as 55 — 47 males, 8 females. In 1890, even though labor migration had been encouraged for nearly six years, the count of Japanese in the United States was only 2,039. After 1898, when Hawaii was annexed and labor contracts discontinued, the capability of moving from the islands to the mainland became smoother. The increase in Japanese immigration was noticeable. The largest number of Japanese came in 1900 — 12,626. Until the Gentlemen's Agreement of 1907, which closed American ports to free Japanese immigration, the annual average was 7,000.

There are some indications that Japanese women were

brought to the United States for Chinese railroad construction workers. Japanese female names such as "Oyuki" and "Ohana" and others can be found on grave markers which date from the 1860s and 1870s and give evidence of the presence of several score of Japanese women at that time. It has been presumed by historians of this era that Japanese slave girls were brought to Denver and other parts of the West at the time of the building of the railroads. The assumption is that these girls were sold by Japanese farmers to Chinese merchants in the pre-Meiji period of Japan's history. It is known that the use of surnames was not introduced into Japan until after 1872 when the custom was enforced under the Meiji government for purposes of taxation. Official emigration from Japan was not sanctioned until 1886; although numerous Japanese emigrated to Hawaii from about 1868 on, United States Census figures do not authenticate the presence of Japanese women in any large numbers before 1886.

Many of the Japanese who immigrated in the early twentieth century came as laborers. They were employed chiefly in agriculture, on the railroads, in lumbering and mining, and in canneries. The earliest Japanese farmers of whom we have records came to Fresno, California, in 1880 as servants to an American who lived in Tokyo. They took on a three-year contract in a vineyard and a few years later returned to Japan. In 1889 they came back to the United States to purchase a farm of their own. In 1888 Kozabura Baba began to work in the apricot orchards of Vacaville, California. His presence made the growers hopeful that more Japanese farm laborers would soon come to the valley. By 1890 more than 300 Japanese were working in the farms and orchards of Vacaville. When beets had become an important crop in 1896, the Japanese came to harvest them. When the beet crop moved to the mountain states around 1903, the Japanese followed. They went to Southern California when fruit became an important crop. By 1901 the Japanese worker was the chief source of labor for grapes and beets in California. By 1904 the Japanese were in the Imperial Valley harvesting cantaloupe. Before long they became farm owners. In 1910 they planted tomatoes, and in 1915 a Japanese by the name of Sato first planted lettuce as a field crop.

In the northern part of the Pacific Coast the Japanese were working in other occupations. By 1892 a thousand Japanese were employed on the Oregon Short Line as construction hands. Actually, the first Japanese in Oregon did not come as laborers. The first Japanese was the bride of Andrew McKinnon, a Scotch skipper from Australia. He came to Portland with his bride in 1880 and built a saw mill which he named Orient Mill, in her honor. Railroad foremen as well as farm owners wanted large groups of workers at one time. The Japanese organized themselves into groups available for such labor. Most of them worked hard, saved everything they received, lived on little or nothing. Their main desire was to earn sufficient money to return to their homeland. These were called "birds of passage" by Americans who resented their thrift and hard work as well as their intention of taking money out of the country. Many Japanese also came for an education. Those who stayed tended to settle in distinct communities because of their language, traditions, and close-knit family ties; and because they were treated as outsiders and foreigners by native Americans.

The number of Japanese in the United States increased rapidly as the nineteenth century closed and the new century began. In 1890 there were 2,039. In 1900 there were 24,326, and by 1910 — 72,157. Most of the Issei immigrants from Japan were in the West. The Japanese moved through the port cities of Seattle and San Francisco and into the surrounding areas. As late as 1940, 90 percent of the Japanese population was concentrated in the Pacific Coast states. Some Japanese, however, made their way further inland. Several colonies of Japanese settled in Texas. These, unlike many of the Japanese immigrants to the West Coast, did not come as sources of cheap labor or as students. Rather, they came with substantial capital to invest in the new country. The Saibara family came from Kochiken bringing $10,000 in capital and accompanied by rice growing specialists, including some graduates from Sapporo Agriculture College. The Saibara party was given free transportation by Pullman to Webster, Texas, where they bought

250 acres of rice land and a cemetery. The descendants of the Saibaras still produce rice in this region.

Another group who devoted their energies to rice growing were the Maekawa family (Mykawa) who arrived in Texas in 1903. So prosperous was their rice growing operation that the railroad built special trackage to convey their produce to the markets. In Houston the Mykawa Road parallels the railroad tracks. There were other exceptions, but the largest number of Issei came to the Western United States or were brought there by recruiters as sources of cheap labor. Like other minority groups, they were frequently used by employers as strike-breakers against the newly formed unions.

Issei laborers were brought to Omaha as laborers in track construction, maintenance of the roadbeds, emergency repairmen for the tracks and trains. Some 12,000 Issei worked on the railroads in the West during the first decade of the twentieth century. During a severe strike against the Cudahy Packing Company 300 Issei were brought in by the company as strike breakers. Knowing little or nothing of American unions or labor procedures, the Issei saw this as an opportunity for economic advancement. Having been recruited by Japanese labor contractors, they had little suspicion of the impact this action on their part would have on their relations with the white workers.

Pueblo, Colorado, was the company town for the Colorado Fuel and Iron Company whose steel mills were the largest west of the Mississippi. During the period of World War I some 300 to 500 Issei worked in this plant. In addition to working in the mills, the Issei worked the coal mines in southern Colorado in and around the Trinidad district. At that time it was not uncommon to pay coal miners by piece work rates on a tonnage basis. Frequently, the Japanese were willing to work for lower wages than the whites and to do so with more industriousness. As the miners' unions began to move forward, the mine owners attempted to offset this economic threat to their profits by recruiting laborers from outside the United States. Negotiations were made with the Italian government for the importation of released convicts. Other arrangements were concluded with the governments of Eastern and Southern European countries. Aside from the lower salaries possible with non-American workers, the owners believed that the conglomeration of languages resulting from these importations would make it almost impossible to unionize the men.

When, despite all these imposed handicaps, the mine workers' union called a strike, Issei were imported to take the places of the strikers who had walked off their jobs. In the violence that followed, striking miners marched with firebrands on the company bunkhouse where the Issei were housed. The Issei barricaded themselves in the building and some twenty were burnt alive. While newly brought Issei were taking the jobs of striking miners, others, more familiar with the situation, were on the side of the strikers. The National Guard was called in to restore order. But tempers were inflamed beyond the point of reason. The strikers refused to disperse and many were shot down by the Guard. In labor history this incident is referred to as the Ludlow Massacre of 1914.

However, not even a majority of the Japanese immigrants were laborers. Many were employed as domestics — striving to earn sufficient money to move up the economic ladder. From 1868 to 1908 only about 39 percent of the Japanese in the United States were laborers. One-fifth were students, another fifth merchants. On the whole, it can be said that the Japanese kept up a higher standard of living than the Chinese or the Mexicans. They lived at a level not unlike that of immigrants from Southern and Eastern Europe. They were eager to learn the English language and established schools for this purpose. Fifteen of such schools were in San Francisco alone by 1909.

The ambition of the Japanese to better their economic condition was looked on unfavorably by native Americans. By 1905 it was quite clear that the Japanese would not remain itinerant laborers if they could help it. They began purchasing and leasing land on their own. True, the only land they could secure was that unwanted by white farmers. However, their tireless labor and frugality made even the most unpromising areas fruitful. Kinji Ushijima, better known as George Shima, was an example of the progressive Japanese farmer. He purchased the only land available to him, some inundated land in the Sacramento delta. Though it took him ten years to do so, he was so successful by 1920 as to have cornered the potato market in San Francisco and was enviously referred to as the "potato king." He operated 60,000 acres and owned barges of his own to carry his produce to market.

Not surprisingly, in the light of the poor relations between the Issei and the American workers and the obvious success of individual Japanese immigrants, the initial impetus of a movement directed against the Japanese immigrants arose from workingmen's groups. In Seattle, the Western Central Labor Union and in San Francisco, the Labor Council both spearheaded actions to remove and/or restrict the Issei. In 1900 the anti-Japanese movement gained momentum. Following on several decades of agitation against the Chinese, opposition to another Oriental group was not surprising. Both labor and "patriotic" groups sought legislation to exclude the Japanese in the same manner as the Chinese had been excluded.

The first formal step against the Japanese was taken by the San Francisco School Board which, in 1906, attempted to segregate Oriental children in separate schools. The Japanese government protested, and President Theodore Roosevelt prevailed upon the San Francisco authorities to rescind the order. In an attempt to settle the problem which increasing numbers of Japanese immigrants seemed to pose, especially in the Pacific Coast states, Roosevelt worked out the "Gentlemen's Agreement" with the Japanese Government. According to the terms of this agreement, which dates from 1907, Japan agreed to refuse passports to laborers unless they were coming to join a husband, parent, or child; to resume a formerly acquired domicile; or to assume control of a previously owned farming enterprise. The agreement did not completely end Japanese immigration to the United States, nor did it end the agitation against the Japanese, but it served to change the type of immigrant admitted and in some ways relieved the tension between the two countries. Before the completion of this agreement, most Japanese immigrants had been male; following the agreement, a large number of Japanese women came to the United

States to become wives of Japanese men already located here. Many of these came as brides in pre-arranged marriages. Between 1907 and 1920 when the "Ladies' Agreement" was reached, 38,000 brides entered the United States from Japan. This fact did much to augment the racial issue and American agitation against the "yellow peril" moved towards total exclusion of Orientals from the United States.

Although a national act excluding the Japanese was not passed until after World War I, many local laws restricted the rights of the Japanese Americans. The state legislature of California passed a number of severely restrictive laws. The California Alien Land Law prohibited Japanese national from buying real property or leasing real property for agricultural land for periods of longer than three years. This act was passed in 1913; ten years later, California's legislature prohibited Japanese-born immigrants from even engaging in agriculture.

Chapter 31

ACCULTURATION AND FAMILY CONTINUITIES IN THREE GENERATIONS OF JAPANESE AMERICANS*

JOHN W. CONNOR

FAMILY SOLIDARITY AND THE IE SYSTEM IN JAPAN

A NUMBER of observers have commented on the importance of the Japanese household or *ie* over the individual. Indeed, Beardsley, Hall, and Ward (1959:216-217) note that in rural Japan the household looms over the individual to such an extent that seldom does the individual think of himself or another apart from his role as a household member. Moreover, the importance of the household is reflected in the practice of filing all personal documents in the name of the household; no separate birth or death registers are kept for individuals. Furthermore, the importance of the household or *ie* over the individuals was recognized by law. Before World War II, the *ie* was legally responsible for its members even while they were away from home (Befu, 1971:40).

The *ie*, then, is a corporate entity that exists through time. As Nakane notes, the *ie* is a continuum from past to future whose members include not only the present generation, but also the dead and those as yet unborn (1970:2-3).

One aspect of the corporate identity of the *ie* is the inculcation of strong emotional bonds and dependency needs in its

*From John W. Connor, Acculturation and Family Continuities in Three Generations of Japanese Americans, *Marriage and Family*, 36:159-165, 1974. Copyright 1974 by the National Council on Family Relations. Reprinted by permission.

416

members. For example, Caudill and Doi (1963:412) state:

> In the early stages of infancy (in the traditional oral stage) there is a great deal of gratification given to the Japanese infant in almost all spheres of behavior. This would encourage the development of a very close attachment to the mother, and a sense of trust in others.

Additional evidence can be found in a recent study comparing the behavior of three- to four-month-old infants in Japan and the United States. In their article, Caudill and Weinstein (1969:14-15) came to these conclusions:

> In summary, in normal family life in Japan there is an emphasis on interdependence and reliance on others, while in America the emphasis is on independence and self-assertion.

Moreover, in an article on family sleeping arrangements, Caudill and Ploth (1966:344-366) were able to demonstrate that the Japanese family sleeping arrangements blurred the distinctions between generations and even between the sexes, and therefore served to emphasize cohesion, strong family bonds, and the interdependence of family members.

This emphasis on the importance of the *ie* over the individual is also to be seen in the care with which the Japanese family members avoid bringing shame to the family. Benedict reports that once a child starts school he becomes in effect a representative of the family. If he engages in behavior that brings shame to the family, he cannot look to the family for support. If the family name has been disgraced, his family will become "a solid phalanx of accusation" (1946:273).

The structure of the *ie* is hierarchical. The authority of the father as household head was enormous and was supported by civil law before World War II. In turn, the importance of hierarchy and the emphasis on the corporate identity of the *ie* leads to the problem of succession. Because of the small size of the land holdings in rural Japan (about two and a half acres), it became common practice to pass the land intact to one son — usually the first born — and ask the remaining sons to seek their fortunes elsewhere. In time, these nonsuccessors would establish branch families of their own and would themselves become household heads.

As successor to the headship the heir was early singled out for special and favored treatment. Siblings were expected to show respect and be deferential to the heir. Indeed, Johnson (1962:91-99) has indicated that the early knowledge of their nonsuccession and their differential socialization, led to an entrepreneurial attitude on the part of the nonheirs.

However, with his favored position the heir was given a number of responsibilities. Upon the assumption of the headship it was his duty to provide for his retiring parents who frequently continued to live with him, his wife, and their children.

Given the importance of the *ie* in Japan it would seem reasonable to assume that those first generation Japanese Americans (Issei) who immigrated to the United States would bring with them not only the belief that the *ie* system was the normal way to organize a family, but they would also have a need to create their own branch families and establish themselves as household heads. In other words, they would attempt to preserve as much as possible of the *ie* ideal and would tend to transmit certain aspects of it to subsequent generations. The subsequent generations would therefore exhibit many of the characteristics associated with the *ie* system in Japan. That is, they would retain a feeling of not wanting to bring shame to the family, they would exhibit a greater sense of hierarchy and order, and have greater dependency and affiliation needs.

THE ISSEI

Reports by a number of authorities (Daniels, 1963; Kitano, 1969; Modell, 1968) on the nature of early Japanese immigration to the United States recorded many uniformities. By and large the vast majority of the immigrants came from southwestern Japan, were of a rural agricultural background, and did not intend to settle permanently in the United States. This latter characteristic coupled with the intense anti-Japanese discrimination of the prewar period, resulted in large numbers of the first generation immigrants (Issei) and their offspring living in more or less self-contained Japanese communities on the West Coast. In these communities it was possible to retain many aspects of the Japanese life-style (Miyamoto, 1939:57-130).

Our interviews with 90 Issei (59 males, 31 females) in the Sacramento area support the conclusions of the earlier writers. That is, the overwhelming majority of our respondents (73%) came from southwestern Japan; they were of a rural, agricultural background, and the average level of education was about eight years, while the average age at the time of emigration was about nineteen years.

The majority of the Issei we interviewed were not the "pioneer" Issei, or original migrants, but rather the *Yobiyose* or summoned immigrants. That is, they were those immigrants who had been called over by an earlier migrating father or uncle. Indeed, when the present average age of the Issei of seventy-three years for the males and seventy-one years for the females is compared with their age at the time of immigration, it can be seen that the majority of the Issei we interviewed arrived here around the time of World War I, or after a substantial number of Japanese had already migrated to the United States.

Despite their being summoned migrants, less than 10 percent stated that they had planned to stay permanently in the United States. The vast majority intended to "make a fortune" and return to Japan. As a matter of fact, most of the Issei maintained some ties with Japan. This can be seen in the fact that 80 percent of them have returned to Japan for at least one visit, and indeed a few have made the trip more than five times.

However, as their ambition of making a fortune proved to be more difficult and take longer than expected, many returned to Japan to obtain a bride, while others relied on relatives to make the necessary arrangements, which often eventuated in "picture-bride" marriages. Well over 90 percent of the Issei we interviewed had their marriages arranged by others.

Given their intent not to settle permanently in the United States, their attempt to preserve as much as possible of the *ie* ideal, their residence in largely self-sufficient Japanese communities, and the often manifested prejudice against them, it is

understandable that many Issei would only be marginally acculturated.

TABLE 31-I

ARITHMETIC DISTRIBUTION ON SUBJECTIVE SELF-EVALUATION
OF DEGREE OF ACCULTURATION

Generation	Japanese Identity (1)									American Identity (10)
Issei	1	2	3	4	5	6	7	8	9	10
Male (N=59)			3.8							
Female (N=31)		2.7								
Nisei										
Male (N=40)					5.5					
Female (N=40)					5.0					
Sansei										
Male (N=64)							7.2			
Female (N=64)							7.0			

The marginal acculturation is apparent not only in their
lack of fluency in the English language, but also in their self-
evaluation as to the degree of their acculturation. As indicated
in Table 31-I, as part of our interview schedule the Issei were
asked to rate themselves on a ten-point scale ranging from a
completely Japanese identity (1) to a completely American
identity (10). The arithmetic mean score of the Issei was 3.8 for
the males and 2.7 for the females.

Once again, an indication of the intent of the Issei to preserve as much as possible of the *ie* ideal can be seen in the fact
that over one-half of them state that they see their children and
grandchildren daily. Moreover, some 46 percent of the Issei
report that they are living with their children. Of those that do
live with their children, approximately 70 percent live with

their sons, while the rest live with the daughter's family. This finding is in close accord with Modell (1968:67-81) who states in his survey of over 1000 Issei that approximately two-fifths of the Issei live with their offspring.

Additional evidence for the preservation of the *ie* ideal in the Issei can be found in the fact that the Issei frequently recorded the birth of their children in the *Koseki* or family register back in Japan. It was this practice that resulted in the problem of the Nisei having dual citizenship before the war. Further evidence can be seen in the responses to the statements depicted in Table 31-II. These statements were administered to 46 male and 38 female Issei, 94 male and 61 female Nisei, 70 male and 54 female Sansei; and 52 male and 102 female Caucasians, who were of approximately the same age and education as the Sansei. The statements were scored on a five-point scale as follows: strongly agree (5), agree (4), undecided (3), disagree (2), strongly disagree (1). The scoring was further categorized in endorsement of an item on either side of neutrality. This score was on an equal distribution basis. Thus, a strongly positive identification would be greater than 3.40; a neutral, or undecided, identification would range from below 3.39 to 2.61; a negative identification would be below 2.60; and a strongly negative identification would be below 1.80.

A glance at Table 31-II discloses that the Issei scored high on all items. Items 1, 2, 4, and 6 are family items directly related to the preservation of the *ie* ideal, while item 3 relates to the emphasis on hierarchy and the authority of the father as discussed earlier. Item 5 also provides some support for the previously discussed inculcation of dependency needs in the child.

Given the insularity, the low acculturation of the Issei, and their intention not to reside permanently in the United States, it would seem reasonable to expect that the Issei would attempt to inculcate in their offspring, the Nisei, essentially the same values of the Issei had learned in Japan, especially the continued importance of the family or *ie* ideal. Our interviewing of eighty Nisei (forty males and forty females) by and large bears this out. Indeed, as indicated in the earlier discussion of the importance of the family over the individual it is understandable that the Issei would emphasize the importance of not

TABLE 31-II

TOTAL MEAN FAMILY ITEM SCORES

Item No.	Item	Category Group and Mean Item Scores			
		Issei (N=84)	Nisei (N=155)	Sansei (N=124)	Caucasian (N=154)
1.	Parents can never be repaid for what they have done for their children	3.86*	3.25	2.99	2.86
2.	In times of need it is best to rely on your own family for assistance rather than to seek help from others or to depend entirely upon yourself.	3.97**	3.66*	3.05	2.95
3.	The best way to train children is to train them to be quiet and obedient.	3.90*	2.72*	2.14	1.93
4.	In the long run the greatest satisfaction comes from being with one's family.	4.33	4.38*	3.69	3.52
5.	The strongest emotional bond is between a mother and her child.	4.19**	3.85*	3.15**	2.76
6.	A man can never let himself down without letting his family down at the same time.	3.85	3.97*	3.31**	2.87

*Significant at the .01 Level (Mann-Whitney U Test)
**Significant at the .05 Level (Mann-Whitney U Test)

bringing shame to the family. As Table 31-III indicates, when the Nisei were asked if the family was stressed when they were young, 80 percent of them answered affirmatively. Moreover, when they were asked if they had been told that one must act in such a way as not to bring shame to the Japanese community, 75 percent of the males and 66 percent of the females answered that such a principle had been stressed.

TABLE 31-III

PERCENTAGE DISTRIBUTION OF NISEI AND SANSEI
REPORTING PARENTAL STRESS ON CERTAIN PRINCIPLES

	Nisei		Sansei	
Principle Reported Stressed	Male	Female	Male	Female
1. Avoid bringing shame to the family				
A. Stressed	80	80	64	65
B. Not stressed	20	20	29	31
C. Don't recall	0	0	6	4
2. Must not bring dishonor to the Japanese Community				
A. Stressed	75	66	44	36
B. Not Stressed	20	26	48	58
C. Don't Recall	5	7	8	6
Number of respondents	40	40	64	64

We also have additional evidence as to the importance of the family in the responses a number of Nisei gave during the interviews. When we raised the subject of excluding a child from the family as a means of disciplining him, one Nisei male said that to do such a thing to a child was worse than beating him. Another Nisei female stated with considerable feeling that her father would lock her in the closet when she was bad. Furthermore, the Nisei had to face this discipline alone. There were no soft-hearted grandparents or kindly aunts from whom they could seek sympathy and comfort.

The values inculcated by the Issei were continually reinforced as the Nisei grew older. Not only did the majority of Nisei attend Japanese language schools, which frequently incorporated within the curriculum the stern moral lessions of the *shusin* or ethics course of the Japanese education system, but the majority of them also resided in the Japanese community. It was the community that was most responsible for the low level of delinquency among the Nisei. As one Nisei who had resided in Sacramento's Japanese community before the war remarked: "You didn't dare step out of line. The first time you did, your parents would be sure to hear about it."

The retention of a number of the values of their parents can be seen in the Nisei responses to several questions they were asked relating to the Sansei. When asked, "What behavior by the Sansei would be most likely to anger or upset you?" the most frequent reply, by 50 percent of the males and 60 percent of the females, was "lack of respect to parents and elders." The next most frequent answer was that of breaking the law or defying authority, which was given by 25 percent of the females and 15 percent of the males. Other opinions given centered upon such subjects as drug taking, demonstrating against the government, and radicalism.

Some indication of the conservatism of many Nisei can be found in their replies to the question, "What Japanese characteristics would you like to see retained in the Sansei generation?" Here again the male-female responses were quite close. The most common response was "respect for parents, elders, and authority," which was given by 60 percent of the males and 58 percent of the females. The achievement orientation of the male Nisei is seen in the reply, "hard work," which was given by 20 percent of the males and 8 percent of the females. A male-female difference was also seen in the response, "humility, endurance, and patience," which was reported by 26 percent of the females and 10 percent of the males. Other responses emphasized the retention of the Japanese language, good manners, and the Buddhist faith.

Additional evidence for the retention of a Japanese identity in the Nisei can be seen in Table 31-I. When asked to evaluate their degree of acculturation on a ten-point scale, ranging from a completely Japanese identity (1) to a completely American identity (10), the Nisei males rated themselves as 5.5 and the Nisei females 5.0. Once again this supports our other evidence that with their bicultural background the Nisei believe themselves to be unique in that they not only see their generation as being midway between the Issei and Sansei (the average is about 45), but also that their generation combines the best of both cultures.

Moreover, with respect to the retention of a Japanese identity and the preservation of the *ie* ideal in the Nisei, it can readily be seen from Table 31-II that they have retained at the very least a strong feeling for the importance of relying upon the family and the warmth and security that comes from being with the family. Table 31-II discloses that in answer to the statement "In the long run, the greatest satisfaction comes from being with one's family" was scored 4.33 by the Issei and even slightly higher at 4.38 by the Nisei. Furthermore, in answer to the statement, "In times of need it is best to rely on your own family for assistance rather than to seek help from others or to depend entirely on yourself," it can be seen that while the Issei scored 3.97, the Nisei still scored 3.66, as compared to 3.05 for the Sansei, and 2.95 for the Caucasian sample. Finally, the statement, "A man can never let himself down without letting his family down at the same time," was scored 3.97 by the Nisei, the highest of any group.

THE SANSEI

When asked to comment on the Sansei (third generation Japanese Americans) the most frequent response by both the Issei and the Nisei was that the Sansei were "completely Americanized." And indeed, when viewed from the Issei and Nisei perspectives it would seem that the Sansei have retained very little of a Japanese identity. As seen on Table 31-I, by their own self-evaluation the Sansei, who are largely in their early twenties, now rate themselves as being over 70 percent acculturated.

Moreover, in our interviewing of 128 Sansei (64 male, 64 female) we discovered that the majority of them participated rather widely in high school and college extracurricular activities, such as being actively involved in school offices, school athletics, etc. Furthermore, the majority of Sansei now have more non-Japanese than Japanese friends. One result of this, of course, is that there has been an increased incidence of both dating and even marriage to non-Japanese. Our data indicate that in Sacramento County from 1961 to 1970, 28.3 percent of all marriages involving Japanese surnamed males and females were with non-Japanese, and indeed, this trend is increasing in recent years. An article appearing in the December 3, 1971, issue of *The Pacific Citizen* indicates that Sansei marriages are even higher in Fresno, California. In that article, Kuhn reports that since 1964 the intermarriage rate rose to 50 percent and has continued to be about the same rate (Kuhn, 1971).

Yet it would be a mistake to assume with the Issei and Nisei that the Sansei have become "completely Americanized." Our research indicates that when compared with a contemporary Caucasian group of approximately the same age and education, a number of Japanese characteristics remain. For example, as part of our research we also administered the Edwards Personal Preference Schedule or EPPS to 201 Sansei (71 males and 130 females) and to 231 Caucasians (101 males and 130 females) of approximately the same age and education. The results clearly disclose that when compared with the Caucasians, the Sansei are significantly more deferent, more abasive, less dominant, more affiliative, less aggressive, more in need of succorance and order, and less in need of heterosexuality than the Caucasians (Connor, 1974).

A further item of contrast may be seen in Table 31-II, wherein, although the Sansei consistently score lower than the Issei and Nisei on all family items, they, nevertheless, consistently score higher than the Caucasian sample.

A final example of evidence for the continuation of Japanese characteristics among third generation Japanese Americans can be seen in the retention of Japanese patterns of child care in the

Sacramento area. This information is available in a study done by Lois Frost under the author's supervision in the spring of 1970 (Frost, 1970). This study was a replication of one conducted by Caudill and Weinstein (1969). The Caudill and Weinstein study consisted of a series of two-day observations made in the homes of thirty Japanese and thirty American first-born, three- to four-month-old infants, who were equally divided by sex and who were living in middle-class urban families. Information was obtained on the behavior of the mother and the child by means of time-sampling. One observation was made every fifteenth second over a ten-minute period on a predetermined set of categories. This resulted in a sheet containing forty equally-spaced observations. Ten sheets were completed for each of the two days, resulting in a total of 800 observations in each case.

Ms. Frost's sample consisted of twenty-one infants, seven males, and fourteen females. When she was completing her study, I advised her to write to Caudill and advise him of her findings. This she did. He, in turn, was most interested in her study and arranged to conduct a series of observations with her in the homes of four infants in order to have a reliability check for observer bias.

Frost's data were then compared and analyzed with Caudill's Japanese and American samples. In an as yet unpublished paper Caudill and Frost conclude that the Sansei mother is combining both the Japanese and American styles of caretaking (Caudill and Frost, 1973). Moreover, their paper indicates that the Sansei mother does more vocal lulling, more breast and bottle feeding, more carrying, and more playing with the baby than the American mother. In these practices she is more like the Japanese mother. Furthermore, while the mother's overall caretaking style and the behavior of her baby are closer to the American than the Japanese response style, there are still some areas in which the baby seems closer to the Japanese baby's behavior. That is, the Japanese American baby does less finger sucking than the American baby and spends less time playing by himself.

In Frost's findings are seen in conjunction with the higher

Sansei needs for succorance, affiliation, nurturance, deference, abasement, and the greater emphasis placed on the family, it is easy to suspect a continuation of dependency needs. Although difficult to demonstrate empirically, all of the above data are clearly supportive of the previously discussed dependency needs fostered in the Japanese family. While not so pronounced as in the Japanese mother, the Sansei mother has retained enough of the Japanese caretaking style so that we are already able to detect discernable differences in her child's behavior at the age of three or four months. Moreover, these differences are exactly the sort of differences we would expect if we were looking for evidence which would indicate the inculcation of dependency needs.

In conclusion, one can see a continuity in both the importance of the family and an attempt to preserve the *ie* ideal in the three generations of Japanese Americans. While the emphasis on the family and the inculcation of dependency needs in the third generation are considerably attenuated in comparison with first and second generations, the emphasis still remains greater than that found in Caucasian Americans.

Finally, when one compares the Japanese American responses on the EPPS with the Caucasian American responses, a question might be asked. That is, is the continuing emphasis on the family, etc., really evidence of the retention of the *ie* ideal, or is it nothing more than a cultural response to the discrimination and prejudice suffered by the Japanese Americans in the larger American society? In other words, are the higher Sansei EPPS scores on deference, abasement, order, etc., really more a result of their minority status than an indication of continuation of Japanese characteristics? While it is difficult to separate such factors, it can nevertheless be rather quickly demonstrated that when the EPPS has been administered in Hawaii, where the Japanese Americans are the largest ethnic segment and are scarcely treated as a minority group, the results are essentially the same as those obtained in our Sacramento Japanese American sample (Arkoff, 1959; Fenz and Arkoff, 1962).

REFERENCES

Arkoff, Abe. Need Patterns in Two Generations of Japanese Americans in Hawaii. *Journal of Social Psychology*, 1959, 50:75-79.

Beardsley, Richard, Hall, John W., and Ward, Robert E. *Village Japan.* Chicago: University of Chicago Press, 1959.

Befu, Harumi. *Japan: An Anthropological Introduction.* San Francisco: Chandler, 1971.

Benedict, Ruth. *The Chrysanthemum and the Sword.* New York, Houghton Mifflin, 1946.

Caudill, William, and Doi, Takeo. Interrelations of Psychiatry, Culture, and Emotion in Japan. In Iago K. Goldstone, ed., *Man's Image in Medicine and Anthropology.* New York: International Universities Press, 1963.

Caudill, William, and Frost, Lois. A Comparison of Maternal Care and Infant Behavior in Japanese-American, American and Japanese Families. To be published in William K. Lebro, ed., *Mental Health Research in Asia and the Pacific*, vol. III. Hawaii: East-West Center, 1973.

Caudill, William, and Ploth, David W. Who Sleeps by Whom? Parent-Child Involvement in Urban Japanese Families. *Psychiatry*, 1966, 29:344-366.

Caudill, William, and Weinstein, Helen. Maternal Care and Infant Behavior in Japan and American *Psychiatry*, 1969, 32:12-43.

Connor, John W. Acculturation and Changing Need Patterns in Japanese American and Caucasian American Students *The Journal of Social Psychology* (Forthcoming, August, 1974)

Daniels, Roger. *The Politics of Prejudice.* Berkeley: The University of California Press, 1963.

Fenz, Walter, and Arkoff, Abe. Comparative Need Patterns of Five Ancestry Groups in Hawaii. *Journal of Social Psychology*, 1962, 58:68-89.

Frost, Lois. Child Raising Techniques as Related to Acculturation Among Japanese Americans. Unpublished masters thesis. California State University, Sacramento, 1970.

Johnson, Erwin. The Emergence of a Self-Conscious Entrepreneurial Class in Rural Japan. In Robert J. Smith and Richard K. Beardsley, eds., *Japanese Culture: Its Development and Characteristics.* Chicago: Aldine, 1962.

Kitano, Harry. *Japanese Americans: The Evolution of a Subculture.* Englewood Cliffs, N. J.: Prentice-Hall, 1969.

Kuhn, Gene. Hirabayashi Challenges Nisei to Fight All Inequalities. *Pacific Citizen*, December 3, 1971.

Miyamoto, Frank. Social Solidarity Among the Japanese in Seattle. *University of Washington Publications in the Social Sciences*, 1939, 11:57-130.

Modell, John. The Japanese American Family: A Perspective for Future Investigation. *Pacific Historical Review*, 1968, 36:67-81.
Nakane, Chie. *Japanese Society*. Berkeley: University of California Press, 1970.

Chapter 32

THE CULTURALLY ADVANTAGED: A STUDY OF JAPANESE-AMERICAN PUPILS*

AUDREY JAMES SCHWARTZ

AMERICANS of Japanese ancestry — who comprise only one-fourth of one percent of the population of the United States — rank higher than any other physically identifiable subgroup on positive attributes like education and income, and lowest on negative attributes like unemployment, crime, and delinquency. With particular reference to education, in California, the home of 34 percent of Japanese-Americans, both Japanese-American men and women rank first of all major racial and ethnic groups in amount of formal schooling. In Los Angeles County, the home of more than half of the state's Japanese-Americans, the median completed school year is 12.4 in contrast with a median of 12 for the total population.[1]

This record in education is qualitative as well as quantitative. As discussed more fully later, comparisons of objective test scores for Los Angeles City public school pupils show that the performance of Japanese-Americans is considerably higher than that of other minority groups and, in general, higher than Anglos.[2] That academic achievement is high for Japanese-Americans in other parts of the country as well is suggested by data from the United States Office of Education.[3]

In short, the educational attainment of Japanese-Americans, both in quantity and quality, has been outstanding in recent years. This fact has stimulated a variety of explanations for their achievement centering largely on cultural values.

There is little consensus, however, on which cultural values

---

*From Audrey J. Schwartz, The Culturally Advantaged: A Study of Japanese-American Pupils, *Sociology and Social Research*, 55:341-351, 1971. Reprinted by permission.

431

— Japanese or American — are responsible for the achievement of contemporary Japanese-Americans. One recent attempt to account for the successful adaptation of Japanese-Americans credits acculturation to middle-class American values:

> If, however, successful adaptation to the larger society consists mainly in acculturation, measured by the ability of a group to share and follow the goals, and expected behaviors of the majority, then the Japanese-American group has been very successful. Japanese-American values, skills, attitudes, and behavior apparently do not differ markedly from those of the average American. "Scratch a Japanese American and find a white Anglo-Saxon Protestant" is a generally accurate statement.[4]

A contrary view supports the centrality of traditional Japanese values to Japanese-American achievement:

> It is one of the major tenets of this report that while the overt behavior of the Nisei may, in many situations, be indistinguishable from the behavior of the white middle class, this arises in considerable part from a Japanese system of values and personality structure.[5]

These traditional values, it is generally agreed, include orientation toward the family unit in its nuclear and extended forms, subordination of the individual to the collectivity, sense of duty, reliance on order and hierarchy, respect for authority, and rational means to attain long-range goals.[6]

The inconsistency in these two conclusions arises from the differences that can be drawn between acculturation of the internalization of the values of an alien culture, on the one hand, and socialization or the learning of norms that are specific to a social situation, on the other. While values are closely related to social norms, they are not the same. Values are

> conceptions of desirable states of affairs that are utilized in selective conduct as criteria for preference or choice or as justifications for proposed or actual behavior. . . . Norms are the more specific, concrete, situation-bound specifications; values are the criteria by which norms themselves may be and are judged.[7]

The first explanation of achievement holds that Japanese-

Americans have internalized many of the values of the American middle class and that they, in fact, utilize the same criteria in evaluating action; the second explanation is more concerned with traditional Japanese values and with the acquisition by Japanese-Americans of the social knowledge to participate successfully in American institutions.

For Japanese-Americans the distinction between socialization to the norms of American institutions and acculturation to American middle class values is justified by the fact that early socialization — and thus socialization more resistant to change — usually takes place within structures that are parallel, rather than identical, to those of the middle class. As members of a distinct minority group, the socialization of young Japanese-American children is circumscribed by the ethnic community "which both protects and impedes the individuals within it."[8] Although ethnic socialization anticipates participation in the systems of the larger society by transmitting the minority group's perception of the operating norms of that society, it is unlikely that it can equally perceive and transmit the value criteria by which these norms are judged.

The empirical determination of the relative import of traditional Japanese values and values of the American middle class to the educational achievement of Japanese-American pupils requires knowledge of (a) the extent to which traditional values are currently held by pupils of Japanese-American ancestry, (b) the extent to which traditional values are similar to those of Anglo pupils, and (c) the relationships between individually held values and academic success for both Japanese-American and Anglo pupils.

The thesis of this article is that the success of Japanese-American public school pupils depends more on the value orientations that differentiate the two groups than upon the value orientations held in common. The acculturation that has taken place thus far does not adequately account for achievement. Value differences related to the orientation of the individual toward the social system persist; these value orientations — which more nearly approximate the values institutionized in the formal educational system than do those of middle-class

Americans — furnish the best explanation for the comparatively high achievement of Japanese-Americans.

What follows is a description of research findings addressed to these issues. First is a description of the research design including the Japanese-American sample and the variable of prime interest; second is a discussion of educational achievement in the Japanese-American community; next is a comparison of the value orientations of Japanese-American and Anglo pupils and the relationships of these orientations to academic achievement; and finally a discussion of the findings.

RESEARCH DESIGN

Data for this analysis were obtained in 1966 from a survey of 2200 pupils enrolled in the sixth, ninth, and twelfth grades of twenty-three Los Angeles City schools. A purposive, nonprobability sampling technique was used to select schools with varying racial, ethnic, and socioeconomic composition, and quota sampling of state-mandated courses (in which there was no "ability grouping") was used within each school. Subsampling within classrooms was not permitted. Of the obtained sample, 254 were classified by visual inspection and by surname identification as Japanese-American. All of these pupils were enrolled in racially mixed schools.[9]

Information about family background, educational and occupational aspirations, educational plans, and value orientations was obtained from pupil responses to a printed questionnaire presented by research personnel in regularly scheduled class periods. Official achievement records were made available for 85 percent of the Japanese-American sample — those whose parents sent their written approval to the school.

About half of the Japanese-American respondents were in the last year of high school (twelfth grade) and the remainder were in the last of junior high (ninth grade) and the last year of elementary school (sixth grade). Pupils from blue collar and white collar homes are evenly represented in the secondary school sample, although there is over-representation of blue collar elementary school pupils. In the interest of clarity, socioeconomic controls for Japanese-American pupils have been abandoned as a comparison of pupils from blue and white collar homes on a number of variables including school performance, value orientations, the relationship between value orientations and achievement, and parents' educational level, showed no large or significant differences.

As used here, the term "value orientation" refers to the various emotional rather than rational outlooks of the pupils. This concept is sometimes referred to by terms like attitudes, beliefs, dispositions, and feelings — the unifying characteristic is that each involves individual sentiments or affect more than cognitive processes. This is not to say that the relationship between the two can be completely severed, but the distinction is useful for analytic purposes. The value orientations treated here are those for which theory and previous research suggest a relationship to school achievement.[10] The variables can be divided into four groups according to the functions they are expected to perform in the attainment of academic success.

1. *The Goals Toward Which the Individual Strives.* These include Occupational Aspirations, Educational Aspirations and Plans, Occupational Rewards (the importance placed on extrinsic rewards like power, prestige, and security in occupational choice), and Idealized School Goals (the ends the school ought to help the pupil attain regardless of whether it does or not).

2. *Activities Appropriate for Goal Attainment.* These variables include Instrumental Orientation (the utility of attending school now for future benefit), Expressive Orientation (the extent to which school attendance affords the pupil pleasure), and Formal School Compliance (the choices the pupil would make between conflicting universalistic school expectations and peer loyalties and his unquestioned acceptance of teacher authority).

3. *The Pupil's Perception of the Feasibility of Attaining His Goals.* These include Self-Esteem (the individual's evaluation of himself in general and in relation to others whom he knows), Faith in Human Nature (the pupil's attitude toward people regardless of his personal knowledge of them), and

Future Orientation (belief that the individual can control his environment and thereby affect his own destiny).

4. *Mode and Intensity of Interpersonal Relations,* that is, whether the individual is inclined to take action without approval of others. These include Orientation toward Family Authority (legitimacy of parental control over pupil activity) and Independence from Peers (sensitivity of the pupil to opinions of his age-mates and their effect on his own action).[11]

EDUCATIONAL ACHIEVEMENT IN THE JAPANESE-AMERICAN COMMUNITY

From all accounts the Issei who came to the United States were relatively well educated for an immigrant population and had high regard for the instrumental value of education for themselves and for their children. Compared with other groups, the Japanese children started school at an earlier age and remained in school longer, and the devotion of their parents to the task of providing them with educational opportunities is largely credited for the relatively high occupational attainment of the Nisei.[12]

The Issei's appreciation for formal education extended beyond its instrumental value, however, and they established parochial schools with instruction in Japanese reading, writing, history, and the like to supplement public education. It was the purpose of these schools to socialize American-born children (who were not sent to Japan for prolonged visits with relatives) to the culture of Japan and thereby ensure its survival in the United States. The language schools flourished until the evacuation of West Coast Japanese during the Second World War. Although only a small number of these schools exist today, many of their cultural transmission functions have been absorbed by other ethnically-oriented voluntary associations.

Emphasis on formal education continues to be characteristic of the Japanese-American community. Sixty percent of all the Japanese-American pupils surveyed in Los Angeles report that their parents have graduated from high school and 30 percent of their fathers and 23 percent of their mothers have attended college. Of the ninth and twelfth grade pupils, 77 percent state that "many" or "some" of their relatives or friends of their parents have had education beyond high school, which implies close acquaintance with college educated persons. Moreover, most pupils have high educational aspirations for themselves: over 85 percent of the secondary school sample indicate that both they and their parents would like them to receive an education beyond high school and the number who expect to do so is almost as high. In addition, the Japanese-American pupils ascribe high educational aspirations to their friends: 95 percent of the twelfth grade, 75 percent of the ninth grade, and 61 percent of the sixth grade report that "all" or "most" of their friends desire to continue their education after high school completion.[13]

The occupational aspirations of Japanese-American pupils are consistent with their educational aspirations and plans. More than 80 percent of the secondary school sample aspire to upper white collar jobs, that is, to jobs that usually require a minimum of four years of college, and only 6 percent aspire to blue collar jobs which call for considerably less schooling. Of further interest is their high ambition for social mobility. A comparison of the status of their own aspirations with that of their parents' occupational level indicates that 68 percent of the ninth grade and 58 percent of the twelfth grade pupils would be upwardly mobile if they enter their preferred occupation. And equally important, less than 5 percent would be downwardly mobile. The excellent achievement record of Japanese-American pupils indicates that these high aspirations are realistic.

A COMPARISON OF VALUE ORIENTATIONS

The Japanese-American and the Anglo secondary school samples were contrasted on the value orientation variables and found to differ significantly on a number of them. In general, Japanese-American vis-á-vis Anglo pupils are more Expressive in their orientation toward school, are more favorable toward

Formal School Compliance and Family Authority, and are less oriented toward the Future in that their sense of personal fate control is low. Nevertheless, they have higher Occupational Aspirations and place greater value on extrinsic occupational rewards.

The two groups are similar in their Idealized School Goals from school attendance and in their Instrumental Orientation toward school activities — both very high in comparison with other ethnic groups — and in their expressed Independence from Peers. The value orientation scores for ninth and twelfth grade Japanese-American and Anglo pupils are presented in Table 32-I.[14] Although they are not presented here, it should be noted that the data from sixth grade pupils are consistent with the findings just discussed.

The Japanese-American and Anglo pupils also differ from one another in the relationship of these value orientations to their academic success as measured by standardized objective tests. Four of the orientations are statistically related to the reading or mathematics achievement of Japanese-Americans and six to similar achievement of Anglos, yet only one — high Faith in Human Nature — is related to achievement in each group.

Related to the achievement of Japanese-American pupils are high Faith in Human Nature (significant at sixth, ninth, and twelfth grades), low Independence from Peers (significant at ninth and twelfth grades), low Self-Esteem (significant at ninth grade), and low Instrumental Orientation (significant at twelfth grade).

Important to the achievement of Anglo pupils are high Future Orientation (significant at sixth, ninth, and twelfth grades), high Faith in Human Nature, orientation toward Family Authority, and, unexpectedly, low orientation toward Formal School Compliance (all significant at ninth grade), and high Self-Esteem (significant at twelfth grade).

DISCUSSION

These findings support the hypothesis that the comparatively

TABLE 32-I

VALUE ORIENTATIONS OF JAPANESE-AMERICAN
AND ANGLO SECONDARY SCHOOL PUPILS

Value Orientation[1]		Ninth Grade		Twelfth Grade	
		Japanese	Anglo	Japanese	Anglo
Expressive Orientation	x score	3.88	3.70*	3.70	3.58
(Scalogram)	s.d.	.59	.77	.83	.90
	% high	84	69**	73	64**
Faith in Human Nature	x score	3.18	3.29	3.50	3.54
(Scalogram)	s.d.	.90	.86	.75	.71
	% high	45	52	64	65
Family Authority	x score	3.11	2.85	2.72	2.55
(Scalogram)	s.d.	1.23	1.37	1.19	1.37
	% high	45	36**	29	27
Formal School Compliance	x score	3.32	3.14	3.22	3.02*
(Scalogram)	s.d.	.78	.89	.95	.96
	% high	52	44	50	39
Future Orientation	x score	2.86	3.05	3.25	3.43*
(Scalogram)	s.d.	.95	.98	.96	.87
	% high	27	40**	54	61
Idealized School Goals	x score	3.77	3.82	3.83	3.79
(Index)	s.d.	.54	.45	.46	.45
	% high	86	86	84	82
Independence from Peers	x score	3.01	3.06	2.97	2.97
(Scalogram)	s.d.	1.11	1.10	1.30	1.28
	% high	30	35	33	32
Instrumental Orientation	x score	3.79	3.73	3.76	3.74
(Scalogram)	s.d.	.45	.49	.45	.48
	% high	86	84	86	82
Occupational Reward Values	x score	3.58	3.37	3.59	3.32
	s.d.	1.05	1.15	1.10	1.18
	% high	26	18**	21	19
Self-Esteem	x score	3.59	3.69	3.76	3.93
	s.d.	1.66	1.60	1.59	1.50
	% high	53	52	56	61
Occupational Aspirations	x score	4.41	4.21*	4.46	4.16*
1. Lower blue collar	s.d.	.90	.88	.91	.95
2. Upper blue collar					
3. Lower white collar					
4. Intermediate white collar					
5. Upper white collar	x score	4.41	4.21*	4.46	4.16*
	s.d.	.90	.88	.91	.95
Base N		67	558	122	473

[1]This table is abridged from Audrey James Schwartz, *Traditional Values and Contemporary Achievement of Japanese-American Pupils*, Los Angeles: Center for the Study of Evaluation, University of California, 1970, Table 8.

*p ≤ .05 for t value of mean differences between Japanese American and Anglo scale scores.

**p ≤ .05 t-test for difference in proportion of Japanese American and Anglo pupils who score "high" on the value orientation.

high achievement of Japanese-American pupils is related more to values that are traditional in Japanese culture than to the acquisition of dominant American values. Although Japanese-American and Anglo pupils are similar with respect to several value orientations, there is little to support the position that the values they hold in common derive from the American middle class. These commonalities, (a) an emphasis on present school attendance for future benefit and (b) a concern for peer group opinion, can logically be derived from the Japanese culture as well as the Anglo.

For example, formal education has customarily been held in high regard in Japan and the literacy rate of that country has been exceptional, even before the establishment of universal schooling in 1872.[15] Futhermore, we have already noted the instrumental orientation of the Issei and Nisei generations in their consumption of public education for the occupational mobility of themselves and their children and in their provision of parochial education for transmission of Japanese culture.

In like manner, sensitivity to peer group approval can be traced to Japanese values which stress "collectivity" over "self" orientations in sio calsystems like the family, employment, and school.[16] The "adolescent society" is now an equally relevant system to Japanese-American youth and their mode of relating to it, like the family and the school, is characteristically one of dependence and subordination rather than individual action.

More telling in the case against acculturation as an explanation of achievement are the *differences* in orientations of Japanese-American and Anglo pupils. Perhaps most germane is the generally favorable view of Japanese-Americans toward hierarchial authority (evidenced by higher Formal School Compliance and Family Authority scores). This finding is consistent with observations of the subordinate-superordinate structure of traditional Japanese culture.[17]

The point to be made here is that Japanese-American pupils seem to reject the notion of individual autonomy. Not only are they oriented toward the "collectivity" and acceptance of its authority structure (which is lineal for the family and school and collateral for the peer social system), they, in comparison with Anglos, express little personal mastery over the future. Whereas Japanese-American pupils indicate exceedingly high educational and mobility aspirations and express significantly greater desire than Anglos for extrinsic rewards — all characteristic of minority groups that have entered the occupational structure at the bottom — their mode of ascent is one of group cooperation rather than individual pursuit. What is more, the presence or absence of the belief that individual action can modify a person's destiny has little relationship to the achievement of Japanese-Americans, in spite of the fact that it is significant and positive for the achievement of comparable Anglos, Mexican-Americans, and Negroes.[18]

Another value that distinguishes Japanese-American from Anglo pupils is their more Expressive orientation toward school: more of them "like school" and more think of school "mainly as a place for having fun." The difference noted in affective involvement may be an example of a more encompassing difference between the two populations that has been noted by others[19] in which the orientation of the Japanese toward social systems is characterized as Gemeinschaft and that of middle class Americans as Gesellschaft.[20]

From a theoretical point of view, it can be argued that the Gemeinschaft orientation tends to inhibit interaction and socialization experiences outside the primary group and thereby presents an obstacle to Japanese-Americans in affectively neutral or Gesellschaft social systems. These data suggest, however, that such obstacles can be overcome with a favorable universalistic orientation toward people in general. The positive relationship between the Faith in Human Nature measure and the academic achievement of Japanese-Americans is a case in point. In other words, given a Gemeinschaft social orientation, ultimate achievement in an affectively neutral system depends upon a universalistic orientation such as Faith in Human Nature: Those who possess the highest degree of the value will achieve the greatest; those who possess the lowest degree will achieve the least.

This is not to say that strong group affiliation in itself is detrimental to achievement; that depends upon the values of the group. For Japanese-American pupils, most of whom perceive their peers with similarly high educational aspirations, dependence upon peer approval is related to scholastic attainment. For the Anglos in this study, however, strong peer affiliation has no significant effect.

Another orientation that is closely associated with dependence upon peers is the evaluation of one's self in comparison with others. Though there is little difference between the measured Self-Esteem of the two groups, its influence is positive for the achievement of Anglos and negative for the achievement of Japanese-Americans. The reason for this negative relationship is unclear. Perhaps reluctance to view one's self competitively with others strengthens the collectivity orientation which has been shown to contribute to achievement, or low Self-Esteem may also influence the strong drive for mobility noted above.

In Summary. Japanese-American pupils have certain advantages for success in the American public school that appear to be rooted in the Japanese culture: first, the traditional family, with its rigid system of obligations subordinating individual interest to those of the group, provides an environment within which children internalize family-defined achievement goals that emphasized educational success and subsequent occupational mobility and are socialized to legitimate means for attaining them; second, the structure of interpersonal relations within the family, which subordinates all members to the authority of the father, anticipates the lineal authority structure of the public school and facilitates the child's adaptation to its bureaucratic organization; and third, the "collectivity" rather than "self" orientation of the family is congruent with the strong peer group affiliation characteristic of contemporary "teen-age" culture which, for Japanese-Americans, is supportive of achievement. This confluence of family, school, and peer values fosters the scholastic attainment of Japanese-Americans, and the affective gratification they receive from school attendance, which further sustains their instrumental efforts, is illustrative of the harmony of their three most relevant social systems.

Anglo pupils, on the other hand, must cope with a disjunction between the goals they hold from school attendance and the means they believe are legitimate to attain them. Like Japanese-Americans they place high instrumental value upon education, but they agree less with the concept of hierarchical authority — a difference that can logically be traced to the greater collateral orientation of the American family. Anglo pupils are less accepting of formal school norms than are Japanese-American pupils who, it appears, have been taught an ideal model of school social interaction. Other investigators have observed the negative influence of Anglo peer groups on individual Anglo achievement.[21] In light of the findings with respect to the positive influence of Japanese-American peer groups on achievement and their favorable orientation toward Formal School Compliance it would seem that the conflict between youth and adults in the school, first brought to attention by Waller[22] does not apply to Japanese-American pupils.

REFERENCES

1. California Department of Industrial Relations, *Californians of Japanese, Chinese, Filipino Ancestry*, San Francisco; Division of Fair Employment Practices, 1965, 26.
2. Audrey James Schwartz, *Traditional Values and Contemporary Achievement of Japanese-American Pupils*, Los Angeles: Center for the Study of Evaluation, University of California, 1970, Table I.
3. United States Office of Education, *Equality of Educational Opportunity*, Washington, D. C.: Government Printing Office 1966, 20.
4. Harry H. L. Kitano, *Japanese Americans: The Evolution of a Subculture*, Englewood Cliffs: Prentice Hall, Inc., 1969, 3. The acquisition of some selected middle class values has been documented by empirical study. See Abe Arkoff, Need Patterns in Two Generations of Japanese Americans in Hawaii, *Journal of Social Psychology* 1959, 50:75-79; Charlotte Babcock and William Caudill, Personal and Cultural Factors in the Treatment of a Nisei Man, in G. Seward, ed., *Clinical Studies in Cultural Conflict*, New York: The Ronald Press, 1958, 409-49; William Caudill and George A. DeVos, Achievement, Culture, and Personality: The Case of the Japanese Americans, in B. E. Segal, ed., *Racial and Ethnic Relations*, New York: Thomas Crowell and Co., 1966, 77-89; Mamoru Iga, The Japanese Social Structure and the Source of Mental Strains of Japanese Immigrants in the U.S., *Social Forces*, 1957, 35:271-78.

5. William Caudill, Japanese-American Personality and Acculturation, *Genetic Psychology Monographs*, 1952, 45:3-102.

6. Ruth Benedict, *The Chrysanthemum and the Sword: Patterns of Japanese Culture*, Boston: Houghton Mifflin, 1946; Leonard Broom and John I. Kitsuse, *The Managed Casualty: The Japanese-American Family in World War II*, Berkeley: University of California Press, 1956; Caudill, *op. cit.*, fn. 5; George A. DeVos, Achievement Orientation, Social Self-Identity, and Japanese Economic Growth, *Asian Survey*, 1965, 5:575-89; Iga, *op. cit.*, fn. 4; Kitano, *op. cit.*, fn. 4; Talcott Parsons, Population and Social Structure of Japan, in T. Parsons, *Essays in Sociological Theory*, New York: The Free Press, 1949, 275-97.

7. Robin M. Williams, Jr. Individual and Group Values, *The Annals of the American Academy of Political and Social Science*, 1967, 371:20-37.

8. Leonard Broom and John I. Kitsuse, The Validation of Acculturation: A Condition to Ethnic Assimilation, *American Anthropologist*, 1955, 57:44-48.

9. The larger ethnic enclaves in the Los Angeles had been destroyed by the evacuation of Japanese in 1942, and subsequent relocation created smaller areas of ethnic concentration. Thus Japanese-American pupils usually attend integrated schools. However, there are several predominantly Japanese-American elementary schools, one of which is included in the sample. For details of the sampling design and description of the schools sampled see Audrey James Schwartz, Affectivity Orientations and Academic Achievement of Mexican-American Youth, doctoral dissertation, UCLA, 1967 or Schwartz, *Comparative Values and Achievement of Mexican-American and Anglo Pupils*, Los Angeles: Center for the Study of Evaluation, University of California, 1969.

10. For a summary of literature relating value orientations to scholastic achievement see Audrey James Schwartz, 1967, *op. cit.*, fn. 9.

11. Value orientation variables for the secondary pupils were created by combining responses to the relevant questionnaire items into scales and indices. Scalogram procedures were used wherever possible. For two variables items were combined into indices rather than scales and the index score implies nothing about the ordering of items of the unidimensionality of the value. Variables for the elementary school pupils were created from responses to single items selected for their discriminatory power in the value orientations of the secondary school pupils. Zero-order correlations among the value orientation variables are sufficiently low to insure statistical independence. For details see Audrey James Schwartz, *op. cit.* fn. 2.

12. Dorothy Swaine Thomas, The Japanese American, in J. B. Gittler, ed., *Understanding Minority Groups*, New York: John Wiley & Sons, 1956, 84-108.

13. The supporting tables with statistical tests of significance for these and

other findings discussed in this paper can be seen in detail in Audrey James Schwartz, *op. cit.*, fn. 2.

14. Since dominant American values are generally believed to be those of white collar Anglos, comparisons were also made between the total Japanese and the white collar Anglo sample. The results are the same as those for comparisons with the entire Anglo sample.

15. Tatsumi Makino, Some Notes on Literacy and Education in Japan, *The Sociological Review*, Monograph 10, September, 1966, 83-93.

16. Talcott Parsons, *op. cit.*, fn. 6, 283 ff.

17. Ruth Benedict, *op. cit.*, fn. 6; Talcott Parsons, *op. cit.*, fn. 6.

18. Audrey James Schwartz, *op. cit.*, fn. 9; unpublished data.

19. William Caudill and H. A. Scarr, Japanese Value Orientations and Culture Change, *Ethnology*, 1962, 1:53-91; Mamoru Iga, *op. cit.*, fn. 4; Forrest E. LaViolette, *Americans of Japanese Ancestry*, Toronto: Canadian Institute of International Affairs, 1946.

20. These orientations, introduced by Tonnies in 1887, are similar to other commonly used concepts like Cooley's primary and secondary groups, Durkheim's mechanical and organic solidarity, McIver's communal and associational relations, and Redfield's folk-urban continuum. Ferdinand Tonnies, *Community and Society*, Trans. and ed., Charles P. Loomis, East Lansing: Michigan State University Press, 1957.

21. For example, James S. Coleman, *The Adolescent Society*, New York: The Free Press, 1961.

22. Willard Waller, *The Sociology of Teaching*, New York: John Wiley & Sons, 1932.

Chapter 33

PERSONALITY CHARACTERISTICS AND ATTITUDES TOWARD ACHIEVEMENT AMONG MAINLAND HIGH ACHIEVING AND UNDERACHIEVING JAPANESE-AMERICAN SANSEIS*

LAWRENCE ONODA

NISEIS (second generation of Japanese in America) were the first generation to enter the American education system and establish themselves as high achievers. Although the Nisei did not have higher intelligence or achievement test scores than Caucasians, the Niseis received significantly higher grades than the Caucasians. Caudill and DeVos (1956) concluded that Niseis have many of the personality characteristics that are valued by the Caucasian teacher such as diligence, obedience, respect for authority figures, cooperativeness, politeness, quietness, and achievement orientation. In essence, Caucasian teachers perceived the Nisei students as closely approximating their concept of a "good student."

Because of the Niseis's high level of academic achievement, the third (Sansei) generation of Japanese Americans became stereotyped as high achievers (Sue & Sue, 1973). Kitano (1962) found, however, that mainland[1] Sanseis's motivation for academic achievement is diminishing in comparison to Nisei's. He implies that mainland Sanseis are becoming more interested in social activities rather than limiting themselves solely to academic pursuits.

*From Lawrence Onoda, Personality Characteristics and Attitudes Toward Achievement Among Mainland High Achieving and Underachieving Japanese-American Sanseis, *Journal of Educational Psychology*, 51:407-412, 1973. Copyright 1973 by the American Psychological Association. Reprinted by permission.

Also, acculturation has had an effect on the personalities of Sanseis. Sanseis have become more acculturated or similar to the Caucasian personality characteristics in contrast to their parents. Sanseis in general have more of a need than Niseis to seek leadership roles, to dominate and control others, and to behave in such a way to elicit the attention of others (Kitano, 1969; Meredith, 1966). In general, Sanseis have less of the traditional personality characteristics that facilitated their parents' academic achievement.

Despite the changing patterns of attitudes toward achievement and the personality characteristics of Sanseis, they have continued to be stereotyped as high achievers. Sue and Sue (1973) imply that Asian Americans, including all Asians not just Sanseis, have been stereotyped with the "success myth." This myth, as it relates to mainland Sanseis, implies two assumptions. First, Sanseis all have similar attitudes toward academic achievement. Second, that they have similar personalities that characterize their high achieving parents. However, not all mainland Sanseis are high achievers possessing the same personality characteristics and attitudes toward achievement. In essence, many have tended to oversimplify the Sanseis population with a narrow and restricting stereotype of being hard working, achievement oriented, shy, humble, cooperative, and intelligent. Mainland Sanseis being labeled with the success myth have higher degrees of anxiety, tension, and frustrations (Watanabe, 1973). Mainland Sanseis receive a tremendous amount of pressure from teachers, counselors, friends, and family members to respond or act with similar attitudes toward achievement and the personality characteristics that identified their parents. Specifically the Sansei underachievers feel added pressures of guilt and shame because they have not fulfilled the expectations of the success myth.

Research has yet to investigate the differences in personality characteristics and attitudes toward achievement of high achieving and underachieving mainland Sanseis. It was anticipated that the personalities of the mainland Sansei underachievers would be less like the traditional stereotype than the personalities of the mainland Sansei high-achievers. Also, it was anticipated that Sansei high-achievers would have more positive personality characteristics than Sansei underachievers. Furthermore, Sansei high-achievers would express more positive attitudes toward achievement and be more likely to attend a college institution than would Sansei underachievers.

Also, acculturation has resulted in significant changes in the personalities of Sansei males and females. When the personalities of mainland Sansei males and females were compared, it was anticipated that Sansei females would show a greater degree of acculturation than Sansei males. Also, there would be no significant differences in the attitudes toward achievement between the males and females.

METHOD

Subjects

The subjects, whose ages ranged from fifteen to seventeen years old, were drawn from the tenth through twelfth graders in all three of the Pasadena City high schools and two of the Los Angeles City high schools. The total sample consisted of 144 subjects (75 males, 69 females) whose family income ranged from $8,000 to $16,000 a year. The median family income was $10,500 for the year of 1970.

Procedures

There were two independent variables: sex and achievement. All students who participated in the study were Japanese-American Sanseis from the mainland. The term Sansei was defined as being the third generation of Japanese in America. If at least one of the parents was a Nisei (second generation), then the student was classified as a Sansei.

Achievement was defined in terms of intelligence test scores on the Lorge-Thorndike Intelligence Test (1962) and an adjusted grade point average (GPA). In computing the GPA, grades received and level of difficulty of the courses were the factors considered. Academic classes such as algebra, English, etc., were weighted by adding half a grade point to the final grade, while no grade points were added to industrial occupational classes or physical education classes. The placement into the four groups was based on a regression equation with X axis being the GPA and the Y axis being the intelligence test score. If the student's actual GPA fell below the expected GPA, he was classified as an underachiever (UA). If the actual GPA met or exceeded the predicted GPA, he was classified as a high achiever (HA). Personality characteristics were evaluated from a phenomenological frame of reference and an attitude questionnaire. The phenomenological measure of the self-concept was the Adjective Check List consisting of 300 adjectives with twenty-four subcategories (Gough & Heliburn, 1965).

In addition, each student was administered the Asian American Survey to measure attitudes toward school and academic achievement (Onada, 1974). Two major subcategories were assessed by the Asian American Survey: attitudes toward school achievement and plans to enter college.

The Adjective Check List was analyzed using the Claremont Graduate School multivariate analysis of variance program (Harrison, 1969) which used a maximum likelihood for the multivariate F ratio. In addition, univariate F ratios for the subscales were calculated. The Asian American Survey was analyzed by a chi-square analysis.

RESULTS

The twenty-four variates of the Adjective Check List were evaluated by the multivariate analysis of variance. Table 33-I contains Wilks's lambda criterion, F ratio, and probability level for achievement, sex, and Achievement x Sex interaction. The multivariate analysis of variance by achievement indicated that Sansei HAs had significantly more positive personality traits between Sansei males and females ($p < .001$). However, the overall F ratio by achievement and sex was nonsignificant.

TABLE 33-I

MULTIVARIATE ANALYSIS OF VARIANCE FOR
THE ADJECTIVE CHECK LIST VARIATES FOR
SANSEIS BY ACHIEVEMENT AND SEX

Source	Wilk's lambda criterion		
	F	df	p
Achievement (A)	2.180	24	.002
Sex (B)	7.730	24	.001
A × B	.875	24	.636
Error		257	

Since the multivariate analysis of variance proved significant for the variables of achievement and sex, univariate analysis of variance tests were conducted on the twenty-four variates of the Adjective Check List. Only the significant univariate test probability levels and the means and standard deviations for the Achievement and sex variables are shown in Table 33-II. The Sansei HAs were significantly higher than UAs on self-control, achievement, dominance, endurance, order, and intraception; but the HAs scored significantly lower than UAs on succorance (p < .044 to p < .001). Sansei males were significantly higher on the number of adjectives checked, defensiveness, achievement, endurance, order, affiliation, and succorance. The Sansei females scored significantly higher in self-confidence, number of favorable adjectives check, and autonomy (p < .012 to p < .001).

The Attitudes Toward School Achievement subscale on the Asian American Survey, which was composed of five questions regarding school achievement, was analyzed by a chi-square analysis. Sanseis as a group expressed more positive attitudes toward school achievement than negative, $X^2(15) = 17.49$, p < .05. However, when HAs and UAs were compared, HAs did not express significantly more positive attitudes toward school achievement when compared to Sansei UAs.

The Plans to Enter College subscale on the Asian American

Survey was analyzed by chi-square analysis. Regardless of sex or achievement, 97 percent of the Sanseis planned to attend college or a trade school, and only 3 percent were not planning to attend any type of post-high school training, $X^2(1) = 7.29$, $p < .001$. This finding would' seem to indicate that Sanseis are not diminishing in their interest for academic achievement. However, there was no comparison between Sanseis and Caucasians on plans to enter college, and thus it is highly possible that Caucasians are likewise increasing in their interest in academic achievement. There were no significant differences between Sansei males and females or between HAs and UAs. It was surprising to find that UAs were just as interested in attending college as HAs. It seems that UAs have been ingrained with the concept that they must attend college.

DISCUSSION

Sue and Sue (1973) indicated that Asians (including Chinese, Filipinos, etc.) have been inaccurately stereotyped with the success myth. The myth, as it relates to Sanseis, tends to perpetuate the concept that all Sanseis are high achievers with similar attitudes toward achievement and have similar personality characteristics. Perhaps the success myth is not true of all Asians, but is clearly evident that Sanseis are maintaining a high level of academic achievement.

The results of the testing program at Pasadena City Schools (1972) indicated that Sanseis tended to score higher on achievement and intelligence tests and have a higher mean GPA than Caucasians and minority students. These findings tend to support the concept that Sanseis as a group have retained a strong interest in academic achievement.

However, the present study was primarily interested in comparing differences in attitudes toward achievement between Sansei HAs and UAs and between males and females. When Saneis were asked to indicate their attitudes toward school achievement and their plans to enter college, there were no significant differences found between the variables of achievement and sex on the Asian American Survey. Sanseis expressed more positive attitudes toward school achievement than negative attitudes. Also, 97 percent of all Sanseis tested planned to enter college after finishing high school. The most unexpected finding was that Sansei UAs did not express more negative attitudes toward academic achievement than Sansei HAs. However, Sansei HAs scored significantly higher on the achievement subscale than the UAs on the Adjective Check List. Sansei UAs described themselves as having less of an interest in achievement and having more doubts and apprehensions about their ability to succeed. The stereotype that Sanseis have a positive attitude toward achievement will probably continue because they, in general, are not rejecting their parents' positive attitude toward education. However, Sansei UAs may not be rejecting their parents' positive attitudes toward achievement, but they have more doubts about their ability to be successful.

Also, it was hypothesized that not all Sanseis can be stereotyped as having the traditional personality characteristics that identified their high achieving parents. It was anticipated that the personality characteristics of Sanseis would be affected by the level of achievement and sex of the person. The statistical analysis of the twenty-four subcategories on the Adjective Check List indicated that there are significant personality char-

TABLE 33-II

SIGNIFICANT PROBABILITIES, MEANS, AND
STANDARD DEVIATIONS BY ACHIEVEMENT

Variable	Univariate p	High achievers (n=88)		Underachievers (n=56)	
		M	SD	M	SD
Self-control	<.001	45.65	10.25	40.79	8.13
Achievement	<.006	44.63	9.15	40.97	7.58
Dominance	<.015	45.57	10.14	43.59	7.54
Endurance	<.005	46.99	12.47	43.28	7.88
Order	<.001	48.26	10.08	41.35	7.31
Intraception	<.044	48.88	9.57	42.78	9.01
Succorance	<.014	51.43	7.53	49.33	8.74

acteristic differences between Sansei HAs and UAs and between Sansei males and females.

The Sansei HAs described themselves as being more self-controlled, serious, sober, responsible, obliging, mannerly, and loyal workers. At times, they show overcontrol or sublimation of their impulses. The Sansei HAs are more likely to champion unpopular or unconventional causes. They perceive themselves as being more concerned with structure and order, which is sacrificed for individuality and self-denial. The HAs described themselves as more intelligent, having a stronger desire and determination to succeed, and having more confidence in their abilities. The HAs see themselves as more strong-willed, forceful, and persevering in their goals. Hence, being more dominant gave them more self-confidence to be forthright.

On the other hand, the Sansei UAs described themselves as more rebellious, arrogant, careless, conceited, cynical, skeptical, and negative toward complacent beliefs. They described themselves as having less self-control and endurance while being more headstrong, irresponsible, complaining, disorderly, impulsive, obnoxious, narcissistic, and ungrateful. In many aspects, they tend to aspire for the gratification of immediate needs rather than seeking the gratification of long-term goals. In general, the UAs described themselves as having more doubts and apprehensions about themselves. The Sansei UAs perceived themselves as less dominant and preferred to stay out of the "limelight," because they are more reluctant to make decisions.

It appears that the degree to which the Sanseis parallel the traditional stereotype of being passive, quiet, and introverted depends upon the level of their achievement. The stereotype that all Sanseis have similar personality characteristics is an oversimplification. Sansei HAs retained more of the traditional Japanese personality characteristics than the Sansei UAs. However, there are certain aspects of the stereotype that were found to be inaccurate or no longer true of Sansei HAs. The Sansei HAs are becoming more outgoing, forceful, strong-willed, and assertive, unlike the traditional stereotype of being passive, quiet, and meek. It was the Sansei UAs that were found to be

TABLE 33-III

SIGNIFICANT PROBABILITIES, MEANS, AND STANDARD
DEVIATIONS BY SEX ADJECTIVE CHECK LIST

Variable	Univariate p	Sex			
		Male (m=75)		Female (n=69)	
		M	SD	M	SD
No adjectives checked	<.001	47.70	9.86	43.74	11.08
Defensiveness	<.001	44.47	9.92	41.22	9.69
Favorable adjectives checked	<.050	42.11	13.63	42.77	11.11
Self-confidence	<.003	41.91	8.81	44.27	7.22
Achievement	<.001	44.88	7.24	40.73	9.49
Endurance	<.004	46.39	8.90	43.89	10.80
Order	<.001	45.84	7.85	42.78	9.28
Affiliation	<.012	46.97	10.94	41.69	10.37
Autonomy	<.001	49.07	7.68	50.76	9.06
Deference	<.005	49.24	8.95	46.92	9.72

more shy, passive, and unassertive. Also, there are indications that Sansei UAs are undergoing more emotional conflicts than previously anticipated. Many mental health workers may have underestimated the seriousness of the personality or identity conflicts that are emerging among the Sansei UAs (Sue & Sue, 1974).

Also, the present study attempted to investigate the differences in personality characteristics between Sansei males and females. It was anticipated that there would be significant differences in the personality characteristics of Sansei males and females and that Sansei females would show a greater degree of acculturation than the Sansei males.

Sansei males are more quiet, reserved, cautious, aloof, moderate, and subdued than the Sansei females. They are more persistent, enduring, idealistic, and concerned about such concepts as truth and justice. Also, Sansei males described themselves as more dependable and controlled, even at the cost of their own individuality. They see themselves as more intellectual, industrious, ambitious, eager to succeed, and more determined to do well. However, Sansei males feel that they are less confident and lacking the ability to mobilize themselves into action. Socially, they are more adaptable, anxious to please, yielding, and retiring.

Sansei females are more emotional, adventurous, wholesome, frank, and helpful than the Sansei males. Although the Sansei females indicated that they are more self-confident, this finding is not totally consistent with the results of the other subscales on the Adjective Check List. On the contrary, Sansei females described themselves as more anxious, apprehensive, critical of themselves, erratic, impatient, intolerant, impulsive, and reactionary than the Sansei males. Also, they expressed more feeling of pessimism about life and restlessness about prolonged interactions. Nevertheless, Sansei females have still retained some of the traditional personality characteristics of being hard working, conventional, dependable, mannerly, and serious. In other words, Sansei females are becoming more assertive, self-willed, independent, dominant, and outgoing than Sansei males. However, this does not mean that Sansei females have totally relinquished all the personality characteristics that identified the Japanese female.

Since this study did not compare Sanseis to Caucasians, it is not possible to generalize these findings to other ethnic groups. However, there still exists a need for further investigation of the implications of the changing personality characteristics among Sanseis. There is some evidence of increased emotional stress, and it is uncertain whether the emotional conflict facing Sanseis is the beginning of a major identity conflict or if there are minor symptoms in which Sanseis will readily adapt.

REFERENCES

Caudill, W., and DeVos, G. Achievement, Culture and Personality: The Case of the Japanese-Americans. *American Anthropologist*, 1956, 58:1102-

1126.

Gough, H. G., and Heliburn, A. B. *Manual: Adjective Check List.* Palo Alto, Cal.: Consulting Psychologists Press, 1965.

Harrison, F. *Quantitative Analysis Computer Program System.* Claremont, Cal.: Claremont Graduate School and University Center, 1969.

Kitano, H. L. Changing Achievement Patterns of Japanese in the United States. *Journal of Social Psychology,* 1962, 58:257-264.

––––––– . *Japanese-Americans: Evolution of a Subculture.* Englewood Cliffs, N. J.: Prentice-Hall, 1969.

Lorge, I., and Thorndike, E. L. *The Lorge-Thorndike Intelligence Tests,* rev. ed. Boston: Houghton Mifflin, 1962.

Meredith, G. M. Amae and Acculturation Among Japanese-American College Students in Hawaii. *Journal of Social Psychology, 1966, 70:*171-180.

Onoda, L. Personality Characteristics of High and Underachieving Japanese American Sanseis. Doctoral dissertation, Claremont Graduate School and University Center, 1974.

Sue, D. W., and Sue, S. Understanding Asian-Americans: The Neglected Minority: An Overview. *Personnel and Guidance Journal,* 1973, 51:387-389.

Sue, S. and Sue, D. W. MNPI Comparisons Between Asian-American and Non-Asian Students Utilizing a Student Health Psychiatric Clinic. *Journal of Counseling Psychology,* 1974, 21:423-427.

Watanabe, C. Self-Expression and the Asian-American Experience. *Personnel and Guidance Journal,* 1973, 51:387-389.

Chapter 34

CULTURAL FACTORS IN GROUP COUNSELING AND INTERACTION*

EDWARD KANESHIGE

THE University of Hawaii has a student population that is somewhat unique in American colleges and universities. When the enrollment is broken down into various ethnic categories, statistics show that the majority of students are of Asian-American background. This is not surprising, since more than half of the population of Hawaii is nonwhite. However, statistics on student use of the university's counseling services, which are provided on a nonfee, voluntary basis to the entire student body, show that the proportion of nonwhite (primarily Asian-American) students who use the services is considerably less. One of the prime reasons for this lack of acceptance and use of counseling services is the inherent conflict between the values of Asian-Americans and the values that are implicit in the counseling process.

Although different orientations in counseling place emphasis on different methods and techniques that are most likely to bring about success the various methods appear to be in general agreement about the desired outcomes. Counseling emphasizes the individual worth of each person and his growth toward greater maturity. This may pose problems for the individual's family and friends, but generally, where there is a conflict, the growth of the individual is considered to be of greatest importance. Understanding the emotional aspect of one's behavior and motivations is another characteristic of counseling. Counselees are encouraged to be expressive of their emotions rather than stifle them. Since counseling is a verbal activity, the full

*From Edward Kaneshige, Cultural Factors in Group Counseling and Interaction, *Personnel and Guidance Journal,* 51:407-412, 1973. Copyright 1973 by the American Personnel and Guidance Association. Reprinted by permission.

and open expression of feelings, problems, conflicts, etc., is a necessary condition.

The values and goals of group counseling are similar to, if not identical with, those of individual counseling. Although each client must be aware of other group members, he is basically working toward his own self-understanding, growth, and maturity. The usual expectation is that one learns more when he is focusing directly on understanding his own dynamics and behavior, but it is possible that significant learning also occurs when one is attempting to aid another individual in understanding his dynamics and behavior.

Most counselors and psychologists accept these goals rather naturally, and they are frequently unaware that the conditions and goals of group counseling run counter to some of the values of their clients. They may not have examined the possibility that some of their fundamental beliefs and premises in counseling are actually contrary to the cultural heritage of some individuals they counsel. Asian-American students encounter a number of conflicts as they participate in the group counseling process — which has been recommended to them as a way of resolving their conflicts.

CULTURAL PATTERNS IN GROUP COUNSELING

Let us first examine some of the conditions, goals, and techniques of group counseling as they relate to the values of one Asian-American group, Japanese-Americans, and then go on to see how the differences in cultural patterns emerge in group interactions.

Will Power

One of the first conflicts that the Japanese-American student faces is his accepting the fact that he has a problem he cannot adequately overcome by himself. This is not as easy as it may seem, since his culture views personal problems and shortcomings as being due to a lack of resolve and determination by the individual. The Japanese-American client finds it difficult to admit that he has a problem when he knows he will be told that he has not tried hard enough. His culture believes that understanding one's motivations may be important but that the primary cause of human failure is insufficient will power.

Consequently, this client sees that taking his problems to a counselor cannot solve the conflict and that the only hope he has is to try harder. If the problem persists and continues to cause pain and unhappiness he develops a fatalistic attitude and bears the burden in stoic fashion. It is therefore not surprising that he somatizes many emotional problems and, if he does bring them to a counseling center, it is only after considerable time and pain.

Nonconfrontation

In many group counseling formats there is only a minimum of structure and direction. The group leader may start each session off, but much of the content and focus is voluntarily initiated and pursued by individual group members. A group member is expected not only to share of himself and his personal concerns but also to become actively involved in the dynamics and problems of other members. To be involved means not only to empathize and be supportive but also to be open and to confront others who are self-deceptive or unable to accept their ability to contribute to a problem's resolution.

The Japanese group member is deterred from directly confronting other group members because he has been taught that it is impolite to put people on the spot; that it is presumptuous on his part to be assertive; and that the group leader is the most knowledgeable person and all should therefore defer to his greater wisdom and judgment. So he finds it difficult to make his share of comments and questions, even when he feels that he has a valid contribution to make.

Humility

A related factor in the degree of participation is the issue of humility. Japanese are taught to be self-effacing because their culture values humility and modesty. "Don't be a show-off or engage in any behavior that smacks of being a braggart" is a common admonition. An example of the way this value works is found in the elementary schools. The teacher asks anyone who knows the answer to a problem or question to raise his hand. She is certain that the problem is not overly difficult and that there are some children who know the answer. However, she is greeted with what appears to be complete nonresponsiveness. No hands go up. No one wants to be a show-off, even though many would enjoy praise and recognition. Similarly, in a counseling group the Japanese client struggles with his desire to volunteer comments and suggestions because of the gnawing feeling that to do so would label him a show-off.

Shame

Another prime value of the Japanese culture is to not bring shame to the family name. The Japanese individual is encouraged to perform deeds that will bring honor to the family, but his failure to attain positive public recognition is not a major consequence. On the other hand, bringing dishonor to the family name is of such importance that family members are repeatedly admonished against performing deeds that could bring disgrace to the family. The Japanese feel that family problems and conflicts are to be resolved within the family circle and that the only image that can be publicly displayed is a socially acceptable and consistent one. Therefore, the admission and display of personal inadequacy, even in a counseling group, is a sign of familial defect, and this brings shame to the family.

Related to this is the Japanese concept that the individual is of minimal importance as compared to the importance of the family. The individual exists and is important only in relation to his group. Thus, the public exposure of family conflicts and the eventual achievement of self-fulfillment is an unacceptable display of selfishness and exaggerated self-importance. Reaction and punishment generally follow swiftly.

The existence of these conflicting values for the Japanese

group is not unique. Every minority ethnic group experiences value conflicts to some extent. Additional problems are created, however, when other group members and the counselor misunderstand or misinterpret the Japanese client's seeming lack of effort to help himself. Being judged as not trying or not wanting to improve because he doesn't ask for help or can't talk about his problems compounds the problems that he has. And to cry out at this unfair judgment seems futile, since it does not alleviate the problem.

CULTURAL PATTERNS IN GROUP INTERACTION

Let us now examine the ways in which the differences in cultural values and patterns show up in interactions among group members from Japanese and Caucasian-Western backgrounds. Four values or patterns of behavior — verbal participation, emotional expression, avoidance of conflict, and acceptance of authority — have been selected to illustrate these differences.

Verbal Participation

Verbal participation is the extent to which an individual verbally participates in the group. Although there are individual differences among members of the same nationality group, anyone who has lived in Hawaii for any length of time would generally agree that Caucasians talk more than Japanese do. It is for this reason that, in the schools, Japanese students are urged, challenged, and encouraged to participate more in classroom discussions, while their Caucasian classmates are gently restrained and encouraged to let their relatively nonverbal fellow students say more.

Let us examine how the verbal participation pattern operates in a group situation. In a group composed of teachers working on improving their self-understanding and their interrelationships, the following exchange took place between a highly verbal Caucasian teacher and a Japanese teacher:

Caucasian Teacher: I don't feel that it's really fair for you local [Japanese] teachers to remain silent and force us [Caucasian teachers] to carry the ball in our discussion with the principal. I feel that it's important that someone speak up for us teachers; but since no one will, I feel that I have to take the responsibility, even though I would prefer not to.

Japanese Teacher: Gee, that's really interesting. What I was thinking while you were talking was that I hoped you would realize that you were talking too much and that you were monopolizing the time. I didn't want to say so, because I felt that it would be impolite for me to do so. Also, I kinda felt that you had a need to talk and be recognized by the group, so I felt that we should be tolerant and understanding of you. Actually, I felt that we were the ones who were behaving responsibly by not speaking out and complaining about your excessive verbalization.

In pursuing this exchange, it became clear that there was a wide difference in opinion as to what talking and silence meant and whether one behavior was more desirable than the other. The Caucasian position seemed to be that (a) a responsible person talks so that something can be accomplished; (b) silence does not accomplish anything; (c) a person who is quiet is either not very bright or does not have any ideas. On the other hand, the Japanese position appeared to be that (a) it is better to be quiet than to ramble on and say nothing or say something that is not well thought out; (b) the talkative person does not think very much because he is too busy talking; (c) the talkative person is essentially an attention seeking, narcissistic individual. The Japanese cultural pattern is to be quiet and listen to others who have more wisdom than you do; the Caucasian tradition is to exercise your initiative and responsibility by talking. If you are uncertain about whether or not to say something, the Japanese view is to remain silent; the Caucasian view is to say it anyway.

Emotional Expression

Emotional expression is defined here as the extent to which

an individual reveals his inner feelings to others. It is closely related to, but not the same as, verbal participation.

In most situations the Japanese person tends to remain non-expressive. He has been raised since childhood not to show his emotions. Thus, although he may be moved by what is occurring in the group, he is almost instinctively restrained from revealing his concern, and his facial expression remains passive. The Caucasian, whose upbringing has nurtured emotional expression, interprets this behavior as demonstrating a lack of feeling about what is transpiring. One Caucasian characterized this behavior as a sign of noncaring, and it brought forth this exclamation from him: "Doesn't this have any effect on you? Don't you care at all?" An individual who is unaffected by another person's suffering and pain is considered almost nonhuman and frequently becomes the focus of anger.

Thus the Caucasian view seems to be that (a) emotional expression is good; (b) the individual who is emotionally expressive is mature and accepting of himself. The Japanese view appears to be that (a) emotional expression is a sign of immaturity; (b) one should strive for adult behavior, and emotional restraint is one example of this.

Avoidance of Conflict

The Japanese culture values the individual who subordinates himself. The individual who sacrifices himself to avoid conflict even when his position may be justified is frequently looked upon with commendation. The individual who insists on his way, even when justified, is often looked upon with disapproval and is frequently condemned. In a verbal dispute, then, the Japanese individual tends to disengage himself from the argument, even when he is convinced that his position has more validity than that of the other person.

Acceptance of Authority

Japanese children are taught very early in life that they are the least worthy and the least knowledgeable and that to be presumptuous is a cardinal sin. They are taught to speak only when absolutely certain, and even then only with extreme modesty. In groups, this type of upbringing is evidenced in the extent to which the Japanese individual wants the goals of the group sessions to be clearly described and specified and his subsequent willingness to stay with the original goals. When it appears that the group is deviating from the original goal, the Japanese individual attempts to get the group back to its original goal. The Caucasian individual sees this conforming behavior as unnecessary and even undesirable and would prefer that the group have the freedom to move in more creative ways. The Japanese person sees this kind of free-flowing behavior as another mark of immaturity and a lack of personal discipline. Imposing rules and regulations is therefore seen as a deprivation of freedom from one viewpoint and as a stimulator of freedom from the other.

THE COUNSELOR'S ROLE

An individual's cultural heritage influences his attitudes and behavior in his daily life. It also influences his acceptance of counseling as a desirable method of increasing his self-understanding and self-worth. Even when he accepts the goals and methods of counseling, however, he may find that his personal values and beliefs are in conflict with them. It is important that counselors understand and recognize the existence of these potential conflicts and that they *do not judge the Asian-American client from the Western-white value orientation.* To do so would hinder or stop the progress of counseling and possibly create even more conflicts for some individuals.

In group counseling, the counselor can work toward (a) helping the Asian-American client overcome the cultural restrictions that hamper his emotional growth and (b) helping other group members grow in their understanding and acceptance of minority group members. The group counselor can do this in a number of ways.

1. He can encourage the Asian-American client to be a more verbal participant by providing a group climate that is suppor-

tive and nonthreatening.

2. He can demonstrate that he understands the uniqueness of the Asian-American by verbalizing some of the cultural value differences and by sensitively recognizing the internal struggle that the Asian-American faces in expressing himself.

3. He can aid the verbally "nonexpressive" and "nonaggressive" Asian-American client who is struggling to express his feelings by minimizing interruptions by other group members. When two group members try to speak at the same time, he can tactfully restrain the more talkative one and encourage the one who has more difficulty in expressing himself.

4. He can reassure the Asian-American client and all group members of the confidentiality in the counseling process.

5. He can try to improve the accuracy of the interpretations made by group members by pointing out and clarifying what is happening, as in the following example:

> *Client #1 [Caucasian]:* I don't see it the same way that you do. I think you're wrong. [*He proceeds to describe his views*]
> *Client #2 [Japanese]:* [*no response*]
> *Counselor [to Client #2]:* Do you feel that your understanding of the situation was right?
> *Client #2:* No. I still feel I was right, and I think that Client #1's explanation doesn't make sense at all.
> *Counselor:* How come you didn't say that?
> *Client #2:* I didn't want to hurt his feelings, and besides, it isn't worth the hassle.
> *Counselor:* It's important that you do express your feelings both for yourself, so you can be understood, and for the others, so that their perceptions can be more accurate.

6. He can challenge aggressive assertions and critical statements made to Asian-American clients by their Caucasian counterparts where he feels that the assertions are only partially accurate. Where he might ordinarily wait for the attacked person to defend himself, the counselor may have to recognize that the "passive" Asian-American client may not defend himself because of his cultural inhibitions. The counselor's actively stepping in and commenting on the statements and behaviors would be important in improving the understanding of what is

happening.

7. He must recognize that he is being a model for all group members, but especially so for Asian-Americans, who value authority. His tone of voice and manner of interaction with each group member are unconsciously and sometimes consciously noted and may do much to encourage or stifle verbal expressiveness.

8. He can help the group process by alerting group members to listen more carefully and to consider the observed behavior from the standpoint of the person being observed rather than that of the observer. "What does it mean to you?" and "What do you think it means to Client X?" are questions that might stimulate group members to think beyond the usual interpretations.

9. He can help the Asian-American client recognize that he is not necessarily denying his cultural identity if he does not always act consistently with his values. The client can be helped to recognize that he can rationally choose to change his pattern of behavior because the new· behavior is more in keeping with the kind of person he wants to be and not necessarily because it is merely conforming to society's codes. For example, he may decide to change his behavior when he understands that his quiet, unassuming, nonassertive behavior is being read by non-Asians as inarticulate, conforming, and obsequious.

In Summary. The group counselor can help the Asian-American client to be more expressive in communicating his feelings and thoughts to the group without negating his cultural values. The counselor can work with other group members in creating an atmosphere that increases the possibility that each individual will be accepted regardless of his background and values. Counseling can be more than therapeutic; it can also be rewardingly educational.

Part VII. Conclusion

Chapter 35

THE EDUCATIONAL CHALLENGE

George Henderson

THIS chapter will summarize data found in earlier chapters as well as present a few additional data. By summarizing educational and community variables pertaining to ethnic minorities, we will better understand the suggested strategies presented in the next chapter.

AFRICAN AMERICANS

The black child begins life with much higher odds against him than a white child. He is more likely to die in infancy than the white baby. If the black baby lives, the chances of losing his mother in childbirth are relatively high; the maternal mortality rate is four times as high as for white mothers. The black baby is born into a family that lives in the inner city (over 70 percent of the 25 million black American population does), usually in the black ghetto. It is a family that is larger than its white counterpart, and it is crowded into dilapidated housing — quarters structurally unsound or unable to keep out cold, rain, snow, rats, or pests.

With more mouths to feed, more babies to clothe, and more needs to satisfy, the black family is forced to exist on a median family income of barely half the median white family income. When the black youngster goes to school, he is usually aware that he is starting down a path that has proved no avenue to adequate living, much less to fame or fortune. And because black children are generally taught in slum schools, usually with inferior teachers, equipment, and facilities, the real gap between black and white students of the same age often approaches five or six years.

Most blacks look at all these conditions, but not all of them see the same social implication. For some the conditions require a change; for others the status quo is fine. The conflicts that center on color do not lead to a single response: Many blacks withdraw, others clown, others assume proud mannerisms, and still others become aggressive or highly suspicious of nonblacks. Those who run to a pride in blackness do not find utopia. Once inside the winner's circle of blackness, a veil of racial discrimination seems to enshroud both the light-skinned and the dark-skinned "victors." This invisible veil, as Ralph Ellison pointed out, is not physical invisibility:

> That invisibility to which I refer occurs because of a peculiar disposition of the eyes of those with whom I come in contact. A matter of the construction of their inner eyes, those eyes with which they look through their physical eyes upon reality .... It is sometimes advantageous to be unseen, although it is most often rather wearing on the nerves. ... You ache with the need to convince yourself that you do exist in the real world, that you're a part of all the sound and anguish, and you strike out with your fists, you curse and you swear to make them recognize you. And, alas, it's seldom successful.[1]

In most communities heavily populated by blacks, low and middle-income groups live in extremely close proximity to each other. This situation is not caused primarily by a natural selection process but by *de facto* housing segregation. Consequently, the plight of poverty-stricken blacks is distorted if only census data are considered. Black "haves" appear less affluent and the "have nots" seem less disadvantaged than they actually are. There is, in short, a much wider gap between black middle and lower classes than is apparent. Both groups closely approximate their white counterparts in income and living styles.

Now let us consider the fact that most blacks are marginal in the dominant white culture.[2] Add to this disadvantage by making them marginal compared with their white socioeconomic counterparts. Finally, make poverty-stricken blacks marginal compared with surrounding middle-income blacks. When all these facts coalesce, one will have a picture of poverty-stricken blacks — a minority group within a minority group. Marginality therefore is characterized by the following conditions: (1) There must be a situation that places two or more cultures (or subcultures) in lasting contact. (2) One culture must be dominant in terms of power and reward potential. This is the nonmarginal of the two cultures; its members are not particularly influenced by or attracted to the marginal culture. (3) The boundaries between the two cultures are sufficiently defined for the members of the marginal culture to internalize the patterns of the dominant group and not be satisfied with the "inferior" group.

Although not all poverty-stricken blacks are marginal, many have become victims of aspirations that they will never achieve and hopes that they will never satisfy.

School Conditions

The more effective elementary, secondary, and higher education schools are accelerating their efforts to teach black pride — to help black children, youth, and adults to find themselves in blackness. For example, in some schools black pride is taught as an integral part of regular school subjects. In such schools Crispus Attucks is becoming as well known as Paul Revere, and the writings of black writers like Langston Hughes, James Baldwin, Gwendolyn Brooks, and Ralph Ellison stand beside those of Charles Dickens, Jane Austen, and Jack London. Even bulletin board displays and school musicals and plays are taking on a black look.

Black students are getting acquainted with nineteenth-century black intellectuals such as Edward Blyden, Martin Delaney, and David Walker. Furthermore, they are learning to respect the revolutionary ideals of Gabriel Prosser, Harriet Tubman, Sojourner Truth, Frederick Douglass, Marcus Garvey, W. E. B. DuBois, Malcolm X, Martin Luther King, Jr.,

Whitney Young, and Frantz Fanon. Gradually, black youth are learning the importance of early twentieth-century black musicians, including Bessie Smith, Jelly Roll Morton, King Oliver, Fats Waller, Louis Armstrong, Perry Bradford, and Duke Ellington.

Literature classes can also double as Black Studies classes. The number of books focusing on black people is increasing at a significant rate. Despite this progress, few black students (or their teachers) learn that *Poems on Various Subjects: Religious and Moral* (1775) by Phillis Wheatley was the first published literary work by a black American. *Escape: Or A Leap for Freedom* (1851), by William Wells Brown, an escaped slave, was the first play by a black American. *The Chipwoman's Fortune* (1932) by Willis Richardson was the first black-authored play on Broadway. *Native Son* (1940) by Richard Wright was the first black novel to achieve classic status. *Annie Allen* (1950) by Gwendolyn Brooks, poet laureate of Illinois, was the first work by a black poet to win a Pulitzer Prize, and *Invisible Man* (1952) by Ralph Ellison received the National Book Award. Equally revealing is the fact that few black students (or their teachers) have read the seminal works of Frederick Douglass, Paul Lawrence Dunbar, W. E. B. DuBois, Booker T. Washington, James Weldon Johnson, and Langston Hughes, to mention a few renowned black writers.

AMERICAN INDIANS

Currently, American Indians and Alaskan natives are at the bottom of the economic ladder. They have the highest rates of unemployment and school dropouts, live in the most dilapidated housing, and in some parts of the country are accorded the lowest social status. These conditions reflect both what white Americans have done to the Indians and what the Indians have not been able to do for themselves.

Unable to realize that we do not have an Indian problem but rather an *American problem*, the Federal government has established government-controlled Indian bureaus, reservations, and assistance programs. Each of these short-sighted solutions has contributed to the psychological emasculation of Indian men, the demoralization of Indian women, and the alienation of Indian children. In other words, most government programs have failed to assist Indians in their efforts to maintain individual dignity and cultural identity while achieving success in the larger society. Yet with missionary zeal, white Anglo-Saxons continue their ill-fated efforts to Americanize the Indians.

Half the 800,000 native American population lives on 40 million acres of reservations in thirty states. Part of their frustration is revealed in the following statistics. Indians have 100 million fewer acres of land today than in 1887. Their average life expectancy is forty-five years. Nearly 60 percent of the adult Native American population has less than an eighth-grade education. Infant mortality is more than 10 points above the national average. The majority of Native American families have annual incomes below $5,000.00; 75 percent have annual incomes below $4,000.00. Indian unemployment is almost ten times the national average.

Feeling trapped and powerless in a world controlled by non-Indians, most rural and urban Indians have not become militant, but instead have withdrawn. Overgeneralizing from this group, representatives of non-Indian cultures pass on stereotypes about shiftless and drunken Indians. There is a saying in some towns, "If you hire an Indian, never pay him the first day if you want him to come back the second day. He'll take the money and drink it but not come back to work." It is not only what is said about Indians that is detrimental, but also what is not said. Until the 1970 United States census, Native Americans were not even listed as an identifiable ethnic group. Little wonder then that from time to time a few automobiles owned by Indians display bumper stickers that say "Custer had it coming."

Conflicts between white and Indian cultures are found on reservations, in small towns, and in big cities. The strains show up in many ways, including juvenile delinquency, adult crime, and alcoholism. Such social pathologies are but symptoms of our inhumanity and insensitivity. Historically, non-Indians have looked at Indian tribes but have failed to see the deplorable social, psychological, and physical deprivations. White teachers and counselors in particular tend to think that because an exceptional Indian student has managed to succeed, the others should also.

School Conditions

One-third of the approximately 280,000 Indian children in schools are in federally operated institutions. Indian schools range from trailers on Navajo reservations to large off-reservation boarding schools. The dropout rate for Indians is twice the national average, their level of educational attainment is half the national average, and their test scores are far below those of other students. Generally, the longer Indian children stay in school, the further behind they get. This *cumulative deficit* partially explains why Indian high school graduates as a group earn 75 percent less than the national average.

Educators concerned about the unfair treatment of native Americans in textbooks are aware of several glaring omissions. By the time white men came, the Indians had already domesticated more than forty plants, had some forty inventions to their credit; were great artists and craftsmen; had music, songs, dances, and poetry; used 150 medicines, surgery and drugs; had discovered rubber, and invented the bulbed syringe. The mythical picture of them as cruel, primitive hunters and nomadic warriors must be replaced by the truth.[3]

Television and movies have exposed American children to the deeds — often distorted to make whites look good — of a few Indian warriors, mainly Cochise, Crazy Horse, Geronimo, Osceola, Red Cloud, and Sitting Bull. Only recently have a small number of American children become familiar with writings about other great native Americans such as Joseph Brant, Chief Joseph, Massasoit, John Ross, Samoset, Shawnee Prophet, Squanto, Tecumseh, Washakie, and Wovoka. This is only the beginning of a long overdue journey into a neglected and embarrassing portion of our past.

Very little is reflected in texts or in historical monuments of the cultures and histories of the diverse peoples called American Indians. Even less has been written about the suffering and degradation that Indians have endured. Only recently have more balanced historical accounts of their displacement and neglect been included in school textbooks. Traditional history books of the nineteenth and early twentieth centuries praised the heroism of white settlers in the development of the North American continent and cheered the subduing of "hostile savages." For example, in the town square of Santa Fe, New Mexico, the oldest settlement in the West, there is the commemorative inscription, "To the heroes who have fallen in the various battles with savage Indians in the territory of New Mexico."

Prior to the federal government's assumption of responsibility for the welfare of native Americans, the Society for the Propagation of the Gospel in Foreign Parts (SPG), established in 1700 by the Church of England, set up several elementary schools and more than 340 missions in the American colonies. The purpose of SPG's missionary activities were quite simple: teach Indians and black slaves their letters and some prayers and hymns.

The first government funds for Indian schools were allocated in the early 1800s. In 1819 Congress passed a law authorizing $10,000.00 a year for the education of American Indians. Most of the money was given to missionary groups for support of church schools for Indians. In 1924 Congress belatedly passed a law making every Indian born in the United States a citizen. With this law came individual state responsibility for the education of Indian citizens.

In 1972 Congress passed the Indian Education Act, creating new educational opportunities for native American and Alaska native children and adults. The act was the outgrowth of three major problems of educating Indian students. They were (1) receiving an inferior quality education, (2) exclusion from management of their own education, and (3) imposition of the educational system of another culture. The act authorized the operation of three different programs to meet the unmet needs of Indians from preschool to college.

While black Americans and native Americans are receiving considerably more attention, Spanish-speaking and Asian Americans receive far less recognition in school materials. Most Anglo writers have had difficulty writing objectively about events such as the Mexican War, the Spanish-American War, and the internment of Japanese Americans at the onset of World War II, since these events represent conflicts between American economic desires and democratic principles. For example, one author described American intervention in four countries thus: Cuba: "The United States was committed to Cuban independence." China: "American missionaries brought education, as well as the Christian religion." The Philippines: "The United States began to help Filipinos develop their country." Mexico: "When the United States sought to encourage the establishment of an orderly government, the Mexicans complained of American interference."[4]

MEXICAN AMERICANS

Mexican Americans reflect a variety of cultural patterns, including those created by their parental heritage and the length of time their families have been American citizens. Second and third-generation descendants of early Spanish settlers are usually affluent, but second and third-generation descendants of agricultural workers tend to be poverty-stricken. There is still a third group: first-generation children of *braceros* — farm workers who have recently migrated from Mexico. The first two groups are likely to be Americanized; they have little knowledge of their Spanish heritage, and they speak little or no Spanish. Children of migrant workers speak fluent Spanish and hold tightly to Mexican customs and traditions. All groups are discriminated against by the Anglos — the white American majority. Indeed, in some communities Mexican Americans are the victims of more discrimination and segregation than blacks.

In many ways Mexican Americans and Puerto Ricans epitomize both racial integration and cultural separatism. This duality is best seen in a brief review of Mexican history. The Aztecs were intermarried with their Spanish conquerors and with Indian tribes hostile to the Aztecs. The children of these mixed matings are called *mestizos*. Also *creoles*, pure-blooded Spanish people born in Mexico, largely disappeared through intermarriage. Blacks from Africa, brought into Mexico during the colonial period as slaves, married Indians, and their offsprings were called *zambos*. *Zambos* and *mestizos* later intermarried, causing the so-called "Negro blood" to disappear.

While they are a racially-mixed people, the heritage of the people called Mexican Americans is quite similar: generally, they are highly religious (mainly Catholic); they are extended family-oriented and give allegiance to *La Raza*, "The Race"; they speak Spanish as their first language; they encourage their children to display good manners and to be especially respectful to older persons; they train their girls for the home and motherhood, and their boys to earn their keep and to protect and honor their families.

Chicanos or Mexican Americans are the second largest minority group in the public schools. The word "Chicano" stems from the Mexican Indian Nahautl word "Mechicano." The first syllable was dropped, and Chicano is left. It is an old term for the American of Mexican descent. Presently the Chicano movement (or Chicanismo) is a commitment to the improvement of life for all Spanish-speaking Americans and Americans of Mexican descent.

School Conditions

The lack of knowledge about cultures other than European is clearly illustrated in the fact that only a few American students learn that the first books printed in the Americas were printed in Mexico, and the first one, *Doctrina cristiana on lengua mexicana* (1540) was written in Nahuatl, the language of the Aztecs. Even fewer students learn that the *Fisica Speculatio* (1560) recorded the laws of gravity one hundred years before Newton, or that Mexicans pioneered the West; mapped and named many mountains, rivers, and fords; and named California, Colorado, Nevada, and New Mexico. Furthermore, Mexicans established numerous settlements, including Las Cruces, Los Angeles, Pueblo, San Antonio, San Diego, San Francisco, and Santa Fe. Finally, for the sake of illustration, only a handful of students learn that most cowboy terminology is Spanish or Indo-Hispanic: adobe, arrejos, chaps, lariat, mesquite, and rodeo, among others.

It is sad that our foremost scholars have praised the significant writings of medieval Europe but not those of Latin or South America. There were bilingual dictionaries in Mexico before 1600, and teacher's guides, *Cartilla para enseñar a leer*, were trilingual — Spanish, Latin, and Nahuatl. But nothing can be done about past omissions. We can, however, prevent similar omissions in the present and the future. American students must also learn about the contributions of such persons as Juan Luis Vives, Alonso de la Vera Cruz, Octaviano Larrazolo, Miguel Hidalgo y Costilla, Rafael Ramírez, José Maria Morelos y Pavón, and Benito Juárez.

Mexican Americans, like American Indians, Asian-Americans, and Puerto Ricans, are truly marginal people. Culturally they are neither black nor white. Their marginality affects individual searches for identity. In most schools the curriculum does not include material with which Mexican Americans can positively identify. In history classes, for instance, they become the villains who massacred the courageous Americans at the Alamo. Most elementary and secondary schools inflict the final blow on the cultural identity of Mexican American children by forcing them to leave their ancestral language at the schoolhouse door. Many students react by adopting a defense mechanism called *ethnic self-hatred*.

Some studies of Mexican American students in junior and senior high schools conclude that in many instances the negative self-images adopted by Mexican Americans are simply coping devices. Recent studies also illustrate the detrimental effects of negative definitions that teachers and administrators hold of the students. Students become aware of the negative views and, in some instances, role-play as people with negative self-images in order to minimize conflicts in school. Submissive acts — "playing dumb" — are ways Chicano pupils manage to coexist with the Anglos.

Most of the 1.7 million or so Mexican American school children in the Southwest have suffered academic failure because of the unwillingness or inability of schools to build a curriculum around their Spanish-speaking background. Yet as early as the 1920s researchers became aware that Mexican American students are better able to achieve in reading and other school-related tasks when they are taught in Spanish. Recently, a few school districts have implemented bilingual classroom instruction.

In Arizona, California, Colorado, New Mexico, and Texas, Mexican Americans comprise the largest minority group in the public schools. Forty percent of all Chicano students who enter the first grade do not graduate from high school. By the time they reach the twelfth grade, three out of every five Mexican American students are reading below grade level. Chicanos are more likely than Anglos to have repeated a grade and seven times more likely to be average for their grade. The problems confronting most Chicano children entering school vividly illustrate the problems of other ethnic minority groups:

1. They are isolated from Anglo children.
2. Their language and culture are excluded from the curriculum.
3. Their neighborhood schools are underfinanced.
4. Teachers treat them less favorably than Anglo students.

Oral language is the most basic concern of any culturally pluralistic curriculum. This is especially true in the early elementary grades, when children depend almost entirely on their ability to communicate orally. Unfortunately for non-English-speaking subcultures, most school materials are based on the false assumption that each child has developed adequate oral language skills.

Just as black English differs from standard English, Chicano Spanish also differs in vocabulary, grammar, and pronunciation from standard Spanish. For example, Chicano dialects often incorporate old Spanish words that were in common use during the seventeenth and eighteenth centuries. Consequently there is a need for well-designed and well-taught bilingual and bicultural instruction.

Less than 2 percent of all Chicano students currently receive state funded bilingual education — the largest number of bilingual programs is found in Arizona and New Mexico. This is so even though in 1974 the U. S. Supreme Court ruled that school districts are required under Title VI of the Civil Rights Act of 1964 to provide special programs for children who speak little or no English. Nationally, more than two million students do not speak English. In addition to Mexican Americans, language minority groups include Native Americans, Puerto Ricans, and Asian Americans.

PUERTO RICANS

A cursory review of related literature shows that Puerto Rican history is not Mexican American history. It is imperative that American students gain an appreciation for the heroic efforts of Puerto Rican leaders such as Ramon Emeterio Betances, Ruiz Belvis, Eugenio Maria de Hostos, and Ruis Rivera. Nor should students be unaware of the political contributions of Munnoz Rivera, Martienzo Cintron, and José Celso Barbosa. Of special significance are the writings of Jose de Diego, Albizu Campos, Luis Muñoz Marin, and Nicolas Guillén. Indeed, there is much more to learning about Puerto Ricans than reading Oscar Lewis' books.

The 12 million Hispanic-American population — native and foreign born — continues to grow at a tremendous rate. New York City and its surrounding communities have been the ports of entry for most of these immigrants. Contrary to popular notion, Puerto Ricans and Mexican Americans are not the only large Hispanic groups in the United States. A sizeable number of legal and illegal immigrants have come from Argentina, Bolivia, Columbia, Cuba, the Dominican Republic, Ecuador, Peru, and Venezuela. Even though the U. S. Census Bureau will conduct its first complete count of Hispanic Americans in 1980, exact figures will not be available for several years. Part of the difficulty in accurately counting and classifying Hispanic immigrants is due to the tendency of non-Puerto Rican Hispanics to list themselves as Puerto Ricans in order to gain full rights as American citizens. (Puerto Ricans are American citizens by virtue of the Jones Act of 1917). Since only a few census takers or school officials are able to distinguish the various Spanish dialects, this deception is seldom caught. In addition to the official count, New York City alone has between 750,000 and 1,000,000 illegal immigrants.

School Conditions

Like the children of other minority groups, Puerto Rican students are frequently plagued by problems revolving around acculturation, language difficulties, and economic barriers. Furthermore, most Puerto Rican parents give little or no parental support to the schools — they are preoccupied with the problems of learning English, finding housing, securing employment, and otherwise trying to survive. When they do turn their attention to the schools, they feel powerless to improve them, controlled as they are by white administrators and teachers. In some communities Puerto Ricans are joining blacks in trying to achieve educational and other gains.

Puerto Rican children are taught very early to respect their elders by bowing their heads. In the schools, however, teachers insist that pupils look at them when giving verbal responses. Other illustrations of cultural differences include the Puerto Rican pattern of little physical contact between the adolescent boy and male adults. Thus, in the classroom boys jerk away when male teachers try to touch them. Still other teachers fail to understand that in some families illness in the home requires everyone to remain home until the sick person's health is restored. Ignorance of such differing cultural norms, or the inability to understand them, results in unjustly labeling students as belligerent or docile or not interested in school. Many teachers not only do not understand cultural differences, they also are insensitive to and often shocked by the accelerated social maturity of slum-dwelling children. Slum children become socially mature at an early age in order to survive. By the time the average slum child is ten or twelve, she has seen too much and done too much. Sex, violence, and crime are all familiar to her.

The more effective teachers, counselors, and administrators seek to understand their own prejudices and cultural limitations before trying to understand and help people from other backgrounds. Much of the turmoil and dissension in recent years in rural and big city schools has arisen because too many administrators and teachers have found the concepts "culturally deprived," "disadvantaged," and "different" to be convenient alibis for failing to provide equal educational opportunities.

ASIAN AMERICANS

Most Asian-Americans live in Hawaii, California, Washington, Illinois, and New York. Each of these groups is beginning to react overtly to patronizing and racist behaviors.

> Many non-Orientals still think of Chinese Americans and Japanese Americans as people who work primarily in laundries and gardens. In academic circles the equally patronizing stereotype of the earnest, bespectacled young Oriental scholar is replacing the older stereotype of the pig-tailed coolie. The new stereotype has grown out of the national reputations achieved by such men as I. M. Pei and Minour Yamasaki, architects; Gerald Tsai, head of the Manhattan Fund; Tsung Dao Lee and Chen Ning Yang, winners of the Nobel Prize in physics; Samuel I. Hayakawa, president emeritus of San Francisco State University; Daniel Inouye, U. S. senator from Hawaii; Toyohiko Takami, dermatologist; and Hideyo Noguchi, bacteriologist.[5]

The plight of the poverty-stricken Asian Americans is vividly captured in San Francisco Chinatown statistics: More than one-third of Chinatown's families are poverty-stricken; three-fourths of all housing units are substandard; rents have tripled in the past five years; more than half the adults have only a grade-school education; one-third of core city residents are more than sixty-five years old; juvenile delinquency is increasing; and the suicide rate is three times the national average.

The educational problems of Asian Americans are compounded by language problems and basic philosophical differences: Asian children are taught to respect older people, deal with others peacefully, observe proper manners, and remember that making money is not the only purpose of education. Non-Asian schools frequently subscribe to a different set of values. Thus racial desegregation of the public schools is opposed by many Asian-American parents who want to maintain their own communities and cultural values.

School Conditions

Until recently the pattern of foreign studies in American schools was clear. In a course inappropriately called "world history" students learned that man's most significant development occurred in Europe and later in the United States. The study of areas beyond Europe entered this version of world history only peripherally, mainly when these areas were "discovered" by Europeans. References to China were usually limited to three or four: when it was a "cradle of civilization," when it was "discovered" by Marco Polo, when it came under European domination, and when it became an "emerging nation." In this version, Japan's "history" begins when it is "opened" by Commodore Perry.[6]

Ethnic studies curricula are teaching the following basic historical facts about Asian-Americans. The three largest American groups of Asian ancestry — Chinese, Japanese, and Filipinos — came to this country during the late nineteenth and early twentieth centuries. Attracted by the gold rush of the 1850s, Chinese were the first to come to America. Later, other Chinese were imported as cheap labor to help complete the transcontinental railway. Gradually overt discrimination increased until the Chinese Exclusion Act of 1882 was passed. This act denied immigration for ten years to Chinese laborers. It was renewed in 1892, and Chinese immigration was suspended indefinitely in 1902. The Exclusion Act also denied citizenship to Chinese born outside the United States. (This act was later applied to other Orientals.)

Almost all Japanese immigration to America occurred between 1900 and 1925. Despite the fact that most Japanese duplicated the European-type immigration pattern (whole families settling in integrated communities), they were discriminated against in the same manner as the Chinese, who mainly came as single males and lived in segregated communities. The "Gentlemen's Agreement" of 1908 between the American and Japanese governments restricted the immigration of Japanese farmers and laborers to the United States.

The most infamous example of Anglo discrimination against the Japanese occurred during World War II, when by Presidential decree the total Japanese population (more than 110,000 people) in California, Oregon, and Washington was evacuated to ten relocation centers in rural areas of America. The barbed wire-encircled barracks communities were patrolled by armed guards. This aspect of American history is usually omitted in American history courses.

The Filipinos came to America in the 1910s, and like other Orientals they were ineligible for naturalization. However, because the United States ruled the Philippines, the early Filipino immigrants carried United States passports and could not be excluded as aliens. In 1935, with the promise of freeing the Philippines, the American government set a quota of fifty Filipino immigrants per year.

After World War II alien Asians became eligible for citizenship, and in 1965 the national origin quota system was abolished. Currently, immigration from the Eastern Hemisphere and dependent areas is limited to 170,000. It is 120,000 for the Western Hemisphere. No more than 20,000 immigrants may come from any one country.

The influx into the United States between 1973 and 1975 of 50,000 school-age Vietnamese and Cambodian children has forced us to focus on the problems inherent in educating Indochinese refugees. Because of their war experiences, a significant number of these children need physical and psychological assistance as well as bilingual/bicultural education. Culturally conditioned to be passive learners, diligent scholars, and respectful of adults, Indochinese students have difficulty adjusting to competitive classrooms, athletically-oriented students, and teacher-student peerlike relationships characterizing American schools.

Attempts to broaden educational perspectives to include cultures in Asia have helped to change the attitudes of American students towards American descendents of those cultures. As our national policies shift, so too do our feelings toward Orientals or Asians. There is, for example, a connection between our feelings toward the Chinese in Asia and Chinese Americans. Because most Americans feel superior to other global cultures, they tend to feel superior to those ethnic representatives within the United States.

Seymour Fersh observed a novel twist to this prejudice: "For some American Orientals, prejudice works the other way; teachers may believe that Chinese, for example, have superior intelligence and work harder than other students. Consequently, more is expected from them and this 'compliment' increases pressure on the learner."[7] More has been done to provide Asian American studies in colleges and universities than in elementary and secondary schools. Even so, the higher education effort is meager.

Despite a growth in ethnic studies, most minorities are antagonistic toward and ignorant about cultures of other minorities. But so too are most Anglo children. To those who argue that ethnic minority content should only be studied by ethnic minorities, James A. Banks gives an eloquent rebuttal:

> The criterion used to determine whether [information about classical Rome and Greece, Medieval Europe, and Italian Renaissance] should be taught is not whether there are students in the class who are descendants of ancient Rome and Greece, or Italy or Medieval Europe. Such a criterion would not be intellectually sound. For the same reasons, it should not be used to select content about other cultures, such as the minority cultures in America.[8]

More than ethnic content is required if minority group students are to be successful in liberating their own communities. In addition to understanding institutionalized racism, minority students must learn strategies for social change. This can be done by actively involving students in counseling and teaching them how social systems work and how they can be altered. This, then, is the educational challenge.

REFERENCES

1. Ralph Ellison, *Invisible Man*, New York: New American Library, 1964, 7-8.
2. At one time or another adolescents, career women, migrants, chiropractors, bilingual persons, monks, the hard of hearing, middle-income groups, Catholics, factory foremen, druggists, and sociologists have all been situationally marginal. See J. W. Mann, Group Relations of the Marginal Personality, *Human Relations*, 1958, 11:77-92.
3. Gertrude Noar, Sensitizing Teachers to *Ethnic Groups*, New York: Anti-Defamation League of B'nai B'rith, nid., 11.
4. William A. Katz, Minorities in American History Textbooks, *Equal Opportunity Review*, June 1973, 3.
5. George Henderson, *To Live in Freedom: Human Relations Today and Tomorrow*, Norman: University of Oklahoma Press, 1972, 134.
6. Seymour Fersh, Orientals and Orientation, *Phi Delta Kappan*, 1972, 53:317.
7. *Ibid.*, 318.
8. James A. Banks, Teaching for Ethnic Literacy: A Comparative Approach, *Social Education*, 1973, 37:746.

Chapter 36

TOWARD A HELPING RELATIONSHIP

GEORGE HENDERSON

SIGMUND FREUD, Erik Erikson, William James, and George Herbert Mead are but a few of the writers who have noted that the self is both the subject and object of individual activity. The self is a doer. It consists of an active group of processes, such as perceiving, thinking, and remembering. It is an object which comprises a person's attitudes, feelings, and evaluations of himself or herself. Specifically, things are not merely happening to ethnic minority students but also are being made to happen by them. The view that our past and current race or ethnic problems in America are only black (or white) problems is an oversimplification of the basic principles of social interaction. Indeed, it is an erroneous oversimplification.

THE SEARCH FOR IDENTITY

We learn from the writings of Carl Jung that all people, regardless of their ethnic designation, strive for psychological unity, equilibrium, and stability.[1] Alfred Adler coined the term "creative self" in an effort to describe an individual's unique processes of interpreting and making meaningful experiences aimed at achieving psychological balance.[2] There is no single response that ethnic minority students make to psychological disequilibrium: Some become hostile, others clown, still others assume proud mannerisms, while many withdraw. The type of adjustment adopted depends upon the sociocultural modes of reaction that have been learned. Evaluating his own experiences, Andras Angyal argued convincingly that the image an individual has of himself or herself may not be appropriate to his/her real needs.[3] Applying this analysis to minority students,

485

their self-concepts are frequently distorted by adverse environmental conditions, causing many of them to project an unreasonably low estimate of their self-worth.

A minority self-concept that is negative can emerge out of school experiences. It can emerge out of conditions similar to those described in this book. Bingham Dai was one of the first researchers to underscore personality problems that are more or less peculiar to minority children.[4] Few writers would disagree that the self-concept of minority children has been contaminated by a color-caste complex. The continual conditions of second-class citizenship have dulled the aspirations of many minorities, young and old.

Somewhat similar to the behavior of Jews in Nazi Germany, minority students' reactions to school failure take on a wide variety of forms: (1) resignation and defeat, (2) heightened in-group feelings, (3) adoption of temporary frames of security, (4) shifts in levels of aspiration, (5) regression and fantasy, (6) conformity to the majority group norms and expectations, (7) changes in philosophy of life, (8) direct action, (9) aggression and displaced aggression. Of these reactions, resignation and defeat, regression and fantasy, conformity to the majority group norms and expectations, and aggression are the behaviors most likely to be expressed by minority students. It is unlikely that a few isolated instances of rejection will cause minorities — or any students — to adopt negative self-concepts. As a result of their continuous inability to achieve academic rewards comparable to their white peers, most minority students do, however, seem to be insulated against positive self-concepts.

The amorphous, nonmembership white middle class has become the positive reference group to which minority students are being encouraged to emulate. For most minority students it is probably true that the definitions of the dominant white culture supersede contradictory minority group definitions. E. U. Essien-Udom summarized the black student's dilemma:

> The Negro cannot choose both the dominant white culture and his own subculture. This sense of suspension between two societies and of dual membership presents enormous impediments to the process of adjustment. Negroes are involved,

subconsciously though it may be, in assertion of membership on one and the denial of membership in the other, or in a feeble assertion of both, or in the denial of the affinity with both.[5]

Ethnic Nationalism

Given the historical and continuing relative deprivation of ethnic minorities in America, the reader may ask: Why do we not see more incidences of minority mob violence, psychiatric maladjustments, and other social pathologies? A strong trend towards ethnic nationalism may be the stabilizing factor.

In a study of children residing in a lower-class neighborhood in Detroit, I made two basic observations: most minorities are marginal in references to their white socioeconomic counterparts, and most minorities seek equality with their white socioeconomic counterparts. Inherent in these assumptions are the following factors:

1. Some minority students believe that they will be accepted as equals by their white socioeconomic counterparts, and they are.

2. Some minority students believe that they will be accepted as equals by their white socioeconomic counterparts, but they are not.

3. Some minority students believe that they will never be accepted as equals by their white socioeconomic counterparts, but they are.

4. Some minority students believe that they will never be accepted as equals by their white socioeconomic counterparts, and they are not.

The failure of most nonwhite ethnic minorities in America to secure equal class and status with whites suggests that the first and third experiences cited above are not predominant. The majority of minority group experiences are of the second and fourth types. Continued rejection has caused many minorities to abandon the American Dream of equality and substitute a new dream: separatism.

George Devereux cautioned that we should not attribute a

single cause to individuals joining a separatist group: "The real point to be stressed is that both organized and spontaneous social movements and processes are possible not because all individuals participating in them are identically (and sociologically) motivated, but because of a variety of authentically subjective motives may seek and find an ego-syntonic outlet in the same type of collective activity."[6]

To low-achieving minority students, separatism may be viewed as an escape from competition with white students. To aspiring minority politicians, it may be viewed as a way to offset the effect of the powerful white political machines. To the minority unemployed, it may be seen as an opportunity to get jobs. In short, separatism attracts many people who have different needs. For example, Chicano separatist groups take lower- and middle-class Chicanos out of the social arena that has white role models for emulation. At first glance, we might surmise that the displacement of white role models is a negative adjustment. It is negative only when acceptance by whites has a strong valence. Otherwise, the devaluation of white role models is both bearable and desirable. For ethnic minorities who feel that they can never achieve maximum success in white society, separatism offers an ethnic society and a new hope.

Like the positive effects of psychotherapy, ethnic nationalism has therapeutic value — it can remove symptoms of ethnic inferiority. The therapy results from changing minority students' view of themselves in a positive direction (black or brown or red or yellow is good), and altering their view of Caucasians and their relation to them (the minority person is equal). When based upon a rigid code of conduct (such as cleanliness, well-mannered behaviors, and abstention from drinking alcoholic beverages and using narcotics), ethnic nationalism contributes to an orderly school. However, when based upon overt aggressive behaviors such as self-defense, it is a threat to school decorum. Contrary to popular opinion, violence is not a black, Indian, Latino, or Asian American nationalist's *raison d'être*. Yet, as in any group process, deindividualization, a reduction of inner restraints in individual members, makes possible the violence potential.

Each year that equal educational opportunity is denied minority students, they agree in increasing numbers with James Baldwin: "White people cannot, in the generality, be taken as models of how to live. Rather, the white man is himself in sore need of new standards which will release him from his confusion and place him once again in fruitful communication with the depths of his own being."[7]

Black nationalism, for example, is a search for "negritude" — a search for black identity. The term negritude was coined in 1939 by Aimé Cesaire, black poet of Martinique, West Indies. White colonialists have forced black people to ask themselves: Who am I? The search for negritude has led to a rediscovery of the past. Gradually, the shame of a once scorned history is giving way to cultures uniquely Negroid. In America there has been a literary back-to-Africa movement. The concept is an emotional antithesis of white colonialists' systematic negation of the black experience. In summary, the search for negritude was shaped first in the lives and writings of Cesaire, Leon Damas in French Guiana, Jacque Roumain in Haiti, Leopold Sadar Senghor and Birago Diop in Sengal. (Other ethnic groups are undergoing similar searches for identity.)

How can educators understand negritude? Perhaps by trying to vicariously feel the pain of Africans brought to this country to be exploited, enslaved, and despised. Educators who are able to gain this type of empathy will be able to appreciate the black drive for freedom. Empathy for other ethnic groups also is needed if the counselor is to be an effective helper.

Many good intentions of counselors go to waste because of their lack of understanding of what is helpful to minority students and what constitutes a helping relationship. To the affected students, this waste of effort may be so negative that it causes them to have a revulsion against all forms of helping. When this happens, helping is seen as a process that benefits counselors more than minority students and counselors are seen as neurotic do-gooders.

PRELUDE TO HELPING

All definitions of help are based on subjective values — something tangible or intangible discovered in a relationship between a helper and a helpee in which the helper aids the helpee in achieving a measure of self-fulfillment. In actuality, help is something that a person discovers for himself or herself. Each person must accept and act on helpful information with the knowledge that the ultimate responsibility belongs to him or her. In the final analysis, help cannot be given to minority students; it can only be offered.

The helping relationship has qualities that are the same whether it is between social worker or therapist and client, counselor and counselee, or teacher and student. The psychological equilibrium underlying the occupational roles resides at a much deeper, more fundamental level. This is true for both the helper and the helpee. Numerous studies suggest that effective help at the emotional level is initiated not so much by technique or special knowledge of the different professions but rather by positive attitudes of the helper. Specifically, research findings suggest that experienced helpers have a better conception of what constitutes a helping relationship than their colleagues who have mastered the theoretical concepts but have little experience. In many instances the man or woman in the street can describe a good helping relationship about as well as the so-called experts.

Some counselors see the helping process as one in which they make intricate diagnoses of minority students and then use a wide variety of helping methods on them. Still other counselors define minority students as being sick and themselves as being well. These are not really helping relationships. On the contrary, they are controlling relationships. When the minority student becomes an object rather than the subject, he or she is no longer the person who acts but instead becomes the person acted upon. Conceptually, a thin line separates wanting to help another person from wanting to change him or her to conform with our expectations.

There is an underlying assumption in the helping professions that a trained person can make a significant contribution to the lives of others if their training has instilled a commitment of effectively using oneself in the helping process. The primary technique or instrument in the helping relationship is the ability of the helper to become an instrument to be used by the helpee to achieve basic needs that must be met (at least from the helpee's perception) and to achieve some measure of self-fulfillment in doing so. From a helper's point of view, this goal of self-fulfillment means that the helpee will become more realistic, self-directing, and self-confident.

One of the most important things about helping in school settings is that the great majority of minority students do not seem to want to be helped. At least they do not appear to want to be helped by their teachers and counselors. Many minority students who ask for help are afraid of it and may try to make sure that no real helping takes place. There are many ways of asking for help. For example, acting out in the classroom may be a plea for help. Consequently, teachers must be aware of these subtle pleas and be prepared to enter into a growth-producing rather than punitive relationship with the acting-out students.

Carl R. Rogers defined the helping relationship as "a relationship in which at least one of the parties has the intent of promoting the growth, development, maturity, improved functioning, improved coping with life of the other."[8] The characteristics that distinguish a helping relationship from an unhelpful one are related primarily to the attitudes of the counselor and the perceptions of the minority student.

Determining what is helpful and what is not depends to a great extent on who is perceiving the situation. In other words, a student may not see a situation in the same way as the counselor. An example of this would be the case of a fight between two students. A counselor may see two students fighting, with one obviously receiving much physical abuse. The counselor also may perceive that the helpful thing to do is to intervene and stop the fight. On the other hand, the student being beaten might much rather take the physical abuse than face the verbal abuse of his fellows, who in all probability will make fun of him for having to be saved by the teacher. Social humiliation can be a much greater pain than physical punishment.

Certain values in a helping relationship must be observed by counselors if the relationship is to be productive in the long run. Doing a chore or making a decision for a minority student may help in the short run, but it will not help the student to become more self-directing in the future. Thus, some helpful values are as follows:

1. The belief that human life, happiness, and well-being are to be valued above all else.
2. The belief that each person is the master of his or her own destiny, with the right to control it in his or her own interest and in his or her own way as long as the exercise of this control does not infringe on the rights of other people.
3. The belief that the dignity and worth of each person shall be respected at all times and under all conditions.
4. The belief in the right of all people to think their own thoughts and speak their own minds.

This final chapter will not attempt to provide a how-to-do-it approach with clearly outlined steps to follow. While lists will be presented, they are done so mainly to summarize various thoughts. Helping relationships do not allow a rigid structure. Therefore, this chapter presents a "be-it-yourself" approach, since teachers and counselors need an attitude of being-for-others. From this perspective, it is more important for the teacher-counselor to be aware than to be an expert. To be aware and to care about the world, values, and life-styles of minority students is a significant aspect of the helping relationship in which teachers and counselors try to promote positive intrapersonal and intergroup relationships.

CHARACTERISTICS OF A HELPING RELATIONSHIP

Carl Rogers further stated that a helping relationship is one "in which one of the participants intends that there should come about in one or both parties more appreciation of, more expression of, more functional use of the latent inner resources of the individual."9 Relatedly, the job of the helper as seen by

Alan Keith-Lucas is to provide "a medium, a situation, and an experience in which a choice is possible."[10] Ideally, through the helping relationship the fears that restrain minority students can to some extent be resolved, and they can find the courage to make a commitment to a course of action and learn some of the practical skills necessary to make this decision a reality. Arthur W. Combs has stated that "the helper's basic beliefs and values rather than his grand schemes, methods, techniques, or years of training are the real determiners of whether or not the helper will be effective or ineffective."[11]

In a classic article entitled "The Characteristics of a Helping Relationship," Rogers asked a series of questions that he felt revealed characteristics of a helping relationship. If a teacher or counselor can answer these questions in the affirmative especially concerning most of their interactions with minority students, then it is likely that they will be or are helpful to their students.

> Can I be in some way which will be perceived by the other person as trustworthy, as dependable or consistent in some deep sense?[12]

This is more than being rigidly consistent. It means being honest and congruent with our feelings so that we are a unified or integrated person.

> Can I be expressive enough as a person that what I am will be communicated unambiguously?[13]

If we are unaware of our own feelings a double message can be given which will confuse the situation and cause the relationship to be marred by the ambiguous communication.

> Can I let myself experience positive attitudes toward this other person — attitudes of warmth, caring, liking, interest, respect?[14]

A professional attitude of aloofness is unhelpful; it creates a barrier or distance which protects scientific objectivity at the expense of establishing a helping relationship.

> Can I receive him as he is? Can I communicate this attitude? Or can I only receive him conditionally, acceptant of some

aspects of his feelings and silently or openly disapproving of other aspects?[15]

The counselor is usually threatened when he or she cannot accept certain parts of the minority student. The counselor must be able to accept those characteristics of the student that he or she cannot accept in himself or herself.

Can I act with sufficient sensitivity in the relationship that my behavior will not be perceived as a threat?[16]

If the student is as free as possible from external threats, then he or she may be able to experience and to deal with the internal feelings that are threatening.

Can I let myself enter fully into the world of his feelings and personal meanings and see these as he does? Can I step into his private world so completely that I lose all desire to evaluate or judge it? Can I enter it so sensitively that I can move about in it freely, without trampling on meanings which are precious to him? Can I sense it so accurately that I can catch not only the meanings of his experience which are obvious to him, but those meanings which are only implicit, which he sees only dimly or as confusion? Can I extend this understanding without limit?[17]

Evaluative comments are not conducive to personal growth and therefore they should not be a part of a helping relationship. For example, positive evaluation is threatening because it serves notice that the student is being evaluated and that a negative evaluation could be forthcoming. Self-evaluation leaves the responsibility with the student, where it really belongs. In essence, the ultimate question becomes, "Can I meet this other individual as a person who is in the process of becoming, or will I be bound by his past and my past?"[18]

Rogers listed four subtle attitudinal characteristics necessary for constructive personality change to occur. (1) The counselor manifests empathic understanding of the student. (2) The counselor manifests unconditional positive regard toward the student. (3) The counselor is genuine or congruent, that is, his/her words match his/her feelings. (4) The counselor's responses match the student's statements in the intensity of affective expression. These four conditions must be communicated to the helpee. In an effort to conceptualize this process, Rogers formulated what he calls a process equation of a successful helping relationship: Genuineness plus empathy plus unconditional positive regard for the client equals successful therapy for the client (G+E+UPR = Success).[19]

Keith-Lucas suggests that the counselor can convey genuineness, empathy, and unconditional positive regard through four statements, including the feelings and actions that accompany them: "This is it," "I know that it must hurt," "I am here to help you if you want me and can use me," and "You don't have to face this alone."[20] These statements contain reality, empathy, and support or acceptance. It should be emphasized that the words of these statements are only one part of the communication process. As an old Indian once said about the treatment his people received from whites, "What you do speaks so loudly I cannot hear what you say!" To be effective, reality and empathy must be conveyed to the minority student.

> Reality without empathy is harsh and unhelpful. Empathy about something that is not real is clearly meaningless and can only lead the client to what we have called non-choice. Reality and empathy together need support, both material and psychological, if decisions are to be carried out. Support in carrying out unreal plans is obviously a waste of time.[21]

Many studies on the nature of the helping relationships support the ideas of Rogers and Keith-Lucas. Various studies indicate three recurring themes as relevant to people who are considering entering the helping professions:

1. The helper's ability to sensitively and accurately understand the helpee in such a manner as to communicate deep understanding.

2. The helper's ability to project nonpossessive warmth and acceptance of the helpee.

3. The necessity for the helper to be integrated, mature, and genuine within the helping relationship.

Let us look now at three characteristics of a successful helping relationship — genuineness, empathy, and acceptance — that seem so vital to a helping relationship.

Genuineness

Lowell wrote, "Sincerity is impossible unless it pervades the whole being, and the pretense of it saps the very foundation of character." To be genuine in a student-counselor relationship requires the counselor to be aware of his or her own inner feelings. If these inner feelings are consistent with the expressed behavior, then it can be said that he or she is genuine and congruent. It is this quality of realness and honesty that allows the minority student needing help to keep a steady focus on reality.

To the nonhumanistic counselor, it may seem that reality is too brutal for the young minority student. Granted, the truth is not always painless; as the old saying goes, "The truth shall make ye free — but first it shall make ye miserable." It is also important to note that being open and honest is not a license to be brutal. A helpful, as opposed to a destructive, relationship is very much like the differences between a fatal and a therapeutic dose of a painkiller — it is only a matter of degree.

In the process of attempting to be transparently real, it is wise for counselors to evaluate their failures, their reasons for being less than honest. To protect minority students from the truth about their skills is to make a very serious judgment about them. It is to say that they are incapable of facing their real educational problems. However, if the counselor only provided honesty in the relationship, it probably would not be very helpful to minority students. The next component in the process, empathic understanding, is also needed.

Empathy

"First of all," he said, "if you can learn a simple trick, Scout, you'll get along a lot better with all kinds of folks. You never really understand a person until you consider things from his point of view —"
"Sir?"
"— until you climb into his skin and walk around in it."[22]

This passage from *To Kill a Mockingbird* accurately depicts the meaning of empathic understanding. It is literally an understanding of the emotions and feelings of another, not by the cognitive process but by a projection of one's personality into the personality of the other. It is a sort of vicarious experiencing of the feelings of the other to the degree that the helper actually feels some of the pain the person is suffering. Empathy requires the helper to leave temporarily his or her own life-space and to try to think, act, and feel as if the life-space of the other were the helper's own. The Spanish writer, Una Muno, wrote, "Suffering is the life blood that runs through us all and binds us together."

The following story demonstrates what is meant by empathic understanding.

In one of Israel's kibbutzim, or collective settlements, there was a donkey. It was a special donkey indeed with long silky ears and large shiny eyes, and all the children loved him dearly. And so when he disappeared one day, all the children were very upset. He had been the favorite attraction of the children's farm. During the morning the children used to come in two's and three's or in entire groups with their teachers to visit the donkey. The little ones would even take rides on his back. In the afternoon the children would drag their parents to the children's farm to see Shlomo, the donkey. But now he was missing, and the children were downcast. The sadness proved to be contagious; and before the day was out, all the kibbutz members had assembled in the large dining hall; and with concern written on all their faces, they were trying to decide what to do next. They had looked everywhere, but Shlomo, the donkey, had not been found.

On this same kibbutz lived an old man, the father of one of the earliest settlers. He had become somewhat senile of late, and children sometimes made fun of him quite openly, although the adults were a bit more circumspect. Well when the entire kibbutz population was gathered in the large new dining hall wondering what to do next, in walked the old man dragging Shlomo, the donkey, behind him. The jubilation was great, the astonishment even greater. While the children surrounded the donkey, the adults gathered about the old man. "How is it," they asked him, "that you of all people have found the donkey? What did you do?"

Well you can imagine the embarrassment of the old man and his joy, too, for never had he been paid so much attention. He scratched his bald pate, looked at the ceiling and then at the floor, smiled, and said: "It was simple. I just asked myself, 'Shlomo,' [for that was the old man's name as well] 'if you were Shlomo, the donkey, where would you go off to?' So I went there and found him and brought him back."[23]

This story illustrates the nature and purpose of empathic understanding. The old man was able to think and feel like the donkey in order to figure out where the donkey was, but was still separate enough to go and get him. It is important that counselors maintain enough objectivity when they become empathic so that they can assist minority students in overcoming educational problems.

Empathic understanding does no good unless it is communicated to the student — to let him or her know that someone has a deep understanding of his or her predicament. This kind of understanding allows the student to expand and clarify his or her own self-understanding. One way of communicating this kind of understanding is through active listening. Active listening is not mere tolerance; a counselor, for instance, has to really care and feel the emotions attached to the student's words. The following four points express what listening with empathic understanding means.

1. Empathic listening means trying to see the situation the way the other person sees it.
2. Empathic listening means one must enter actively and imaginatively into the other person's situation and try to understand a frame of reference different from one's own.
3. Empathic listening does not mean maintaining a polite silence while we rehearse what we are going to say when we get a chance.
4. Empathic listening does not mean waiting alertly for the flaws in the other person's argument so that we can correct her or him.[24]

Once counselors are behaving genuinely and have empathic understanding toward the minority student, the next step, which often occurs simultaneously, is acceptance.

Acceptance

In Rogerian jargon, acceptance of the minority student means that the counselor will feel and show unconditional positive regard for him or her. It is worth repeating that counselors must be congruent or consistent in both their feelings and expressions of acceptance for minority students. If counselors do not really accept minority students yet attempt to express acceptance, they will be giving a double message — acceptance and rejection. In such a case, the best that can happen is that minority students will perceive these counselors to be phonies. The worst that can happen is that students' self-esteem will be damaged. Double messages occur when feelings do not coincide with words. For instance, a counselor's words may say, "I accept you and respect your feelings." But the nonverbal messages which reflect more deeply-held feelings are difficult to correct because the owner does not have as much control over them as over words. Small children know this and are perceptive enough to sense these feelings. The words of Joe Louis to one of his boxing opponents illustrate this point: "You can run but you can't hide from me."

The basic reasons for demonstrating acceptance are to build a relationship based upon trust and openness, to establish a situation in which the minority student is able to gain respect for self, and to develop an atmosphere through which the student can come to respect others. The process involved in this aspect of the relationship is caring, and support is given through helpful feedback. Feedback is simply the expression of reactions to a behavior. In a sense, the student will perceive the counselor's attitude of respect as an either/or thing: either the counselor does or does not respect him or her. This may be an oversimplification, but if the student perceives it in this manner, then the consequences of that perception are real.

To the extent that counselors can be themselves as persons, expressing their real selves, hopefully they will have empathic understanding and liking for their students. In searching for the helping relationship, it would be wise to remember the following Zen poem:

It is too clear and so is hard to see.
A man once searched for fire with a lighted lantern.
Had he known what fire was,
He could have cooked his rice much sooner.

AND WHAT ELSE?

This section deals briefly with the various views of human beings, the healthy minority student, social class and poverty, and social helping — a sort of potpourri. In other words, it deals with the question asked by the little girl after being given a long list of information and data: "And what else?"

Views of Human Beings

Every human being has a totally unique inner nature. This inner self ("real self" according to Arthur Janov, "inner nature" according to Abraham H. Maslow) has characteristics which may be described in different ways. Maslow lists several ways of characterizing the inner self in *Psychology of Being:*

1. The inner self is biologically based. It is, in many ways, unchangeable or at least unchanging.
2. Each person's inner self is unique to him/her.
3. We may only discover the inner self; we cannot add to it or subtract from it.
4. The inner self is good or neutral — not bad.
5. If the inner self is allowed to develop, happiness is the result.
6. If the inner self is denied or suppressed, sickness develops.
7. Because the inner self is not strong or overpowering, it may easily be suppressed by socialization.
8. Yet, even though denied, the inner self does not disappear. It merely persists underground forever pressing for self-actualization.[25]

Janov believes that the core of each person is the real self.

The real self has real needs which must be met early in life to survive. Hunger, the need to be held, and the need to be loved are all real needs.[26] Obviously, if a child is not fed, he or she will die. This real need is universally recognized. The need to be held was not completely recognized until World War II, when the Nazis put infants into a room and only fed them. As a result of not being held, all the children died. The need to be loved is as universally recognized as it is misunderstood. The real self must be fed with real love — the unconditional love Eric Fromm talks about or the ok-ness Thomas A. Harris describes. If an adult does not get real love, he or she will not die but will instead split with the real self in order to survive.

Some characteristics are frequently confused with the inner self. Some of these characteristics are entrenched in political philosophy, public education, religion, and superstitution. Biblical phrases such as "spare the rod and spoil the child," for example, imply some basic instinct in humans toward evil. Superstition, added to religious phrases such as these, implies that the evilness must be beaten out of the person so that "the demon won't creep out." Hence, the inner self is often considered evil.

Certain defensive feelings, such as jealousy, hate, and hostility, are often thought to be inborn in human beings. According to A. S. Neill, this is not true. Neill worked with children in his Summerhill School and found that after psychological treatment children could refrain from expressing feelings of hate, hostility, and jealousy. Because they had learned these things, they could learn to refrain from expressing them.[27]

Janov claims that primal patients do not express (or have) feelings of hate, hostility, or jealousy. According to Janov, anger may be real or unreal; fear may be real or unreal; guilt may be true guilt or socialized guilt. Hence, these feelings are not always inborn in the individual.

Defenses are not part of the real self but are added to the individual for protection, which is not protection at all. Transactional analysts say that defenses are seen in games, manipulations, ulterior transactions, and similar endeavors undertaken by children and adults. We are not born manipulators; we are taught to be manipulators. Maslow believed some defenses are desirable. He further believed that frustration, deprivation, and punishment are ways to fulfill and feed our inner selves. Whether they are expressing the real or unreal self, a disproportionate number of low-achieving minority students display jealousy, hate, and hostility. And an equal number become manipulators in order to survive in the academic game.

Humanistic education may be viewed as a phenomenological, personalistic, existential view of students who are engaged in a continuous process of becoming. What this means is that all students are basically good and their behavior is a function of the perceptions that they have or their world and themselves. The environment's effect on the individual is filtered through each person's perceptual apparatus. Thus a child may in reality be living in a ghetto, but if she does not perceive herself to be a ghetto dweller, then that perception has more effect on her behavior than her environment. A counselor may be open, flexible, and democratic but if a student perceives him to be closed, rigid, and authoritarian, then the consequences of that perception will stifle the student-counselor interaction.

Humanistic education takes a relativistic view of reality. It leaves the individual at the center of decision making and responsibility. If one holds to the behavioristic or Freudian views of humanity, the individual is no longer considered the initiator of his or her acts and thus is no longer responsible. The Freudian view of the helping relationship tends to make helping a manipulative relationship, with the helpee being the object rather than the subject of the relationship.

Many basic needs affect a relationship. Maslow divided our basic needs into five major categories:

1. Physiological needs (food, water, and shelter).
2. Safety or security needs (freedom from physical and psychological attacks).
3. The needs for love, affection, and belonging.
4. Esteem (self-concept) needs.
5. The need for self-actualization.

Until the first four needs are met, the fifth need, which is a rather abstract concept of potentiality and self-development, is virtually unseekable.[28] A disproportionate number of ethnic minority children do not have their physiological and safety needs met.

In another vein Donald Snygg defines self-concept and its development as the basis of human values, and he suggests three pertinent points for the counselor to be aware of:

1. The basic goal of all individuals is for a feeling of increased worth, of greater personal value. (This goal is never completely reached.)

2. Given one success, a degree of self-enhancement, human beings usually will aspire to more success.

3. Satisfaction of the need for greater personal value can be and is sought in a number of alternative ways.[29]

High grades, consumer goods, and personal experiences are of value to the student only as they contribute to the feeling of positive self-worth.

Creativity is a goal often sought by counselors for their minority students, but the authoritarian nature of traditional counseling methods prevents most minority students from being creative. The key requirement for creativity is freedom. In most schools too many structural barriers block the path of personal freedom. Studies comparing the maze-learning ability of rats raised in a cage and periodically run through mazes with that of free-roaming rats concluded that the free-roaming rats out-perform the caged rats in maze-learning and in more complex behavior. But rats are not people!

In counseling sessions that minority students perceive as authoritarian, social dimensions become more than a boundary; they become barriers to openness. Students become prisoners cut off from communicating with their jailors. Under these conditions minority students can easily become defensive, psychological cripples. In the following passage, Earl C. Kelley describes this process and the lack of sensitivity of educators to it:

> Defenses are necessary, provided they do not become so impervious that they imprison that which they defend. It

often happens that defenses are inadequate for the dangers of living. This happens most often to the very young, who have tender psychological selves and inadequate protection. In these cases, which are numerous, the self becomes damaged, and in serious cases crippled. These psychological cripples have to behave as cripples do, and their actions are at wide variance with what is "expected" of them in our culture. From this group society gets its criminals, its deviates, its so-called insane. The person is crippled by conditions over which he has little control, and then because he behaves in a crippled fashion we say he is delinquent, or "insane."

This is not because we are inhuman, or devoid of human compassion. It is because we cannot see the psychological self. Our hearts go out to the physical cripple, and great deference is properly paid to him. If we could see the psychological cripple our blame, hostility, and rejection would be changed to love, and tender nurture. We would not expect him to step lively, and look out for himself. We would cease to subject him to the many forms of rejection which we have devised for those who do not conform.[30]

It should be obvious from the preceding discussion that both the counselor's and the minority student's frame of reference are important in understanding the counseling relationship. The question now arises: What are the criteria for a socially and psychologically healthy minority student? One answer, of course, is that the healthy person is mature — which is what the next section is about.

The Healthy Minority Student

William James said, "An unlearned carpenter of my acquaintance once said in my hearing: 'There is very little difference between one man and another; but what little there is, is very important.'" We have already built a case for the assumption that the inner self is good and desirable. We may also assume that a healthy minority student is a person who *is* his or her inner self, and that a healthy minority student who is his or her inner self is self-actualizing. Or stated another way, health is self-actualization. The healthy minority student is one who is free to make choices. He or she is free to sift through alternatives and choose which alternative is best. He or she is free because of this awareness of alternatives.

All people have options. All people make choices every day. Yet not all choices are made out of awareness. An example of making an unaware choice is losing control of one's temper and blaming others for this loss, i.e. "You made me angry." An example of making a choice through awareness is expression of direct anger. If anger is turned inward, it becomes depression. If anger is turned outward without responsibility, it becomes hostility. If anger is expressed outwardly with responsibility and directly at the source of anger, the result is anger with awareness. Even in extreme cases of life and death, people make choices.[31]

The healthy minority student is a self-regulated person. Self-regulation is learned early in life and continues to strengthen and develop as the individual matures. Self-regulation means the right to live freely, without undue outside authority. The healthy minority student operates in the here-and-now. He or she is primarily concerned with the present — not the past. And to repeat for emphasis, the healthy minority student is aware of choices and accepts responsibility for his or her behavior. What about the healthy counselor?

In addition to displaying traits similar to the healthy minority student, the healthy counselor is a perceptive person. He or she does not see everything in dichotomous terms — good or bad, childish or mature, and so forth. The healthy counselor has insight into the behavior of minority people yet does not exploit that insight. He or she uses insight to empathize with the suffering of students. On the same note, that insight gives him or her the ability to vicariously identify with the pleasures of minority students as well.

Robert R. Spaulding found significant positive correlation between the height of the self-concept and the degree to which the teachers in his study were calm, accepting, supportive, and facilitative. A negative correlation was found when teachers were dominating, threatening, and sarcastic.[32] Morris L. Cogan found that students with warm, considerate teachers produced large amounts of original art and poetry,[33] while C. M. Christensen found the warmth of teachers significantly related to the vocabulary and mathematical achievement of students.[34] Horace B. Reed found that teachers and counselors character- ized by students as considerate, understanding, and friendly had a favorable influence on students' interest in science.[35]

It is also important to note Frank C. Emmerling's conclusion that teachers and counselors who accept students, perceive them positively, and attempt to understand them facilitate an im- proved learning climate.[36] Several studies have shown that if a teacher has a positive perception of the student, i.e. if he or she thinks the student is a capable learner, the student does better academically. It is extremely important that teachers and coun- selors be aware of their belief and value systems. Robert M. Thomas described four aspects of a counselor's value system that are important in the counseling process. (a) A counselor is often unaware of his or her philosophical principles until forced to look at them. (2) Some of the counselor's values con- flict with others. (3) The values counselor's espouse are often different from their actions. (4) Some counselor values are im- possible to realize because they are inconsistent with the facts of life.[37] Gilbert C. Wrenn made five suggestions which are both values and principles to be followed as a basic humanistic counseling credo:

1. I shall strive to see the positive in the other person and praise it at least as often as I notice that which is to be cor- rected.

2. If I am to correct or criticize someone's action, I must be sure that this is seen by the other as a criticism of a specific behavior and not as a criticism of himself as a person.

3. I shall assume that each person can see some reasonable- ness in his behavior, that there is meaning in it for him if not for me.

4. When I contribute to another person's self-respect I in- crease his positive feelings toward me and his respect for me.

5. To at least one person, perhaps many, I am a person of significance, and he is affected vitally by my recognition of him and my good will toward him as a person.[38]

Social Class and Poverty

Counselors should be aware of some other ideas about helping. Specifically, most writers suggest that four things must occur before minority students ask for help:

1. They must recognize that something is wrong which they can do nothing about without help.
2. They must be willing to tell someone about the problem.
3. They must give that person some right to tell them what to do.
4. They must be willing to change in some way.

All of this is very threatening to the student's equilibrium and self-concept. In school this puts low-achieving minority students in a particularly difficult situation because of their relatively low self-esteem. To them, seeking help may be a degrading process. For this reason Vincent F. Calia challenged the idea that the student must come forward directly and ask for help before a positive relationship can be established.[39] As noted earlier, students may ask for help indirectly through various forms of acting out.

As to the actual kind of helping relationship established with minority students from the lower socioeconomic classes, Frank Riessman warned that male adolescents from this group dislike talk and have a strong preference for action.[40] In fact adolescents in most groups tend to be secretive and afraid to talk about their inner feelings. When there is difficulty in verbalizing feelings, human relations structured exercises can be helpful as a medium for opening up communication. Group exercises can spark verbalization and the ventilation of feelings, and psychodrama and role-playing can offer opportunities for students who are less verbal to express their feelings in an action-oriented environment. Unfortunately, many of the human relations exercises are too difficult for most counselors to manage without further training.

Numerous studies have focused on the helping relationship with disadvantaged minority students. August B. Hollingshead and Frederick C. Redlich observed that therapists have more positive feelings toward patients whose social class standings are comparable to their own.[41] It seems reasonable then that teachers and counselors also tend to have more positive feelings for students of their own socioeconomic class. George Banks, Bernard G. Berenson, and Robert R. Carkhuff found that helpers who are different from their helpees in terms of race and social class have the greatest difficulty effecting constructive changes, while helpers who are similar to their helpees in these respects have the greatest facility for doing so.[42] This does not rule out effective cross-cultural counseling.

It is important to note that ethnic minority students need more (or a different kind of) attention than other students. Of course this is an over-generalization, since each student should be looked at individually in order to determine his or her personal needs. Even so, it is imperative that counselors be cognizant of barriers created by ethnic or social class differences. If Black students are hesitant to trust a white counselor, for example, it may be because they do not trust members of that particular ethnic group, or it may be because the counselor's nonverbal messages say "stay away." Rather than guess, it is better to ask the students what they think the difficulty may be. If done tactfully, this will get the issue out in the open with a minimum of defensiveness. It may be that the students are not aware of their own nontrusting behavior, or the counselor may have been projecting his or her own nontrusting attitude onto the students. In any case, it is best to get and keep these feelings, perceptions, and thoughts out in the open so that trust can be built. This does not mean that helping relationships are always nice and sweet. The following interview with a student tells of a helping relationship that he had with a teacher that was not always pleasant.

> He was my teacher for three years in junior high school, and I gave him hell. I was a devil then and hated the guy. That's what I thought then, but it wasn't only hate. He didn't let me get away with a thing in class, and lots of times he'd keep me in after school to talk things over. He told me exactly how he felt, and I remember I told him lots of things. . . . I don't know why exactly. . . . I think, because I trusted him.

Now that I think of it, that teacher never told me he was right and I was wrong. He said there were things I was doing he couldn't allow, or something like that, and he told me why. I told him how I felt about the kids in the class and how boring school was. He listened to it. We never got to see eye to eye on lots of things, but we knew where we stood. I know now that I learned more from him in those talks than I did during four years in high school. I didn't know it then, but he taught me to think and to see what I was doing. After a while he had enough, I guess, and I don't blame him. He gave me up for lost, I suppose, and he'll never know how much he helped me. It took me years to find it out.[43]

Social Helping

Most of minority students' problems are rooted in their social environments. Certainly family therapy is an alternative. Another alternative is social action designed to change organizations. Donald H. Blocher observed that one of the reasons why many counselors are continually frustrated is because the problems they are called upon to solve are themselves the products of other institutional or community organizations.[44] If counselors really want to be helpful, some of them will have to be active in community change. But the most significant changes that they can make involve their own schools and neighborhoods.

Frequently a minority student's development depends not on his or her adjustment to an existing classroom situation but instead on being moved to another classroom. This kind of environmental change is not without a theoretical foundation; it is modeled after milieu therapy, preventative and community or social psychiatry. We can take as our illustration the model of milieu therapy, in which the hospital environment serves as a therapeutic instrument, and patterns of human relationships are consciously attuned to the treatment or developmental needs of the residents.

When applying this model to the school, it too becomes clear that more often than not nonwhite students do not get the institutional treatment they need because school resources are not attuned to their needs. Combs listed seven suggestions for what counselors can and must do if each minority student is to be aided and allowed to become a fully functioning person:

1. Regard each student as a vital part of the curriculum.
2. View students positively because whatever diminishes the student's self — humiliation, degradation, failure — has no place in education.
3. Provide for individual differences.
4. Apply the criteria of self-actualization to every counseling experience.
5. Learn how things are seen by the students.
6. Allow rich opportunities for individuals to explore themselves and their environment.
7. Help the young to become independent.[45]

Since sensitivity to their won feelings is a prerequisite to effective helping, it may be beneficial for teachers to undergo some type of sensitivity training. A study by Edward W. Schultz and Judith Wolf indicates that a large number of teachers are in need of some kind of experiential training.[46] A series of studies by Carkhuff and others show extensive evidence for the idea that educators trained in such programs are more successful in helping students and have more of the characteristics of the helping relationship.

If the research studies reviewed are correct in their assertion that helping can be accomplished only on the terms of the healthier person in the relationship, then it becomes necessary to have some criteria for determining who and what a healthy person is. Rogers defined the fully functioning person as a person who lives life as an ongoing, becoming process. Such a counselor is able to accept his or her present feelings and able to trust and act on feelings of what is right in a way that involves the courage to be. These educators are psychologically mature. Gordon W. Allport developed six criteria or psychological characteristics of the mature person.

1. A mature person extends his/her self-concept by caring, belonging, identifying with, and working towards causes other than his/herself.
2. A mature person accepts himself/herself.

3. A mature person is capable of intimacy and love — love that is given unconditionally.

4. A mature person functions with efficiency and accuracy in perception and cognition. He or she is able to solve problems of the real world without panic, pity, and resignation.

5. A mature person maintains balance and keeps his or her perspective through insight and humor.

6. A mature person has a clear comprehension of life's purpose.[47]

It is important that counselors be mature. In an effective helping situation the minority student will ultimately be able to do everything that the counselor does at nearly the same level at which the counselor is functioning. Counselors who have not gotten themselves together are not able to assist students.

Many studies have been conducted which indicate the importance of the interpersonal relations between the counselor and the minority student. The implications of these studies should be self-evident. Student-counselor relationships may be for better or worse, i.e. the development of minority students' social adjustment may be helped or retarded because of the type of relationships they have with their counselors. Helen H. Davidson and Gerhard Lang found that when students feel that teachers value and respect them, they are likely to value and respect themselves.[48]

Other researchers comparing patients' reports on the therapeutic experience with psychoanalytic, nondirective, and Adlerian therapists have found them to be more or less the same fundamental relationship. The ideal counselor is seen in almost the same way as the ideal therapist. The various helping professions are really quite similar in terms of interpersonal styles and relationships. Donald Super and Arthur Combs noted that counselors in their study described the ideal counselor in much the same way that therapists describe the ideal therapist. This gives support to the idea that common characteristics of a helping relationship exist and that relationships that are helpful are very similar in the various helping professions.

Three major assumptions about the universality of helping

should be remembered. (1) We all at times have emotional problems which we experience as unpleasant and painful. (2) We all seek help for our personal problems. (3) We all offer help to others who are experiencing emotional difficulties. When William Menninger was asked how many people suffer from emotional illness, he answered, "One out of one of us." The help we all seek may come from a spouse, a colleague, a friend, or a counselor. And it is clear that a part of our needs must be met in relation with others. The nature of this relationship was captured in the following passage:

> You and I are in a relationship with each other. Yet each of us is a separate person having his own needs. I will try to be as accepting as I can of your behavior as you try to meet your own needs. I will even try to learn how to increase my capacity to be accepting of your behavior. But I can be genuinely accepting of you only as long as your behavior to meet your needs does not conflict with my meeting my own needs. Therefore, whenever I am feeling nonaccepting of you because my own needs are not being met, I will tell you as openly and honestly as I can, leaving it up to you whether you will change your behavior. I also will encourage you to do the same with me and will try to listen to your feelings and perhaps change my behavior. However, when we discover that a conflict-of-needs continues to exist in our relationship, let us both commit ourselves to try to resolve that conflict without the use of either my power or yours. I will respect your needs, but I also must respect my own. Consequently, let us strive always to search mutually for solutions to our inevitable conflicts that will be acceptable to both of us. In this way, your needs will be met but so will mine. As a result, you can continue to grow and achieve satisfaction and so can I. And, finally, our relationship can continue to be a healthy one because it will be mutually satisfying.[49]

SUMMARY

It has been proposed that counselor preparation criteria include success working in an open setting where ethnic group problems are explored and alternative solutions are considered.

Counselor commitment to cultural pluralism is exemplified by those who demonstrate a willingness to both accept change and to change themselves.

The role of the counselor in implementing ethnic and cultural pluralism includes the following dimensions of intergroup relations: identity consciousness, validation of differences, minority group advocacy, collaborative and cooperative strategies, conflict resolution, and risk-taking.

Validation of differences suggests that counselors go beyond simply valuing cultural dissimilarities; they must take an active stance in protecting cultural differences. Minority-group advocacy requires "placing one's self in another's shoes; it means supporting work toward the goals identified by persons from another group; it means listening rather than telling. . . . Advocacy thinking should lead to a clarification of differences between persons, and to a recognition of when it is or is not possible to collaborate."[50]

Counselors can best serve themselves and their counselees when they recognize and prepare for conflict situations. Conflict is inevitable in society. It can be a destructive force that breeds differences, hostility, and alienation, or it can become a creative force that encourages open and constructive problem solving.

Minority counselees and their counselors should understand that social change requires risk-taking. Risk nothing, or everything, and your commitment is likely to be questioned. Risking something specific in a thoughtful, calculated manner seems to be the best strategy for change. This can be done successfully in individual and group counseling sessions which utilize affective and cognitive formats. Whatever format is used, the risks should be clearly identified.

It is hazardous enough to risk educational and employment opportunities or peer approval or ethnic identity with one's eyes open, to do so in ignorance is to invite needless failure and pain. Ethnicity complicates human interactions; it is not an irreversible asset or liability. Hopefully this book of readings has added a measure of understanding about ways to effectively counsel ethnic minority and majority persons. However, no amount of readings is an adequate substitute for humane behavior.

While considered essential for competent counseling/therapy of women, the following principles adopted in 1979 by the American Psychological Association's Division of Counseling Psychology are paraphrased below to fit females and ethnic minorities:

1. Counselors/therapists must be knowledgeable about sex differences and ethnic minorities, particularly with regard to historical, psychological and social issues.
2. Counselors/therapists must be aware that assumptions and precepts of theories relevant to their practice may apply differently to females, males, ethnic minorities and non-minorities. Counselors/therapists must be aware of those theories that prescribe or limit the potential of female and ethnic minority clients, as well as those that may have particular usefulness for female and minority clients.
3. After formal training, counselors/therapists must continue throughout their professional careers to explore and learn of issues related to females and ethnic minorities.
4. Counselors/therapists must recognize and be aware of various forms of oppression and how these interact with sexism and racism.
5. Counselors/therapists must be knowledgeable and aware of verbal and nonverbal process variables (particularly with regard to power in the helping relationship) as these affect females and ethnic minorities in counseling/therapy so that the counselor/therapist-client interactions are not adversely affected. The need for shared responsibility between clients and counselors/therapists must be acknowledged and implemented.
6. Counselors/therapists must have the capability of utilizing skills that are particularly facilitative to females and ethnic minorities in general and to specific female and minority clients in particular.
7. Counselors/therapists must ascribe no preconceived limitations on the direction or nature of female and ethnic

minority client's life goals.

8. Counselors/therapists must be sensitive to circumstances where it is more desireable for a female or an ethnic minority client to be seen by a female or an ethnic minority counselor/therapist.
9. Counselors/therapists must use non-sexist and non-racist language in counseling/therapy, supervision, teaching and publications.
10. Counselors/therapists must not engage in sexual activity with their clients.
11. Counselors/therapists must be aware of and continually review their own values and biases and the effect of these on their female and ethnic minority clients. Counselors/therapists must understand the effect of female and minority group role socialization upon their own development and functioning and the consequent values and attitudes they hold for themselves and others. They must recognize that behaviors and roles need not be sex or ethnic based.
12. Counselors/therapists must be aware of how their personal functioning may influence their effectiveness in counseling/therapy with female and ethnic minority clients. They must monitor their functioning through consultation, supervision or therapy so that it does not adversely affect their work with female and minority clients.
13. Counselors/therapists must support the elimination of sexism and racism within institutions and individuals.

REFERENCES

1. Carl G. Jung, *The Integration of the Personality*, New York: Farrar and Rinehart, 1939.
2. Alfred Adler, The Fundamental Views of Individual Psychology, *Journal of Individual Psychology*, 1935, 1:5-8.
3. Andras Angyal, *Foundations for a Science of Personality*, New York: Commonwealth Fund, 1941, Chapter 6.
4. Bingham Dai, *Sociological Foundations of the Psychiatric Disorders of Childhood*, Pennsylvania: Child Research Clinic, 1946.
5. E. Essien-Udom, *Black Nationalism: A Search for an Identity in America*, Chicago: University of Chicago Press, 1962, 24.

6. George Devereux, as quoted in Neil J. Smelser and William T. Smelser, eds., *Personality and Social Systems*, New York: John Wiley & Sons, 1963, 29.

7. James Baldwin, *The Fire Next Time*, New York: The Dial Press, 1963, 110-11.

8. Carl R. Rogers, The Characteristics of a Helping Relationship, *Personnel and Guidance Journal*, 1958, 37:6.

9. *Ibid.*

10. Alan Keith-Lucas, *Giving and Taking Help*, Chapel Hill: University of North Carolina Press, 1972, 46.

11. Arthur W. Combs, *Florida Studies in the Helping Professions*, Gainesville: University of Florida Press, 1969, 3.

12. Rogers, *op. cit.*, 12.

13. *Ibid.*

14. *Ibid.*

15. *Ibid.*, 13-14.

16. *Ibid.*, 14.

17. *Ibid.*, 13.

18. *Ibid.*, 14.

19. See Carl R. Rogers, The Process Equation of Psychotherapy, *American Journal of Psychotherapy*, 1961, 15:27-45.

20. Keith-Lucas, *op. cit.*, 70.

21. *Ibid.*, 88.

22. Harper Lee, *To Kill a Mockingbird*, New York: Popular Library, 1960, 34.

23. Alfred Benjamin, *The Helping Interview*, Boston: Houghton Mifflin, 1969, 47.

24. Frank H. Drause and Donald E. Hendrickson, *Counseling Techniques with Youth*, Columbus, Ohio: Charles E. Merrill, 1972, 39-48.

25. Abraham H. Maslow, *Toward a Psychology of Being*, New York: D. Van Nostrand, 1962, 3-5.

26. Arthur Janov, *The Primal Scream*, New York: Dell, 1970.

27. A. S. Neill, *Summerhill*, New York: Hart, 1960.

28. For a discussion of Maslow's and Rogers' concepts see George Henderson, *Human Relations: From Theory to Practice*, Norman: University of Oklahoma Press, 1974, 236-40.

29. Donald Snygg, The Psychological Basis of Human Values, in Donald L. Avila, Arthur W. Combs, and William W. Purkey, eds., *The Helping Relationship Sourcebook*, Boston: Allyn & Bacon, 1971, 86.

30. Earl C. Kelley, Another Look at Individualism, in Avila, Combs, and Purkey, *ibid.*, 315.

31. An excellent literary work focusing on suicide as a choice is found in Hermann Hesse, *Steppenwolf*, New York: Holt, Rinehart & Winston, 1963.

32. Robert R. Spaulding, Achievement, Creativity, and Self-Concept Correlates of Teacher-Pupil Transactions in Elementary Schools, in Celia B. Stendler, ed., *Readings in Child Behavior and Development*,

2d ed., New York: Harcourt, Brace, 1964, 313-18.

33. Morris L. Cogan, The Behavior of Teachers and the Productive Behavior of Their Pupils, *Journal of Experimental Education*, 1958, 27:89-124.

34. C. M. Christensen, Relationship Between Pupil Achievement, Pupil Affect-need, Teacher Warmth and Teacher Permissiveness, *Journal of Educational Psychology*, 1960, 51:169-74.

35. Horace B. Reed, Implications for Science Education of a Teacher Competence Research, *Science Education*, 1962, 46:473-86.

36. Frank C. Emmerling, A. Study of the Relationship Between Characteristics of Classroom Teachers and Pupil Perceptions, unpublished Ph.D. dissertation, Auburn, Ala.: Auburn University, 1961.

37. Robert M. Thomas, *Social Differences in the Classroom: Social-class, Ethnic and Religious Problems*, New York: David McKay, 1965, chapter 1.

38. Gilbert C. Wrenn, Psychology, Religion; and Values for the Counselor, *Personnel Guidance Journal*, 1958, 36:43.

39. Vincent F. Calia, The Culturally Deprived Client: A Reformation of the Counselor's Role, *Journal of Counseling Psychology*, 1966, 13:100-105.

40. Frank Riessman, Role Playing and the Lower Socioeconomic Group, *Group Psychotherapy*, 1964, 17:36-48.

41. August B. Hollingshead and Frederick C. Redlich, *Social Class and Mental Illness*, New York: John Wiley & Sons, 1958, 176.

42. George Banks, Bernard G. Berenson, and Robert F. Carkhuff, The Effects of Counselor Race and Training Upon Negro Clients in Initial Interviews, *Journal of Clinical Psychology*, 1967, 23:70-72.

43. Benjamin, *op. cit.*, 92-93.

44. Donald H. Blocher, *Developmental Counseling*, New York: Ronald Press, 1966, 87-96.

45. Arthur W. Combs, What Can Man Become?, in Avila, Combs, and Purkey, *op. cit.*, 197-212.

46. Edward W. Schultz and Judith Wolf, Teacher Behavior, Self-Concept, and the Helping Process, *Psychology in the Schools*, 1973, 10:75-78.

47. Gordon W. Allport, *Pattern and Growth in Personality*, New York: Holt, Rinehart & Winston, 1961, 283-304.

48. Helen H. Davidson and Gerhard Lang, Children's Perceptions of Their Teacher's Feelings Toward Them Related to Self-Perception, School Achievement, and Behavior, *Journal of Experimental Education*, 1960, 29:107-18.

49. Thomas Gordon, A Theory of Healthy Relationship and a Program of Parent Effectiveness Training, in J. T. Hart and T. M. Tomlinson, eds., *New Directions in Client-Centered Therapy*, Boston: Houghton Mifflin, 1970, 424-25.

50. Richard C. Larson and Larry F. Elliott, Planning and Pluralism: Some Dimensions of Intergroup Relations, *Journal of Negro Education*, 1976, 45:95.

NAME INDEX

SUBJECT INDEX

529